TEACHING SPEECH
IN TODAY'S
SECONDARY SCHOOLS

TEACHING SPEECH IN TODAY'S SECONDARY SCHOOLS

CHARLES L. BALCER
SAINT CLOUD STATE COLLEGE

HUGH F. SEABURY
STATE UNIVERSITY OF IOWA

HOLT, RINEHART AND WINSTON, INC.
NEW YORK   CHICAGO   SAN FRANCISCO   TORONTO   LONDON

Copyright © 1965 by Holt, Rinehart and Winston, Inc.
All rights reserved
Library of Congress Catalog Card Number 65-14616

20786—0115

Printed in the United States of America

PN
4086
.B35

ACKNOWLEDGMENTS

The Authors are grateful to the following companies and organizations for permission to quote from books published by them:

Appleton-Century-Crofts, Inc., a division of The Meredith Publishing Co., *The English Language Arts in the Secondary Schools* prepared by The Commission on the English Curriculum of The National Council of Teachers of English, copyright © 1956, Appleton-Century-Crofts, Inc.; *Speech, Its Techniques and Disciplines in a Free Society*, 1st ed., by William Norwood Brigance. Copyright, 1952, Appleton-Century-Crofts, Inc.; *A Challenge to Secondary Education*, edited by Samuel Everett. Copyright 1935, D. Appleton-Century Company, Inc.

American Book Company, *On Teaching English* by H. F. Seely, New York, 1933.

Artcraft Press, *Teaching Speech* by Loren Reid, Columbia, Missouri, 1960.

The Bobbs-Merrill Co., Inc., "The Place of Speech Training in an Integrated Curriculum" from *Education* (September 1955).

Central States Speech Journal, "The Need for Developing Responsible Speaking" by Carl A. Dallinger (Spring 1958), "High School Students Can Take Phonetics—and Like It" by Don Rasmussen (Fall 1955), with permission of the authors.

Educational Policies Commission, *The Purposes of Education in American Democracy*. Washington, 1938.

Harcourt, Brace & World, Inc., and George Allen & Unwin, Ltd., London, *Language in Thought and Action*, 2nd ed., 1964, by S. I. Hayakawa.

Harper & Row, Publishers, Inc., *The Bases of Speech*, 3rd ed., by Giles W. Gray and Claude M. Wise, New York, 1959.

Harvard University Press, Report of the Harvard Committee *General Education in a Free Society*, Cambridge, Mass.: Harvard University Press, copyright 1945 by the President and Fellows of Harvard College.

George G. Harrap and Company, Ltd., *The Language and Mental Development of Children* by A. F. Watts, London, 1944 and D. C. Heath and Company, New York.

ACKNOWLEDGMENTS

D. C. Heath and Company, *How We Think* by John Dewey, New York, 1933.

Holt, Rinehart and Winston, Inc., *Argumentation and Debate*, edited by David Potter, copyright 1954; *Curriculum Planning: For Better Teaching and Learning* by J. Galen Saylor and William M. Alexander, copyright 1954; *Developing Vocal Skills* by Theodore D. Hanley and Wayne L. Thurman, copyright 1962; *Speech for Everyday Use*, rev. ed., by E. G. Andersch and L. C. Staats, 1960.

Iowa High School Forensic League for materials and ideas.

The Journal of the National Education Association, "What Are Desirable Social-Economic Goals for America?" by Joy Elmer Morgan (January 1934); "A Bill of Rights for the New Age," prepared by a Committee of the NEA (November 1934); "Classroom Control in the High School" by Emelie Ruth Dodge (March 1958); copyrights 1934, © 1958 by the National Education Association.

The Key Reporter, "An Outsider Looks at Education" by John Kirkland Clark (Winter 1938).

J. B. Lippincott Company, *The New American Speech* by Wilhelmina G. Hedde and William N. Brigance, 1957; from *The Story of Language* by Mario Pei. Copyright, 1949 by Mario Pei. Published by J. B. Lippincott Company.

McGraw-Hill Book Company, *Basic Voice Training for Speech* by Elise Hahn, Donald E. Hargis, Charles W. Lomas, and Daniel Vandraegen Copyright 1957; *Speech-Code, Meaning, and Communication* by John W. Black and Wilbur E. Moore. Copyright 1955. McGraw-Hill Book Company. Used by permission.

The Macmillan Company, *Reorganizing the High School Curriculum*, 3rd ed. by H. B. and F. J. Alberty, 1962; *The Improvement of Voice and Diction* by Jon Eisenson, 1958.

G. & C. Merriam Company, *A Pronouncing Dictionary of American English*, copyright 1953.

Michigan Speech Association, "Curriculum Guide for Basic Speech."

National Association of Secondary-School Principals, *The Bulletin:* "Dramatics in the Secondary School," Vol. 33 (December 1949); "Critical Problems in the Administration of Student Activities," Vol. 36 (February 1952); "A Basic Secondary Course in Public Speaking," Vol. 36 (May 1952); "Speech and Society," Vol. 32 (January 1948); "Speech and the Guidance Program," Vol. 32 (January 1948); "What Speech Can Contribute to High School Education," Vol. 29 (November 1945).

National Council for the Social Studies, *Housing America: A Source Unit for the Social Studies*, by John M. Haefner and others, Bulletin 14, 1940.

Pinault-Truszinski & Co., Architects, design of speech facilities for Cathedral High School.

Prentice-Hall, Inc., *Speech in the Classroom* by Donald H. Ecroyd. © 1960; *The Teaching of Speech* by Andrew T. Weaver, Gladys L. Borchers, and Donald K. Smith, 1952, by permission of Prentice-Hall, Inc., Englewood Cliffs, New Jersey.

Putnam's & Coward-McCann, *Art as Experience* by John Dewey. New York: Minton, Balch and Company, 1934.

The Ronald Press Company, *Speech Criticism—The Development of Standards for Rhetorical Appraisal* by Lester Thonssen and A. Craig Baird. Copyright 1948 The Ronald Press Company.

Russell Sage Foundation, *Behavioral Goals of General Education in High School* by Will French and Associates. New York, 1957.

Saturday Review, passage from p. 20 October 27, 1956 issue.

Scott, Foresman and Company, excerpts from *Language and Its Growth—An Introduction to the History of Language* by Harry F. Scott, et. al. Copyright © 1935 by Scott, Foresman and Company, Chicago.

Speech Association of America, quotations from three SAA publications.

State of Iowa Department of Public Instruction, *A Descriptive Handbook*, 1957 and *How Good Is Your Local School System*, Bulletin No. 100.

Traynor & Hermanson, Architects, sketch of the speech class room for the Detroit Lakes High School.

ACKNOWLEDGMENTS

Particular appreciation is extended to the following individuals for quoted materials:

Mary Adams, for the List of Units.

Sister Ambrose, O.S.B., Saint Boniface High School, for evaluation sheets and other materials.

Barnet Baskerville, "The Critical Method in Speech."

Donald N. Dedmon, for the tournament record form.

Marceline Erickson, for suggestions to help individual teachers upgrade speech education, Committee on Secondary School Speech, Central States Speech Association.

Marnell Fliger, for the Pairings Worksheet and the Table of Rank Values of Students.

Dennis Franke and Rev. Norman White, for "Appreciation of Great Music."

Frank W. Hart, *Teachers and Teaching by Ten Thousand High School Seniors,* 1934.

Paul Heinberg, "Rank Value of Students" scale.

Arthur Housman, for permission to quote from his personal philosophy of speech.

William S. Howell, Donald K. Smith, and David W. Thompson, rating blanks from *Speech, Debate, and Drama in Contest and Festivals.*

Donald E. Malmgren, Debate Tabulation Form.

Elizabeth Moodie Prather, for her 1957 statement of speech-teaching philosophy.

Arthur J. Przybilla, one-act play rehearsal schedule.

Ronald R. Reid, for a statement of philosophy of speech teaching.

James Robinson, evaluation sheets from *Oklahoma High School Speech League Official Handbook.*

F. Fulton Ross, for permission to quote from his personal philosophy of teaching speech.

To our teachers, who taught us much; to our students, who taught us more; and to future teachers and students of speech and speech education—may they learn from it.

Speech is civilization itself. The word, even the most contradictory word, preserves contact—it is silence which isolates.
—THOMAS MANN
THE MAGIC MOUNTAIN

Preface

Teaching Speech in Today's Secondary Schools is intended primarily for college students who are preparing either to teach speech or direct speech activities. It also is designed as a reference work for neophyte teachers who feel a need for help in getting started, and for experienced teachers who may desire a refresher in methods and materials for teaching speech and directing speech activities.

This book offers detailed, practical suggestions based on sound theory supported by the results of experimental studies. Most of the procedures, methods, and suggested handling of problems are based on the combined experiences of the authors as teachers for approximately fifty years in high schools, state colleges, and universities; some are the result of the teaching experiences of colleagues and friends.

The basic philosophy of the book rests on these beliefs: (1) Speech education should occupy a prominent place in American secondary education. (2) The teaching of speech should be closely and effectively oriented to the objectives of our democratic society and secondary education. (3) Successful teachers of speech are dedicated to stimulating and guiding students in their achievement and development as individuals, communicators, and citizens. (4) The effective teaching of speech may be difficult, time- and energy-consuming, but it is rewarding; and (5) with an increasing emphasis upon curricular, extra-class, and interscholastic speech education in high schools in the United States, teachers and directors must be equipped and ready to handle all phases of speech activities and education.

Obviously, no one book can cover the entire field of speech education and answer every possible question. This book is designed to present in sufficient detail the most effective methods and to discuss those materials which are both desired and desirable for teaching speech. It is also intended as a springboard to additional reading and investigation, a starting point for potentially qualified and dedicated teachers of speech.

The authors wish to express appreciation to colleagues and friends for suggestions, especially to Sister Annerose, O.S.B., Arthur Housman, and Robert H. Wick.

Special gratitude is extended to our wives and children for their many months of patience.

C.L.B. and H.F.S.

Saint Cloud, Minn.
Iowa City, Iowa
January 1965

CONTENTS

Preface		ix
1	SPEECH EDUCATION: ITS CONTRIBUTION TO EDUCATION AND SOCIETY	1
2	THE TEACHER OF SPEECH	42
3	THE HIGH SCHOOL STUDENT	66
4	THE TEACHER IN THE CLASSROOM	95
5	BASIC APPROACHES TO TEACHING SPEECH	115
6	THE RESOURCE UNIT IN TEACHING SPEECH	221
7	EVALUATING, TESTING, AND GRADING IN SPEECH EDUCATION	241
8	FACILITIES, EQUIPMENT, TEACHING AIDS, AND TEXTBOOKS	269
9	DIRECTING A CO-CURRICULAR SPEECH PROGRAM	284
	Appendix: Checklist for Teachers of Speech	415
	Index	419

CHAPTER 1

Speech Education: Its Contribution to Education and Society

Speech education has different meanings for different individuals. In its broadest sense, it embraces all experiences in the home, school, and community through which speech is learned. It refers to the contributions which parents, teachers, and, in fact, all our friends and associates make consciously or unconsciously to our learning to talk. It includes the effect on our speech by speakers to whom we listen.

Speech education is interpreted sometimes to mean only one phase of a curricular or, more often, an extracurricular program of speech training. This training may be corrective with appropriate compensations for defects not subject to correction by speech-handicapped students. The training may consist of coaching of a limited number of students who elect to develop their abilities in declamation, debate, dramatics, or some other types of speech performance. Neither corrective training nor coaching can serve best the speech interests, needs, and abilities of all students in a high school.

Usually, speech education refers to the theories, principles, methods, procedures, techniques, materials, devices, and activities utilized by teachers and other speech specialists to stimulate and broaden speech interests, satisfy the speech needs, and develop the speech abilities of all students to a high level of their individual capacities for learning to talk. In short, speech education refers, usually, to the teaching and learning of speech as an important means for helping all students—the so-called normal, the handicapped, and the talented—to become at least adequately adjusted, responsible, and effective communicators and citizens.

But speech education is a title which may refer, as it sometimes is used to refer, to "teaching and learning *to teach speech*." The results of much experience and some significant research are available to give insight and guidance to teachers and potential teachers of speech concerned with "how to arrive at what is best to teach," "how best to teach it," "for what purposes and outcomes to teach it," "how to prepare professionally and personally to teach it," and "how the teaching and learning of speech can be developed and made to fit efficiently, effectively, and harmoniously in the whole educational program in the high school."

Every one of these concepts of speech education has significance for the teacher of speech. He must know that his students learn speech initially by imitating the speech of their parents. He must know that all teachers have an influence, even if inadvertent and unconscious, on students' ideas, on their arrangement of their ideas, on their vocabularies and language, and on the quantity and quality of their comprehension and use of audible symbols and visible bodily action in talking. Obviously, the concepts of speech education by which students can learn speech and the methods and materials for teaching speech hold significance and interest for teachers of speech.

Answers to many questions about objectives, methods, and materials in teaching speech may be inferred from our understanding of the objectives of our society and of secondary education to which speech education, like any other part of the program of the high school, must contribute efficiently, effectively, and harmoniously.

Societal Objectives

Our society, like any other, is composed of people who are united by a common interest and who pursue the achievement of objectives which, to the extent that they are successfully achieved, lead to desired outcomes.

A society is not necessarily a community, a nation, or a government. On the contrary, nations and governments may be subservient to the society and to entities or institutions used by the society as means to facilitate the achievement of its objectives.

The ultimate objective of our American democratic society is to effect, maintain, and perfect an environment which affords for each individual full opportunity and incentive for him:

1. to develop his interests, abilities, and personal attributes or qualities to the maximum level of his potential as a person and worthy member of a democratic society.

2. to exercise responsibly and effectively all freedoms, privileges, and rights safeguarded by a democratic society for the happiness and welfare of himself and others.

3. to pursue, with the excellence and conscience of which he is capable, his freely chosen mission compatible with the preservation or survival, progression or growth and perfection, prosperity or success and well-being, and power or ability to direct the destiny of our American democratic society and thereby to provide equal opportunities for all.

4. to realize and enjoy the respect inherent in a democratic society for the worth and dignity of man.

This ultimate societal objective is, on the one hand, necessarily lofty, extravagant, and ideal. It must be so to appeal to the best and highest motives of all men and women as they determine societal and individual policies and courses of action. No less than an ideal objective can give right and sufficient direction to members, individually and collectively, of our American democratic society. No less than an ideal ultimate objective should guide our living, thinking, communication, and courses of action. On the other hand, our ultimate objective, like all enabling objectives subordinate to it, must hold hope and promise for achievement of significant outcomes desired by the individual as well as by the collective body of members identified by our American democratic society.

Lofty, extravagant, and ideal objectives which are sound can be everlastingly practical and workable to the extent that they are inspiring, hopeful, full of promise, challenging, rewarding to the extent achieved, and influential in our living, thinking, communication, and action as members of our American democratic society and its institutions.

The Evolution and Endurance of Our Objective

Our objective was the concern of men many centuries before America was discovered. Democracy was conceived in the Greek cities from which our democratic concepts and standards were inherited. By 348 B.C., a utopian society was visualized by Greek philosophers and statesmen. Plato,[1] with a vision of Utopia, devoted himself, as recorded in *The Republic*, to the evolution of an ideal state and system of state education. The objective of the state was clearly to serve man, as implied in Plato's concept of a democratic state:

> A State, I said, arises, as I conceive, out of the needs of mankind; no one is self-sufficing, but all of us have many wants. Can any other origin of a state be imagined? There can be no other.[2]

[1] Plato, *The Republic*. Trans. by Benjamin Jowett. New York: The World Publishing Co., 1946.
[2] *Ibid.*, p. 66.

Likewise, the objective of state education, as conceived by Plato and recorded in *The Republic,* was to realize the supreme values of human life. State education was, therefore, the necessary foundation, concern, and primary function of the state.

Although concepts and standards of a democratic society and of state education were modified during 2,000 years and more, the ultimate objective of society persisted, as is evidenced in our Declaration of Independence:

> We hold these truths to be self-evident, that all men are created equal, that they are endowed by their Creator with certain inalienable Rights, that among these are Life, Liberty, and the Pursuit of Happiness. That to secure these rights, Governments are instituted among men, deriving their just powers from the consent of the governed. That whenever any Form of Government becomes destructive of these ends, it is the Right of the People to alter or to abolish it, and to institute new Government, . . .

This declaration reflects the utopian society, the ideal state, and the system of state education which were the dreams of the Greek philosophers and statesmen. The great vision and wisdom of those who drafted it resulted in thinking, communication, and action which gave hope for a free American democratic society in which government would guarantee to all people equality of opportunity, and place responsibility on each individual for contributing his fair share of successful effort to the defense and support of the society.

The conflict between our concept of our freedoms and our concept of our responsibilities seems to be clearly evident in our Declaration of Independence and in the Preamble of our Constitution. This conflict was the focus of thinking and communication during the period from 1787 to 1791, as it is today, and resulted in action which seems to be continuous.

The first Ten Amendments to our Constitution, or the Bill of Rights, adopted in 1791, shifted the direction of our Constitution and its Preamble to give strength to the dignity and worth of the individual, with government as his means and servant, not the end or his master. Above all, the individual and his beliefs, emotions, sensations, and thoughts were thereby guaranteed freedom from interference and, as a supreme value, were guaranteed privacy as the most valued right. Nevertheless, socially responsible and effective exercise of the right were ever to be his greatest challenge and, simultaneously, the greatest challenge to education as the primary and perhaps supreme function of the state.

In the period of over 170 years since 1791, successful pursuit of democratic objectives has been achieved by an increased number and percentage of us, individually, as well as collectively.

THE EVOLUTION AND ENDURANCE OF OUR OBJECTIVE

Opportunities for self-development have improved, even if equal opportunity has not been achieved. Our liberties have been enlarged, often by the supreme sacrifice of freedoms and even of lives during wars and other forms of strife to maintain union, justice, tranquillity, and the blessings of liberty. Through the thinking, communication, and action of men, our democratic society and its institutions have been preserved, have prospered, and are respected by people throughout the world. Nevertheless, a re-examination of our societal objectives has been accomplished, especially during the twentieth century, as conditions and crises have seemed to demand.

In 1931, conditions made mandatory a re-examination of objectives as evidenced by a resolution adopted in a national meeting of educators:

> *Whereas*, The widespread economic disturbance through which the United States and other nations of the world are passing is evidence of serious social-economic maladjustment, and
>
> *Whereas*, The education of the people of a democracy determines its methods of dealing with social-economic problems,
>
> *Therefore Be It Resolved*, That the Board of Directors of the National Education Association recommends to the President of the Association the appointment of a committee to propose to the Association desirable Social-Economic Goals of America, and that the committee indicate the materials and methods which the schools of the nation should use to attain these goals.[3]

Six outstanding scholars[4] presented, after at least three years of study, "Ten Desirable Social-Economic Goals of America"[5] to give direction to America, its government, its schools, its enterprise, and its social and economic life, and to lay the foundation for a new outlook in the life of the people:

> 1. To increase opportunity for everyone to be wellborn under conditions which will conserve his innate strengths and capacities.
>
> 2. To provide opportunity for everyone to realize his rights to protection from accident and disease.
>
> 3. To assure each individual the fullest possible opportunity and incentive to gain command of the knowledge, skills, and techniques of communication such as spoken and written language, numbers, music, and drawing; to share far-flung contacts with men, goods, and ideas; to

---

[3] Joy Elmer Morgan, "What are Desirable Social-Economic Goals for America?" *The Journal of the National Education Association*, vol. 23, no. 1 (January 1934), p. 6.

[4] Members of the Committee: John Dewey, Willard E. Givens, Fred J. Kelly, Leon C. Marshall, Robert C. Moore, and Edward A. Ross.

[5] Committee of the National Education Association, "A Bill of Rights for the New Age," *The Journal of the National Education Association*, vol. 23, no. 7 (November 1934), p. 205.

understand our institutional life and problems of the day and their appropriate solutions; and to develop a critical appreciation of standards and values which reflect the experience of the human race and which actuate human conduct.

4. To multiply opportunities which foster the development of initiative, ability to weigh facts, resistance to prejudice, independence in thinking and judgment, expression of individual differences, and cooperative and socially contributory action.

5. To afford counsel and guidance as to vocations for which youths should fit themselves, training which underlies reputable modes of making a living according to individual liking and social need, and placement and advancement which result normally from efficient work in their respective occupations.

6. To guarantee to everyone a minimum income that will provide a reasonable standard of living.

7. To avail everyone with trustworthy information from unprejudiced, unbiased sources.

8. To guarantee to everyone equal chance to attain to his fullest possible development consistent with his duties, responsibilities, and service in proportion to his abilities; compensation in proportion to services rendered; and general diffusion among the people of the knowledge, the ethics, the idealism, and the spirit which as nearly as possible shall make this equality actual and effective.

9. To assure everyone the widest sphere of freedom compatible with the equal freedom of others.

10. To afford the means and incentive for everyone to act in conformity with the highest good of all other members of society and increasingly of the world.

These objectives were presumed by the Committee to be most desirable for Americans to pursue and most likely to lead to what the greatest number of Americans desire. The objectives might be said to be enabling objectives for achieving the more lofty and perhaps more extravagant ultimate objective of liberty and its blessings. Freedom of worship, of the press, and of speech were not admittedly valued less than heretofore but security was valued more than ever before. Therefore, the ten objectives which were evolved by 1934 were probably more hopeful and promising during the depression which had struck with suddenness and intensity. In fact, these objectives were probably designed to bolster morale, and to give people direction for recovering at least a degree of prosperity. Many Americans were without opportunity for employment. Too many were in breadlines. Too many had exhausted their savings. Many were demoralized by a curtailed and meager life. They sought freedom from want and freedom from fear. They demonstrated diminished confidence in obtaining rewards for their efforts in a free democratic society and some loss of faith in democracy itself. Likewise, education seemed to be wasteful and somewhat removed from serving the needs of Americans. However, even as their spirits were low, conditions were changing slowly and improved until a different set of needs arose.

Within less than ten years, societal needs resulted in ambitious, united, and supreme effort by Americans to achieve economic and military objectives mandatory for survival and for victory in World War II. Production, training programs, technological developments, medical and scientific advancement, and all available human resources and effort went into high gear. The outlook of Americans changed from depression and defeatism to prosperity and victory and restored faith in democracy as a way of life.

In 1960, fifteen national *Goals for Americans*[6] were proposed for achievement. The President's Commission,[7] administered by The American Assembly, Columbia University, as requested by President Eisenhower who founded the Assembly in 1950, expressed the hope that their recommendations would evoke discussion because, under the democratic process, active discussion is the path to a national consensus. The objectives seem to be especially significant because: (1) they recognize and are consistent with the democratic objectives which are traditionally American; (2) they counter objectives of 1934 under the New Deal of the Roosevelt administration; (3) they reflect confidence in the ability, determination, and resourcefulness of our free American democratic society and its system of enterprise; (4) they express faith in Americans and give clear and specific direction to them in enlarging their liberties at home; (5) they, for the first time in a statement of societal objectives, give direction to American and other free world initiative, enterprise, and leadership in meeting the menace and threat by any totalitarian state or combination of states to the extension of freedom throughout the world; (6) they summon Americans to exercise responsibly their sustained and cooperative effort for enlarging their liberties at home and extending freedom abroad; and (7) they provide ultimate objectives and suggest a framework and function for free American education and, in turn, speech education to the extent that it can contribute significantly to education and to society.

In the words of the President's Commission, "Goals at Home" were:

1. To achieve equal treatment of men and women . . . to expand their opportunities for self-development and self-expression.

2. To . . . assure every man and woman equal rights before the

[6] The President's Commission on National Goals, *Goals for Americans*. Englewood Cliffs, N.J.: Prentice-Hall, Inc., 1960.
[7] The Members of the Commission: Henry M. Wriston, Frank Pace, Jr., Erwin D. Canham, James B. Conant, Colgate W. Dorden, Jr., Crawford H. Greenewalt, Alfred M. Gruenther, Learned Hand, Clark Kerr, James R. Killian, Jr., and George Meany.

law, and an equal opportunity to vote and hold office, . . . and to participate fully in community affairs.

3. To preserve and perfect the democratic processes in the United States to clear the way for individual initiative. . . .

4. To strengthen and enhance the effectiveness of education at every level and in every discipline.

5. To advance knowledge and innovation on every front. . . .

6. To enable individuals to have maximum freedom in their choice of jobs, goods, and services.

7. To stimulate the economy to grow. . . .

8. To promote and encourage technological change. . . .

9. To achieve a supply-demand equilibrium in agriculture. . . .

10. To remedy slum conditions, . . . seek solutions for haphazard suburban growth. . . .

11. To meet the demand for medical care. . . .

The "Goals Abroad," in the words of the President's Commission, were:

12. To help to build an open and peaceful world.
13. To maintain the defense of the free world.
14. To attain disarmament.
15. To preserve and strengthen the United Nations.

All these societal objectives, proposed by various committees and commissions, are enablers for achieving the ultimate objective of our American democratic society to effect, maintain, and perfect an environment affording full opportunity and incentive to think, communicate, and act as responsible, effective, and respected persons and citizens. The greatest strength of our society rests in the potentialities of its citizens. Our system of public education has grown out of our concern for stimulating and guiding each individual to the achievement of the maximum of his ability to participate in the responsibilities and privileges of our society. Therefore, the ultimate educational objective is closely correlated with the objectives which the society has set up for itself. The ultimate educational objective in free public education is accomplished, in so far as it is accomplished in our high schools, by making a change, a difference, an improvement in boys and girls, in their attitudes and qualities, their intellects, their work and play, their emotional balance and control, and, in fact, their adaptation, influence, cooperation, and control and direction of their interests, abilities, and energies. This improvement seems to be revealed in their behavior as boys and girls and in their later behavior as adults. Our attitude toward the importance and worthwhileness of public education, and toward any part of its program, seems to be closely correlated with our impressions of its effect in helping individuals to become responsible and effective adult citizens in cooperative pursuit of our society's objectives.

Educational Objectives

Educational objectives are presumably either parallel or subordinate to our societal objectives. In either event, the educational objectives of the high school are presumed to be in consonance with the societal objectives. Also, the objectives of the high school are enabling objectives through which, to the extent that they are achieved in secondary education, the high school makes its contribution to the societal objectives.

The "Cardinal Principles of Secondary Education" is probably the most widely and best known statement of objectives for the high school. The seven objectives are (1) health, (2) command of fundamental processes, (3) worthy home membership, (4) vocation, (5) civic education, (6) worthy use of leisure, and (7) ethical character.[8]

These seven objectives have been widely employed by faculties in elementary and secondary schools. Likewise, they have been praised because they suggest outcomes of secondary education in the development of adolescents by specifying attributes regarded as desirable for adults. Possibly they have been praised because they are meaningful and, at the same time, general enough to permit a variety of interpretations and thereby enable teachers to serve various objectives in the name of the "Cardinal Principles of Secondary Education." On the other hand, they have been criticized adversely because they allegedly specify attributes regarded as desirable for adults. They seem to give little recognition to the developmental problems of adolescents, such as understanding their parents and having their parents understand them, of making adjustment to their physiological changes, of social relationships with each other and especially relationships with the opposite sex, of gaining and maintaining status acceptable to their peers, and their problem of satisfying adult standards of behavior. In fact, they seem to neglect desirable educational outcomes such as intellectual growth, economic efficiency, scientific knowledge, social competence and responsibility, and international and even national understanding. Nevertheless, they are broad educational objectives which give broad direction to many secondary school programs.

In 1938, the Educational Policies Commission of the National Education Association stated *The Purposes of Education in American Democracy*.[9] This Commission filled in some of the gaps in the "Seven Cardinal Principles of Secondary Education" and gave more specific direction to secondary education. Also, the Commission changed the focus from outcomes of

---

[8] Commission on the Reorganization of Secondary Education, "Cardinal Principles of Secondary Education," *United States Office of Education Bulletin No. 35*. Washington: Government Printing Office, 1918. p. 9.

[9] Educational Policies Commission, *The Purposes of Education in American Democracy*. Washington: National Education Association, 1938.

education regarded by adults as desirable for adult citizens to aspects of growth of the high school student as a person and citizen. These objectives center on the development in each individual of significant aspects of growth. In the words of the Commission,

> These aspects center around the person himself, his relationships to others in home and community, the creation and use of material wealth, and socio-civic activities. The first area calls for a description of the educated person; the second, for a description of the educated member of the family and community group; the third, of the educated producer or consumer; the fourth, of the educated citizen.[10]

The broad fourfold classification of educational objectives and the slightly less than fifty specific objectives proposed by the Commission and published by the National Education Association in 1938 follow:

1. *The Objectives of Self-Realization*

The Inquiring Mind. The educated person has an appetite for learning.
Speech. The educated person can speak the mother tongue clearly.
Reading. The educated person reads the mother tongue efficiently.
Writing. The educated person writes the mother tongue effectively.
Sight and Hearing. The educated person is skilled in listening and observing.
Intellectual Interests. The educated person has mental resources for the use of leisure.
Esthetic interest. The educated person appreciates beauty.
Character. The educated person gives responsible direction to his own life.

2. *The Objectives of Human Relationships*

Respect for Humanity. The educated person puts human relationships first.
Friendships. The educated person enjoys a rich, sincere, and varied social life.
Cooperation. The educated person can work and play with others.
Courtesy. The educated person deserves the amenities of social behavior.
Appreciation of the Home. The educated person appreciates the family as a social institution.
Conservation of the Home. The educated person conserves family ideals.
Homemaking. The educated person is skilled in homemaking.

[10] *Ibid.*, p. 47.

Democracy in the Home. The educated person maintains democratic family relationships.

3. *The Objectives of Economic Efficiency*

Work. The educated producer knows the satisfaction of good workmanship.

Occupational Information. The educated producer understands the requirements and opportunities for various jobs.

Occupational Choice. The educated producer has selected his occupation.

Occupational Efficiency. The educated producer succeeds in his chosen vocation.

Occupational Adjustment. The educated producer maintains and improves his efficiency.

Occupational Appreciation. The educated producer appreciates the social value of his work.

Personal Economics. The educated consumer plans the economics of his own life.

Consumer Judgment. The educated consumer develops standards for guiding his expenditures.

Efficiency in Buying. The educated consumer is an informed and skillful buyer.

Consumer Protection. The educated consumer takes appropriate measures to safeguard his interests.

4. *The Objectives of Civic Responsibility*

Social Justice. The educated citizen is sensitive to the disparities of human circumstance.

Social Activity. The educated citizen acts to correct unsatisfactory conditions.

Social Understanding. The educated citizen seeks to understand social structures and social processes.

Critical Judgment. The educated citizen has defenses against propaganda.

Tolerance. The educated citizen respects honest differences of opinion.

Conservation. The educated citizen has a regard for the nation's resources.

Social Applications of Science. The educated citizen measures scientific advance by its contribution to the general welfare.

World Citizenship. The educated citizen is a cooperating member of the world community.

Law Observance. The educated citizen respects the law.

Economic Literacy. The educated citizen is economically literate.
Political Citizenship. The educated citizen accepts his civic duties.
Devotion to Democracy. The educated citizen acts upon an unswerving loyalty to democratic ideals.

These specific objectives provoke both praise and blame. Some educators praise them for being specific, meaningful, and useful guides for our schools. Some praise them for their emphasis on social adjustment and on the development in each boy and girl of the knowledge, understanding, abilities, and attributes or qualities basic and necessary for intellectual growth, vocational preparation, civic responsibility, and self-realization. Yet others may complain because the objectives fail to focus on intellectual growth. Still others may complain because the objectives seem to place equal emphasis on attaining desired outcomes unequal in importance. Also, teachers may complain because the objectives are too specific as directives for elementary and secondary education. Nevertheless, all of us may accept the 43 objectives, as a whole, as best of those suggested for guiding faculties in our high schools.

In 1944, "The Imperative Needs of Youth" was formulated under the auspices of the National Association of Secondary School Principals. The ten imperative needs, as formulated by high school administrators, follow: (1) salable skills; (2) health and physical fitness; (3) citizenship; (4) family life; (5) purchase and use of goods and services; (6) scientific knowledge and methods; (7) appreciation of beauty; (8) wise use of leisure time; (9) respect for others, ethical values, and cooperation; and (10) ability to think, express thoughts, read, and listen.[11]

The statement of the ten needs of youth is an extension of the "Cardinal Principles of Secondary Education." They focus attention on outcomes regarded by adults as desirable for well-rounded adult citizens. If the imperativeness of the needs is not accepted by boys and girls in high school, it is accepted presumably by many of their elders. Since the statement of imperative needs of youth was formulated by a committee of principals and adopted by our foremost national organization of principals, the list of ten desired outcomes is presumed to be used widely by teachers in high schools in the United States.

In 1945, The Harvard Committee transmitted to President James Bryant Conant, Harvard University, its report on "The Objectives of a General Education in a Free Society." The Committee of twelve consulted hundreds of other people across the nation. Numerous concepts basic to

---

[11] National Association of Secondary School Principals, *Planning for American Youth*. Washington: National Education Association, 1944.

EDUCATIONAL OBJECTIVES 13

objectives of the high school were proposed by members of the Committee.[12] In the words of their report, a very few of the concepts follow:[13]

> ... a supreme need of American education is for a unifying purpose and idea. As recently as a century ago, no doubt existed about such a purpose: it was to train the Christian citizen. ... a diversity of education which, if it has many virtues, nevertheless works against the good of society by helping to destroy the common ground of training and outlook on which any society depends. ... it seems that a common ground between some, though not all, of the ideas underlying our educational practice is the sense of heritage. ... there is doubtless a sense in which religious education, education in the great books, and education in modern democracy may ... work together to the same end, which is the belief in the idea of man and society that we inherit, adapt, and pass on. ... that of the dignity of man. To the belief in man's dignity must be added the recognition of his duty to his fellow men. ... Belief in the dignity and mutual obligation of man is the common ground between these contrasting but mutually necessary forces in our culture. ... It [general education] is used to indicate that part of a student's whole education which looks first of all to his life as a responsible human being and citizen; while the term, special education, indicates that part which looks to the student's competence in some occupation.[14]

Responsible citizens who are competent in their occupations are, at once and always, to be desired as members of society. The Harvard Committee recognized both general and special education as means to responsible citizenship and occupational competence. They emphasized the essential areas of knowledge and attributes of mind and character comprised by general education and basic to successful pursuit of life, liberty, and happiness. However, for our purpose, "The Objectives of a General Education in a Free Society" as recommended by the members of the Committee are important:[15]

> 1. To think effectively. By effective thinking we mean, in the first place, logical thinking; the ability to draw sound conclusions from premises. ... logical thinking is the capacity to extract universal truths from particular cases and, in turn, to infer particulars from general laws. More strictly, it is the ability ... to analyze a problem into its

---

[12] The Members of the Committee: Paul H. Buck, John H. Findlay, Jr., Raphael Demos, Leigh Hoadley, Byron S. Hollinshead, Wilbur K. Jordan, Ivor A. Richards, Phillip J. Rulon, Arthur M. Schlesinger, Robert Ulich, George Wald, and Benjamin F. Wright.

[13] Reprinted by permission of the publishers from Report of the Harvard Committee, *General Education in a Free Society*. Cambridge, Mass.: Harvard University Press, 1945, by the President and Fellows of Harvard College.

[14] *Ibid.*, pp. 42–58.

[15] *Ibid.*, pp. 65–78.

component elements, and . . . to recombine these . . . so as to reach a solution. . . . the three phases of effective thinking, logical, relational, and imaginative, correspond roughly to the three divisions of learning, the natural sciences, the social studies, and the humanities, respectively.

2. To communicate thought. The ability to express oneself so as to be understood by others is obviously inseparable from effective thinking. . . . Good speech and writing are the visible tests and signs of good thinking. . . . You cannot say something unless you have something to say; but in order to express your ideas properly you also need some skill in communication. . . . Communication is not speaking only but listening as well; you cannot succeed in communicating your ideas unless the other person wishes to hear and knows how to listen. . . . communication breaks up into the four related skills of speaking and listening, writing and reading. . . . In its character as the sharing of meanings it is the instrument by which human beings are welded into a society. . . . In a free and democratic society the art of communication has a special importance.

3. To make relevant judgments. The making of relevant judgments involves the ability of the student to bring to bear the whole range of ideas upon the area of experience. The essential thing is that the teacher should be constantly aware of the ultimate objectives, never letting means obscure ends, and be persistent in directing the attention of the student from the symbols to the things they symbolize.

4. To discriminate among values. Discrimination among values involves choice. The ability to discriminate in choosing covers not only awareness of different kinds of values but of their relations, including a sense of relative importance and of the mutual dependence of means and ends. . . . There are the obvious values of character, like fair play, courage, self-control, the impulse of beneficence and humanity; there are the intellectual values, like the love of truth and the respect for the intellectual enterprise; there are the esthetic values, like good taste and the appreciation of beauty. . . . Discrimination in values is developed by the study of all the three areas of learning. . . . Values are rooted in facts; and human ideals are somehow a part of nature.

These four objectives are recognized universally. They are accepted as supreme objectives of secondary education. However, they are probably seldom proclaimed by faculties as guides for their programs in our high schools. Most teachers maintain that the subjects they teach serve to help their students to think effectively, to communicate thought, to make relevant judgments, and to discriminate among values. But these teachers may be too busy helping their students to grasp the subject matter of courses, to gain understanding of the subject matter, and to develop skills in courses in which skills are desired outcomes to permit these students or their teachers to be concerned with these high objectives. A teacher is probably justified in saying that his subject, course, or other specialty does contribute something to each of the four abilities. He may find it difficult to explain how his carefully organized course, units, or assignments result in any significant contribution to these objectives of general education in the high school. He may question whether he should be concerned with general education in the high school. If he is teaching government, history, literature, or physics, he may state frankly that he has no time to focus on helping students to think effectively or to express themselves clearly. Nevertheless, he may be justified in his assertion that the concepts, vocabulary, and language which students learn in his course or specialty contribute to the achievement of these objectives. Opportunities may be found in all courses in the high school to contribute directly and effectively to achieving these ideal objectives.

In 1948, Dr. Magdalene Kramer, a past president of the Speech Association of America, indicated eight goals of universal education:[16]

1. It should, first of all, prepare a man to earn a living.

2. It should provide opportunities and the necessary resources for him to develop a "well-furnished mind."

3. It should aid him in the cultivation of the power to think: to reason, to investigate, to test new ideas, to evolve new concepts, to make decisions on the basis of pertinent data, to distinguish fact and opinion, to analyze propaganda, to form sound judgments, to build worthy values, and to solve problems.

4. It should foster with great care the development of articulate human beings, who are aware of their moral accountability for any ideas expressed.

5. It should cultivate within the individual a social consciousness and responsibility, as well as develop the ability to cooperate with others and to recognize the rights of others.

6. It should cultivate the creative and appreciative talents.

7. It should help the individual to formulate estimable moral values.

8. It should provide the means for discovering those individuals who are endowed with the special qualifications for leadership, and also provide the experiences which will enable the potential leaders to grow to the fullest of their capacity.

From these suggested functions of universal education one can easily infer objectives which reflect and give added meaning to the objectives stated by the Harvard Committee. Those indicated by Kramer may not be adopted by faculties in many high schools, yet they are probably widely employed, in essence, in most secondary schools. They suggest that the objectives of general education are inseparable from those of special educa-

[16] Magdalene Kramer, "The Role of Speech in Education: A Re-Evaluation," *Quarterly Journal of Speech*, vol. 34 (April 1948), pp. 23–27.

tion and that the problem of our faculties in high schools is to maintain a balance in their perspective and in their individual and collective programs.

In 1953, Havighurst indicated problems bothersome to adolescent boys and girls who feel the need for immediate solution of their problems. These ten problems, stated as desirable and desired outcomes,[17] indicate objectives for achievement by teachers who are interested in stimulating and guiding students in their growth to full maturity and stability as persons and citizens:

1. Achieving new and more mature relations with age-mates of both sexes.
2. Accepting a masculine and feminine social role.
3. Accepting one's physique and using the body effectively.
4. Achieving emotional independence of parents and other adults.
5. Achieving assurance of economic independence.
6. Selecting and preparing for an occupation.
7. Preparing for marriage and family life.
8. Developing intellectual skills and concepts necessary for civic competence.
9. Desiring and achieving socially responsible behavior.
10. Acquiring a set of values and an ethical system as a guide to behavior.

Although the solution of these problems can hardly be the primary concern of teachers in our high schools, their neglect may result in a lack of progress by students in satisfying their felt needs. Preoccupation by adolescent boys and girls with their problems recognized by these ten objectives may make it difficult, and in some cases almost impossible, to pursue the achievement of any other objectives. Until they achieve sufficient maturity and stability in facing and solving their developmental problems, they are not likely to be challenged by other concerns by their teachers and by themselves. Even though adolescent boys and girls may not admit or even recognize why they do not make academic progress, the cause may be, and often is, immaturity, instability, and lack of confidence. Lack of academic progress by high school students, based on the developmental problems of youth implied by these objectives, may have given impetus to the widespread development of guidance programs in secondary education during the last fifteen years. However, most thoughtful teachers would hardly expect guidance counselors alone, no matter how well prepared the counselors might be, to be successful in satisfying the developmental needs of adolescent boys and girls. These teachers might indeed welcome opportunities for helping students to solve their develop-

[17] Robert J. Havighurst, *Human Development of Education.* New York: David McKay Company, Inc., 1953.

mental problems by contributing a portion of their energy and time to stimulating and guiding students in achieving the ten objectives suggested by Havighurst.

In 1955, a committee of the White House Conference on Education prepared a statement of programs and services from which can be inferred at least fifteen objectives as guides for planning by high school faculties:[18]

1. A general education as good or better than that offered in the past with increased emphasis on the physical and social sciences.
2. Programs designed to develop patriotism and good citizenship.
3. Programs designed to foster moral, ethical, and spiritual values.
4. Vocational education tailored to the abilities of each pupil and to the needs of the community and nation.
5. Courses designed to teach domestic skills.
6. Training in leisure time activities such as music, dancing, avocational reading, and hobbies.
7. A variety of health services for all children including both physical and mental inspections and instruction aimed at bettering health knowledge and habits.
8. Special treatment for children with speech or reading difficulties and other handicaps.
9. Physical education, ranging from systematic exercises, physical therapy, and intramural sports, to interscholastic athletic competition.
10. Instruction to meet the needs of abler students.
11. Programs designed to acquaint students with countries other than their own in an effort to help them understand the problem America faces in international relations.
12. Programs designed to foster mental health.
13. Programs designed to foster wholesome family living.
14. Organized recreational and social activities.
15. Courses designed to promote safety, including instruction in driving, swimming, civil defense, et cetera.

These White House educational objectives reflect the objectives stated earlier. They parallel closely our societal objectives. They give additional, new emphasis and impetus to general education with recognition of "Special treatment for children with speech or reading difficulties and other handicaps," "Instruction to meet the needs of abler students," "Programs designed to acquaint students with countries other than their own in an effort to help them understand the problem America faces in international relations," "Organized recreational and social activities," and "Courses designed to promote safety." They give meaning to the development of ". . . a student's whole education which looks first of all to his life as a

[18] The Committee for the White House Conference on Education, *A Report to The President.* Washington: Government Printing Office, 1956. pp. 8–9.

responsible human being and citizen," and ". . . to the student's competence in some occupation."[19] Judging by the number of educators and laymen in the White House Conference, they reflect outcomes of education desired by representative citizens of the United States.

In 1957, the Iowa State Department of Public Instruction set forth twelve objectives to help elementary and secondary schools give direction to their own school programs and to suggest direction for education for adults:[20]

1. To develop and maintain sound physical and mental health.

2. To achieve a growing command of the fundamental learnings: the three R's, facility in speech, skill in listening, map reading, skills in science and mathematics, and respect for all fields of organized knowledge.

3. To establish an understanding of and belief in oneself.

4. To work easily and effectively with others.

5. To understand and respect our democratic heritage: respect for for authority, concern for the common welfare, belief in the will of the majority, and the practice of democracy in group relations.

6. To develop ability to use personal resources wisely: material resources such as money and goods and human resources such as physical energy and mental endowment.

7. To build a personal system of moral standards and spiritual values: to do work honestly and well, to make reasonable decisions without undue delaying action, to show genuine respect for the feelings of others, to see life's funny side with gentle humor, to act consistently as responsible citizens, and to grow in understanding and practice of spiritual qualities which include a faith in a power greater than oneself.

8. To grow in an awareness and enjoyment of things of beauty.

9. To develop wholesome leisure-time interests: to choose activities that will promote physical well-being, stimulate the intellect, expand creative interests, increase social enjoyment, practice civic duties, and make life more vital and significant.

10. To grow increasingly in good judgment and intelligent action: to detect problems, to apply effective means of arriving at solutions, and to put their decisions into action.

11. To develop an inner compulsion for lifelong learning: to inspire young people with the freshness of intellectual excitement, to give meaning and purposes to their life, and to enable them to grow, year by year, in their zest for learning.

12. To thoughtfully consider and plan for a career: to open up the field of occupational possibilities, to give some exploratory experi-

---

[19] The Harvard Committee, *op. cit.*, p. 51.

[20] The State of Iowa Department of Public Instruction, *A Descriptive Handbook*. Des Moines, Iowa: The Department, 1957.

ence, and to develop the skills and attitudes which are helpful to young people regardless of the specific careers they may finally choose.

These twelve objectives point to tasks of all education as interpreted by the Iowa State Department of Public Instruction in helping local school systems and faculties to direct their own programs. Basic to the interpretation are assumptions which were stated by the Department:[21]

> There seems to be a growing understanding that education is the most important public service in the United States today. Many will agree that the future of our country, in large measure, is to be found in its classrooms. . . . the social and governmental policy of the American people is based upon democratic principles. Thus, it follows that education and democracy must develop together. Probably the best measure of the success of an educational program is the degree to which our young people grow into effective, participating citizens. . . . Progress in the achievement of a given purpose is likely to mean the strengthening of all others.

Contributions of Speech Education

A comparative study of our educational objectives of the last half century with our societal objectives of the last two centuries reveals that the former are either parallel or subordinate to the latter. In some instances, they are identical. Without exception, they give direction and commitment to secondary education to provide a variety of experiences which will satisfy the interests and needs of the individual and develop his abilities and desirable personal qualities, and also serve our democracy. The seeming conflict between the best interests of the individual and those of our representative democracy is in reality no conflict when one considers that an individual apart from social relations is a myth—or a monstrosity.[22] An individual, living in a democracy, has no desirable interests, needs, and abilities which are incompatible with those of a democratic society. Education can neither permit the group to exploit the individual nor the individual to disregard the interests of the group. Secondary education and all its parts, including speech education, should provide a variety of guided experiences for the perpetuation of the individual as a person and as a member of society and, by doing so, perpetuate that kind of society. The best measure of the value of a program of speech education, and of any other program in a high school, is the degree to which it contributes, or can contribute, to the

---

[21] State of Iowa Department of Public Instruction, *How Good Is Your Local School System?*, Bulletin No. 100. Des Moines, Iowa: The State of Iowa, 1958. 36 pp.

[22] William H. Kilpatrick, *The Educational Frontier*. New York: Appleton-Century-Crofts, Inc., 1933. p. 291.

aspects of growth of each boy and girl as a responsible and effective person, student, and citizen.

Speech education, the teaching and learning of responsible and effective speaking, has long been a concern of thoughtful men. As citizens of the Greek cities conceived democracy, they were faced with the requirement for regulations governing organized and responsible speaking. Likewise, they were concerned with effective speaking as imperative in a democracy in which people were responsible for governing themselves. Although speech education as it is known today may not have been practiced in the Greek cities, something of the kind was started in Sicily by 400 B.C. People who gain the freedom to govern themselves recognize their obligation to adapt to one another, to cooperate, and to exercise influence through speech. Because speech is used daily in more ways to solve more problems, to settle more issues, and to reap more dividends than any other human activity which is subject to human development, speech education has evolved as a function of education.

Its value and the need for more emphasis on it have both been recognized in the writings by authorities in speech and by progressive educators. Thonssen and Baird commented succinctly on the educational requirements of a democracy and on the value of speech and speech education:

> Democratic society is based upon the premise that the collective body of the common people is competent to exercise supreme authority in the state. In such a scheme, the power of public address must be a force of no mean proportion. If each citizen is to be—or is as Aristotle put it in his *Politics*—a "political animal," and if speech is to be the instrument by which advantage and disadvantage, truth and justice, are to be sustained, it follows that each man must be something of a statesman and of an advocate in his own right. Each citizen must serve as a balance wheel in an exceedingly complex political mechanism.[23]

That each man in a democracy must be something of a statesman and of an advocate in his own right was the basic assumption, point of departure, and frame of reference accepted by Brigance in his book, *Speech: Its Techniques and Disciplines in a Free Society*:

> These, in brief, are that speechmaking in the beginning grew out of man's first attempts at self-government, that it is inherent in a free society, that a course in speechmaking ought to be based on this concept, and speech training in a free society ought to be recognized as being essentially at variance with that in countries where governments

---

[23] Lester Thonssen and A. Craig Baird, *Speech Criticism: The Development of Standards for Rhetorical Appraisal*. New York: Copyright 1948, The Ronald Press Company, p. 468.

CONTRIBUTIONS OF SPEECH EDUCATION 21

are sustained by thought control. . . . The significant fact is that a theory of public address grew swiftly and inevitably out of the compulsion laid upon the people to govern themselves by persuasive talk.[24]

Progressive educators, as well as progressive speech educators, have expressed the need for more emphasis on speech education. Dewey in *How We Think* wrote:

> Speech . . . is the great instrument of social adaptation; and with the development of speech adaptation of the baby's activities to and with those of other persons gives the keynote of mental life. . . . It [language] is continually used in all studies as well as in all of the social disciplines of the school. . . . It is a distinct object of study. . . . That problem [of the school in respect to speech] is to direct pupils' oral and written speech, used primarily for practical and social ends, so that gradually it shall become a conscious tool of conveying knowledge and assisting thought.[25]

Dewey in his *Art as Experience* further recognized the need for emphasis on speech education:

> Moreover, events that are familiar and customary are those we are least likely to reflect upon; we take them for granted. They are also, because of their closeness to us, through gesture and pantomime, most difficult to observe. Communication through speech, oral and written, is the familiar and constant feature of social life. We tend, accordingly, to regard it as just one phenomenon among others of what we must in any case accept without question. We pass over the fact that it is the foundation and source of all activities and relations that are distinctive of internal union of human beings with one another.[26]

Hochmuth, a leading educator in speech, wrote in the *Bulletin of the National Association of Secondary School Principals*:

> Since communication is the social mechanism by which people relate themselves to each other, it is imperative that an attempt be made to perfect its use. The assumption that because one is able to make utterances he needs nothing further is false. It always has been. Farseeing educators will recognize that we cannot be seriously concerning ourselves with the problem of active and responsible citizenship so long as we do little or nothing to facilitate the process of cooperation.[27]

[24] From *Speech: Its Techniques and Disciplines in a Free Society*. 1st ed., by William Norwood Brigance. Copyright 1952, Appleton-Century-Crofts, Inc. pp. vii and ix. Reprinted by permission of Appleton-Century-Crofts.

[25] John Dewey, *How We Think*. New York: D. C. Heath and Company, 1933. pp. 207 and 238–239.

[26] John Dewey, *Art as Experience*. New York: Putnam's & Coward McCann, 1934. pp. 334–335.

[27] Marie Hochmuth, "Speech and Society," *The Bulletin of the National Association of Secondary School Principals* (January 1948), p. 32.

O'Connell presented a case in support of speech education as a vital part of education in our kind of society:

> Speech is the common bond possessed by all men and the most universal means of communication.... By ... a conscious program of speech education, we contribute to the two basic aims of all education which are: (1) self-realization of the individual, and (2) social adjustment of the individual.... Because speech education helps to develop thinking, articulate participation, and consciousness of responsibility, social adjustment, therefore, becomes easier as we find the speech trained individual taking part more fully in the democratic process vital to this type of life.[28]

This statement by O'Connell expresses our concern that the "teaching and learning of speech" contributes significantly to the student's achievement of the objectives of secondary education. But neither speech education nor any one program in secondary education is expected to contribute significantly to the student's achievement of all objectives. No educationally minded teacher would either make such a claim or act as if he believed it. But each program and each teacher in a high school is expected to make an important contribution to students' achievement of at least one of its objectives. A teacher of speech should, of course, concern himself with the objectives of the high school in which he teaches, with planning his program to effect their maximum achievement by students, and with giving maximum cooperation and support to the high school's entire program.

The teacher of speech, like any other teacher, should be concerned with the contribution of speech education to the achievement of all school educational objectives, thereby satisfying to a maximum degree the needs of the society that supports the school and its program. To this end, the following consideration of possible contributions by speech education can be helpful.

The competent teacher of speech will recognize that the effective program of speech education is based on facts secured from various disciplines, such as psychology, linguistics, communication, social science, and physiology. One listing of important elements included: (1) speech is learned, not inherited, (2) speech is complicated, (3) the act of speech is unified, and (4) the requirements of speech vary in differing cultures.[29]

The importance of communication in our present-day world is indisputable. Education for effective "oral" communication is paramount for the individual and the modern society in which he is living. With radio, television, and communcation satellites, perhaps at no time in man's history

---

[28] William V. O'Connell, "Speech and the Guidance Program," *The Bulletin of the National Association of Secondary School Principals* (January 1948), p. 137.

[29] Special Committee on Contests of the Speech Association of America, "A Program of Speech Education," *Quarterly Journal of Speech* (October 1951), pp. 348–349.

is thoughtful, proficient, and continuously effective communication more important than today. As a man could be the center of attention in a New England town meeting, so he can be an important center of attention of the whole world today on radio and television. We have only to reflect on the problems brought about by a failure in communication—personal, social, national, and international—to recognize the importance of effective speaking and listening.

All those interested in America's secondary schools—administrators, teachers, parents, taxpayers, and students—have shown a concern for the all-round and continuous development of students as responsible and concerned members of a school and of the ever enlarging community. They conceive of a "successful" school as one that formulates a program that is so consistent with the interests, needs, and abilities of its students that one is able to see the results of their education in the behavior of its graduates. The importance and significance of the high school program is thus reflected by the degree that the products of such a program become responsible, informed, intelligent, and effective adult citizens in the society.

Since it is imperative that future teachers of speech understand the importance of their work, the following consideration of the contribution of speech education to the educational goals of the high school is presented.

1. *Health.* "To help students develop and maintain sound physical and mental health and fitness" is implicit in every set of objectives of secondary education. Health is normally considered the jurisdiction of the teacher of physical education, the school nurse, the parents, and physicians. A well-qualified teacher of speech has exceptional opportunity to contribute to his students' development and maintenance of a healthy mental outlook. By his choice of reading assignments, with continual concern for reflective thinking, the well-prepared teacher of speech can stimulate and guide students to explore health problems. He knows that the best teaching and learning of speech compels students' understanding of themselves, of the control and use of their bodies, of right habits of living, and of the importance of a high standard of physical and mental health. He recognizes his obligation to be acquainted with the physiological, the neurological, the psychological, and the genetic bases of speech as well as its social and other bases.[30]

2. *Command of the Fundamental Processes.* "Reading, writing, and arithmetic" have been extended since 1918 to include "ability to think, express thoughts, read, and listen" as imperative needs of youth. Clark, President of the New York State Board of Law Examiners, made the point in 1937 that

---

[30] Giles Wilkeson Gray and Claude Merton Wise, *The Bases of Speech.* New York: Harper & Row, Publishers, 1934.

> . . . every physical process in which every individual constantly engages is almost never adequately taught or effectively learned. . . . the first two physical processes in which the newborn child engages—breathing and the use of the vocal cords—are usually sadly neglected in the course of our educational process. . . . In the great majority of cases a child learns to speak solely by the imitation process. . . . Two suggestions occur to the observer. The first is that at the start and at frequent intervals stress be laid upon the acquisition of proper speaking methods. The second is that every person who undertakes to participate in teaching should pay enough attention to the primary processes so that he or she should be a living exemplar of the qualities I have outlined.[31]

Seely, in his *On Teaching English,* recognized a need for more emphasis on speech education in organized education. He wrote:

> Undoubtedly oral expression is at once the most natural and direct means of intercourse possessed by man . . . formal and formidable species of oral performance, oratory and debating, have been prominently included in the curriculum almost from the beginning of organized education. . . . What man actually does and needs to do it better, more happily, and more meaningfully will give us our first cues to the direction education should take.[32]

Featherstone, writing on "The Place of Speech Training in an Integrated Curriculum," supported the need for speech education in our schools.

> Every curriculum should provide opportunity for the student who wishes to major in speech arts, just as it provides for the student who wishes to major in modern languages, science, or industrial arts. Furthermore, every school should provide for the clinical aspects of speech training. . . . Every teacher should try to feel his personal responsibility for the better speech habits of his pupils. . . . He should, first of all, set a good example, because much learning takes place by imitation. . . . There is no phase of general education that has been so sadly neglected.[33]

Communication, the act of sharing meanings, consists of four fundamental and vitally essential processes: speaking, listening-observing, writing, and reading. Speaking is defined as the act of projecting sound waves or light waves, or both, which we call audible symbols or visible bodily

---

[31] John Kirkland Clark, "An Outsider Looks at Education," *The Phi Beta Kappa News Magazine,* vol. 3, no. 1 (Winter 1938), p. 1. (Excerpts from an address delivered before the Phi Beta Kappa Council, Atlanta, Georgia, September 10, 1937.)

[32] H. F. Seely, *On Teaching English.* Chicago: American Book Company, 1933. pp. 155–157.

[33] W. B. Featherstone, "The Place of Speech Training in an Integrated Curriculum," reprinted from the September 1955 issue of *Education,* by permission of the publishers, The Bobbs-Merrill Co., Inc., Indianapolis, Indiana.

action to which we hope the listener will attach the meaning we intended. The counterpart of speaking is listening, which is defined as the act of attaching meaning to audible symbols, or visible bodily action, or both. Basic to both speaking and listening is speech manifested by audible symbols and bodily action used by a speaker to stir up ideas and affective states in a listener or listeners. Obviously, neither the ideas nor the affective states intended by the speaker will be stirred up in the listener unless the listener attaches to the symbols and action the meaning intended by the speaker. However, neither a set of audible symbols nor visible bodily action used by a speaker constitute speech, because speech is not merely vocalizing, enunciating, pronouncing, articulating, and gesturing.

Speech, as used by public speakers, by actors, by oral interpreters, by conversationalists, by discussers, by debaters, by declaimers, and by listeners, includes (1) ideas selected for communication under the conditions of the speech situation, (2) arrangement of the ideas for the purpose of getting from the listener the response desired by the speaker, (3) phraseology of the selected thoughts in language appropriate for the listener in the speech situation, and (4) projection of sound waves or light waves, or both, to stimulate in the listener the meanings, attitudes, ideas, and affective states desired by the speaker in the listener. Effective speech is, therefore, that speech which serves maximum efficiency in self-expression and in communication. It is (1) purposeful, (2) easily understood, and (3) provocative of thought, ideas, affective states, or action, or all of these, in terms of the purpose of the speaker.

Speech education is a process of stimulating and guiding the continuous and all-round growth of the individual by (1) satisfying and broadening his speech interests and needs, (2) developing his speech abilities (a) to use effectively audible symbols and visible bodily action to stir up ideas and affective states in other persons and (b) to interpret the audible symbols and gestures used by other persons to stir up ideas and affective states in him, and (3) developing desirable personal attributes such as alertness, initiative and industry, imagination and resourcefulness, cooperation, reliability, and integrity and self-direction in discharging responsibilities promptly and well.

Although every student began to get some command of these fundamental processes at home and in the kindergarten, the primary, and the elementary schools, every student in high school, every college student, and, in fact, every individual has a speech need as he attempts to exercise his freedom of speech in speech situations in which he finds himself in the school and in the community. Many high school and college students do not speak with clarity and fluency. They have a speech need if we interpret it as either a lack of speech capacity or a lack of developed speech ability, or of both, to enable them to adjust to and to exercise influence in situations and groups in which they find themselves. If we interpret speech ability as the individual's speech capacity developed so that he can adjust to, and exercise influence in, any situation or in any group in which he finds himself, we may accept as vitally essential speech education and the contribution it can make to his growth by developing his speech abilities and his desirable personal attributes to the highest level of his capacity.

3. *Worthy Home Membership.* Problems of home life cannot all be delegated to the social science or home economics teacher. At present, we find much concern and criticism about the absence of much real "family living." Readings, discussions, speeches of many different kinds, plays, role playing, et cetera, dealing with family relationships can enable the teacher of speech to help his students and the school achieve, to a significant extent, this cardinal objective of secondary education.

4. *Vocation.* Helping students discover aptitudes for and interest in possible vocations is within the province of the modern secondary school. The teacher of speech can include a unit on vocations as part of the class work—taking advantage of the students' interest in their future education and work. In such a unit, the value of speech ability, and awareness of the drawbacks when they are deficient in it, can be most helpful to the students. A teacher of speech can encourage supplementary readings on a vocation of interest to a student and help him develop his ability to express himself clearly and accurately by reporting his findings to the speech class. Such assignments could also help students become acquainted with each other's vocational problems and aspirations.

5. *Citizenship.* Informed, intelligent, and active citizenship is the foundation of democracy. In a class in speech, the wise teacher will unobtrusively foster better citizenship. Respecting the rights of others, welcoming disagreement and debate, recognizing the importance of compromise, and analyzing arguments and evidence as the basis of decisions can be encouraged in class discussions and in other assignments. Effective citizenship includes seeking facts, discussing and debating issues, forming tentative attitudes until more knowledge is available, and utilizing Dewey's steps in reflective thinking:[34]

> (1) to recognize the problem, (2) to analyze the problem and the circumstances related to it, (3) to formulate tentative solutions as a basis for thinking, (4) to reason the tentative solutions and their possible consequences, and (5) to promote the solution which will be best for himself and society.

[34] John Dewey, *How We Think.* New York: D. C. Heath and Company, 1933. pp. 107–115.

The teacher of speech can help students to be able and willing to use these steps in reflective thinking so that they can think better about problems with multiple solutions. To do so can probably be classified as a real contribution in helping students and the school in the achievement of informed, intelligent, and active citizenship.

6. *Worthy Use of Leisure Time.* With increased automation and a shorter work week in prospect, the teacher of speech can share with the teachers of art, music, English, and physical education a responsibility for equipping students to use their increased leisure time wisely. This means much more than their being idle or even harmlessly occupied. Cousins stated, and we believe wisely:

> ... leisure does not carry with it automatically the birth and growth of purpose. It does not of itself make visible new horizons or lead to adventures in the fulfillment of an individual's potential. It is as neutral as the calendar. ... If all that was required here were increased emphasis upon hobbies, the problem would be non-existent. What is actually required is the making of a new man—someone who has confidence in the limitless possibilities of his own development, someone who is not intimidated by the prospect of an open hour, someone who is aware that science may be able to make an easier world but only man can make a better one.[35]

Each individual is confronted with an increasing amount of free time resulting from man's substitution of machinery for his own labor in satisfying his wants. Since man's use of his free time can degrade or elevate him, impoverish life or enrich it, and breed mediocre living or stimulate rich living, education, especially secondary education, has a responsibility for engaging students in worthwhile experiences and pleasures and in helping them to pursue similar experiences and pleasures as adults.

Jacks, writing on *The Education of the Whole Man,* supported the importance of effort in the secondary school to achieve the objective of worthy use of leisure time:

> A good system of education ... would aim at the liberation of our creative powers and the guidance of them by many paths to forms of beauty. So educated we should spend less of our leisure in yielding to its sumptuary temptations ... and more of it to developing our creative possibilities and so asserting our unfettered freedom, and our essential nature, as human beings. And we should enjoy our leisure a thousand times more, and, in addition, we should be less of a nuisance to one another.[36]

[35] Norman Cousins, *Saturday Review,* October 27, 1956, p. 20.
[36] L. P. Jacks, *The Education of the Whole Man.* London: University of London Press, Ltd., 1931. pp. 130–131.

Speech education can contribute in many of the best ways to the achievement of this educational objective. It need not be limited to engaging students in the usual speech experiences such as "speechmaking," discussion and debate of problems to challenge their intellectual power, oral interpretation of poetry and prose which will likely be lasting in its interest to themselves. Untapped opportunities are available in "Readings in Drama" in which students can develop their understanding and enjoyment of plays that have an impact on our insight, interest, outlook, imagination, and language, and on social, economic, political, and personal problems and issues. Films, recordings, acting of scenes, legitimate and television drama, oral reports, and substantial research papers can augment the reading and discussion of plays by world-famous playwrights to elevate and enrich life, and to contribute to the achievement of the worthy use of our leisure time. Likewise, "Readings in Public Address" can help students develop their understanding and appreciation of public addresses by speakers recognized for their persuasive and inspirational speeches and speaking on our social, economic, educational, political, and personal problems, and courses of action; our beliefs, imagination and language; and our speaking, writing, listening, and reading. Again, recordings, platform and television speakers and speaking, oral reports, and substantial research papers can augment our reading and discussion. Perhaps it is not too much to suggest that a unit on the criteria of rhetorical criticism, based on the writings of Plato, Aristotle, Cicero, Quintilian, and modern theorists may challenge lasting interest and pursuit of enrichment worthy of our leisure time.

7. *Ethical Character*. In a democratic society, ethical character becomes paramount among the objectives of the secondary school. Emphasis upon the achievement of this objective should help students to develop their sense of personal responsibility and initiative and the spirit of service. Teachers, by their example, can help. Helping students to recognize that there *are* standards of rightness, and helping them to define and clarify these standards as they speak, listen, and write, are accomplishments toward which all teachers of speech can aim.

In 1938, the Educational Policies Commission of the National Education Association advocated that high schools concern themselves with attaining the objectives of self-realization, human relationships, economic efficiency, and civic responsibility among all their students.[37] A brief examination of these objectives, and the part that speech education can play in helping students and the school to achieve them, can help the teacher of speech to understand better how his subject matter and activities can contribute to a realization of desirable outcomes.

[37] Educational Policies Commission, *op. cit.*

1. *Self-Realization.* One of the most fundamental objectives of secondary education should be to help individuals make the most and best of themselves. The authors of "What Speech Can Contribute to High School Education" remarked about the educated person:

> No individual can grow up emotionally and intellectually without learning to speak well. As a man refines his speech, he builds up his personality, intellect, and emotional balance and control. Man, the speaking animal, cannot rise to his full stature without developing his most distinctive capacity, a capacity in which there is a fusing of four basic elements: (1) mental attitudes and processes, (2) visible action, (3) voice, and (4) oral language. Well-rounded training in these four elements advances a student toward self-realization.[38]

Speech education can help to reduce feelings of inadequacy and insecurity brought about by poor performance. In any endeavor to do one's best, one must first discover his strong and weak points and then plan an informed and intelligent program for strengthening his strong points and improving the points on which he is weak, eliminating the weaknesses or compensating for them. The wise teacher of speech can keep this in view in planning a course of study, a unit, or extra class or interscholastic speech activities.

Speech education can contribute to self-realization by pursuing its basic objective of helping students to think. Does one think before he speaks; is thinking simultaneous with speaking; or does one speak before he thinks? A. F. Watts explained what he apparently thought to be the relation of thought to speech:

> It is clear that both the infant and the unsophisticated adult have to try out their thoughts by uttering them aloud before they can feel sure that they know what they are. . . . On the other hand, it is also clear that to be educated persons a great many thoughts occur with unmistakable identity in advance of their expressions in words, so that they can truthfully say that many ideas occur to mind before passing into speech.
>
> It would appear that our more familiar thoughts become matched sooner or later with words sufficiently adequate for their effective expression, so that whenever the occasion occurs for their "release" they are apt to become expressed time after time in the same forms. This being so, our having an idea may in many cases be no more than experiencing a feeling that the appropriate verbal response is about to follow. . . .
>
> When, however, thought is tentatively following new tracks and breaking fresh ground, it is another matter. In this case, we must give

---

[38] Andrew T. Weaver, Glen G. Eye, Gladys L. Borchers, "What Speech Can Contribute to High School Education," *The Bulletin of the National Association of Secondary School Principals* (November 1945), p. 10.

our thoughts words to make them known. Then we find out what we think by expressing it. . . .[39]

Speech is closely allied with self-realization. Much of our impressions about people come from what they say and how they say it. The effective teacher of speech can help his students to use the sort of speech which characterizes the kind of person they are interested in becoming. Any course in speech which does not reflect itself in competent, careful, and acceptable speech can hardly be termed successful. In our diagnosis of the speech interests, needs, abilities, and capacities of our students, in our helping them to become oriented in principles and practices of speech and to develop their speech abilities, our students grow in desirable personal attributes and in personal stature. Charles H. Woolbert summed up, over thirty years ago, the place of speech education and speech in personal development when he wrote:

> In a strikingly justifiable sense, speech training is training in personality. Vague as that term is, still it suggests always one's powers of expression; bodily carriage, movement of head, arms, hands, torso; richness and flexibility of voice; mastery of language; fertility, timeliness, and fitness of concepts, ideas, feelings, and attitudes—the outward marks of an inward grace, the expression of one's selfhood; the revelation of one's character and even of the soul itself. And the aim of training in personality must always be stated in terms of richness of life, social adaptability, and ability to take one's place in the life of the race.[40]

2. *Human Relationships.* Any modern society places great emphasis upon learning to get along with other human beings. This is especially true in a democratic society like ours. Social contacts, for most people, are the very center of all their finest experiences. Imagine most social situations without speech, if you can, and you will easily see how necessary speech is to their social existence. Helping students to express themselves clearly, acceptably, and effectively in all types of social situations will result in their better social adjustment.

It is important for the high school student to get "off on the right foot" in his face-to-face relationships with other students, to make the right impression with adults, to communicate effectively and acceptably with his family and friends, to be able to say what he wants to say in his classes, and to express his convictions wherever they may be.

---

[39] Reprinted from A. F. Watts, *The Language and Mental Development of Children.* Boston: D. C. Heath and Company, 1944. pp. 20–21. By permission of D. C. Heath and Company and of George G. Harrap and Company, Limited, Publishers.

[40] Charles H. Woolbert, *A Course of Speech in Speech Training and Public Speaking for Secondary Schools.* New York: The Century Company, 1925. (A report of a special committee of the National Association of Teachers of Speech.)

CONTRIBUTIONS OF SPEECH EDUCATION 31

Getting along with people in other nations is important, now that we have the prospect of becoming "one world." United States diplomats and even our President have recognized the value of speaking directly with the heads of foreign nations and their representatives in "getting the picture," "feeling them out," and reducing tensions and promoting more peaceful relations.

3. *Economic Efficiency.* Education for economic efficiency requires speech education. Most people discuss jobs, decide upon specific jobs, apply for positions, and hold these positions and jobs in no small part through competent, acceptable, and effective speech. In our modern business world, the need for purposeful, easily understood, and attention-holding speech is obvious in telephoning, holding conferences, interviewing, dictating letters and memoranda, and "delivering" formal speeches and reports. These are all necessary in winning and keeping business success.

4. *Civic Responsibility.* The ability to express oneself and to communicate with others is important in discussing political matters and in solving local, state, and national problems. To be a good and active citizen, one needs to be able to think and express his thoughts clearly. With our wonderful tradition of "free speech" in America, we must help our students realize that speech is really free only in proportion to how good it is. We must be concerned with raising the quality of speech, speaking, and "speech-making," not just increasing the amount. As teachers of speech, we are obligated to help our students use this precious freedom of speech wisely, holding them responsible for *what* they say as well as *how* they say it.

Speech education can contribute to the achievement of the *Behavioral Goals of General Education in High School* reported by French and his associates.[41] They undertook to analyze the function of the high school and to indicate an organized consensus of the expectations that citizens and educators hold for the American high school. As indicated in the title of their report,

> . . . the common idiom of this study is that of behavior: What should the student be able and willing to *do*, in an observable way, as a consequence of his high school education?[42]

French and his associates seem to feel strongly that it is the school's responsibility to stimulate and guide students in their behavioral choices. They stated:

> This study has assumed from its inception that the high school should be an active, responsible social agency helping youth to develop

---

[41] Will French and Associates, *Behavioral Goals of General Education in High School*. New York: Russell Sage Foundation, 1957.
[42] *Ibid.*, p. 14.

common kinds and levels of behaviors in all aspects of living, competence in which the making of choices is essential if students are to capitalize their own personal resources and to continue to do so independently in their post-high school or college life.[43]

As a basis for their report, they used the objectives of self-realization, human relationships, economic efficiency, and civic responsibility advocated by the Educational Policies Commission. They showed the relationships of these objectives and some of the most commonly required subjects to the behavioral outcomes proposed. The subjects and other school experiences which are generally relied upon for the achievement of the objectives are listed. Then, the proposed behavioral outcomes which ought to be evident if the objectives are achieved are set forth in the report.

Even a cursory examination of the book, *Behavioral Goals of General Education in High School*, will reveal that speech education is tied in closely with the goals and that it can affect greatly the desired behavior. Such behavioral outcomes under Self-Realization as "Improving in His Ability to Communicate and to Recognize and Use Good Standards," and "Becoming Sensitive to, and Competent in, the Use of Logical Thinking and Problem-Solving Processes" can be, and usually are, part and parcel of any course and of most activities comprising speech education. "Improving and Understanding Control of Emotional Self" and "Physical Self" are outcomes for which teachers of speech strive. As a matter of fact, teachers of speech have long recognized that the "behavior" of their students after their experiences in speech education was perhaps the only valid test of the effectiveness of the program. Speech education can and ought to make a contribution to the behavioral objectives and to the realization of desirable behavioral outcomes.

Speech education can make a contribution to the development of abilities implied by the objectives set forth in the *Harvard Report*.[44] This report enumerated four abilities: (1) to think effectively, (2) to communicate thought, (3) to make relevant judgments, and (4) to discriminate among values.

Speech education can help students to develop *effective thinking*. In order to "make" a speech, it is necessary to scan many sources of materials and select pertinent information. Students will have to organize and develop their ideas in a logical sequence and arrive at a sound conclusion. While this is being done, effective thinking is involved. Such thinking is important in every class in school. There is a necessity for research, organization, and development in all classes. The teacher of speech and the teachers in the other classes can probably be more helpful to

[43] *Ibid.*, p. 44.
[44] Harvard Committee, *op. cit.*, pp. 64–79.

students in transferring to these other classes skills of effective thinking learned in speech education. Then too, the same motivation, procedure, and skills need to be applied in voting, choosing a vocation, planning a budget, and everyday social intercourse.

Speech education is vital to the act of expressing oneself so as to be understood by others. *To communicate thought* through speaking is vital to one's education and adjustment in society. During every day in school and in the community, we must speak and answer questions, ask questions, persuade others to our way of thinking, give directions, and make generalizations.

Learning the techniques of analyzing, classifying, reasoning, evaluating, drawing conclusions, and formulating attitudes and beliefs is necessary in the *making of relevant judgments* in any given situation. These techniques are learned in the process of preparing for "speechmaking," oral interpretation, discussion, participating in a play, and so on. In the various activities of increasingly complex speech situations, the ability to make informed and intelligent judgments is essential, and, in making these judgments, students can become increasingly able and willing to exercise judgment.

Effective research and thinking are necessary and basic to *discrimination among values*. It is imperative that both extensive and intensive consideration be given to educational, societal, moral, economic, and physical values that are ever present to persuade us and to affect our behavior. Only from our extensive and intensive consideration of these values can we select those worth calling our own.

Concern for the relationship of speech education to the educational goals of America prompted two Interest Groups of the Speech Association of America—Speech in the Elementary Schools and Speech in the Secondary Schools—to adopt jointly a policy statement concerning "Speech in the Public Schools" in 1958. This policy statement reads:

> In the United States, public education has assumed the responsibility for teaching all children and youth in grades one through twelve those skills which are generally understood to be essential to the development of self-reliant, self-sustaining, and socially effective individuals and citizens. Prominent among those skills are the language arts—listening, speaking, reading, and writing. We hold that, since listening and speaking are the most frequently used of the language arts, systematic instruction in the discipline commonly designated as speech ought to be provided for all pupils at all school levels. We hold, too, that . . . *all pupils* at all school levels *are entitled to instruction in speech by teachers trained in speech and in methods of teaching speech.* We, therefore, recommend that: (1) the elementary school curriculum provide specif-

ically for instruction in speech for every pupil in every grade, and (2) there be specific provision for instruction in speech for every pupil in the secondary schools.

Objectives of Speech Education

The administrator of a high school has a right and an obligation to exercise leadership in determining its objectives, its program of study and activities, and the desired outcomes. Along with teachers, parents, and the boys and girls themselves, he has an obligation to analyze each aspect of the program of study and activities and its contribution to the total program of the school. Likewise, the administrator has responsibility, and should have the commensurate authority, for making the high school program a single whole to accomplish the objectives for which the high school is supported. The whole program and each of its parts are expected to contribute to the attainment of sound educational objectives in keeping with our democracy, all of which are the *ultimate objectives* of speech education.

In a high school, the aims of speech education, including dramatics, forensics, and speech, are, of course, to be evolved under the leadership of the administrator. He, along with teachers, parents, and the boys and girls themselves, has an obligation to analyze the objectives and each of the other aspects of the program. However, the well-qualified teacher of speech, like the well-qualified teacher of any other program of study in the school, will probably be expected to recommend to the administrator a statement of objectives and an outline of the program of study and experiences for the high school. If the teacher of speech demonstrates his understanding of the total program of the school and how speech education can fit into it to serve sound objectives and to achieve desirable outcomes, he will probably be delegated by the administrator to assume responsibility, with commensurate authority, for the success of the program of speech education. Then, if he demonstrates that he can assume this responsibility without interfering with other important programs in the school, he will feel no restraint. If he understands his program and its relation to the school, and shows competence by virtue of his preparation and ability, good judgment, initiative and industry, and resourcefulness, he will probably be given a free hand and support by the administrator, other teachers, students, and parents.

Although ultimate aims of speech education are enabling objectives of the school, the teacher of dramatics, forensics, and speech needs to determine the immediate and specific objectives of his program. Therefore, the following goals may be helpful to him:

1. To help *all* students to develop their individual speech interests and

abilities to a high level of their individual capacities and to become responsible and effective persons in the school and community by providing for the (1) *analysis and evaluation* of students' speech interests, needs, abilities, personal attributes, and capacities; (2) *knowledge and understanding* by students of principles, fundamentals, and practices of speech and listening; and (3) development of students' speech and listening and students' personal adjustment and growth in desirable personal and speech attributes through (a) corrective training and appropriate compensation for students who have speech handicaps, (b) curricular offerings consisting of a variety of increasingly complex experiences in dramatics, forensics, and speech for all students, and (c) extra-class and interscholastic experiences in dramatics, forensics, and speech for students who have specialized interests and abilities in speech and its component areas such as extemporaneous speaking, oral interpretation, discussion, dramatic art, original oratory, performances on radio and television, declamation, parliamentary practices, and combinations of these component areas.

2. To stimulate interest in dramatics, forensics, and speech through intra- and interschool specialized speech activities.

3. To develop and to promote a high standard of work by challenging students to a high level of performance in dramatics, forensics, and speech.

4. To bring the results of teacher and student efforts in speech and its component areas to the student body, to parents, and to other members of the community through school assemblies and community programs.

5. To sustain and improve relationships and to develop cooperative projects with other departments in special areas in the school.

6. To sustain and improve relationships and to develop cooperative projects in research, teaching, and service with speech clinics and speech correctionists as a means to provide maximum opportunity for students with speech handicaps.

7. To participate *creditably* in specialized dramatic, forensic, and speech activities in the high school and within a reasonable distance from the school, and with concern for the educational speech development of high school students.

Although the teacher of dramatics, forensics, and speech may desire to help *all* students in the high school to develop attitudes, knowledge, understandings, abilities, and personal attributes needed and desirable in every school and community, he will need to select speech activities which he will emphasize and, if he is the sole teacher of speech in a large high school, select the individuals to be served by speech education. However, the competent teacher of speech will likely recognize the following as desirable outcomes of speech education and infer from them immediate, specific, and enabling objectives:

1. Adjustment, self-confidence, poise, and an appropriate degree of

personal dignity, integrity, and humility in speech situations typical of the school and community.

2. Understanding and appreciation of the characteristics, desirability, principles, fundamentals, and practices of responsible and effective speech.

3. Recognition of standards of acceptable speech for individual attainment.

4. Initiative, ability, and responsibility in (a) increasing and improving ideas and maintaining individual integrity in the use of ideas in talking with others, (b) organizing ideas clearly for others, (c) analyzing, developing, supporting, and testing ideas, (d) analyzing data and drawing sound inferences, (e) comprehension and use of language, (f) developing and exercising control of purposeful, well-coordinated, meaningful, and unobtrusive bodily action which is responsive to meaning in talking with others, (g) developing and exercising control of clear, flexible, well-modulated, and unobtrusive voices which are responsive to meaning in talking with others, (h) developing purposeful, easily understood, and unobtrusive enunciation, articulation, and pronunciation, and (i) courteous, analytical, and discriminating listening and observing.

5. Appreciation for freedom of speech and responsibility of self and others in exercising it for the best interests of others and self.

6. Background, maturity, stability, scholastic attainment, personableness, and ability and willingness to receive criticism, suggestions, and guidance for self-improvement.

7. Purposeful self-direction for the good of others and self as each develops and exercises (a) alertness, interest, initiative, and industry, (b) imagination and resourcefulness, (c) cooperation, dependability, reliability, and integrity in discharging responsibilities promptly and well, (d) active participation in classroom activities and in co-curricular, extracurricular, and interscholastic dramatic, forensic, and speech experiences, and (e) efficient and wise use of time and of desirable influence on others.

Although opportunities may well be provided for students to develop their individual speech abilities and desirable personal and speech attributes to a high level of their capacities in a variety of increasingly complex and guided experiences in dramatics, forensics, and speech, the primary aim of speech education is *not* to make *public speakers* but to enable *all* students to become *proficient speakers* in public and private life in the school and community; *not* to make students *platform* or *public readers* but to enable *all* students to become *skillful readers* so as to gain information, insight, understanding, and enjoyment; *not* to make *stage* or *television actors* and *actresses* but to enable *all* students to develop self-confidence, self-control, poise, effectiveness, and a degree of humility in all sorts of speech situations.

Summary

Speech education embraces (1) all of the speech experiences through which speech is learned, (2) curricular and extracurricular speech training in schools, (3) the teaching and learning of speech to help all students to become at least adequately adjusted, responsible, and effective persons, communicators, and citizens, and (4) teaching and learning *to teach speech*.

The objectives, the kinds of speech experiences, the methodology and materials for teaching and learning speech, and the desired outcomes of speech education as a part of secondary education are outgrowths of our American democratic society. Therefore, answers to many questions about speech education are to be found in our understanding of our society and of secondary education to which speech education must, if it is to be most effective and beneficial, contribute efficiently, effectively, and harmoniously.

The ultimate objective of our American democratic society and its institutions is to effect, maintain, and perfect an environment which affords for each individual full opportunity and incentive (1) to develop his interests, abilities, and personal attributes to a maximum level of his potential as a person and worthy member of a democratic society; (2) to exercise responsibly and effectively all the freedoms, privileges, and rights safeguarded by a democratic society for the happiness and welfare of himself and others; (3) to pursue, with utmost excellence and conscience, his freely chosen mission compatible with the preservation, progression, prosperity, and power to direct the destiny of our American democratic society and thereby to provide equal opportunities for each of the persons of whom it is comprised; and (4) to realize and enjoy the respect inherent in a democratic society for the worth and dignity of man. Therefore, realization by all men of the supreme values of human life is the ultimate outcome desired from our society, government, and public education, including speech education designed to stimulate and guide each student in his growth as an increasingly responsible and effective communicator.

Basic to our concepts and standards of society and education are self-evident truths inherited from Greek philosophers and statesmen of over 2,000 years ago. Such self-evident truths as equal opportunity for all men, freedom to pursue their individual objectives with equal rights *restrained only by their unequal endowments of capacity and their unequal abilities*, government subservient only to the people to guarantee to them equal opportunities, freedom, and rights constitute the framework for American institutions and endeavors. These truths, evidenced in the American Declaration of Independence, the Constitution, the Bill of Rights, the Social-Economic Goals for America, and *Goals for Americans* at home and abroad during the 1960's, constitute a framework of reference for American elementary and secondary education. This frame of reference pinpoints the need and focus for free public education for all Americans: freedom to pursue their individual objectives with equal rights restricted only by their unequal endowments of capacity and their unequal abilities.

Education for *all* at public expense was proposed by Americans during the 1820's as their cooperative effort (1) to provide training for their vocations and (2) to improve their lives. Although unequal endowments of capacity imposed restrictions on the freedom of Americans to pursue their individual objectives, their strength lay partly in their combined capacities. Their unequal abilities did not deter Americans' cooperative effort to provide common education to help each individual develop his abilities and thereby to minimize restrictions on his freedom. The dignity and worth of the individual became an increasingly important and meaningful concept in American education. Their strength lay partly in their greater abilities as a result of their common education.

Since 1850 and especially since 1900, secondary education has been increasingly concerned with the all-round and continuous growth of the individual as a responsible and effective person, communicator, and citizen. This concern is evidenced by (1) the seven "Cardinal Principles of Education" in 1918; (2) *The Purposes of Education in American Democracy* in 1938 which are noted for their specificity, meaningfulness, and usefulness as guides for our high schools; (3) "The Imperative Needs of Youth" in 1944 formulated by our National Association of Secondary School Principals with emphasis on "ability to think, express thoughts, read, and listen"; (4) "The Objectives of a General Education in a Free Society" in 1945 proposed by the Harvard Committee of twelve to satisfy a supreme need of American education for a common ground of training and outlook on which society depends: (a) to think effectively with the three phases of logical, relational, and imaginative thinking corresponding to the three divisions of learning, the natural sciences, the social studies, and the humanities respectively, (b) to communicate thought with emphasis on having something to say and skill in communication as the instrument by which human beings are welded into a society, especially in a free and democratic society, (c) to make relevant judgments involving the ability of the student to bring to bear the whole range of ideas upon the area of experience, and (d) to discriminate among values involving a choice between values of character, intellectual values, and esthetic values; (5) eight goals of universal education by Dr. Magdalene Kramer, until lately Professor of Speech and Speech Education at Columbia University, which give added meaning to the objectives stated by the Harvard Committee; (6) ten bothersome developmental problems designated by Havighurst in 1953 indicating direction for teachers interested in stimulating and guiding students in their growth to full maturity and stability; (7) fifteen programs and services proposed by The Committee for the White House Conference on Education in 1955 implying objectives which parallel closely the societal objectives and which can easily serve as guides for planning by teachers of speech; and (8) twelve objectives proposed by the Iowa State Department of Public Instruction in 1957 seeking to bring about a partnership between education and democracy.

The contribution of speech education to the achievement of educational and societal objectives has long been accepted by thoughtful men. Citizens of the Greek cities recognized the need. A kind of speech education was started by 400 B.C. in Sicily. Likewise, authorities in speech and also progressive educators have expressed the need for more emphasis on speech education. They agree that effectiveness in speaking is a mark of an educated person. They also agree that speech can be taught and that provision should be made for it in the secondary schools.

If teachers of speech are to accept their full responsibility, they must have a clear-cut understanding of education and its relationship to our democratic society which supports education, and of speech education and its relationship to secondary education of which speech education is a part, and how the various facets of speech education can contribute to its own objectives and how it can thereby help students in high schools to realize the desired outcomes of secondary education and of democracy in which speech education has long been deeply rooted.

Projects

1. Define "speech," "speech education." Compare your definitions with those given in typical high school speech texts.

2. Evaluate your state course of study in communication, English, or speech, or the appropriate curriculum bulletin. What are its stated objectives? What guiding philosophy of speech education is expressed?

3. List the specific obligations which you believe a teacher of speech has towards democracy.

4. Interview various business and professional men to find out how important they believe speech ability is in their work. Compare their responses with responses of teachers in both high school and college.

5. Thomas H. Briggs wrote: "The first duty of the school is to teach pupils to do better the desirable things that they are going to do anyway. . . . Another duty of the school is to reveal higher activities and to make them both desired and to a maximum extent possible." What implications do these statements have for the teacher of speech and for the teaching of speech in high school? Present a written statement of your reactions.

6. Study the ten desirable goals offered by the Committee on Social Economic Goals of America. How can speech education contribute directly to the achievement of these goals?

7. What good is freedom of speech to persons who are not proficient in speaking? In bringing to bear in speech situations the ideas and details of their experiences in the school, the home, and the community? What is the relationship between freedom of speech and the ability to organize ideas for speaking, to phrasing ideas, and to speaking clearly and distinctly? Prepare a written statement of your answers and be prepared to explain your reactions to the class.

8. Carl A. Dallinger stated: "The teaching of speech is rooted deeply in the democratic tradition. In most of the countries of the world our subject would not be included in the educational program. The foreigner frequently is amazed to find in our curricula a subject called speech. Our own colleagues often are amazed that in our teaching we are as much or more concerned with ideas as with posture and pronunciation. But if we can lead our students to some better understanding of the essence of democracy and to some concept of the importance of responsible speaking in the democratic way of life, then we may find some satisfaction in knowing that we are not teaching in a vacuum, but that we are performing a real service in the preservation of our tradition." Outline your reactions in preparation for a five-minute talk with the class.

9. Read Gladys L. Borchers' "A Reaffirmation in Support of Essentials in Secondary Speech Education," *The Speech Teacher* (November 1959). React to her point of view.

10. Present to your instructor your written statement of the imperative needs of youth, including their needs resulting from their developmental problems. Be prepared to state in class your reasons for believing in the imperativeness of the needs which you include in your statement.

11. Select one societal objective. Show how one educational objective can, to the extent it is achieved, contribute to the achievement of the societal objective. Then, explain how speech education can contribute to the achievement of the educational objective.

Selected Bibliography

ALY, BOWER, "Speech in the Service of Tyranny and Freedom," *The Speech Teacher*, vol. 3, no. 2 (March 1954), pp. 81–85.

ANDERSON, LESTER W., and LAUREN A. VAN DYKE, *School Administration*. Boston: Houghton Mifflin Company, 1963.

ARNOLD, CARROLL C., "The Case Against Speech: An Examination of Critical Viewpoints," *Quarterly Journal of Speech*, vol. 40, no. 2 (April 1954), pp. 165–169.

SELECTED BIBLIOGRAPHY

AUER, J. JEFFERY, "Speech and the Satellite," *The Speech Teacher*, vol. 7, no. 4 (November 1958), pp. 281–288.

BAKER, VIRGIL L. and RALPH T. EUBANKS, "Democracy: Challenge to Rhetorical Education," *Quarterly Journal of Speech*, vol. 46, no. 1 (February 1960), pp. 72–78.

BARNES, HARRY G., "Basic Concepts of Speech Education," *The Speech Teacher*, vol. 1, no. 1 (January 1952), pp. 14–19.

BORCHERS, GLADYS L., "A Reaffirmation in Support of Essentials in Secondary Speech Education," *The Speech Teacher*, vol. 8, no. 4 (November 1959), pp. 300–303.

BRADEN, WALDO W., ed., *Speech Methods and Resources*. New York: Harper & Row Publishers, 1961.

CLEVENGER, THEODORE, JR., "The Teacher of Speech and Free Speech," *The Speech Teacher*, vol. 5, no. 2 (March 1956), pp. 91–101.

CORTRIGHT, RUPERT L., "The Speech Age Makes New Demands upon Education," *The Speech Teacher*, vol. 2, no. 1 (January 1953), pp. 1–6.

DALLINGER, CARL A., "The Need for Developing Responsible Speaking," *Central States Speech Journal*, Spring 1958, p. 23.

HANSEN, KENNETH H., *Public Education in American Society*. Englewood Cliffs, N. J.: Prentice-Hall, Inc., 1956.

HARRINGTON, ELBERT W., "The Role of Speech in Liberal Education," *Quarterly Journal of Speech*, vol. 41, no. 3 (October 1955), pp. 218–222.

KNOWER, FRANKLIN, "Speech Education for All American Youth," *The Bulletin of the National Association of Secondary School Principals*, vol. 32, no. 151 (January 1948), pp. 7–11.

NILSEN, THOMAS R., "Free Speech, Persuasion, and the Democratic Process," *Quarterly Journal of Speech*, vol. 44, no. 3 (October 1958), pp. 235–243.

OGILVIE, MARDEL, *Teaching Speech in the High School: Principles and Practices*. New York: Appleton-Century-Crofts, Inc., 1961.

REID, LOREN, *Teaching Speech*, 3rd ed. Columbia, Missouri: Artcraft Press, 1960.

RICHEY, ROBERT W., *Planning for Teaching*, 2nd ed. New York: McGraw-Hill Book Company, Inc., 1958.

ROBINSON, KARL F. and E. J. KERIKAS, *Teaching Speech: Methods and Materials*. New York: David McKay Company, Inc., 1963.

SEABURY, HUGH F., "A Basic Secondary Course in Public Speaking," *The Bulletin of the National Association of Secondary School Principals*, vol. 36, no. 187 (May 1952), pp. 27–44.

———, "Objectives and Scope of the Fundamentals Course in Speech in the High School," *The Speech Teacher*, vol. 3, no. 2 (March 1954), pp. 117–120.

CHAPTER

2

The Teacher of Speech

The success of a program of speech education in a high school depends largely on the teacher of speech.

Modern classrooms, the latest textbooks, ample audio-visual aids, an alert and able group of students, interested and cooperative parents, and an understanding and able administrator do not make a successful program of speech education, important as these factors are. They are not a substitute for an able teacher of speech, who sets the tone of the class and the spirit of the program. He, together with the administrator and other teachers, sets the tone and spirit of the high school.

Reactions to teachers and to their teaching by students, teachers, and administrators can help all teachers determine for themselves what constitutes a "successful" teacher.

Some twenty years ago, Hart collected, compiled, and analyzed the reactions of 10,000 high school seniors who were given the opportunity to tell teachers what students like and dislike in teachers and their methods. These high school seniors were asked to think of the teacher they "liked best" and set down their reasons; similarly, to think of the teacher they "liked least of all"; and, finally, to indicate if the "best liked" teacher was also the "best" teacher. If, in their judgment, the "best liked" teacher was not the "best" teacher, the students were to indicate how the "best" teacher differed from the "best liked" teacher. Their reactions can help the teacher of speech to determine for himself what makes for success or failure in teaching. The ten most frequently mentioned reasons for liking a teacher best are listed in the order most frequently cited by the 10,000 high school seniors:[1]

1. Is helpful with school work, explains lessons and assignments clearly and thoroughly, and uses examples in teaching.
2. Cheerful, happy, good-natured, jolly, has a sense of humor, and can take a joke.
3. Human, friendly, companionable, "one of us."
4. Interested in and understands pupils.
5. Makes work interesting, creates a desire to work, and makes class work a pleasure.
6. Strict, has control of the class, and commands respect.
7. Impartial, shows no favoritism, and has no "pets."
8. Not cross, crabby, grouchy, nagging, or sarcastic.
9. "We learned the subject."
10. A pleasing personality.

In contrast to these attributes of the "best liked" teacher, the following were the ten most frequent reasons for their disliking a teacher:[2]

1. Too cross, crabby, grouchy, never smiles, nagging, sarcastic, loses temper, and "flies off the handle."
2. Not helpful with school work, does not explain lessons and assignments, not clear, and work not planned.
3. Partial, has "pets" or favored students, and "picks on certain pupils."
4. Superior, aloof, haughty, snooty, overbearing, and does not know you out of class.
5. Mean, unreasonable, hard-boiled, intolerant, ill-mannered, too strict, and makes life miserable.
6. Unfair in marking and grading and unfair in tests and examinations.
7. Inconsiderate of pupils' feelings, bawls out pupils in the presence of classmates, and pupils are afraid and ill-at-ease and dread class.
8. Not interested in pupils and does not understand them.
9. Unreasonable assignments and homework.
10. Too loose in discipline, no control of class, and does not command respect.

Eighty percent of these high school seniors reported that the teacher they liked best was also the best teacher, that is, the one who taught them most effectively. The twenty percent who indicated some other teacher as best gave the following differences between the best-liked teacher and the best teacher:[3]

[1] Frank W. Hart, *Teachers and Teaching by Ten Thousand High School Seniors.* New York: The Macmillan Company, 1934. p. 131.
[2] *Ibid.*, pp. 250–251.
[3] *Ibid.*, pp. 278–279.

1. More exacting in standards of work, stricter in marking, and "we learned more."
2. Better at explaining lessons and assignments and work is better planned.
3. Knows the subject matter and can 'put it over' better.
4. Stricter, more rigid discipline.
5. Makes the work more interesting.
6. Is less friendly.
7. More serious, more businesslike, keeps closer to the subject, and more conscientious.
8. Less understanding of pupils and less interested in pupils.
9. More sarcastic.
10. Less attractive.

The teacher needs the cooperation of his students if they are to learn effectively. The students' viewpoint of what an effective teacher is can help the teacher to understand his task better.

Teachers' Judgment of an Effective Teacher

Not only have students indicated their idea, but teachers themselves have tried to determine what they believe an effective teacher is. A panel of faculty members at Macalester College in Saint Paul, Minnesota, stated, during a discussion at a convocation in the summer session of 1957, what they believed to be eight basic qualifications of an outstanding teacher. They agreed that, at any level of instruction, a "top" teacher must have (1) a sense of mission, (2) love of people, (3) love of his work, (4) intellectual honesty, (5) thorough knowledge of his subject, (6) a nonauthoritarian attitude, (7) understanding of students, and (8) the ability to create student interest.

Most teachers and most teachers of speech probably agree that these eight basic qualifications suggest necessary characteristics of a teacher of speech, a director of plays, and a coach or director of forensics.

Administrators' Concepts of a Superior Teacher of Speech

The concepts by administrators in the secondary school of a superior teacher of speech offer helpful suggestions as any teacher of speech attempts to evaluate himself. Eye reported in *The Quarterly Journal of Speech*[4] the following concepts by two superintendents and two principals on what constitutes a superior teacher of speech:

[4] Glen C. Eye, "What Constitutes a Superior Teacher of Speech?"; L. M. Fort, "The Qualifications Necessary"; Matthew L. Dann, "The Superior Teacher of Dramatics"; and A. E. Rupp, "The Superior Teacher of Debate," *The Quarterly Journal of Speech*, April 1948, pp. 216–221.

1. The good speech teacher should have the personal qualities that would make him or her welcome and desirable company for others of the same age group. . . .

2. The teacher should be capable of establishing and maintaining good social relationships in the community without apparent strain upon either the teacher or the community.

3. There should be evidence of a broad liberal education and thorough professional training. . . .

4. The instructional skill of the teacher should be of the quality that brings pupils eagerly to class and leaves them reluctant to have the period end. The teacher should be able to identify pupil development, measure the degree of progress, and interpret the results to professional colleagues and lay people.

5. The good teacher should recognize that pupil development depends in part upon experience other than class activities.

6. The speech teacher should work toward the broadest possible offering in his own field but he should not permit his enthusiasm for the field of speech to stifle cooperation with his colleagues in other fields of teaching.

7. The teacher should be as concerned for the development of the slow pupil as for that of the bright pupil.

8. The good speech teacher should not
    a. falsely believe that making speech a required course is a terminal achievement,
    b. assume that speech is a cure for all educational, social, economic, national, and universal ills,
    c. look upon the auditorium as private domain, indestructible, and uncontestable, and
    d. blame the administrator for all obvious shortcomings of the speech program.

Fort, a superintendent, added some specific qualifications he felt necessary for an effective teacher of speech:

1. The ability to make a good speech.

2. A teacher who insists upon speech for the average boy and girl— a philosophy that speech is for everybody.

3. A teacher who has initiative—who is continually discovering ways and means for promoting speech activities in the community.

4. A speech teacher who is so thoroughly informed in his field that I can turn to him for the answers to the questions that continually arise in speech studies.

Dann enumerated qualities of a superior teacher of dramatics:

Understanding of . . . young people. Skill in presentation of ideas. . . . Willingness to work hard in preparation. . . . Enthusiasm for working with youths coupled with enthusiasm for his subject. Judgment of literary material. . . . Ability to select the best participant for each part in a play. Capability . . . of superior demonstration whenever needed. Capable and willing to maintain high professional standards. . . .

Rupp, in discussing the ideal teacher of debate, emphasized the need by the teacher of debate for a sound foundation in speech, in the social sciences, and in other areas. He stated that the ideal teacher of debate must be

. . . alert, open-minded, ready to re-evaluate the evidence at any time . . . well-read . . . possess a keen, analytical mind . . . must like young people . . . and also be a good teacher of speech.

Some Factors Which Guide Administrators

Some administrators keep in mind factors which guide them in employing teachers of speech and in helping these teachers to improve "on the job" through in-service training. An understanding of these factors can help prospective teachers of speech and teachers of speech who are in service:

1. An administrator looks for evidence that the teacher of speech has a philosophy of speech education and the ability to express it. He has a right and an obligation to know the teacher's philosophy. It will influence and probably determine the objectives and practices of the teacher in his classes and in his direction and supervision of extra-class and interscholastic speech activities. Likewise, it will indicate the impact of the teacher on the program of speech education and the impact of both teacher and his program on the total program of the school.

The administrator may ask the teacher of speech for a statement of his philosophy, or he may ask questions whose answers will reveal it. From his interview with the teacher, the administrator may learn much of the teacher's philosophy. Later, the teacher's philosophy of speech education will be revealed by his actual work. Answers to such questions as the following will probably reveal the teacher's philosophy of speech education:

a. What is his chief concern as a teacher of speech? Speech education for all students? For the gifted? For the handicapped? For the "average" student?

b. What is his conception of the role of speech in society? In everyday living? In the school? In the community?

c. What is his attitude toward his place and the place of speech education in the total program of the school? Is he a teacher, first and foremost, as he thinks of himself? Is he a "coach"? Is he a "director"? Does he seem to see any difference in the functions of the three?

d. What is his conception of speech education? Required course for all? If so, in what grade or grades? Elective courses for whom? In what grade or grades? For what purposes? Emphasis on content or "delivery"? Does he seem to visualize speech education as a program of student performances only? What relationships does he seem to see between speech education and other programs of study and activities in the school?

e. What is his attitude toward extra-class and interscholastic speech activities? Valuable experiences for students? Related to courses in speech education? Success dependent on a record of winning interscholastic speech contests? Publicity? Overly interested in trying to make a name for himself?

f. What is his conception of the place of play production in the high school? Class project? Public performances in an auditorium? An indoor or outdoor spectacle?

g. What is likely to be the kind and quality of the plays he selects for production? Plays that make possible artful production and performance by a few students only? Plays that provide opportunity for many students to achieve excellence of performance and to develop the maximum level of their capacities? Plays that are inherently worthwhile for the educational growth and enjoyment of students and an audience?

h. How well is he likely to handle students in debate practice? In play rehearsals? How many rehearsals will he need, how long will he rehearse, and how late will he rehearse the students? Will he have a rehearsal schedule publicized in advance? Will he be concerned about demands on students' time? Is he likely to manage debate practices and play rehearsals in a businesslike way? How will he manage the extra details connected with play production and travel for participation in interscholastic forensic events? Money? Transportation? Lodging? Recordkeeping?

i. Will he likely be a cooperative, dependable, and considerate teacher of speech who will exercise high integrity and judgment? What evidence does he present to indicate that he is well prepared and certified to teach in a high school or junior college?

j. What will likely be his attitude toward his students? Other teachers? Administrators?

These questions and many others concerning the teacher of speech and his function in the school are fair questions to which the administrator has a right and an obligation to know the answers.

Also, the teacher of speech has a right to know the attitude of the administrator toward speech education. If the administrator is one who wants an outstanding record in declamation, debate, and drama, and is interested in the number of "superiors" won at speech contests, the teacher of speech should know it. If the teacher of speech accepts the position, he is obligated to give the administrator of the high school what he wants, because the administrator is responsible for the school program and its success, and therefore should have commensurate authority. If the philosophy of the administrator is that speech education is to provide a valuable experience for as many students as possible—which is the generally accepted view by administrators—then the teacher of speech should take that fact into consideration when accepting the position and in guiding the extra-class and interscholastic program.

The philosophy of the administrator who evaluates the program in relation to the number of "superiors" may be altered by the teacher of speech as he works toward an acceptance of speech taught as a significant communicative experience for all students rather than as an exhibition by a few. The teacher of speech may well utilize at first the wishes of the administrator in regard to "winners" or high ratings. However, even if the success of a program of speech education, a program of athletics, or a program of music education is measured in ribbons or medals or trophies, there may be a noticeable increase in the interest and participation by students during the following year. Conversely, no awards result oftentimes in a noticeable decrease in the interest and participation during the following year. Of course, much depends on how the awards are acquired. If the teacher of speech and his students seek the awards by limiting the number of participants, using the same participants many times for the purpose of winning, conniving in any questionable manner to beat other students with less than excellence of participation and complete honesty and integrity, or driving themselves beyond reason simply to win, the teacher of speech had better take stock of his motives and procedures and those of his students. On the other hand, neither the teacher of speech nor his students are justified in doing less than their best in achieving excellence of participation in whatever events, curricular or interscholastic, they may be engaged. If excellence of performance is evident, the teacher of speech and his students should be proud to accept awards. What better argument than that supported by excellence of interest, effort, performance, achievement, and growth of students can be offered by an alert teacher of speech for the inclusion of a course in speech education in the curricular offerings of the high school? When a curricular base for speech education has been achieved, it is often possible to obtain approval for broadening the program to include additional courses. This takes time. The teacher of speech should be prepared to work patiently, persistently, and effectively for what he believes is the best program of speech education in his school.

2. A very important factor which the wise administrator keeps in mind when employing teachers of speech and in helping them improve "on the job" through in-service training is the relationship of speech education to the total program of the school. The administrator of a high school tries to keep the faculty working together in the best interests of the education

of all the students. His job, in this respect, is quite easy when each faculty member accepts willingly the fact that he or she is a member of the whole group and that the goal of the whole group is primary. At the same time, the wise administrator considers it important to help in the organization of situations so that each teacher can teach, and each group of students within the whole group can learn, all or more than the teacher teaches. The speech teacher must realize that speech education is an integral part of, but not more important than, the total program. The teacher of speech needs to consider also that speech education is one of many important, integral parts of secondary education and that some other part of the total program may be just as important as speech education in its contribution to the objectives of secondary education. Teachers are, in a sense, crusaders for a better school and a better community, but teachers of speech should not be "crusaders" who believe that speech education is first and foremost in the program. An ardent "crusader" for a strong department of speech education can easily kill his chances for building up cooperation by the administrator and other faculty members and any chances for his realization of their interests in speech education. Cooperation by the teacher of speech with other faculty members and his good human relations with them are important. Since many students interested in speech education will also be involved in other activities, there must be a give-and-take for their interests, time, preparation, and achievement. Thus, the teacher of speech must be willing to cooperate with the director of the band, the director of the choir and chorus, the advisers of the newspaper and annual, the coaches of athletics, and with the administrator and all other teachers in the high school.

3. The speech habits of the teacher of speech can well be a concern of the administrator. The teacher of speech whose speech reflects good thinking, worthwhile ideas based on knowledge in breadth and depth, and ability to engage in cooperative sharing of ideas and thinking is likely to be an asset. If his voice is clear, flexible, well-modulated, unobtrusive, and responsive to meaning, he tends to stimulate a favorable reaction to a program of speech education. Such qualities make a difference in the attitude of students, other teachers, and people in the community toward the teaching of speech as well as toward the teacher. Students are likely to be acutely aware of the speech of the teacher of speech. They are likewise increasingly aware of the speech habits of their other teachers and of other people as they are conscious of excellence of speech by their teacher of speech. He should serve as a model for his students. To some degree the community will judge the program of speech education by his speech.

The effective teacher of speech should have had a variety of speech experiences prior to the time he began to teach, and he can go on participating in a variety of speech experiences during his tenure as a teacher. Too often teachers do not make use of the opportunities available.

The teacher of speech can be one of the most important public relations persons on the staff of the high school. As such, he can do much through his speaking to promote the school and the total educational program of the school and, at the same time, the program of speech education in the school. Prospective teachers of speech should make every effort to prepare themselves by participating, while in college, in speech activities such as discussion, oral interpretation, debate, drama, radio, and television. Thus, as members of the faculty of a high school and as members of communities they will be more effective as a result of their practical knowledge of speech situations.

4. Another factor the administrator considers is the teacher's preparation. Speech education for the teacher is important if he is to be in a position to give his students real help in their pursuit of the objectives of speech education. No longer should the administrator assign classes in speech and extra-class work in speech to a teacher who is not well prepared for it. Obviously, preparation in teaching English per se does not qualify a teacher to teach speech. Teachers of English would be the first to admit that they are not qualified to teach speech unless they have successfully completed courses, or the equivalent, in fundamentals of speech, oral interpretation, discussion and debate, dramatics, stagecraft, speech science, speech pathology, and parliamentary procedures which are usually included in the preparation of teachers of speech.

Teachers who are assigned to teach speech, discussion and debate, or play production in the high school, and who feel that they are inadequate for the task, can find worthwhile opportunities for preparation in colleges and universities. These opportunities may lie in workshops in speech and dramatic art for teachers during summer sessions. These workshops are usually aimed at giving them some help to do an effective job of teaching speech and directing students in dramatic art and forensic activities. Workshops in speech and dramatic art for high school students are, in some colleges and universities, closely allied with workshops for teachers, so that teachers can engage in laboratory practice in teaching dramatics, forensics, speech, voice and speech development, and radio and television with the supervision by faculty members in departments of speech and dramatic art. However, teachers and high school students who participate in these workshops are probably helped most by realizing that they can learn much more by working in the area of speech education than during the workshops.

Most administrators are concerned about the prospective teacher or the teacher who has "specialized" in only one aspect of speech such as debate, acting, or speech on radio and television. The teacher of speech in a high school needs background in *all* aspects of speech education. Administrators would be happy to have in their high schools dedicated and able teachers who have specialized in speech and speech education. True, in some of our larger high schools the administrators are able to bring to their high schools teachers who have specialized in one aspect of speech, but even in these schools, the teacher who has specialized is in a better position to succeed if he has prepared in all areas of speech education.

A committee of the Speech Association of America, in its recommendation to the North Central Association, summarized the training which the members of the committee believed necessary for teaching speech:

> The educational record of the teacher who develops and participates in the speech program should disclose specialized college or university training in the seven topics: Fundamentals, Reading Aloud, Discussion, Debate, Public Speaking, Drama and Theatre, Radio and Television, and Motion Picture. If speech is the major teaching subject, the teacher may have emphasized (1) oral reading, theatre and drama, or (2) public speaking, discussion, and debate, or (3) radio and television; nevertheless, the teacher will have had supporting courses in all areas of speech. In semester hours, the record will show 20-26. If speech is the second teaching field, the teacher will have had at least one course in each of the areas of speech; in terms of semester hours, the teacher's record will show 16-20.[5]

In 1960 the Secondary School Interest Group of the Speech Association of America recommended to the Legislative Assembly of the Association certain minimum requirements for certification of teachers of speech in secondary schools. The Legislative Assembly adopted, on December 28, 1960, the resolution entitled "A Resolution Adopted by the Legislative Assembly of the Speech Association of America:"

> Resolved: That the Legislative Assembly endorses the following statement of minimal requirements for certification of teachers of speech in secondary schools:
>
> Section I. *General Requirement.* For permanent certification in speech, the teacher should offer at least twenty-four semester hours in speech, taken at an accredited college or university, and distributed as specified in Section II. For provisional, temporary, or "second field" certification, the teacher should offer at least eighteen semester hours in speech, taken at an accredited college or university, and distributed as specified in Section II.
>
> Section II. *Subject Area Preparation.* To insure breadth of prepara-

---

[5] Committee of the Speech Association of America, "Recommendation to the North Central Association," *Quarterly Journal of Speech*, October, 1951.

tion, each certified teacher of speech should have completed at least one course in each of these divisions: (A) *Speech Sciences and Processes*, such as phonetics, physiology of the voice mechanism, basic speech development, voice, articulation, et cetera; (B) *Theatre and Oral Interpretation*, such as oral interpretation, acting, directing, technical theatre, play production, radio, television, et cetera; (C) *Speech Correction*, such as speech correction, speech pathology, clinical practices in speech correction, et cetera; (D) *Public Address*, such as public speaking, discussion, argumentation, debate, radio, television, et cetera.

Section III. *Professional Preparation.* In addition to the preparation specified above, the teacher certified in speech should offer at least one course in methods of teaching speech in the secondary school, together with appropriate student teaching.

Certification of speech correctionists or therapists should follow the certification requirements of the American Speech and Hearing Association.

Orville A. Hitchcock, Executive Secretary of the Speech Association of America from 1951 to 1954 and Director of the Association's placement bureau during those years, gave this advice to teachers of speech:

> ... prepare yourself thoroughly. To me, thorough preparation means that you should be broadly educated, both generally and within the field of speech. As Aristotle and other classical writers pointed out long ago, rhetoric deals with all subject matter. So does poetics. Assuming adequate preparation in speech itself, the wider your knowledge beyond the field, the better teacher of speech you will be. ... It is a basic truth that "you can't speak speech." What you speak is the knowledge and experience of mankind.
>
> You must also remember that in speech we are concerned with people, helping them to improve. To do so, you must really understand people, know what motivates them, what makes them what they are. A speech teacher must not only know about such things; he must also be a student of human nature.[6]

Hitchcock also advocated "breadth within the field of speech," and said that "It is dangerous to become too much of a specialist." He cited as one reason for his belief the large percentage of teaching positions that are combination positions—speech combined with another field such as English or social studies, or a combination of a number of different areas within the province of speech. Another practical reason for breadth within the province of speech education is the close relationship between the various phases of speech. Each supports the others. Hitchcock stated:

---

[6] Orville A. Hitchcock, "How to Get a Job as a Teacher of Speech," *The Speech Teacher*, vol. 4, no. 4 (November 1955), pp. 225–230.

I do not see how you can be a good teacher of public speaking without having had work, for example, in speech pathology and dramatic interpretation. By the same token, I do not see how you can be an effective speech pathologist without having studied the various types of speaking (public speaking, discussion, reading aloud) that your students are certain to be called upon to do.[7]

All evidence indicates that at least a major, or the equivalent, in the field of speech education is desirable. A minor appears to be an absolute minimum.

In 1959 a special committee of the North Central Association on the certification requirements by the Speech Association of America supported the viewpoint that there is danger in

> ... the incorrect assumption that the fields of English and speech are the same and that the teachers do the same kind of job. Speech is not Oral English. Speech instruction consists of much more than having the student stand up and vocalize. Speech teachers must be trained to cope with student problems of emotional adjustment in all kinds of audience situations. They need to know how to teach strong preparation and logical structure as the basis for "thinking on one's feet," or extemporaneous speaking from notes; they are obliged to teach and insure clarity in oral communication through careful attention to the language of *practical discourse* (they are not primarily concerned with the language of fine literature); they must stress simple, clear sentence structure for *instant* intelligibility; they are obliged to teach audience analysis, usable means of vocal emphasis and bodily action to gain and hold the attention of the audience. Furthermore, they must know how to help boys and girls make effective voices out of ineffective ones, substitute standard for substandard diction, and train the body to aid and not hinder in all communication.
>
> The English teacher does not do these things as a regular part of English instruction. Typical preparation patterns for English and speech teachers of necessity are different and, in the opinion of the Speech Association of America, these differences should be recognized in teacher certification requirements. Handling students in speech learning situations demands good preparation specific to that job. Such responsibility should not be handed to just anyone with inferior training.[8]

The committee of the Speech Association of America assumed, and stated the assumption boldly for the purpose of making the point obvious, that most teachers of English who teach speech are not prepared to teach it. The teaching of English can be a full-time job. If it is a full-time job and if teachers of English are conscientious and dedicated to teaching English

[7] *Ibid.*, p. 227.
[8] *The Speech Teacher*, vol. 8, no. 2 (March 1959), p. 118.

as most of them are, they have neither a primary interest in teaching speech nor the time to teach it. If teachers of English were to teach speech by choice, as some of them do, it would appear that they would do so because they believed the teaching of speech to be more important than the teaching of English or else because the teaching of English could be taught better by teaching speech.

Similarly, if teachers of speech are conscientious and dedicated to teaching speech as most of them are, they have neither a primary interest in teaching English nor the time to teach it. If teachers of speech were to teach English by their choice, as apparently few of them do, it would appear that they would choose to teach English either because they believed the teaching of English to be more important than the teaching of speech or because the teaching of speech could be taught better by teaching English.

Some teachers of English have prepared to teach speech and some teachers of speech have prepared to teach English. In both cases, the preparation appears to serve these teachers well in helping them to be more effective teachers of English and speech, respectively. Every teacher recognizes his need for much more and much broader preparation, and is probably the first to admit it. Of course, every teacher in the secondary school is a teacher of speech, consciously or unconsciously. The problem of the teacher of speech, like that of other teachers, is to prepare himself to make a significant contribution as an effective teacher.

5. An administrator is interested in the attitude of the teacher of speech toward his students and their attitudes toward the teacher. Without good student-teacher relationships, students are likely to learn little in the classroom. If students like and respect the teacher, they are likely to learn and to conduct themselves well in his classroom and in his presence outside of class. If they respect the teacher but do not like him, they may learn in spite of their not liking him. If they like the teacher but do not respect him, they can hardly be depended on to learn and are likely, sooner or later, to embarrass the teacher with their antics of friendship and their lack of learning. If they neither like nor respect the teacher, they will probably learn nothing in his class. Perhaps one of the most serious mistakes a teacher can make, especially during his first year of teaching, is to be too friendly with his students in an effort to have them like him. After they are out of control, it is difficult, and sometimes impossible, for the teacher to regain control of the same group of students again, even though it has been done with the help of the administrator. The teacher should be friendly with his students but never sentimentally so, and never so friendly that he cannot take charge of them in a situation where his supervision is needed. If he has the respect of his students, his ability to take charge at once is considerably enhanced.

Students may respect a teacher for any of several reasons, such as their respect for his knowledge of his subject, his standards of achievement by his students, his ability to teach, his fairness, his efficiency, his sincerity, and, perhaps above all, his sincere interest in his students, their problems, their achievement, and their all-round and continuous development. It is difficult for many teachers of speech, as well as for other teachers, to determine what is the best proportion of friendliness, fairness, and firmness to maintain so as to do their best as teachers. And yet, friendliness, fairness, firmness, enthusiasm, and sincerity reflect the attitude of the teacher of speech toward his students and help to determine the student-teacher relationships in and out of his classroom. Firmness with students at the beginning of a course may be helpful in establishing good student-teacher relationships. Firmness may be modified as rapport in the classroom permits relaxation and greater friendliness, but fairness, enthusiasm for students' learning, and sincerity should always prevail.

The teacher of speech often has excellent opportunities for guidance in his relationships with students. If the teacher is interested in his students, he is likely to be interested in their problems. One teacher of speech, in working with a student in original oratory, discovered in the course of conversations with the student a home situation that was causing the student such anxiety as to impair his scholastic achievement. Other members of the faculty seemed to be "riding" the boy unfairly about his poor work, his laziness, and other faults. When these members of the faculty were informed of the impending break-up of the student's home, they could better appraise his work and understand why he was failing. Also, the teacher of speech helped the student by referring him to the guidance counselor for assistance in adjusting to the crisis.

6. The inability of a teacher of speech to direct extra-class activities satisfactorily is one of the biggest problems of the principal of a high school. Some teachers of speech manage extra-class dramatic and forensic activities very well and, at the same time, teach effectively students in their classes. Some direct the extra-class activities well but neglect their classroom activities, which constitutes a problem for both the principal and the teacher. But the teacher of speech who is unable to cope with the antics of the play cast, the debate squad, or members of the radio club presents a problem of concern to the principal. Since many of these extra-class activities are conducted after school or in the evening, the problem can become serious. Many principals have had to report to the auditorium to help maintain order while a play was being rehearsed. Obviously, the director of a play should not allow such a situation to develop. The director who needs help in supervising his play rehearsals finds himself in this position because he does not insist upon the cast's cooperation from the very first rehearsal. The director needs to have definite plans made for

students not on stage during rehearsal. Many directors of plays can learn from basketball and football coaches who are often masters at making use of practice time in an organized fashion. These directors and all teachers in a high school should acquaint themselves with school policies and regulations covering after-school and evening meetings and make sure that rules are observed. They should assume vigorous leadership in their special extra-class responsibilities.

7. The teacher of speech should be a competent bookkeeper and recordkeeper. Almost all modern extra-class activities involve the handling of money. Royalty payments for plays and ticket sales for plays and festivals can become bothersome if the teacher neglects such matters. Efficient keeping of records so that information is quickly available for Awards Day, newspaper articles, and similar uses is a responsibility of the teacher who sponsors extra-class and interscholastic events in a high school. Every teacher of speech should be prepared for such duties as ticket sales, information for newspaper stories, and awards assemblies. The efficient and wise teacher will closely supervise student assistants who can, and should, handle the "leg work" of ticket sales; insist upon accurate records; check up frequently on ticket sellers; and deposit daily in the office of the principal the cash received. A special notebook for keeping a record of the speech contests and festivals attended and of the names of students who participated and their ratings and awards can save much time.

8. Probably all principals of high schools feel that it is important that the teacher of speech organize the program of speech education so that the administration, the students, the teacher of speech, and all other teachers affected by the program of speech education know where they are going. Again, the basketball and football coaches have well-planned seasons for both practice and performance. Teachers of speech, directors of plays, and directors of forensic activities should also organize their activities so that as many students as possible can participate and so that other teachers know when to schedule their activities to minimize conflicts and to use efficiently the time allotted. Also, parents of students involved in extra-class and interscholastic speech activities need to know such things as where their sons and daughters are and why, when they are going and returning, arrangements for transportation and supervision, and what money is to be paid by the students or parents. The wise teacher of speech may plan with the principal to obtain parental approval, as well as approval by other teachers, of students' participation in extra-class events and especially for their travel and participation in interscholastic events. The teacher of speech seems to be shocked sometimes when parents and other teachers display a strong interest in his plans for "his" students' activities. Sometimes he

imagines that other teachers in the school, including the basketball and football coaches, are not required to obtain advance approval of their plans. Unfortunately, not all such plans are approved in advance by all concerned. Sometimes these unapproved plans are executed with resulting conflicts and even more serious consequences. Most plans for curricular, extra-class, and interscholastic activities in a high school are the result of the combined judgment of teachers, parents, and students under the leadership of the administrator of the high school.

Although it is impossible at times for teachers of speech to determine far enough in advance the details of interscholastic forensic programs, opportunities, and responsibilities, each teacher of speech should be alert and responsible for obtaining this information as soon as possible and sharing it with the students, teachers, and parents who are involved in the program or affected by it. Furthermore, the teacher of speech, together with the principal, as necessary and possible, should seek the cooperation of teachers of speech and principals in other high schools to set up in advance of the beginning of the school year a schedule of interscholastic events. In fact, many states have organizations, consisting of administrators and teachers, to set up an annual school calendar of extra-class and interscholastic activities in which schools plan to participate. The trend in coordinating and planning these school events seems to be toward determining the events to be published on the calendar at least one school year in advance. Copies of the calendar of school activities are made available to the administrators of the high schools in the state. Teachers of speech may well be, and oftentimes are, alert and foresighted enough to work with their high school administrators to have listed on the calendar for state-wide distribution the forensic and dramatic art events planned in their high schools.

Obviously, the principal of a high school should be completely informed on all plans for extra-class and interscholastic activities. His office will undoubtedly keep a calendar of events, in addition to the calendar by the state-wide organization, on which all extra-class and interscholastic events are to be listed at the suggestion of his teachers and after they are approved. The efficient and wise teacher should provide the principal with opportunity to approve or disapprove all plans for extra-class activities, especially interscholastic activities. Principal and teacher may both arrive at the point at which the office of the principal needs and wants only to be informed of all that is going on in the school, except possibly in the case of special innovations which may best involve the combined judgment of the teacher and the principal. In the case of special innovations, the principal has a right and an obligation to exercise his judgment in the planning of the event and in affirming the plan or rejecting it.

The teacher of speech may well be concerned with the soundness of his philosophy of his rights and responsibilities in a high school. It would probably be fruitful for him to check aspects of his philosophy against what other teachers of speech have indicated as their philosophies. In order to do this best, it could be to the advantage of each teacher of speech, present and prospective, to write out his "Philosophy of Teaching Speech" and evaluate it.

In 1958 the Central States Speech Association inaugurated "Outstanding Speech Teacher Awards" for young teachers with less than five years of teaching experience, so as to promote effective speech education in the Central States area. As one of the requirements, applicants for these awards were invited to submit a statement of their philosophies of teaching speech. Such statements may offer valuable help to potential and prospective teachers of speech as well as to teachers with much experience in speech education.

Arthur L. Housman, Professor of Speech and Drama at Saint Cloud, Minnesota, State College, wrote:

> I believe fundamentally that speech is a learned process; that the process of speechmaking is complex and is related to all activities of man in social intercourse; that the act of speech is unified; that good speech is dependent upon the worthiness of the speaker, his objectives, and his ability to organize and deliver intelligently a sum of worthwhile material; that good speech demands great mental and physical effort; that good speech demands vocal and physical skill developed through the discipline of training; that good speech depends upon the speaker's sense of responsibility to himself, to his audience, and to his society; that good speaking results best from the integrated and related activities of public speaking, debate, discussion, drama, and oral interpretation which utilize the same basic technical tools, and which are provided fundamentally with the same set of circumstances in the speech situation: a body of content, an agent of oral delivery, and an audience.
>
> I believe, further, that the pressing increase of modern man's need for speech education in a society responsive to instantly available media of mass communication imposes upon the teacher of speech the greatest personal responsibility which he must understand and accept if he is to fulfill himself personally and professionally.

Ronald F. Reid, Assistant Professor of Speech and Director of Forensics at Washington University, Saint Louis, Missouri, replied:

> My philosophy of speech education requires that both content and skill be taught. Public speaking, for example, should include a study of content—the principles of persuasion, the history of rhetorical theory, and the like. It should also teach public address as a skill; in other

words, it should produce speakers who are clear and persuasive. Teaching either content or skill alone is not enough.

My philosophy also requires that a speech teacher be broad in outlook, that he consider himself a *teacher* first, a *speech teacher* second. This principle has several implications:

1. A speech course should be a liberal arts course in the broadest sense, one concerned with the whole student. The teacher, therefore, should prevent, as best as he can, speeches on trivial subjects and those which are exclusively 'occupation centered.' He should encourage, for example, engineering students to grapple with political issues and political science majors to concern themselves with, say, literary questions.

2. The speech teacher should look beyond his particular specialty into other areas of speech, and indeed other disciplines, for knowledge. Psychology, literature, history, rhetoric, logic—all these fields, and many others, have relevance for speech training.

3. The speech teacher should feel free, indeed obligated, to consider ethics. We must be candid enough, both privately and in our classes, to acknowledge that some insidious techniques are persuasive and that speech can be used to help an evil cause; but we must never overlook ethical considerations.

My philosophy requires, furthermore, that speech education be available to all students. The speech therapist works with the speech handicapped. All speech teachers—whether their specialty be public speaking, dramatics, radio, or something else—have a responsibility to cooperate with the therapist. Superior students should be encouraged to participate in co-curricular activities.

Finally, my philosophy requires that the speech teacher also be a student. He must study, especially in speech and the fields most closely allied to this area of speech. And he should make some scholarly contribution to research in his field. His study is in reality a part of his teaching, for the good teacher must know much and must be constantly stimulating himself intellectually in order to stimulate his students.

Another Award Winner of the 1958 Central States Outstanding Speech Teacher Award was F. Fulton Ross, then a high school teacher of speech in the Central Senior High School at Davenport, Iowa. His philosophy of speech was embodied in a series of objectives listed as desirable for achievement in the teaching of speech:

I should like to express my personal philosophy of the teaching of speech by setting forth objectives listed as desirable for achievement in the teaching of speech. . . .

1. To develop an awareness of the significance of speech as our fundamental means of communication.

2. To develop an appreciation for freedom of speech and the responsibility of the individual in using it.

3. To develop within the individual self-confidence, poise, and control in speech situations.

4. To develop within the student a realization of the importance of the quality and integrity of ideas expressed in speaking situations.

5. To help the individual develop proficiency in pronunciation, articulation, and enunciation.

6. To develop the ability of the individual to organize ideas clearly for oral presentation.

7. To help the student increase his vocabulary and thereby develop his ability to choose words and use language in speaking.

8. To develop the individual's ability to express himself through voice and bodily action.

9. To develop in the individual the ability to listen and observe courteously, analytically, and discriminatingly.

Elizabeth Moodie, then Instructor in the Speech and Hearing Laboratories of the University of Nebraska, formulated her philosophy of speech education from her experiences in the area of speech correction:

> My training and experience are limited to the area of speech therapy. Thus, my beliefs in regard to the teaching of speech have developed with reference primarily to this area. I feel that the techniques of teaching are less important than the atmosphere which is built between the student and teacher. One begins to teach by accepting the student where he is and respecting his ability to grow. An atmosphere where the student is free to experiment with new ideas, to make mistakes, and to evaluate his performance seems to me to lead to effective teaching. We do not actually teach a person to change his manner of speaking; rather, we assist the child or adult in making new observations which enable him to make the changes.

Judging from these statements, teachers of speech agree on certain basic aspects of a sound philosophy. Effective teachers of speech seem to have incorporated into their teaching these beliefs:

1. *All* students can be helped by speech instruction: those with defects, those "normal," and those with talent.

2. Speech education and training should provide for social integration.

3. The proper program of speech education is personal and practical.

4. The purpose of speech is not "exhibitionism."

5. Concern for the individual in the classroom is mandatory.

Summary

The teacher of speech determines largely the caliber, quality, and success of speech education in a high school. As a human being living and working among other human beings, he necessarily strives to be liked and respected by students, teachers, administrators, parents, and others in his sphere of influence.

Effective teaching seems to be the best criterion by which most high school students judge a teacher to be their "best" teacher. However, the "best-liked" teacher, even when students judge him not to be their "best" teacher, seems to be "best-liked," because he is exacting in his standards, stricter in marking, and more effective in helping them to learn.

Teachers have agreed that a "top" teacher is one with a sense of mission, who loves people, his work, who is intellectually honest, thoroughly knows his subject, is not authoritarian, understands his students, and is able to create student interest. A "top" teacher of speech is probably one who has all eight of these basic qualifications.

Administrators have expressed their belief that the "superior" teacher of speech is (1) personable, (2) socially competent, (3) liberally and professionally educated, (4) skillful in the motivation of students and in the evaluation of their achievement and development, (5) cognizant of the relationship of student development and student experiences outside of class, (6) enthusiastic about speech and speech education without stifling his cooperation with other teachers and their fields of teaching, (7) mindful of the value of speech education for all students, (8) reasonable in his conception of the domain, role, and effect of speech education in the high school, (9) hesitant to blame the administrator for shortcomings in the speech program in the high school, (10) able to make effective speeches in the school and community, (11) familiar with the findings of research in speech and speech education as well as in teacher education, (12) understanding and enthusiastic in working with high school students, (13) sound in judging the value and suitability of subject matter for the educational development of high school students, (14) capable of injecting demonstration, when needed by students, in teaching dramatics, forensics, and speech, and (15) interested in developing and maintaining high professional standards.

Factors considered by wise and conscientious administrators who have a right and an obligation to know the attitudes, capabilities, and potentialities of teachers of speech in high schools are: (1) the teacher's philosophy of speech and speech education including extra-class and interscholastic dramatic, forensic, and speech activities, (2) the relationship of speech education, as an integral part of the total educational program of the high school and to each of its other integral parts, (3) the effect of the speech abilities, speech habits, and speechmaking on students, other teachers, parents, and others who are influenced by the teacher and who influence him, (4) the breadth and depth of preparation within the field of speech, liberal arts, and professional teacher education, (5) attitude of the teacher toward high school students and their attitude toward the teacher with assurance of mutual respect and fondness, (6) the ability of the teacher to direct at least satisfactorily extra-class and interscholastic dramatic, forensic, and speech activities to serve sound objectives of speech education, and (7) preparation and ability as a bookkeeper and record-keeper to assume responsibility for budgets, receipts, expenditures, information for newspaper stories, names and ratings of students in interscholastic events, information for awards assemblies, et cetera, related to activities within the scope of the program of speech education in the high school. These factors of administrative concern are indicative of judgments which may be exercised by principals of high schools. However, the teacher of speech has a right to know the attitude of the principal toward speech and speech education and an obligation to cooperate with him in working toward acceptance of speech taught as a significant communicative experience for all students.

A teacher of speech is responsible for evaluating periodically his philosophy of speech education which affects his choice of objectives, his methodology and materials, the standards by which he evaluates student achievement and growth, and the outcomes of his efforts in a high school and community. Doing so, he will likely find fruitful the philosophies of speech education as expressed by other educators. Each prospective teacher of speech may well write and evaluate his "Philosophy of Teaching Speech."

Projects

1. Write a paper on "The Ideal Speech Teacher" or on "Speech Teachers I Have Known."

2. Construct a rating scale for evaluating teachers of speech.

3. Read Robert W. Richey's chapter on "Competencies for Teaching." Construct your self-appraisal form for your evaluation of teacher-competency.

4. Discuss with your classmates the reasons why you and they are particularly interested in speech and speech education. Then, outline a brief talk for the class on what influenced you.

5. Write a paper on "Qualifications of a Director of Plays" or "Qualifications of a Director of Forensics."

6. Formulate *your* philosophy of the teaching of speech.

7. Outline what you believe to be the necessary requirements for certification to teach speech at the secondary school level. How does your statement of requirements compare with your own state's requirements?

8. Prepare to discuss the relationship of speech education to the total educational program of a high school.

9. State your position on "The Right and Obligation of the Teacher of Speech in a High School to be a Model 'Speechmaker' in the Community." Support your position.

10. Write a paper on "The Strengths and Weaknesses of my Preparation for Teaching Speech in a High School." In the paper indicate measures which should be taken to help prospective teachers of speech to be better prepared.

11. Prepare to explain to the class your conception of the difference between "liking" and "respecting" a teacher. Support your concept.

12. Outline your ideas of how a director of a play or the director of forensics in a high school can best manage students during after-school and evening rehearsals and practice.

13. List ways in which you believe bookkeeping and recordkeeping can be used to advantage by a teacher of speech who assumes responsibility for extra-class and interscholastic dramatic, forensic, and speech activities.

14. Reflect on the merits and demerits of the "Outstanding Speech Teacher Awards" inaugurated by the Central States Speech Association in 1958. Be prepared to present to the class the results of your thinking about the innovation of 1958.

15. Read the series of articles in *The Speech Teacher* on "Great Teachers of Speech." Be prepared to state why you believe each of the teachers was designated as a great teacher of speech.

16. Read Ernest W. Henrikson's article in *Speech Monographs*, September 1959, pp. 221-226, on "Some Relations Between Personality, Speech Characteristics, and Teaching Effectiveness of College Teachers." What help can Henrikson's ideas be to the teacher of speech in a high school?

17. Prepare to state in class your reactions to "Responsibilities of the Speech-English Program" by Donald C. Bryant. Be prepared to defend your reactions.

Selected Bibliography

"A Program of Speech Education—The North Central Association," *The Quarterly Journal of Speech*, vol. 37, no. 3 (October 1951), pp. 347-358.

BALCER, CHARLES L., "The High School Principal and the Teacher of Speech," *The Speech Teacher*, vol. 4, no. 3 (September 1955), pp. 182-186.

BARR, A. S., and ASSOCIATES, "The Measurement and Prediction of Teacher Efficiency," *The Review of Educational Research*, vol. 25, 1955, pp. 261-269.

BRYANT, DONALD C., "Critical Responsibilities of the Speech-English Program," *The Speech Teacher*, vol. 10, no. 4 (November 1961), pp. 276-282.

BURNS, KENNETH, "A Report on Teacher Training in Speech," *The Speech Teacher*, vol. 9, no. 3 (September 1960), pp. 192-199.

CURVIN, JONATHAN, "Alexander M. Drummond," *The Speech Teacher*, vol. 12, no. 1 (January 1963), pp. 10-12.

DE BOER, JOHN J., "The Relation Between Speech and English in the Curriculum of the Secondary School," *The Speech Teacher*, vol. 11, no. 2 (March 1962), pp. 101-104.

DONNER, STANLEY T., "Ralph Dennis: A Great Teacher," *The Speech Teacher*, vol. 11, no. 3 (September 1962), pp. 214-220.

HABERMAN, FREDERICK W., "Toward the Ideal Teacher of Speech," *The Speech Teacher*, vol. 10, no. 1 (January 1961), pp. 1-9.

HARGIS, DONALD E., "The General Speech Major," *The Quarterly Journal of Speech*, vol. 36, no. 1 (February 1950), pp. 71-77.

HARRINGTON, ELBERT W., "The Role of Speech in Liberal Education," *The Quarterly Journal of Speech*, vol. 41, no. 3 (October 1955), pp. 219-222.

HOCHMUTH, MARIE, "Great Teacher of Speech: III. Wayland Maxfield Parrish: Teacher and Colleague," *The Speech Teacher*, vol. 4, no. 3 (September 1955), pp. 159-160.

HUCKLEBERRY, ALAN W., "The Relationship between Change in Speech Proficiency and Changes in Student Teaching Proficiency," *Speech Monographs*, vol. 17, no. 3 (November 1950), pp. 378-389.

KNOWER, FRANKLIN, "A Philosophy of Speech for the Secondary School," *The Speech Teacher*, vol. 1, no. 2 (March 1952), pp. 79-85.

KONIGSBERG, EVELYN, " 'Speech Education for All': Do We Mean It?—A Committee Report," *The Speech Teacher*, vol. 2, no. 3 (September 1953), pp. 191-195.

LEWIS, R. F., "Quality Standards for the Speech Teacher," *The Speech Teacher*, vol. 10, no. 1 (January 1961), p. 64.

LILLY, EMILY KIMBALL, "Great Teachers of Speech: I. The Young Lew Sarett," *The Speech Teacher*, vol. 4, no. 1 (January 1955), pp. 22-23.

MCBRIDE, MALCOLM R., "Great Teachers of Speech: IV. Frank M. Rarig," *The Speech Teacher*, vol. 4, no. 4 (November 1955), pp. 231-232.

NELSON, SEVERINA E., "Great Teachers of Speech: II. Charles Henry Woolbert," *The Speech Teacher*, vol. 4, no. 2 (March 1955), pp. 113-117.

NILES, DORIS, "The Beginning Speech Teacher as Director of the High School Assembly," *The Speech Teacher*, vol. 10, no. 4 (November 1961), pp. 291-297.

OKEY, L. LA MONT, "Thomas Clarkson Trueblood Pioneer, 1856-1951," *The Speech Teacher*, vol. 11, no. 1 (January 1962), pp. 10-14.

PETERSON, GORDON E., "Giles Wilkeson Gray," *The Speech Teacher*, vol. 10, no. 1 (January 1961), pp. 10-12.

REID, LOREN D., *Teaching Speech*, 3rd ed. Columbia, Missouri: Artcraft Press, 1960.

ROUSSEAU, LOUSENE, "Great Teachers of Speech: James Milton O'Neill," *The Speech Teacher*, vol. 10, no. 2 (March 1961), pp. 95-99.

SELECTED BIBLIOGRAPHY

SEIFRIT, WILLIAM C., "The General Speech Major: Ten Years Later," *The Speech Teacher*, vol. 10, no. 1 (January 1961), pp. 34-40.

SKINNER, TED, "A Study of Speech Major Requirements," *The Speech Teacher*, vol. 10, no. 4 (November 1961), pp. 302-303.

SIMON, CLARENCE T., "The Teacher and His Graduate Work," *The Speech Teacher*, vol. 1, no. 4 (November 1952), pp. 231-236.

SMITH, DONALD K., "What Are the Contemporary Trends in Teaching Speech?" *The Speech Teacher*, vol. 10, no. 2 (March 1961), pp. 87-94.

SMITH, JOSEPH F., "Maud May Babcock, 1867-1954," *The Speech Teacher*, vol. 11, no. 2 (March 1962), pp. 105-107.

SPECIAL COMMITTEE, Secondary School Interest Group, Speech Association of America, "Fundamentals of Speech: A Basic Course for High Schools," *The Speech Teacher*, vol. 8, no. 2 (March 1959), pp. 93-113.

TRAUERNICHT, MAXINE M., "Woolbert as a Teacher," *The Speech Teacher*, vol. 9, no. 3 (September 1960), pp. 200-206.

WALTER, OTIS M., "On the Teaching of Speech as a Force in Western Culture," *The Speech Teacher*, vol. 11, no. 1 (January 1962), pp. 1-9.

WEAVER, ANDREW T., GLADYS L. BORCHERS, AND DONALD K. SMITH, *The Teaching of Speech*. Englewood Cliffs, New Jersey: Prentice-Hall, Inc., 1952.

WICHELNS, HERBERT A., "James A. Winans," *The Speech Teacher*, vol. 10, no. 4 (November 1961), pp. 259-264.

CHAPTER 3

The High School Student

In forty years, from 1910 to 1950, enrollment increased from slightly more than one million to over six million students in our high schools.[1] Estimates were that from 1961 to 1963 the projected high school enrollment would increase by over two million.[2] Some statistical projections indicate that the number of students in our high schools by 1970 will exceed twelve million. Those born during World War II are now graduating from our high schools and many of them are entering our colleges. Meanwhile our increased annual birth rate of perhaps 5,000,000 promises an ample number of high school students in the United States during the next twenty years.

Since the United States is committed to the philosophy of secondary education for all young people and since speech education for all American youth is becoming an integral part of secondary education, we can expect a large enrollment in courses within the program of speech education.

The teacher of speech, like every other teacher, in a junior or senior high school will need to know in advance as much as he can about the students in his classes and in speech activities. With the growing number of students comes the likelihood of an increase in the individual differences in students. Even with all the information the teacher can obtain in advance

---

[1] United States Office of Education, "Progress of Public Education in the United States of America," *Biennial Survey of Education in the United States, 1954–56.* Washington: Government Printing Office, 1959. p. 11.

[2] Information supplied by Office of Education, Department of Health, Education, and Welfare, *Statesman's Yearbook, 1958.* London: Macmillan and Company, Limited, 1958. p. 107.

about his students, there will be differences indicated by intelligence quotients ranging from 50 to 160, by wide variations in home backgrounds, educational and vocational interests, temperament, special talents, and by the heterogeneity resulting from school consolidations, shifts in population, and differences in incentives. However, background materials on the adolescent are almost inexhaustible. Most prospective teachers of speech will have had courses in adolescent psychology from which they can get some theoretical background on the physical, mental, and emotional development and characteristics of the teen-ager. Without it, the teacher of speech may be disappointed, disillusioned, and ineffective in the classroom.

Adolescence marks a period of change. Students in this phase of growth require patience, understanding, and sympathy from a teacher, especially since so much of the work in speech education may be of a "performance" nature which places a premium on adjustment, self-confidence, poise, group approval, and cooperation.

The National Council of Teachers of English Curriculum Commission formulated a list of characteristics of junior and senior high school students based securely on the psychology of adolescents.[3] A thorough study of these characteristics should help the prospective teacher of speech better to understand junior-senior high school students.

STUDENTS Physical, Mental, and Emotional Characteristics	STUDENTS Language Characteristics
Level: 12-15 Years	
1. Go through a period of rapid growth and development, making many new adjustments necessary (many girls are approximately a year ahead of boys in physical and organic maturity).	1. Desire to have fun, a fact which manifests itself in language expression related to sports, amusements, and humorous situations; develop increased maturity in interests through clubs and teamwork; show interest in language activities related to animals, adventure, mystery, collections, and explorations, but resist tasks requiring lengthy application; girls show interest in sentiment and romance.
2. Undergo internal changes involving heart, gland, and bone	2. Desire to be interesting is manifested in the individual's pursuit

[3] Commission on the English Curriculum of the National Council of Teachers of English, *The English Language Arts in the Secondary School*. New York: Appleton-Century-Crofts, Inc., 1956. pp. 16–20.

STUDENTS
Physical, Mental, and
Emotional Characteristics

structure; the heart grows faster than do the arteries, thus causing a strain on the heart and often conflicts and emotional upsets.

3. Need emphasis on good posture; possess relatively poor coordination; often feel they do not "belong"; evidence marked concern and interest in their accelerated growth and changing bodies, and take increasing pride in personal appearance.

4. Have wide intellectual interests as a group but growing specializations of interest on the part of the individual; are more capable of intellectualizing their own experiences than at earlier levels but often are hampered by their emotions; are alert, active, and curious about everything; want facts; are still interested in firsthand experiences but are increasingly capable of learning vicariously.

5. Often feel socially insecure and may compensate by making themselves conspicuous in one way or another hoping for group approval; are more interested in approval, but need and desire adult support at times; desire to understand themselves, to be interesting, and to have freedom with security; experience anxiety over financial, social, and family insecurity; desire satisfying vocational experiences for immediate needs and for building for the future.

STUDENTS
Language Characteristics

of his own welfare, and in human relationships, with increasing social sensitivity to reaction of individuals and group in language situations.

3. Desire to understand and express themselves through dramatization and imaginative thinking; show wide variation in educational attainment; desire to realize their capacities as shown in their atempts to understand personal abilities and to seek interests that will fulfill their recognized language needs.

4. Desire to become informed and to discuss ideals by which men live (manifested in hero worship); and express a challenging mental attitude toward social problems, and a concern about right and wrong.

5. May display marked aggressiveness in speech and a tendency toward constant argumentation; show a liking for parliamentary procedures; enjoy hobbies involving use of much technical knowledge and skill and employ a more logical approach to solving problems; establish habit of reading periodicals and books related to interests; experience a need to express a new awakening to beauty.

STUDENTS
Physical, Mental, and
Emotional Characteristics

STUDENTS
Language Characteristics

Level: 15-18 Years

1. Reveal great individual differences in intelligence, scholastic achievement, background, and interests; increasingly wide variations in groups of older children because of the additional years of living and differing experiences.

2. Complete their physical changes and have grown-up-looking bodies; require adequate food, sleep, and precaution against fatigue; are aware of physical characteristics of themselves and others; admire physical vigor and courage; tend toward awkwardness; become concerned about sex, pair with the opposite sex, as well as go in crowds.

3. Have strong feelings for their group; are extremely sensitive to the opinion of the group; give

1. Reveal great variations in degrees of development in the various language arts; a small percentage have developed the ability to write creatively, but a greater number probably have powers that are undeveloped; often show reluctance in sharing their production; manifest far less difference in reading interests between sexes than between individuals; exhibit a wide range in ability in various aspects of language power; an individual may be skillful in one or more abilities (as reading or speaking) and immature in aspects of others (as skill in spelling or punctuation in writing); range from almost total inadequacy to to a successful degree of fluency in oral expression; increase in writing skills as their thinking becomes more clarified; acquire skill in discriminative use of many types of instructional materials.

2. Extend language experiences in the treatment of mature problems, including relationships among persons, sexes, economic classes, races, political parties, nations and periods of history; boys seek fiction and talk about physically vigorous and morally courageous heroes; girls enjoy romantic stories.

3. Increase in power to think together in large groups (whole classes), to share opinions, and

STUDENTS
Physical, Mental, and
Emotional Characteristics

importance to the gang and seek its approval and acceptance; remain inherently conservative as to group pattern; become increasingly aware of the importance of cooperation with others in classroom and school activities; have strong feelings of loyalty.

4. Have considerable feeling of insecurity; may replace lack of assurance and security by rowdyism; often cover shyness and sensitivity by apparent indifference; often indulge in conspicuous behavior and employ various other devices for gaining attention.

5. Are growing increasingly independent of parents and other adults; resent domination; respect adults without feeling dependence on them; are curious about people in the adult world and seek vocational guidance.

STUDENTS
Language Characteristics

to reach a common feeling and understanding; are so preoccupied with radio and television programs popular with the group, and with activities, pleasures, and friends that it is necessary that all reading and expression suggested by the school be meaningful to them in order to compete successfully for their out-of-school time; are willing to use their specific talents for the group (e.g., poster-making, lettering, running machinery, writing verses, planning programs); cooperate because of group loyalty.

4. Make considerable use of slang and swearing in their speech since it serves not only to furnish a form of expression for their emotions, but also to attract attention of adults and to show belongingness in their own group; are interested in dramatics for personal satisfaction and to gain status within the group.

5. Desire intensely to gain information on their special interests, so are easily led toward becoming good readers; appreciate the importance of vocational success and are willing to master necessary language skills and adult standards; many delight in expressing opinions, very often in a critical way; are willing to "sharpen" their powers of discrimination to select from many sources those literary experiences including books, periodicals,

STUDENTS Physical, Mental, and Emotional Characteristics	*STUDENTS* Language Characteristics
	music, radio programs, plays, etc., which best fill their needs.
6. Have intense emotions and sensory impressions; subordinate intellectual drives to emotional and social needs; are uncertain or questioning with regard to values, particularly in respect to such areas as meaning of life and nature of success; desire insight into themselves; seek understanding of self, asking: "What am I like as an individual? Why am I as I am? Why do I do as I do?", frequently alternating between self-reliance and self-distrust.	6. Have begun to see remote goals and are willing to go through experiences and practices in language even though tedious, because of the values anticipated in successful accomplishments; develop interest in becoming informed as to human relationships and issues; enjoy the beautiful in nature, literature, and human beings; strive to acquire beauty for themselves as a means of securing favorable reaction, as expressed in words, from the group.

The behavioral characteristics of adolescent boys and girls are of vital importance to the teacher of speech because an understanding of them provides a basis for motivation and for arousing interest. Knowing about the adolescent and his need to discover and to understand himself, understanding what problems bother him, can guide the teacher of speech in making his subject matter and activities meaningful to the student. Adolescent boys and girls seem to worry about their social adjustment, health, their future, personality, using time wisely in school and out, family relationships especially when the family seems not to understand the boy or girl, social approval by other adolescents and by adults, and about money. Awareness of these problems, or at least these problem areas, helps the teacher of speech to a better understanding of the interests and needs of adolescent students in his classes and activities.

Individual Needs

To stimulate the interests and satisfy the needs of the student, the teacher should know these interests and needs. A wide range of interests, needs, abilities, and levels of achievement by students in a class is a challenge to the best teacher of speech. Thus, besides knowing the general characteristics of the adolescent, the teacher of speech needs to assemble information on the individuals in his class. Before school starts, every teacher will have access to the records of his students. These records give valuable information on the individual's health record, family data, tests results, special interests, scholastic record, out-of-school travel and experiences, behavioral anecdotal records, and much more. The autobiographical theme is used by many teachers of speech as an assignment early in the school year for such information. Other teachers invite each student to write a confidential letter to the teacher telling about himself, his interests, his hopes and aspirations in the class and in school, his problems, why he likes certain subjects in school best and why he likes other subjects least, what he likes best to do when he has nothing to do, where he has traveled, what extra-class activities he likes best, and what concerns him at home and in school. Also, he may, of course, confide in the teacher about any other special interests and problems. The student should be urged to write the letter in excellent form, using good paper, correct heading and salutation, margins, paragraphing, sentence structure, language, spelling, punctuation, and closing. It is the teacher's job to help the student determine what to write about and to take pride in how he presents this information. If this assignment is to be effective, the student will find the teacher recognizing bits of information in the letter as the teacher talks with the student, calls upon the student to perform in the class, and suggests topics for expository and descriptive talks so that the student knows certainly that the teacher is using the information to help him do his best. Without violating any confidences, the teacher will make it evident to other students also that he is sufficiently interested and informed to help each of them progress in achievement and growth.

With all of this information about adolescents and about each individual student in the class, the effective teacher will concern himself with the "speech interests, needs, abilities, and capacities" of his students. He will want to study them to determine their group tendencies and individual differences. Otherwise, he cannot begin with them "where they are" and take each of them expeditiously toward the desired and achievable goals.

The teacher will want to appraise

1. the adequacy of each student's self-confidence, self-control, poise, and adjustment in a variety of increasingly complex speech situations.

2. the intelligence, background, maturity, stability, and interests of each student for achieving outcomes of the course, consonant with desirable outcomes of secondary education,

3. each student's personableness, alertness, adaptability, initiative, industry, resourcefulness, cooperativeness, vigor and force, sincerity, tact, and interest in self-improvement,

4. the worthiness and clarity of each student's objectives as he speaks,

5. each student's initiative and ability to recognize problems, topics, and propositions in the school and community which can profitably be considered in the course,

6. each student's initiative and ability to structuralize, or make a framework, and to organize his ideas within and around the structure,

7. each student's initiative and ability to select and organize clearly explanatory and supporting details which are related to his ideas and which explain or document his ideas,

8. each student's phraseology, including his vocabulary, word choice and pronunciation, and use of language in talking,

9. each student's purposefulness, responsiveness, and control and use of his bodily action and voice in speaking,

10. each student's skill in enunciation and articulation,

11. each student's choice of material for reading aloud and his interest and ability in reading aloud from the printed page,

12. each student's interest and ability to observe and listen courteously, analytically, and discriminatingly,

13. each student's knowledge and understanding of principles, fundamentals, and practices of speaking, reading aloud, acting, and listening and observing,

14. each student's appreciation for freedom of speech and responsibility of himself and others in exercising it, and

15. the satisfaction each student gets from participating in the activities of the course and from achieving desirable and desired outcomes of his participation.

Although the appraisal and diagnosis of the students and their "speech interests, needs, abilities, and capacities" by the teacher will be a continuous process during the course or courses and activities, the teacher will want to make his initial effort during the first few days of the course. As previously mentioned, he may begin his appraisal before the course begins by consulting the individual records of the students in the central office of the school. However, the appraisal and diagnosis may be continued through each student's

1. completing a carefully devised autobiographical form which can reveal to the teacher the student's interests, needs, and abilities in speaking and his professed attitude toward speaking and toward speech situations.

2. making a short autobiographical talk in which he elaborates on topics suggested by the teacher, so that the teacher can know more about him, the better to help him.

3. taking carefully devised voice and articulation tests, prepared and administered by the teacher or by a speech correctionist in the school

or county, to reveal the student's use of loudness, pitch, quality, and duration of his voice and to reveal defects in enunciation and articulation as well as more serious speech handicaps.

4. making and playing back voice and speech recordings, if a tape or other recorder and reproducer is available, to reveal to the teacher and to the student his voice properties and his use of them, his speech rate, emphasis, inflection, and variety, his sustaining of thought, his directness, distinctness, and intelligibility as he speaks and reads aloud, and perhaps the clarity of his organization and excellence of his phraseology.

5. choosing and reading aloud prose and poetry to enable a prepared speech teacher to diagnose his speech interests, needs, abilities, and capacities in reading aloud.

6. making a short expository or persuasive speech to enable the well-prepared teacher to diagnose his adjustment, attitude, ideas, ability to organize, initiative and ability to document and support his ideas, his phraseology, his bodily action, et cetera.

7. taking paper-and-pencil tests which are carefully designed to indicate his understanding of principles, fundamentals, and practices of speaking, reading aloud, and acting.

8. participating in conferences with the teacher to analyze his speech interests and needs and to make plans for developing his speech abilities and his desirable personal attributes.

After the appraisal and diagnostic performances by the student, the teacher should have a short private conference with each student in which the instructor's reactions to the speaking, reading, and acting are discussed. This conference can be invaluable for establishing rapport with each student and securing his confidence. Also, the conference can lead to high motivation of the student if he and the teacher can arrive at a clear objective for the student to achieve with the teacher's help, establish in the student's mind reasons why he needs to achieve the objective, determine how the student can gain it, and generate mutual enthusiasm for the student's initiating, sustaining, and persisting in his efforts toward his goal.

Typical speech problems of secondary school students likely to be recognized by the teacher as a result of the appraisal and diagnosis are (1) poor adjustment to speech situations, (2) lack of vocal control and vocal flexibility, (3) poor articulation, (4) unacceptable pronunciations, (5) language inadequacies, (6) lack of organizational techniques, (7) inadequate use of developmental and supporting materials, (8) poor choice of basic ideas, (9) failure to adapt to the immediate speaking-listening situation, (10) poor listening habits, and (11) speech defects.

Although accurate diagnosis of the student's speech interests, needs, abilities, and capacities is desirable and necessary, it is no substitute for excellent teaching to enable the student to become oriented to principles, fundamentals, and practices of the course in speech education and to develop his ability to talk well. Without such appraisal and diagnosis, it is hard to know where to begin, whether any progress is being made, or whether the objectives of speech education have been accomplished and to what extent when the course is ended.

Suggested Appraisal Methods and Materials

If a teacher of speech is to make his maximum contribution to his students, he must ". . . strive to know the child's inmost thoughts and deepest feelings."[4]

The high school student's inmost thoughts and deepest feelings probably focus on problems which hamper or promote the development of his abilities to his highest capacity. Likewise, his social, economic, and educational background, his family status, history, and composition, his personal and speech history, the speech experiences and situations he encounters, or his personal interests, needs, and abilities may hamper or promote the development of his speech abilities.

As the teacher of speech understands his students and their problems, he can help them choose and plan experiences and thus develop their speech capabilities.

Not every working method or every set of working materials for the appraisal of the speech interests, needs, abilities, and capacities needs to be used for every student. But any or all of the following sets of methods and materials may be used in studying each individual and as a member of a group:

1. *Autobiographical Form.* No single item in any autobiographical or other form is with certainty significant for the appraisal of a student's speech interests, needs, abilities, and capacities. Some items may seem unrelated to students' speech needs and abilities, but the answer to any single group of items may supply the key to the interests, the need, or the ability. The items in the autobiographical form, considered as a whole and coupled with the teacher's observation of a student as he lives, works, and plays, individually and as a member of a group, may help in providing challenging, appropriate, and worthwhile speech situations and experiences for the student. Of course, each teacher of speech may devise his own autobiographical form to fit his students, or he may draw upon "My Autobiography" below for items in using whatever form he devises.

[4] Samuel Everett and Associates, *A Challenge to Secondary Education.* New York: Appleton-Century-Crofts, Inc., 1935. p. 137.

MY AUTOBIOGRAPHY

The information herein presented is to enable my teacher to get acquainted with me and to help me with my problems as they arise during my progress in speech education. In order to help the teacher to help me, I shall carefully and completely answer *all* questions and fill in *all* blanks.

NAME _____ CLASSIFICATION (Grade 9, etc.) _____
HOME ADDRESS _____ TELEPHONE _____
FATHER'S NAME_____ ADDRESS _____
MOTHER'S NAME _____ ADDRESS _____
GUARDIAN'S NAME _____ ADDRESS _____

I. *General:* I was born on the _____ day of _____ in the year of _____ at (town or city) _____ in the (state) _____.
Since my birth I have lived in these places: (Underscore) on a farm, in a small village of about 500 or less, in a town of more than 500 but less than 10,000, in a city of more than 10,000 but less than 50,000, in a city of more than 50,000. My family lived in _____ for _____ years before I was born. I (have, have not) visited those places. I have lived with my father and mother for _____ years, my father alone for _____ years, my mother alone for _____ years, with persons other than my father or mother for _____ years.

II. *Family:* There are _____ of us living in our house. My father is _____ years old. He was born in _____. His nationality is _____. He has lived in this vicinity about _____ years. He died _____ years ago. My father completed _____ grades in grade school, _____ years in high school, _____ years in college, and _____ years in _____. His present occupation is _____. He has also been a _____. My mother is about _____ years of age. She was born in _____. She has lived in this vicinity about _____ years. She died _____ years ago. My mother completed _____ grades in grade school, _____ years in high school, _____ years in college, and _____ years in _____. My mother (underscore) is living, makes a home for us, is an invalid, does not live in our home, works outside of the home, is deceased. My mother (does, does not) do the homework. She has done _____.

I have _____ brothers and _____ sisters. Some of the facts about my brothers and sisters are given in the outline below:

Name	Age	School	Grade	Married	Occupation	Where Living

III. *Home:* I shall underline the items below which describe our home and its conveniences: library; dictionary; encyclopedia; many books, few books, no books; many magazines, few magazines, no magazines; many newspapers, few newspapers, no newspaper; less than five books, five to twenty-five books, twenty-five to fifty books, fifty to one hundred books, over one hundred books; piano, other musical instruments: _____, _____, _____; radio, radios; television, television sets; a room alone for me to study, a desk for me alone to study, other satisfactory arrangement for me to study; my regular duties in the home are _____, _____, _____; I (am, am not) allowed to drive the family car; I drive a car regularly, irregularly; I do not drive; I reach school by walking, bus, other means: _____.

IV. *Health:* My health is (underline) good, fair, poor. My eyesight is (underline) good, fair, poor. My hearing is (underline) good, fair, poor. My speech is (underline) good, fair, poor. My physical defects are _____. I (do, do not) eat breakfast regularly. I sleep (regularly, irregularly) about _____ hours of each twenty-four.

V. *Social:* I (do, do not) dance. I attend church (underscore) regularly, irregularly, frequently, none. I like to go to Sunday School (underscore) regularly, irregularly, frequently, none. I go to the movies about _____ times a month. I listen to television about _____ hours per week. My favorite television programs are: (1) _____, (2) _____, (3) _____. I would rather be (underscore) in school than at home, at home rather than in school. I would rather be (underscore) with others than alone, alone than with others. Five of my school friends are: _____, _____, _____, _____, _____. I (do, do not) like to go to parties. I go to about _____ parties per month. I belong to the following clubs and societies: _____, _____, _____, _____, _____. When I finish school, I would like to live in the country, a town, a city, because _____.

VI. *Interests:* When I have time of my own these are the things I like to do: _____, _____, _____, _____, _____. I am underlining the items below which I enjoy: classical music, semiclassical music, music other than classical, motion pictures, dancing, parties, conversing with friends, reading, athletics, hiking, lectures, bicycling, games, travel, school, making things, cooking, collecting stamps, playing musical instruments, writing stories, other: _____, _____, _____. My favorite magazines are: _____, _____, _____. The books which I have most enjoyed during the last year are: _____, _____, _____. I have traveled in the following foreign countries and states of the United States: _____.

In my travels, I was most impressed by _____, _____, _____.

VII. *My Future Occupation and My Education:* The occupations in which I am somewhat interested for myself are (List them in order of choice): (1) _____, (2) _____, (3) _____. The occupation of my first choice takes _____ years in high school, _____ years in college, and _____ years of professional or other training. The occupation of my second choice takes _____ years in high school, _____ years in college, and _____ years of professional or other training. The occupation of my third choice takes _____ years in high school, _____ years in college, and _____ years of professional or other training. Courses in high school which I believe will best enable me to prepare for my career: (1) _____, (2) _____, (3) _____. My father would like for me to be a _____. My mother would like for me to be _____. I (do, do not) like to go to school. I would like to stay in school through the _____ grade and then take _____ years in _____. I (do, do not) want to go to college. I (do, do not) expect to go to college. As a rule, I spend _____ hours at home studying my lessons. I have earned money in these ways: _____.

VII. *Speech—Previous Training and Activities:* (I shall place a letter X in the blanks after those activities in which I have participated.) Debates _____, class reports _____, reading prose aloud _____, reading poetry aloud _____, storytelling _____, class plays _____, club plays _____, assembly plays _____, community plays _____, one-act plays _____, longer plays _____, operettas _____, minstrel shows _____, choral speaking _____, public speaking _____, speech drills _____, radio broadcasts _____, television telecasts _____, voice training _____, speech correction program _____. Other speech activities in which I have taken part, either in or out of school are: _____, _____, _____. I (did, did not) have any speech training in the grade school.

IX. *Speech—Attitude:* (I shall place a letter X in the blanks after those items which are true concerning me.) I volunteer to recite in class _____; I recite only when asked to recite _____; I dislike to talk in class _____; teachers seldom call on me to recite _____; teachers frequently call on me to recite _____; I like to converse with my friends outside of class _____; I like to make speeches _____; I like to read aloud _____; I like to participate in a play _____; I like to appear in public _____; I hesitate to lead in a conversation _____; I like to debate _____; I like to participate in speech activities _____. When I stand in front of a group to talk, my knees shake _____; my voice seems different _____; my mouth gets dry _____; I forget what I was going to say _____; I get over my nervousness after I have talked for a few minutes _____.

X. *Speech—Voice and Sounds:* (I shall place a letter X after those items which tend to describe my voice and speech sounds and a O after those which do not.) I speak clearly and distinctly _____; I often have to repeat to make people understand me _____; I stutter _____; I lisp _____; I have difficulty with some speech sounds _____; I speak with a foreign dialect _____; I have difficulty in making my voice carry _____; I get tired if I talk very long at a time _____.

I believe my voice is (underline) clear, flexible, well-modulated, audible, unobtrusive, responsive to meaning, pleasant, unpleasant, too loud, too weak, too high pitched, too low pitched, thin, coarse, breathy, nasal, denasal or dull as if I had a cold, well-used, misused, harsh, hoarse-husky, infantile, metallic.

The speech sounds with which I have difficulty are (underline all with which you have difficulty): s, z, sh, wh, w, th, ch, r, l, t, d, f, v, ing, tle. Others which bother me are: _____, _____, _____, _____, _____.

XI. *Speech—Performances:* (I shall place a letter X after those statements which are true concerning me and a O after those which are false.) When I am requested to prepare a speech or oral report, I get nervous immediately _____; it is difficult for me to choose a topic _____; to decide what my purpose is _____; to know how to prepare _____; to make an outline _____; to find suitable material _____; to plan a conclusion _____; to know how to begin _____; to remember my audience _____; to remember the situation in which I shall speak _____; to make my speech the right length _____; I resolve I will get more experience in making speeches _____.

When I am called upon to speak to a group, I am not nervous _____; I do not forget what I am going to say _____; I seem to be able to express myself well _____; I can make the group understand me _____; I feel very much at ease _____; I find myself using my hands _____; the groups seem to be interested in my talk _____; I like to make speeches _____; I like to read aloud _____; I resolve that I will develop my speechmaking ability _____; I resolve that I will develop my ability to read aloud _____.

XII. *Speech—Needs and Abilities:* (These are the ways in which I believe my speech might be improved.) _____

These are the speech activities in which I would like to participate before I graduate from high school: _____

XIII. *Speech—Comments of Mine* which I believe might help the teacher to get acquainted with me and to help me with my speech problems: (Give any information not already requested.) _____

2. *Guide for Recording Speech.* This guide is suggested for recording the speech of each student in a beginning course in speech. The recording of a student's speech can be a challenge to him to do his best, especially if he is given an opportunity to prepare in advance. It can give the teacher of speech an opportunity to appraise and diagnose the student's speech, his speaking, reading aloud, voice, speech sounds, poise, pronunciation, interests, and the attitude and personal attributes evidenced as he makes his recording. The alert teacher can do a considerable job of teach-

ing, especially if he, the student, and two or three others in the class meet to help the student appraise and diagnose his speech. Obviously, the whole class, assuming that there are no more than fifteen or twenty students, can profit by the reproduction of the recording and their appraisal and diagnosis. However, if the teacher can manage it, each student may engage in study and activity which may be educationally more profitable than hearing more than three to five recordings. The problem is to maintain high interest in whatever worthwhile activity the students are engaged. If each recording is retained for use later, a second recording, or even a third one, may be compared to the first to determine what changes have been effected in the student's speech. Of course, the teacher should plan, with his students, their guide for making a recording, preferably a number of guides so that no more than three to five students use any one guide such as the following.

GUIDE FOR RECORDING SPEECH OF A STUDENT

I. Say: My name is (give your name as it is on the school records).

II. Say: I was born (where and when). I have lived in (where for most of your life). I have traveled (where). I enjoy (what two or three things especially). My favorite television programs are (what two or three). I like to read (what books, periodicals, newspapers, other).

III. Say something about your hobby or hobbies or your principal interests.

IV. Read the following selection as if you were telling a story to a radio audience:

>   A young fox named Reynard saw his shadow at sunrise on Wednesday and said, 'I'll have either a deer or a camel for lunch today. And I think I'd better start out right now to look for it, if I want to find one or the other by lunchtime. I'll probably have to walk many miles hunting for it, because I'm sure there is nothing around here.'
>
>   After a while he passed four or five older foxes who were running along a narrow path in the forest. They'd seen their shadows early that morning, and were also searching for some large animals to eat for lunch. At noon our young fox went back to join them where they'd stopped to rest near the edge of a small body of water. They were tired and hungry, too, but, when they looked at their shadows again, they said, 'A mouse will do.'

V. Read for meaning the following rhymes by Edward Lear:

>   There was an old man who said, 'Well!
>   Will nobody answer this bell?
>   I have pulled day and night,
>   Till my hair has grown white,
>   But nobody answers this bell!'

SUGGESTED APPRAISAL METHODS AND MATERIALS 81

>There was an Old Person of Burton
>Whose answers were rather uncertain.
>When they said, 'How d'ye do?'
>He replied, 'Who are you?'
>That distressing Old Person of Burton.

VI. At this point, converse with your teacher and respond to his questions about everything you will have said and read. Your teacher will initiate the conversation and ask questions.

VII. Say: (Give date and repeat your name.) That's all.

The teacher will want to have a number of paragraphs loaded with speech sounds to substitute for the story of the young fox named Reynard. He will want paragraphs loaded with the various sounds to test students' enunciation and articulation, including some sounds in the initial, medial, and final positions in words. Also, he will want to make substitutions in whatever guide he uses for the rhymes by Edward Lear. By making the substitutions, he can tend to keep the interest high and, at the same time, test the enunciation and articulation of each student. He will want to be alert in the conversation with the student after the speaking and reading so that the student can hear the difference between the way he speaks in making a speech and the way he speaks in reading from the way he speaks in conversation. Although the recording per se can be a profitable educational experience, the high point of the experience can result from the analysis of the recording. In fact, the value of the recording will be determined largely by the teacher's stimulation and guidance of the student to analyze the recording, determine improvements which the student wants to make, set forth a plan for the desired improvements, and execute the plan persistently until the desired change is effected in the student's speech, speaking, speechmaking, and reading aloud.

3. *Diagnostic Form for Speech and Hearing.* The teacher of speech will probably want to make his adaptation of this form which is used in the Saint Cloud State College, Saint Cloud, Minnesota, to appraise and diagnose the speech and hearing of each student.

SPEECH AND HEARING DIAGNOSTIC FORM

Name (please print) _____ Age _____
                           (Last)   (First)
Name of high school attended _____
Languages spoken at home _____
Accidents or operations on face, throat, or ears _____
Check any of the following you may have had:

1. Running ears
2. Repeatedly severe colds
3. Ear ache
4. Loss of permanent teeth
5 Bands or braces on teeth
6. Chronic throat or sinus condition
7. Hearing difficulties

Check interest or participation in:
1. Radio
2. Debate
3. Public Speaking
4. Speech Correction
5. Acting
6. Scene Construction
7. Costuming
8. Interpretation
9. Lighting

Semester(s) of Speech taken in High School _____
Semester(s) of Speech offered in High School _____
            Do not write below this line

VOICE QUALITY Superior ___ Acceptable ___ Poor ___ Needs Correction___
Pitch _____ Too low _____ Too high _____ Monotonous _____
Placement _____ Heady thin _____ Throaty _____ Nasal _____
Volume _____ Weak _____ Too loud _____ DeNasal _____
Tension _____ Breathless _____ Tense Throat _____ Explosive _____
SPEECH Superior ___ Acceptable ___ Poor ___ Needs Correction ___
    General Rhythm _____ Stress _____ Intonation _____
Vowel Faults
    Special Problems
Consonant Faults
    Special Problems
RECOMMENDATIONS
_____1. Special remedial work
_____2. Return for recheck for Speech ___ Hearing ___ within ___ weeks
_____3. No further attention required
_____4. Other_____

    4. *Voice and Articulation Evaluation Form.* This form for use by any qualified teacher of speech for his evaluation of the voice and articulation of each student can be helpful by suggesting to the teacher criteria by which to appraise and diagnose the student's voice and articulation, by serving as a convenient means for helping each student to develop his concept of elements of voice, articulation, pronunciation, tempo, and projection, and by serving to stimulate and guide each student to effect improvement in elements of each of the categories designated on the form.

VOICE AND ARTICULATION EVALUATION FORM

NAME OF STUDENT: _____ DATE _____
DIRECTIONS: Circle the number opposite each category which indicates your evaluation of the student's voice, articulation, and pronunciation.

(1) Much Below Average, (2) Below Average, (3) Average, (4) Above Average, (5) Much Above Average. Under each category, check the words and phrases which apply. Space is provided for comments which are solicited.

Voice Quality: 1 2 3 4 5
  Breathiness
  Harshness
  Metallic
  Improper nasality
  Throaty
  Falsetto
Articulation: 1 2 3 4 5
  Accurate
  Indistinct
  Overprecise
  Omissions
  Substitutions
  Distortions
Pronunciation: 1 2 3 4 5
  Generally acceptable
  Misplacement of accent
  Selection of inappropriate sounds
  Pronunciation of unrequired sounds
  Unfamiliarity with some words

Pitch: 1 2 3 4 5
  Generally effective
  Too high a level
  Too low a level
  Lack of variety
  Pitch pattern
Tempo: 1 2 3 4 5
  Generally effective
  Too fast a rate
  Too slow a rate
  Too staccato
  Too legato
  Lack of variety
  Time pattern
Projection: 1 2 3 4 5
  Generally effective
  Too loud
  Too weak
  Lack of variety
  Loudness pattern

General Impression Made by the Voice: (Underline words which describe) friendliness, lack of friendliness; vitality, lack of vitality; alertness, dullness; carefulness, carelessness; confidence, lack of confidence.

Comments:

Observer

5. *Speech Analysis Form.* Although this form for use by a competent teacher for analyzing the speech of a student appears, as a result of a cursory examination, to serve a purpose similar to that served by other forms for speech analysis, it differs considerably by focusing attention on the speaker, the speaker's speech, and the speaker's speaking and reading.

SPEECH ANALYSIS FORM

Speaker _____ Section _____
Observer _____ Date _____

Instructions: Either encircle the proper term under each heading or write exceptions after the term.

EXCEPTIONS

I. Speaker's Bearing and Manner
   Self-confident
   Purposeful
   Communicative
   Poised

II. Speaker's Speech
    Purposeful
    Easily understood
    Minimum of distractions
    Gets desired response

III. Speaker's speaking and reading
     Meaning: Understood   Communicated
     Mood: Understood   Communicated
     Stress: Accurate   Effective
     Phrasing: Accurate   Varied

     Pronunciation: Acceptable   Consistent
     Tone: Well initiated   Well supported
     Quality: Pleasant   Controlled
     Volume: Varied   Controlled
     Pitch: Varied   Controlled
     Rate: Varied   Controlled
     Rhythm: Consistent with meaning

IV. Speaker's Speech Sounds (Vowels, consonants, diphthongs. Note especially: substitutions, omissions, lisp, excessive nasalization, glottalization, retraction, and slackness.)
    Enunciation:
    Articulation:
    Sounds properly varied:
    Sounds properly aspirated:

6. *Diagnostic Blank—Voice and Speech Analysis.* This blank for use by a competent teacher of speech offers suggestions for appraising and diagnosing a student's voice and his speech in relationship to his employment of voice and speech in reading aloud and in speaking. Also, it offers suggestions for comparing and contrasting the employment of voice and speech in reading aloud with the use of voice and speech in speaking.

DIAGNOSTIC BLANK
VOICE AND SPEECH ANALYSIS IN READING AND SPEAKING

Name _____ Date _____

Items	Reading	Speaking

I. Volume
  A. Too loud
  B. Too soft
  C. Lack of variety
  D. Satisfactory
II. Pitch
  A. Too high
  B. Too low
  C. Lack of variety
  D. Fixed Pattern
  E. Proper inflection
III. Quality
  A. Breathing
  B. Harsh
  C. Metallic
  D. Improper nasality
  E. Full, resonant
IV. Rate
  A. Too fast
  B. Too slow
  C. Satisfactory
V. Articulation
  A. Indistinctness
  B. Over-preciseness
  C. Satisfactory		

General Impression of Voice and Speech

1. Favorable: suggesting friendliness, alertness, sympathy, strength, vitality, and culture.
2. Unfavorable: suggesting dullness, indifference, indecision, carelessness, unfriendliness, distrust.

7. *Speaker Rating Form.* This speaker rating form is suggested for use by a teacher of speech who needs to appraise and diagnose a student as a speaker who is "making a speech." An analysis of this speaker rating form compared with an analysis of each of the other forms already presented will reveal that the emphasis in the speaker rating form is much different than the emphasis in the other forms.

SPEAKER RATING FORM

SPEAKER _____ DATE _____
TOPIC _____
SECTION _____ TEACHER _____

INSTRUCTIONS: Please *complete* one of these forms for each speaker, during and/or immediately after his speech. Rate him on each of the five criteria listed, using the following RATING SCALE: 5—excellent, 4—above average, 3—average, 2—below average, 1—unsatisfactory. After rating him on each of five criteria, write the sum of the five ratings after TOTAL. Record your comments that explain your rating.

CRITERIA	COMMENTS	RATING
TOPIC: Adapted to interests and background of speaker and audience? Appropriate for occasion? Properly narrowed? Of significance?		
CONTENT: Ideas interesting? Significant? Related to topic? Specific? Valid? Varied? Sufficient? Adapted to purpose and audience?		
ORGANIZATION: Introduction, purpose, body, and conclusion apparent? Division of significant ideas clear and logical? Transitions clear?		
DELIVERY: Communicative, conversational, direct, fluent, varied? Voice clear and used well? Enunciation clear? Articulation distinct? Pronunciations acceptable? Language clear, intelligible, accurate, varied, vivid, appropriate?		
GENERAL EFFECTIVENESS: Speaker purposeful, easily understood, attention holding? Speaker's purpose realized?		

TOTAL: _____
JUDGE _____
(Signature)

Continue comments on back as desired.

SUGGESTED APPRAISAL METHODS AND MATERIALS 87

8. *Reading Aloud Rating Form.* This form is suggested for use by a competent teacher of speech for rating a student during and after his reading of a selection of prose or poetry. Although a rating can be inferred from the comments on each of the elements involved in reading aloud either prose or poetry, the teacher's objective is to appraise and diagnose the reader, his selection, his interpretation, and his projection.

READING ALOUD RATING FORM

READER _____ DATE _____
SELECTION _____ AUTHOR _____

CRITERIA	COMMENTS

CHOICE OF READING:

UNDERSTANDING OF THE READING:

PROJECTING OF THE EMOTION:

USE OF PHYSICAL ACTIVITY:

USE OF VOICE:

ARTICULATION AND PRONUNCIATION:

COMMUNICATIVENESS:

OTHER COMMENTS:

CRITIC

9. *Speech Interview Outline.* An interview is a purposeful conversation in which the interviewer or, in this instance, the teacher of speech tactfully appraises or diagnoses the speech of the interviewee or student. A speech interview outline is, likewise, a guide for the interviewer. The outline may be used by a well-prepared and competent teacher of speech to (1) establish friendly relations with the student, (2) obtain information concerning the student's attitude and speech needs in speech situations, (3) obtain information concerning the student's particular speech interests and abilities, (4) discover the causes of the student's speech difficulties, (5) give information and suggestions with which the student may meet his

speech needs and develop his speech abilities, and (6) engage the student in a satisfying and a broadening speech experience.

The conversation may occur in private or in the presence of other students, depending, at least in part, on the specific purpose of the interview and on the probable effect of the interview on the student. If the student is made overconscious of how he talks or how he is expected to talk, he will probably converse little. Likewise, he may converse little in the presence of others if attention is focused directly upon either his particular speech ability or speech defect. Dewey offered this advice for the interviewer:

> Insistence upon avoiding error instead of attaining power tends also to interruption of continuous discourse and thought. Children who begin with something to say and with intellectual eagerness to say it are sometimes made conscious of minor errors in substance and form to the point that the energy that should go into constructive thinking is diverted into anxiety not to make mistakes, and even, in extreme cases, into passive quiescence as the best method of minimizing error.[5]

Some students will be more likely to have something to say and greater intellectual eagerness to say it if they are in the presence of others. Surely all high school students should be encouraged to recognize and to overcome their speech difficulties and to develop their abilities in speech situations with other students. But for purposes of the interview by the teacher of speech they may well be engaged in purposeful conversation apart from other students.

The following outline can serve as a guide in an interview by a competent teacher of speech whose purpose is to discover and to diagnose the particular speech needs of a student. It can serve best, usually, after other appraisal and diagnostic methods and materials have been accomplished, and, more especially, if other methods failed to reveal to the teacher the cause of the student's speech deficiencies. The teacher should study the student's cumulative record before the interview. The important results of the interview should become a part of the student's cumulative record.

SPEECH INTERVIEW OUTLINE

STUDENT'S NAME _____ SEX _____
DATE _____ AGE _____
INTERVIEWER OR TEACHER OF SPEECH _____
   I. Background Information from Cumulative Record _____
_____

---

[5] John Dewey, *How We Think*. New York: D. C. Heath and Company, 1932. p. 246.

SUGGESTED APPRAISAL METHODS AND MATERIALS 89

Reasons for the Interview _____

II. General Appearance, Physical Bearing, and Bodily Activity
   General Appearance   Well developed _____
      Neat _____ Clean _____ Pride in appearance _____
      Remarks _____
   Physical Bearing   Strained posture _____ Careless posture _____
      Well poised _____
      Remarks _____
   Bodily Activity   Awkward _____ Too active _____ Too passive _____
      Coordinated _____
      Remarks _____

III. Speech Attitudes, Emotional Control, and Inhibitions
   Eye contact and movement _____
   Enthusiasm _____ Too serious _____
   Poised and controlled _____ Effeminate manners, if male_____
   Nervous and irritable _____
   Overly aggressive _____ Masculine manners, if female_____
   Overly humble _____ Communicative _____
   Indifferent _____ Antagonizes _____
   Remarks _____

IV. Voice and Voice Control
   Loudness
      Too loud _____ Too soft _____ Monotonous _____
      Adaptable to the situation _____
      Remarks _____
   Pitch
      Too high _____ Too low _____ Monotonous _____
      Acceptable and flexible _____
      Remarks _____
   Quality
      Muffled _____ Metallic _____ Nasal _____
      Denasal _____ Lacks support_____ Hoarse-husky _____
      Infantile _____ Harsh _____ Lacks resonance _____
      Clear _____ Pleasant _____ Rich _____ Resonant _____
      Flexible _____ Controlled _____
      Remarks _____
   Duration
      Enduring _____ Jerky _____ Rapid _____
      Inactive _____ Inaccurate _____ Flexible _____
      Remarks _____

V. Speech Sounds
   Pronunciation of syllables
      Overly meticulous _____ Careless _____ Correct _____
      Remarks _____

Enunciation of vowel sounds
  Clear _____ Muffled _____ Strained _____
  Remarks _____
Articulation of consonant sounds
  Overly precise _____ Agile _____ Acceptable _____
  Remarks _____
  Foreign accent _____ Nationality _____
  Remarks _____
VI. Speech Defects
  Organic
  Facial paralysis _____ Lips _____ Teeth _____
  Tongue _____ Palates _____ Other _____
  Remarks _____

  Functional
  Remarks _____

VII. Summary of the Important Results of the Interview
  _____
  _____

Cumulative Record System

The cumulative record of each student in a high school belongs in the office of the principal. Of course, the office of the guidance counselor may be adjacent to the office of the principal or the guidance counselor may have an office within the principal's office. No teacher or other person in the school is entitled to remove from the central office the cumulative record of a student, but each teacher does have the right and, if he wants to know a student, the obligation to consult his students' cumulative records.

During the process of appraisal and diagnosis of the speech interests, needs, abilities, and capacities of students, some system for the cumulation of records is necessary. One manila folder for each student can be simple and convenient. Folders kept in a file are easily accessible to students, parents, and teacher of speech as well as to other teachers. All records, except those of a confidental nature, may be kept in the office of the teacher of speech or in his classroom.

Each student can profit by studying his own record from time to time. Confidential matter should be kept under lock and key, but the other records of the appraisal and diagnosis of the student's speech should be available to him. Findings by the teacher of speech which hold significance as a part of his permanent record may, and should be, transferred to the office of the principal. The cumulative record of each student prepared by the teacher of speech may be supplemented during the course of a semester or longer by outlines, papers, written examinations, test papers, and other evidences of activity by the student. This record should include all the findings of the appraisal and diagnosis which may be helpful in stimulating his speech interests, meeting his speech needs, and developing his speech abilities. An appraisal of a student also helps him to gain insight into the field of speech and into the possibilities for the improvement of his speech. The results of working methods and materials for the diagnosis of students' speech become increasingly valuable in developing a variety of complex speech experiences for students in all sorts of speech situations.

Orientation of Students to Basic Speech Concepts

Although the teacher of speech will want, initially and continuously, to appraise each student's speech, his orientation in desirable attitudes and basic concepts, and his development of speech ability and good personal attributes, the student need not know when the emphasis on appraisal leaves off and the emphasis on his orientation begins. Nor should he know when the emphasis on his orientation leaves off and the emphasis on his development begins. The three are not mutually exclusive but are interrelated and interactive. No one of the three can be accomplished without contributing to the accomplishment of the other two. However, all three cannot be accomplished best by an overemphasis on one.

The teacher of speech should make clear to each student that the speech classroom is really a laboratory where the student needs to "experiment" to discover those techniques which serve him best as a communicator, person, and active member of a group. By observing others, by being evaluated by the teacher, and by having many opportunities to speak, the student can develop his speech and his desirable personal attributes. Many students need to be impressed with such basic concepts as the following:

1. *Speech is learned, not inherited.* Although a person is born with *capacity to speak,* he is born without *ability to speak.* A discussion of this concept can help the student to see that some of his problems are caused by faulty learning. Sometimes what he has learned must be unlearned if he is to progress in developing purposeful, easily understood, efficient, and effective speech.

2. *Adjustment is learned.* "Stage fright" is a common experience. Discussion of what it is, that it is common, that it can be controlled, and that it can be useful will help many students. Repeated speech performances develop courage and ability that can gain for the student satisfaction and enjoyment and so lessen the fearful feeling of "stage fright."

3. *All speakers must have "content"—something worthwhile to talk*

about. Very often students feel that because we may start with factors of delivery in our speech course, delivery is the most important factor. In fact, speech has been closely identified with delivery and, as a result, many teachers may think of *delivery* and *speech* as synonymous. The teacher of speech should, from the first, insist upon the recognition by the student of the need for worthwhile "ideas." Content is important. Power seems to be rooted in knowledge, even though "delivery" may, in some cases, be more persuasive than poor ideas. Content and "delivery" are most powerful.

4. *Effective speech has a purpose*. The effective speaker should know what his purpose is and should organize and "deliver" his speech so as to do his best to achieve his purpose. Unless the speaker knows what he is trying to do, it is doubtful if the listeners will.

5. *Effective speech is well organized and adequately developed*. Since speakers are concerned with communicating their ideas, feelings, and needs to a listener, the student should recognize the importance of a well-organized presentation and one that is adequately developed and supported.

6. *Effective speech depends upon phraseology*. An understanding of language and its use is important. Recognition of semantic problems that can arise unknowingly, vocabulary suited to the listener, the need for specific, concrete, and vivid word choice—all can help the student communicate more effectively.

7. *Communication is a two-way process*. The teacher of speech should warn his student not to forget the listener. Speaking to a specific audience and preparing for that audience are vital. Therefore, audience analysis should be emphasized.

These concepts are typical of many that the wise teacher will pursue in the program in speech education. Of course, they are not all taught or even mentioned at the beginning of the course but they are ones that the student will recognize as important as he learns to be a more effective oral communicator.

Summary

This chapter has proposed to put the focus on the student and his personal development. The entire program of speech education in any high school can be built upon the ability and willingness of a competent teacher of speech to organize the program of speech education, including all courses and activities in it, so that each student's speech interests and needs are discovered and appraised, his speech interests are stimulated, guided, and broadened, his speech concepts and understanding supported by insight, and his speech abilities and desirable personal attributes are developed. A knowledge of the adolescent in general, an understanding of each student specifically, and a working knowledge and understanding of methods and materials for appraising the speech assets and liabilities of each student can be helpful to the teacher of speech.

Projects

1. Psychologists have identified at least four basic needs which they indicate must be met if people are to be happy and well adjusted. They include (1) the need to establish and maintain self-respect, (2) the need to belong, (3) the need to establish and maintain a role, and (4) the need for love and recognition. Do you agree that these are important? If so, why? If not, why not? How can the teacher of speech utilize this information in the program of speech education? Be prepared to explain.

2. Make an intensive study of one high school student utilizing all the information available to you. Be objective and keep your own judgments out of your case study until you have all of the facts available to you. Then, prepare to report the facts to the class and to state your conclusion or conclusions based on the facts in your case study.

3. What types of information might a junior-senior high school have in its files that a teacher of speech should study in appraising and diagnosing the speech interests, needs, abilities, and capacities of students?

4. Define "speech interests," "speech need," "speech ability," "speech capacity," "speech experience," and "speech situation."

5. A school administrator once wrote to the director of the bureau of educational research at a large university asking the director to suggest a standardized test for use as a final examination in a general course in speech education in a high school. If you were that director, how would you respond? Why?

6. Select one or more of the physical, mental, and emotional characteristics of adolescents and write a paper illustrating how a teacher of speech might use the characteristics you select in some specific assignment in speech education.

Selected Bibliography

BLAIR, ARTHUR WITT, and WILLIAM H. BURTON, *Growth and Development of the Preadolescent.* New York: Appleton-Century-Crofts, Inc., 1951.

BRIGGS, THOMAS H., J. PAUL LEONARD, and JOSEPH JUSTMAN, *Secondary Education,* rev. ed. New York: The Macmillan Company, 1950.

COLE, LUELLA, *Psychology of Adolescents,* 6th ed. New York: Holt, Rinehart and Winston, Inc., 1964.

Landis, Paul H., *Adolescence and Youth*. New York: McGraw-Hill Book Co., Inc., 1952.
Little, Wilson, and A. L. Chapman, *Developmental Guidance in Secondary Schools*. New York: McGraw-Hill Book Co., Inc., 1953.
Malm, Marguerite, and Otis G. Jamison, *Adolescence*. New York: McGraw-Hill Book Co., Inc., 1952.
Rothney, John, *The High School Student*. New York: Holt, Rinehart and Winston, Inc., 1953.
Seidman, Jerome, ed., *The Adolescent*, rev. ed. New York: Holt, Rinehart and Winston, Inc., 1960.
Wattenberg, William W., *The Adolescent Years*. New York: Harcourt, Brace, & World, Inc., 1955.

CHAPTER 4

The Teacher in the Classroom

Although beginning teachers may be prepared by education, training, and experience as indicated in Chapters 1 and 2 and may be confident of understanding the students they will teach as suggested in Chapter 3, many still feel uncertain about getting started. Although a teacher understands the basic principles underlying teaching, the methods and techniques of carrying out those principles in the classroom may not be as readily available as he wishes. It is to this end that this chapter is presented.

The teacher is *ready* to meet students in the first sessions of a class in speech education. The problems of getting started, of providing the students with an adequate orientation in speech and speech education, of classroom control, and how to improve himself and his teaching may plague the beginner.

This is not a problem of the teacher of speech alone. All suggestions in this chapter are basic to all learning and to the general principles of education. However, because the personal relationship between teacher and student in a class in speech education is close and because the teacher must concentrate on each student and his performance to stimulate and guide him, these techniques become especially important to the teacher of speech.

Classroom Control

Many new teachers of speech feel adequately prepared to teach, but often are uneasy in coping with classroom behavior. Of all the questions most frequently asked about methods of teaching speech, those concerning "discipline" and "classroom control," rank first. Textbooks or lectures do not usually deal with flying missiles, strange noises from unknown quarters, out-of-control discussion, chronic tardiness, impertinence, effrontery, or other obstructions to classroom progress. This is because the same classroom problem rarely arises twice, so a pat answer is worthless. Also, as Loren D. Reid pointed out,[1] each teacher has a different impact on the students; consequently, each teacher must develop his own way of handling a problem.

There are, however, certain basic principles that will guide the new teacher. Surveys of what adolescents regard as qualities of a good teacher indicate "fairness" as an important one. The teacher must build a reputation for fairness by playing fair. Emelie Ruth Dodge[2] pointed out that to do so, these principles must be followed:

> Don't threaten unless you can, and intend to, fulfill the the threat. Don't promise unless you can, and intend to, fulfill the promise. It will take only one unfulfilled threat or promise to assure your boys and girls that you are no exception to their rapidly crystallizing conviction that adults are three-quarters hot air.
>
> Don't break a rule for anyone unless the entire class can see that it is an emergency. There are times when exceptions must, of course, be made; but when these cannot be postponed and handled in private conference, the class should be allowed to see that an exception is necessary.
>
> Stick to school rules yourself. Frequently, it is not required that you observe them; however, do not break rules or equivocate before your students. . . . Don't wander into your classroom late and expect your status to excuse you.
>
> Always tell students the truth. . . .
>
> Keep your classroom rules short and simple. Don't establish long lists of do's and don'ts.
>
> Always make your demands clear to everyone ahead of time. Don't give a pupil a chance to say: "But I was absent the day you gave us that!" Write your requirements and assignments on the board to be copied into notebooks, or give out mimeographed sheets. Then make absolutely certain that these instructions are understood.

Problems of discipline often arise when the teacher loses the attention of the class. Knowledge of and enthusiasm for the subject matter and teaching are imperative requisites of excellent teaching. Students tend

---

[1] Loren D. Reid, "On First Teaching Speech," *The Speech Teacher*, vol. 1, no. 1 (January 1952), pp. 5–7.

[2] Emelie Ruth Dodge, "Classroom Control in the High School," *The National Education Association Journal*, March 1958, pp. 180–181.

to respect you as a teacher and as a person when they realize that you know what you are talking about. Preparing a course or bloc of study or a resource unit may seem dull and tedious, but an overview of your plan for a semester or even for a year is essential. Coming to class each day prepared to utilize every minute of the class period can minimize the possibility of unpleasant situations arising. Students who are not really busy often cause trouble. Plan your lessons carefully with varied activities so as to take into account students' relatively short attention spans. On the other hand, don't crowd too many activities into one class period. Be flexible and responsive to the mood of the class. Students who are unchallenged and idle and students who are pushed beyond their capacities create problems. They are likely to be restless, uncooperative, and even defiant.

Students who are interested and busy are more likely to be model students than are idle students, even if they are "intelligent loafers." Each student needs to be motivated. However, no student is likely to be motivated until he sees an objective clearly, a need for his achieving the goal, how he can attain the objective, and see some hope of satisfaction in accomplishing his objective or from his efforts. Careful planning, skillful practice, and everlasting enthusiasm by the teacher of speech for the students' success in learning are basic to the students' motivation.

In spite of your every effort to be fair and to plan carefully for each day's work, you will probably encounter some disciplinary situations. If so, try to handle them as unobtrusively as possible on an individual basis. Speak quietly and privately to the offender. Tell the student to stop whatever he is doing and go on with what you were doing without waiting for an answer. Asking the student if he will stop only invites an answer —probably an impudent one. You may, of course, send the offender out of your classroom. It hardly seems advisable to waste the time of the class just to discipline one student. Some teachers feel that sending a student to the principal's office lessens their prestige with the students and makes the next occasion more difficult. This does not necessarily follow. If you send a student to the principal's office or to the disciplinary officer in your school, you should follow up, at the earliest opportunity, by checking with this school official yourself and explaining the situation. Basically, however, every teacher should always try to discover why the situation developed by analyzing his own remarks and actions as well as the behavior of the students.

Other specific suggestions that have been made for the guidance of effective classroom control include:

1. Don't talk down to your students. They resent it if you adopt

a condescending attitude and belittle their abilities or backgrounds. Treat each student with all the respect he deserves.

2. Be pleasant and friendly, but not chummy. Loyalty is a dominant quality in adolescents; when they have accepted you as a friend, you may be surprised to discover the extent of their loyalty.

3. Keep your sense of humor. It is easier and more satisfying to share a joke that amuses the class than to try to frown down hilarity, only to see it grow with your attempts to suppress it.

4. Stand at the door at the beginning of the period. This gives you a good opportunity to show general friendliness, greet students who have been absent, and exchange casual remarks with others.

5. Avoid punishing the whole class for misbehavior, however widespread the action may seem to be. Mass punishment aligns the whole group against the teacher.

6. Do not publicly praise or reprimand an individual student. If the attitude of the class is not favorable, a "good" student may react rudely if singled out for unwelcomed commendation. Scolding a student publicly not only embitters him but sometimes enlists the rest of the class on his side—against you. Always focus your praise on the excellence of effort, performance, achievement, or growth by the student rather than the student himself. Likewise, focus your suggestions on the work of the student on the assumption that he wants to improve rather than on the student himself.

In summary, the most sensible way to handle classroom control is by not allowing problems to develop in the first place. Discipline is most successful when it is preventive rather than punitive; but if it must be punitive, make it swift and sure. Some teachers may imagine that the worst will happen but it seldom does. We should all remember that the troublesome students are troubled young people. A few of them may have emotional problems and disturbances calling for special attention, but most of them are merely boys and girls whose problems you can help them solve.

Getting Started: First Assignments

The success of a class in speech may, like a speech, depend upon its good beginning. The first assignment poses a special problem. The teacher wants to provide an assignment simple enough to enable students with different abilities to achieve some sort of success. He wants to challenge all students to do their best. He wants to discover needs and abilities that will provide a basis for future work for each student.

The logical place to start is by getting acquainted with your students. Many teachers of speech wisely use the first class period to have each student relate to the others something about himself: name, special interests or hobbies, what subject or extra-class activity he likes best, what he likes least, an unusual experience of his, et cetera. Of course, the teacher may lead and be alert to lead and to ask questions of each student as well as to manifest a sincere interest in what each student has to say. Other teachers pair off students and have them introduce each other to the class, after the students have obtained the necessary information. In either event, the teacher can then indicate to the students that the "first speech—the hardest one—is over and everyone survived!" After this autobiographical type of assignment, the teacher may spend the remainder of the first class period discussing with his class the general outline of the course, the objectives, any special rules and regulations, his grading system, and so on.

To obtain helpful and more lasting information, many teachers of speech have each student complete a speech inventory *after* the autobiographical talks or introductions. Although a detailed and lengthy autobiographical form is presented in Chapter 3, the following examples of shorter and typical inventory forms may be used after the autobiographical talks or introductions:

A PERSONAL INVENTORY

The information requested in this inventory is solicited in the hope that your instructor will be in a better position to help you achieve maximum efficiency in communication by knowing as much as possible about you. The information requested is to be kept confidential. It should in no way affect your grade in this course. Please answer the questions fully and honestly.

GENERAL
1. Name _____ 2. Age _____
3. Address _____ 4. Telephone _____
5. Class _____
6. Where were you born? _____
7. Where else have you lived? _____
8. What languages in addition to English do you speak fluently? _____
9. In what foreign countries have you traveled? _____
10. Do you have considerable difficulty speaking and understanding English? _____

EDUCATION
11. Where have you gone to school? _____
12. What subjects in the curriculum did you elect to take? List those not actually required _____
13. What were your favorite subjects? _____
14. How well do you do in English composition? _____

APTITUDES
15. In what vocational activities do you excel? _____

INTERESTS
16. What are your special hobbies? _____

17. Of what clubs or special organizations are you a member? _____

18. What newspapers or magazines do you read? _____

19. Who is your favorite author? _____
20. What is the most boring book you have ever read? _____
21. What extra-class activities do you most enjoy? _____

PERSONAL ATTRIBUTES
22. Generally speaking, do you avoid situations that require your verbal participation? _____
23. Are you quite often intolerant of other people's ideas? _____
24. Do you have many very close friends? _____
25. Do you readily admit in the face of evidence that you are wrong? _____
26. Do you quite frequently give vent to your emotional feelings in loud outbursts? _____
27. How easily can you adjust to new ideas or to new ways of doing things?

28. Do you usually feel quite nervous when facing an audience? _____

29. To what extent are you given to stuttering or stammering? _____

30. Are you overly sensitive to criticism? _____ 31. To what extent do you butt in when others are talking? _____

EXPERIENCE
32. What positions of leadership have you accepted in high school? _____

33. Have you had previous experience in public speaking? _____ debate? _____ oratory? _____ group discussion? _____ drama? _____ radio or TV? _____ oral interpretation? _____

SELF-DIAGNOSIS
34. Describe in detail the difficulties which you think this course should help you overcome.

BRIEF PERSONAL INVENTORY

1. NAME _____ 2. AGE _____
3. ADDRESS _____ 4. PHONE _____
5. Father's Occupation _____ 6. MAJOR _____
7. Other High Schools Attended: _____ 8. DATES _____
9. Favorite High School Subject _____

10. Extra-class activities in which you have participated _____

11. List hobbies, interests, etc. _____

12. Newspapers you read regularly _____
13. Magazines you read _____
14. Books you have read in the last year _____

15. Class schedule for this quarter:

Course	Hour	Instructor
_____	_____	_____
_____	_____	_____
_____	_____	_____

16. School organizations and activities you are interested in _____

17. Are you employed? _____ 18. Number of hours weekly _____
19. List what you feel have been your main problems in oral communication? _____

20. In what do you need the most work to improve your ability to communicate effectively? _____

21. What do you hope to gain from this course? _____

If the teacher of speech is prepared and alert as a questioner, he can make the first class period in a course in speech education very interesting and challenging and set a high tone by leading a discussion in which he asks a series of questions. If he will step in front of his class, have the questions well in mind, keep his eye on everybody in the class, call on everybody in the class by name or otherwise to contribute to the elicited answers, and ask questions with the skill of an Art Linkletter, the teacher of speech can draw students into an interesting, exciting, and worthwhile first class period and perhaps two class periods. These questions are basic and may be used: What is speech? Effective speech? "Good" speech? Differences between effective and "good" speech? Fundamentals of speech? Why do we talk? In what kinds of speech experiences and situations do we participate? For what good reason or reasons do you imagine you are required to study speech or why did you elect to study speech? How can our speech best serve us in other courses and activities in and out of this high school? How can your speech best be improved to serve you? In what speech experiences should we participate in this course? Which of these experiences do you believe would be most interesting? Which of these experiences could be most helpful to you? How? How can we identify our speech needs? Our speech abilities? How can you know if your speech is improving? How can we know if our speech is acceptable?

Before the end of the first class period, the teacher may well ask each student to bring to class on the second day his statement of what speech is, his statement of what constitutes effective speech, and his statement of what "good" speech is. On the second day, each student may be called upon to read his statements and the papers probably ought to be collected by the teacher. Obviously, during the first class meeting, the teacher of speech will need to be well-prepared, alert, skillful in questioning, ready to recognize rapidly and well the contribution of each student, swift and tactful in challenging unsound contributions, and capable of keeping the students "on the move" to think through each question.

After the initial class meeting and after the ice is broken, the next step is to assign an interesting, challenging, and profitable activity for the students. This should provide the teacher with an opportunity to observe the student in a speech situation so as to draw some conclusions on individual interests, needs, abilities, and capacities. There are many types of beginning assignments and the teacher will want to exercise his imagination in planning them. Most experienced teachers of speech have their favorite beginning assignments which have proved to be successful for them.

Laura Crowell has indicated that the first speech should meet the following criteria:[3]

> 1. A first speech should give the student a successful and satisfying experience in communication.
>
> 2. A first speech should constitute an effective basis for the next speech experience.
>
> 3. A first speech should call each auditor into the most effective listenership possible.

After analyzing the assignments often used—a speech about one's own fears and his reactions to them, telling a personal experience, expressing a firm conviction, presenting a demonstration speech with blackboard or equipment, or both—she recommends the "process-inquiry speech." In this speech each student will prepare to explain a process which may be characterized as well-known to him through actual experience, relatively unfamiliar to the rest of the class in its operation, and involving steps related to physical activity. No object, blackboard drawing, or notes may be used. During the speech each student who is speaking will watch for hands raised by those who find something unclear to them.

---

[3] Laura Crowell, "The Process-Inquiry Speech," *The Speech Teacher*, vol. 1, no. 3 (September 1952), pp. 167–168.

GETTING STARTED: FIRST ASSIGNMENTS 103

The speaker is to clarify each point as well as he can. Teacher and students are free to raise questions at any time.

Loren D. Reid suggested that, since students speak better than they read aloud, informal speaking should precede oral interpretation. He recommended the use of conversation and interviewing activities as the first assignment.[4]

Group discussion—a panel forum—is recommended by Waldo W. Phelps[5] as a first assignment in a class in fundamentals of speech in a high school. His suggested plan covers the first week of school and involves student selection of topics which will allow them to participate primarily on the basis of past observations and experiences and using their own facts, organizing discussion groups of five to eight students each, a lecture-discussion of the mechanics of group discussion, time during class for planning sessions of each panel forum to work as a group exchanging information, and discussions from the groups of twenty-five minutes each.

E. C. Buehler[6] stated a very important point when he wrote

> ... no time period in the entire course is as crucial as the opening days. This is when students are especially impressionable and susceptible to suggestions and directions. This is strategically the time to get the class rolling, establishing personal relationships between teacher and students, reduce the initial feelings of apprehension, and generally build those essential attitudes of faith toward the course, toward themselves, and toward the teacher.

Although Buehler's concern was with a class in fundamentals of speech in college, his statement can well be adopted for application in a speech course in high school. His suggestions indicate that he assigns, on the first day, the writing of a confidential letter by each student to the teacher. The student's letter, due on the third day, includes information about his home, family, and community life; speech experiences and training; evaluation of personal speech needs; professional or occupational goals and interests. Also, the first day, students are paired off and given time to secure information for introductions.

The second day is devoted to the introductions and the next assignment is given. The second assignment consists of two-minute speeches with half the class ranking in importance and giving reasons for ranking the six factors of life: (1) friends, (2) education, (3) religion, (4) money,

---

[4] Loren D. Reid, *op. cit.*

[5] Waldo W. Phelps, "The Panel-Forum as a First Assignment in the Secondary School Speech Fundamentals Class," *The Speech Teacher*, vol. 1, no. 3 (September 1952), pp. 163–166.

[6] E. C. Buehler, "The First Seven Days of the College Beginning Speech Class," *The Speech Teacher*, vol. 7, no. 4 (November 1958), pp. 303–304.

(5) family, and (6) health. The other half of the class makes the same approach to six professions and evaluates them as to which has contributed most to civilization: (1) the preacher, (2) the farmer, (3) the scientist, (4) the artisan, (5) the politician, and (6) the teacher.

On the third day these speeches are given, letters are collected, and the next assignment is given: two-minute speeches with one-half of the class told that

> You and a companion are to live two years in a lighthouse isolated from the rest of the world. You can take only three books other than the Bible and can have sent to you, for the duration of your stay, two magazine subscriptions. Which three books and two magazines would you choose? Support your selections.

The other half of the class is told that

> Nine people are stranded on a desert. A helicopter can save only five. They are: an army captain, his fiancée, a twelve-year-old boy, a wealthy society woman, a noted scientist, the president of General Motors, the governor of your state, a famous movie star, and a little-known preacher or priest. Whom would you save and why?

The fourth day is devoted to these speeches and to the next assignment—a four- or five-minute demonstration speech. The class is divided into three sections and the fifth, sixth, and seventh class periods are devoted to these speeches. The teacher offers no evaluation until the demonstration speeches.

John T. Auston[7] indicated that the following sequence can help minimize those problems connected with the opening speech and the subsequent exercises on gesture and voice: an opening speech announced as an ungraded project on a topic describing a simple operation such as "How to Wind a Watch" or "How to Put On Lipstick," et cetera. This can be followed by a second speech in which the student is asked to describe, with bodily action, an exciting personal experience such as an automobile accident or a winning play in a football game. The third speech assignment can be an exercise in vocal animation and can be of the "complaint" or "gripe" variety in which the student registers any dissatisfaction he may have experienced over such an injustice as "grading practices" or "seating policies at basketball games," and the like. All speeches should be limited to two or three minutes.

Other initial activities which have been used are: short announcements, reading aloud selections chosen by the student or prepared for read-

[7] John T. Auston, "Supplementary Methods for Secondary Speech," *The Speech Teacher*, vol. 2, no. 2 (March 1953), p. 9.

ing by the teacher, pantomime, choral speaking, tape recordings, and voice and articulation tests.

The teacher of speech has, indeed, a wide selection of assignments with which to start a course in speech education. Many teachers have found that an original speech, in which each speaker agrees or disagrees with a proverb or maxim, has proved most satisfactory. Another assignment may be the oral reading of such material as an editorial, news item, sports article, and the like. From these assignments, one can easily move to a recording, a voice and articulation test, or to other assignments emphasizing adjustment to the speech situation, effective use of bodily action, or other fundamentals of speech. It is also easy to make a transition from these activities to such more specialized speech activities as discussion, oral interpretation, parliamentary procedure, debate, and so on.

Suggestions for Improved Teaching

Getting a class in speech education started on the right foot toward improvement is a vital first step in teaching speech. Keeping the students on the road with a minimum of detours is also important. Teachers of speech, especially beginning teachers, may welcome these suggestions which have been developed through experience by successful teachers of speech:

1. Prepare an individual manila folder for each student. Include in the file folder for each student information obtained from the student's cumulative record in the offices of the principal and guidance counselor, the completed speech inventory, and all pertinent evidence of achievement and develovment by the student. Use the contents in discussing student progress with the student or with his parents, or both. Develop the habit of placing all pertinent information concerning the student and his speech interests, needs, abilities, and capacities, except confidential information, in the student's manila file folder.

2. Become acquainted with the textbooks, manuals, curriculum guides, reference books, and periodicals such as *The Speech Teacher, The American Educational Theatre Journal, The Quarterly Journal of Speech, Speech Monographs, The English Journal* for both junior and senior high school and the college edition, regional speech and English publications, and any other publications pertinent to speech and the teaching of speech as they become available for the class and for the teacher.

3. Examine the permanent records of your students to learn their special talents and abilities as well as their interests, needs, and capacities for development in your class.

4. Use a variety of teaching methods and materials and be alert for special opportunities for motivation: assembly programs, special events

such as school council elections, class meetings, community clubs and meetings, field trips, et cetera. Don't overlook the possibility of using games, contests, and prizes as intra- and extra-class activities for stimulating achievement and growth by students. After a round of talks a prize may be awarded to the student voted by the class as having done the best job and to the student voted by the class as showing the most improvement. A five-cent pencil may be just the item to be awarded as a prize, because the inherent worth of the item is not as important as the recognition of the student's having done his best, having done the best job, or having shown the most improvement. Be careful that the students do not become too competitive, resulting in improper emphasis by the class.

5. Since students learn by example, invite students to do out-of-class observations and submit written reports on convocation-lectures, sermons, occasional addresses, radio and television addresses, radio and television actors and actresses, et cetera.

6. Use assignment sheets in which you as the teacher of speech have indicated clearly what is expected, dates of class meetings when speaking assignments are scheduled, the reading assignments, due dates on outside speech reports, lists of sample topics, criteria for selecting topics, criteria for evaluating speechmaking, and so on.

7. Be prepared—in case your "time sense" is lacking and your fifty-minute lesson is completed in half the time—with supplementary activities for effective use of every minute of class time. Many teachers of speech announce early in the semester that any spare time left over during regularly scheduled speaking periods will be devoted to impromptu speaking. Students may be asked to suggest topics for use at such times. Impromptu individual pantomimes are also used effectively.

8. Until you feel secure in what you are doing and where you are going, make out a detailed lesson plan for each day's work. Plan your work and work your plan but not so rigidly that you cannot adjust to whatever situation that develops. Detailed plans can help to remind you about immediate and long-range aims and objectives of each day's lesson.

9. Check yourself continually so that you don't become deluded into believing that "saying something is the same as teaching it." And do not make the error of assuming that your students know more than they really do because, if you do, you may seldom make your points simple and clear to them.

10. Avoid the following pitfalls:

a. Do your best not to be easily influenced by discussions in the teachers' lounge. Experienced teachers do not know all the answers, and their impressions of individual students may be no better guide than your own. On the other hand, experienced teachers do know some of the answers, and their impressions of individual students can often help you to find your own answers. Listen, reflect, think independently, exercise your own best judgment, and assume responsibility for your own decisions and action.

b. Become familiar with school policies and regulations, especially those that relate to after-school and evening events, field trips, use of the auditorium, use of any and all facilities in the school in which others have an interest and for which they have use, et cetera.

c. Do not feel that to seek help, counsel, and advice is a sign of weakness or poor preparation. This is what supervisors and principals are for. However, do not seek to have supervisors and principals take on your responsibilities. Consider the likely effect and the question of ethics in stating or suggesting to your students that your supervisor or your principal is responsible for a decision or a permission when your students have every right to look to you for it.

d. Accepting responsibilities on too many committees or in too many organizations—both in school and in the community—may seriously handicap your work as a teacher of speech in the classroom. Remember that your main job is teaching in the high school. Conserve your strength for excellence of teaching.

e. Attend meetings of your own professional organizations: local, teachers' associations, staff meetings, and state and regional meetings. Conduct yourself as a member of a profession.

f. Keep careful and accurate records and prepare records and reports on time.

g. Do not close your mind to new ideas and practices. Always be alert for new and better ways of achieving your aims in the speech classroom. Doris Niles recommends a "notebook for neophytes" which has much merit.[8]

Suggestions to Help Individual Teachers Upgrade Speech Education

Excellent teaching is a combination of personal attitude and attributes of firmness, fairness, and friendliness, proper subject matter background, understanding of effective teaching methods and materials and ability to apply them, effective planning, a variety of teaching methods and materials, voluntary student participation, professional cooperation with other teachers and with administrators, and effective evaluation.

Teachers of speech in high schools and colleges suggested ways and means by which individual teachers can help upgrade speech education and thereby maintain a high level of effectiveness.

[8] Doris Niles, "Notebooks for Neophytes," *The Speech Teacher*, vol. 8, no. 2 (March 1959), pp. 129–133.

Marceline Erickson, as chairman of the standing committee on Secondary School Speech, reported the following suggestions during the Convention of the Central States Speech Association in Chicago in April, 1960:

    1. Allow yourself time to re-think the purposes and scope of speech so you have a new and deeper faith in its potentials. Think of speech as a first-class, not second-rate, activity. Your own philosophy colors the philosophy of your students and your colleagues.

    2. Join and be an active member of your state, central states, and national speech organizations. From these contacts you can "hold on" with new courage in your own situation. You learn that others are in the "same boat as you are." You find yourself better able to cope with the frustrations in your situation and more appreciative of your opportunities.

    3. If you have had limited training in speech, you may want to read one, two, or three books in the speech field—particularly those in the area of speech for which you have responsibilities. Give yourself time to think about what you have read.

    4. Try to meet and discuss common problems with other teachers in speech work in your area.

    5. Try to attend and take your students to attend speech clinics, speech laboratory days, and festivals sponsored by colleges and universities in your area. Such experiences will help in motivating and upgrading speech activities.

    6. Recognize the use of the speech activities of speaking, reading aloud, discussion, and listening in English, social studies, and other classes. As students learn to use the activities of speech, their attitude toward speech improves.

    7. Use the drama club as an opportunity to give more students a knowledge of and experience in play reading, acting, and stagecraft.

    8. Exchange programs with a nearby high school so that your students have a chance to meet and talk with other students interested in speech.

    9. The high school assembly offers opportunity to acquaint more students with better quality and more artistically handled interpretative readings, speeches, plays, and discussions.

    10. Capitalize on opportunities to tie in activities in speech with student government, pep rallies, Homecoming, banquets, and so on.

    11. Capitalize on using competent student readers, speakers, and acting groups for certain civic and community clubs. Such programs can make more townspeople aware of speech activities and gain their support. However, protect yourself against having to furnish programs on the instant or at the sacrifice of some school curricular or extra-curricular responsibility.

    12. Consider trying to establish chapters of National Forensic League or National Thespians in your school. Some teachers claim national affiliation gives stature and prestige to speech activities.

13. Present awards for honors in speech activities at the assembly in which athletic, music, and other awards are given.

14. Use television and radio to introduce high school students to outstanding actors and actresses, readers, and government leaders. Help them have a greater awareness and appreciation for their skills. Plan to see some of these programs as a group with discussions immediately afterward. Help students be more discriminating listeners and viewers.

15. Take students interested in speech activities to district, regional, and state speech contests so that they may hear better high school readers and speakers. Let them see and hear how good such readers and speakers can be.

16. Try to add to your own speech training by attending night classes, summer school, or Saturday classes. Consult a speech teacher in the college of your choice for competent advice on speech work to suit your needs.

17. Try to discuss with your principal or superintendent the goals of speech, so that he becomes aware of your sincerity and your concern for high school students. Try to establish a common bond of interest. . . .

18. Help students and colleagues understand that speech has a body of knowledge to be understood and skills to be learned. Help them understand in all cases that ideas are to be shared.

19. Help students come to know that speech activities can be fun.

Deductive and Inductive Teaching of Speech

Very often much of our teaching of speech has been by the deductive method of teaching. In this method a general principle or rule is stated or a definition given. Examples are presented to illustrate the rule, principle, or item stated. Then, the student must use this information in his own speaking situations. To illustrate: many teachers announce to their classes that effective bodily action should be "purposeful," because it can help the individual communicate ideas, feelings, and mood. Then, by illustrating or by demonstrating, the teacher indicates examples of nonpurposeful movements such as swaying, excessive pacing, playing with a pencil, jingling coins or keys, and poorly motivated gestures. The teacher of speech can, by so doing, put on quite a show. Then, his students are expected to understand the basic concept of purposeful bodily action and to demonstrate its effective use. Very often we tend to overlook the danger that many students will lack a clear understanding of the concepts upon which the principle or rule is based and thus become confused or discouraged.

A simple definition of inductive teaching in speech is: the student gets his generalizations from observing what happens when he and his classmates speak. From these observations and relevant discussions of them with the teacher and his fellow students, he can gain insight into basic concepts of speech and the principles arising from them.

Inductive teaching is much slower, less precise, requires much more careful planning on the part of the teacher, and demands more patience than does deductive teaching. But the results of inductive teaching are usually more satisfactory and lead usually to more lasting satisfaction. The individual student learns better the basic concepts and retains them longer by reaching conclusions as a result of his own inductions. The student is likely to feel that he has had a part in arriving at the generalization or principle and that it is not something that the teacher or the textbook has told him to remember. Therefore, it will probably mean more to him.

One of the most successful examples of the inductive method of teaching was presented some years ago at an annual convention of the Speech Association of America by Wanda Mitchell, a teacher of speech in Evanston Township High School, Evanston, Illinois. She and twenty or twenty-five of her students came into Chicago to present a demonstration lesson. Each of her students had been asked to bring some object with him and to demonstrate it for an audience of teachers of speech. To begin with, one student was asked to tell and demonstrate how his item worked—using bodily activity as a necessary part of his explanation. Then, another student was asked to join the speaker at the front of the class so that the demonstrator could tell the new person "how" to operate the object. In telling how the object worked, the demonstrator used language but without bodily action. This pattern was repeated several times. Since the use of bodily action was necessary in telling best how the object operated, the demonstrator found it difficult, using language only. After each of these demonstrations, no conclusions were stated and no implications were discussed. Also, after the demonstrations, other students drew slips of paper on which descriptive sentences had been typed. Typical sentences were "He only came up to here on me!" and "You should have seen the one that got away!" Each student was asked to read his statement as expressively as possible, using no bodily action, and then to reread it using whatever appropriate bodily action he felt would help communicate the idea and feeling.

After these and other such activities, the teacher asked a class secretary to record on a blackboard what the other members of the class said they had learned about visible bodily action during the class period. Eventually, the members of the class arrived at the generalization that effective bodily action is necessary for effective speaking, that the bodily action should be "purposeful," and that the purposeful bodily action should parallel and contribute to the speaker's purpose.

SUMMARY

This method of instruction, clearly illustrated in the demonstration lesson, can be applied to other concepts of speech education. The alert and effective teacher is well aware of this method of inductive teaching and uses it often.

Summary

The beginning teacher of speech is likely to be apprehensive about his success in working with students in the classroom. In fact, every capable and conscientious teacher should be concerned about his impact on his students and their learning, regardless of their effect on him and his teaching. He needs to be concerned about problems of "discipline," "classroom control," and management of his classes as he focuses his attention on each individual student and the performance and development by the student. Unless he has planned well for all of his students, some students in a class in speech education get no benefit, though the teacher strives to stimulate and guide them in speech performance.

Although each teacher must develop his own special ways for establishing rapport with students in his class, he can be guided by such basic principles as: (1) playing fair with all students and showing no favoritism, (2) making neither threats nor promises without fulfilling them, (3) applying the rules of the school without equivocation and with consistency except in cases of emergency which can be recognized by the students as emergencies, (4) always telling students the truth without any attempt to bluff even if it means admitting to students that you do not know the answers to some of their questions, (5) stating a minimum of short and simple rules rather than a long list of do's and dont's, and (6) making assignments clear, definite, and understood by all students so that no student can claim successfully that he did not understand the assignment.

Well-motivated students are busy. Each student is likely to be well-motivated and busy if he sees his objective clearly, his need for achieving it, believes he can attain it, and recognizes the likelihood of his satisfaction in accomplishing it. Careful planning of each bloc, unit, project, and lesson, skillful teaching, and everlasting enthusiasm by the teacher of speech for students' success in learning are basic to students' learning and to the solution of problems of "discipline," "class control," and management in a class and in extra-class speech activities.

Students tend to like and respect teachers who like and respect them. Students tend to respect and to be devoted to teachers who are friendly but not chummy, firm, and, above all, fair and reasonable in all their relationships with students, other teachers, and administrators. Careful daily preparation, a sense of humor, alertness in meeting students at the door of the classroom, recognition of each student wherever he is, preventive rather than punitive discipline when possible, swift and sure punitive measures when necessary, speaking softly and privately to troubled and troublesome students, anticipating students' problems and demonstrating interest in helping them to solve their problems, and complimenting students for their successes are basic and vital factors of excellent management in the classroom and in extra-class activities.

"Getting started" in a class and in each meeting of the class is basic to success by the teacher and by the students. At the beginning of each class and of each extra-class activity, the teacher who is well prepared and who has planned carefully wants to challenge each student to do his best. Although mastery of subject matter and methodology by the teacher is important, he needs to know the students, their "longcomings," and their "shortcomings." The logical place to start is by getting acquainted with the students. The speech inventory, guided autobiographical talks, discussions led by the teacher, and different kinds of brief speech performances by each student can help the teacher and the students determine individual differences and group tendencies and specific speech interests, needs, abilities, and capacities.

The opening days of a course in speech education constitute a crucial time period for establishing personal relationships between the teacher and his students, reducing feelings of apprehension, and building faith in the course and benefits to be derived from it. The teacher of speech can have a carefully devised roster of challenging activities from which to draw in making assignments such as initial introductions, interviewing, group discussion led by the teacher, thought-provoking speechmaking, short announcements, reading aloud selections chosen by the student, pantomime, choral speaking, tape recordings, voice and articulation tests, and original speeches in which each speaker agrees or disagrees with a proverb or maxim.

The teacher of speech who is willing to learn, who has adequate preparation in the field of speech education, and who believes in the worthwhileness of speech education for all students will likely succeed. He will be alert and receptive to suggestions, regardless of their source, and to counsel and advice by his supervisor and principal. His mind will be open to new ideas and new practices. His understanding of school policies and regulations will help him to proceed cooperatively and harmoniously with his colleagues and with students to organize and expedite his part of the school program. His records and reports will be up-to-date, accurate, and complete. His improvement "on the job" will result in his growth and in the upgrading of speech education in the high school.

Projects

1. Prepare to explain to the class how a teacher of speech can be friendly with students and, at the same time, gain and maintain their respect for him as a teacher and person, how friendship and respect are related, and how friendliness may lead to loss of a teacher's effectiveness in a class.

2. List problems with which you expect to be confronted during your student teaching or during your first year of teaching. Interview successful teachers of speech for their reactions to your list of problems. Discuss possible solutions or answers to each of your anticipated problems. Present these problems and their possible solutions to the class.

3. Prepare to explain the relationship of each of the following concepts to the teaching of speech and to achievement by students in speech activities: (a) Motivation results from having a specific objective to be achieved, a recognition of the need for achieving it, and insight into a method for achieving it; (b) Reaction is essential to learning and, in fact, all learning is directly proportional to the quantity and quality of reaction by the learner; (c) Concentration, by which a student learns, means focusing his full attention or the full power of his mind on what he is learning; (d) Comprehension refers to gaining insight into the organization of an idea or ideas enabling the learner to understand the governing principle revealed by the organizational pattern for retention and application; (e) Repetition, essential to learning, does not guarantee learning; and (f) Learning results from motivation, organization, reaction, concentration, comprehension, and repetition.

4. What is the function of each of the following activities or steps in teaching and learning speech: (a) Preview, (b) Question, (c) Read, (d) Verbalize, and (e) Test? Explain, first, how each function can be best accomplished, and, second, what good can result from accomplishing it. Be prepared to support your position.

5. Formulate a unit or at least one lesson plan in which you plan to teach by using the inductive method. As a student teacher, teach it to your present class and evaluate your success.

6. Make a list of possible first assignments for use in a beginning course in speech education. Compare your list with the lists made by other members of the class.

7. Make a list of the characteristics of a good assignment for a first course in speech education. Be prepared to justify to the class all characteristics on your list.

8. State your position on the proposition, *"Resolved:* That a pretest is essential for all assignments by a teacher of speech."

9. Consider: The ability to direct thinking through questioning is one of the most valid proofs of teaching skill. Then, design a series of questions to develop understanding of speech, effective speech, good speech, and fundamentals of speech. Compare your questions with those devised by other members of the class.

Selected Bibliography

Braden, Waldo W., ed., *Speech Methods and Resources.* New York: Harper & Row, Publishers, 1961.

Ecroyd, Donald H., *Speech in the Classroom.* Englewood Cliffs, N. J.: Prentice-Hall, Inc., 1960.

Giroux, Isabelle, "Improving Methods of Teaching in the Secondary School," *The Speech Teacher*, vol. 3, no. 1 (January 1954), pp. 49-53.

Ogilvie, Mardel, *Teaching Speech in the High School: Principles & Practices.* New York: Appleton-Century-Crofts, Inc., 1961.

Reid, Loren, *Teaching Speech*, 3rd ed. Columbia, Mo.: Artcraft Press, 1960.

Robinson, Karl F., and E. J. Kerikas, *Teaching Speech: Methods and Materials.* New York: David McKay Company, Inc., 1963.

Weaver, Andrew, Gladys Borchers, and Donald K. Smith, *The Teaching of Speech.* Englewood Cliffs, N. J.: Prentice-Hall, Inc., 1952.

CHAPTER 5

Basic Approaches to Teaching Speech

If one were to investigate the various curricular patterns of teaching speech in secondary schools today, he would find at least five distinct ones. In some high schools the teaching of speech is incorporated into the everyday work of the English class and is taught somewhat incidentally by its emphasis during oral book reports, class discussions, and oral reading of literature. In other high schools a separate unit in speech education is included in the English class. In this pattern, speech may or may not be taught by the regular teacher of English. Some high schools have a teacher of speech move into the English class to teach a unit of five or six weeks' duration, relieving the teacher of English of this part of the course. A third pattern has an elective course in speech education offered usually at the junior or senior class level. This elective course usually offers concentration on dramatic-type activities during the first semester and on forensic-type activities during the second semester, or vice versa. A fourth pattern includes a required course in speech education for *all* students in the high school. The fifth pattern is a combination of two or more of the other patterns. Evidence of these patterns is revealed in the descriptions of programs of speech education in high schools in the United States.[1]

[1] For a description of programs of speech education in the United States, consult: The Speech Association of America, "Speech Education for All American Youth," *The Bulletin of the National Association of Secondary School Principals*, vol. 32, no. 151 (January 1948), pp. 179-199; The Speech Association of America, "A Speech

Four approaches to the teaching of speech are available for use by the teacher, no matter what curricular pattern prevails or how much time and emphasis are placed on speech education. These four approaches are the "fundamentals" approach, the "activities" approach, the "subject matter" approach, and a combination of two or three of these approaches. Regardless of the approach used, the primary goal of the teacher is to help students develop their speech knowledge, understanding, abilities, and desirable speech attributes as communicators, persons, and citizens.

The "Fundamentals" Approach

The "fundamentals" approach in teaching speech refers to the teacher's directing the attention and effort by the students to effect improvement of each of the fundamentals of the students' speech such as basic content or ideas, organization of ideas, developmental or supporting details, and adjustment to the speech situation. Likewise, the teacher may focus attention and effort on a part of one fundamental of speech such as loudness or pitch of the students' voices. Also, the focus may be on one of the personal speech attributes such as imagination, resourcefulness, or initiative in speech. The teacher organizes and builds a unit, project, or lesson plans to effect improvement in a fundamental of speech, or in a part of it, or in one of the personal speech attributes. The students study, read, discuss, drill, and practice on a fundamental in an effort to improve and develop it. If the students are, for example, careless in their articulation, the teacher may set out to effect distinct articulation by the students. If they need help in the organization of ideas for communication, the teacher helps them to learn how better to organize ideas. Naturally, the teacher will realize that speech is an integrated act and that all fundamentals of speech are important in speaking; but, for the sake of concentration, emphasis, and individual improvement, only one of these fundamentals may be the focal point of learning at any one time. Obviously, subject matter related to the fundamental is important for consideration by the students and by the teacher. Also, speech activity is important in teaching a fundamental of speech. However, both subject matter and activity are, in the fundamentals approach, means by which the fundamental is understood and its development is effected. Of course, imagination or any other personal speech attribute subject to human learning and development can be a focal point in learning with both subject matter and activity serving as necessary means for understanding and developing the attribute.

Program for the Secondary School," *The Bulletin of the National Association of Secondary School Principals,* vol. 38, no. 199 (January 1954), pp. 157–193; *The Speech Teacher,* vol. 6, no. 4 (November 1957), pp. 285–299.

The commonly accepted fundamentals of speech include: (1) basic content or ideas; (2) organization of ideas; (3) developmental or supporting details; (4) adjustment to the speech situation; (5) bodily action for purposes of communication; (6) voice usage; (7) enunciation, articulation, and pronunciation; (8) language; (9) adaptation in the speech situation; and (10) listening.

1. *Basic Content or Ideas.* The teacher of speech is responsible for helping students recognize that speech is most effective when the speaker has something worthwhile to say. This applies to all types of speech, that is, conversation, public speaking, oral interpretation, acting, discussion, debate, storytelling, and others.

One of the age-old questions is, "How responsible is the teacher of speech for what his students talk about and what they say about it in his class?"

A teacher of speech may say that he cannot evaluate students' topics which are, to him, complex and technical or outside his range of knowledge. Another teacher of speech may deny responsibility for *what* his students talk about or what they say about it. He will likely affirm his responsibility for concentrating on *how* his students speak and contend that the concern of a teacher of speech is limited to factors of delivery. A third teacher may weigh heavily the ideas and the way ideas are organized and developed and supported, with less emphasis on delivery. And finally, a fourth teacher who is well prepared in subject matter and methodology of speech education, knowledgeable in related areas of subject matter, and alert, thoughtful, and skilled in asking questions may lead his students to see that the *subject matter* of their speech, speaking, and speechmaking is inseparable from the *manner* of their speaking.

Each teacher of speech must decide for himself just what his position and responsibilities are in teaching speech. However, any program of speech education tends to become insignificant and may even be harmful to students if the teacher does not insist that all speech subject matter used by students in his class must be worthwhile and that his students must be responsible for their topics, subject matter, and statements. He can question the meaning of statements by students, distinguish between facts and opinion, request the source of developmental and supporting details, challenge mere assertions, detect fallacies and evaluative judgments alleged to be factual, encourage his students to examine and re-examine their reasoning and conclusions, explore hasty generalizations, analyze assumptions underlying arguments and assertions, suggest investigation of additional information related to a topic, and otherwise encourage and help students to develop their abilities and willingness to be investigative, informed, analytical, critical, discriminating, accurate, and skilled and responsible speakers and listeners.

If students select topics on speech or on speech education such as "How to Organize a Speech," "Preparing a Role in a Play," "Voice Production," "How to Speak Distinctly," or "The Duties of a Leader in Discussion," the teacher of speech is, indeed, likely to assume responsibility for what his students say and the way they speak. Of course, the teacher of speech should be the best guide available in helping his students to speak accurately on topics within the scope of speech and speech education. But is the teacher less responsible if his students elect to speak on art, literature, science, social studies, or other subjects? If the teacher cannot assume responsibility for what his students say in his class, he may seek help from teachers who are specialists in areas from which his students draw topics and ideas. The very least he should do is teach his students how to get information to document what they say.

Perhaps one question asked most frequently by high school students of speech is "What shall I speak about?" Without guidance, many students will probably select overworked, trite topics they do not care about and so handicap themselves in holding the interest of the class. With such topics they will have neither fun nor benefit. Students who are permitted to speak on such worthless topics can hardly grow in their speech, speaking, or speechmaking. Also, members of the class who have to listen will show their lack of interest, and so discourage the speakers that no one will gain a thing from the experience.

In courses in speech education in high schools, time is devoted to speechmaking and other kinds of speech performances. Whenever speeches by students are scheduled, both the teacher and the students face the problem of selecting the topic. The teacher must deal with the problem of how best to help students to select materials for speech experiences.

On the one hand, the teacher needs to help students to learn to select their own topics. Consistent with the objectives of democracy and democratic procedure, freedom of choice of topics and materials and freedom of expression are essential in our classrooms if students are to learn to make wise choices and to assume responsibility for them. Students who are to be taught democracy must be encouraged to exercise freedom of choice and freedom of expression, always.

On the other hand, the teacher of speech can easily forego the teaching of democracy by assigning the topics on which his students will speak. Likewise, he can determine, to a great extent, the content and ideas which will be expressed by his students and accepted by him. In his conscientious effort to guarantee significant achievement and growth by his students in their successive speech performances, the teacher wants to be assured that his students will speak on appropriate, challenging, and worthwhile topics. Experience may have taught him that students who select their own topics frequently do badly. So he may assign topics to them. Likewise, he may assign problems for their discussion, propositions for their debate, and selections for their oral interpretation. Knowing probably better than his students their backgrounds, interests, needs, abilities, and capacities, he can assign topics and materials that will, collectively if not individually, improve their speech performances in his class. In 1958, Neher[2] undertook to determine whether learning and development of speech ability are faster and better when high school students choose their own topics, when they choose their topics with guidance by the teacher of speech, or when they are assigned the speaking topics. Her statistical analysis of the results of her experimental study of these three methods for selecting topics for speechmaking "showed statistically significant improvement in speech performance" by students when the teacher assigned the topics on which they spoke during three successive rounds of speeches. Neither the students who selected their own topics nor the students who selected topics with guidance by the teacher showed any real improvement during the three successive rounds of speech performances. However, even if the findings of Neher's experiment were a sound basis for concluding that students will improve more rapidly and more significantly when the teacher of speech assigns each student his topic, the advantage gained in speech performance might be offset by their being denied the opportunity and right to learn to choose their own topics with guidance by a qualified teacher of speech.

Stimulation and guidance of students in choosing topics and materials as a part of their preparation for their speech performances are essential. Research on theories of learning attests that mental effort starts with and is directed by a problem.[3] The problem of choosing topics on which to speak and the consequent problem of selecting content with which to develop the topic are major obstacles to good speech performances by high school students. The obstacles must be surmounted and the problems solved by each student with the teacher's help. No teacher of speech can be most effective, regardless of how effective he is in teaching skills of delivery, without concerning himself with the topics and content used by his students in their speech performances. If his instruction is to be most effective, he will neither permit his students to use topics or content which is not educationally appropriate, challenging, and worthwhile nor will he assign topics or dictate the content used by them in speechmaking, oral interpretation, discussion, debate, or any other speech activity or performance. He will apply three types of control patttterns, as reported by

[2] Nancy Neher, "An Experimental Study of Methods for Selecting Topics for Speechmaking," Unpublished M.A. Thesis (State University of Iowa, August 1958).

[3] James B. Stroud, *Psychology of Education*. New York: David McKay Company, Inc., 1956, p. 422.

Cronbach,[4] in his effort to help his students learn to make wise choices of topics and content to serve increasingly well their individual achievement and development in speaking, oral interpretation, and acting. The results of the study of the three control patterns reported by Cronbach support the conclusions that (1) when the teacher does not participate in the direction of activities, students are disturbed because of their own low accomplishment, wasted energy, and low persistence, (2) teacher-controlled activities result in relieving anxiety by setting definite standards, and (3) when students have some self-authority but are teacher-guided, their members have greater acceptance of the goals, understanding of the task, and self-direction.[5] These conclusions lead one to believe that benefits accrue from both student-teacher cooperation and teacher-domination techniques.

Most writers in speech education who advise students on the selection of topics and content state that they should consider the audience, the occasion, the objective to be served, and the speaker. The teacher can guide his students in their analysis of these four major criteria for their selection of topics: (1) The background, interests, maturity, and likely receptivity of classmates or other members of the audience of the student speaker should help to determine the topic and ideas selected by him; (2) The occasion, including the reason for meeting, the time of the meeting, and the time limit for the speaker, may dictate the topic and influence largely the choice of content, especially if the occasion is a special event, real or imaginary; (3) The objective of the speaker and of his speech affects the topic and content with which the objective can likely be achieved rather than the content and topic determining whether the speaker's objective is to inform, describe, explain, provoke thought, convince, actuate, or entertain; and (4) The personal experiences, interests, hobbies, beliefs, personal opinions, school courses, current events, and so on, of the speaker constitute a major criterion by which the student, with stimulation and guidance by his teacher, selects his topic and content.

Most textbooks in public speaking include lists of topics as sources of suggestions to students, but the teacher of speech should be prepared to suggest topics as examples. As he listens to various speeches, he builds lists of topics from which he can draw in his classes to stimulate and guide his students. Although a single topic may serve more than one objective in speechmaking, some topics are better for describing than for convincing.

Suggested student objectives which should result from emphasis by the teacher on the selection of topics include: recognition of the importance of

[4] Lee J. Cronbach, *Educational Psychology*. New York: Harcourt, Brace and World, Inc., 1954, p. 459.
[5] *Ibid.*, p. 459.

worthwhile ideas in speech performance; practice in selecting and limiting topics; opportunities for student examination of his own experiences and interests as sources of ideas; awareness and critical evaluation of the ideas of others in their speeches; examination of textbooks on public speaking for suggestions; and the great advantage of a working knowledge of the school library in finding information on speech topics.

Suggestions for teaching the selection of topics and content include:

(a) Read references in the bibliography at the end of this chapter and discuss factors which should be considered in selecting a topic for speaking.

(b) Make a list of topics which would be appropriate, challenging, and worthwhile for use by high school students in your course in speech education. Point out other situations in which these same topics would not be suitable.

(c) Assume that you, at some point in your course in speech education in a high school, decide to invite each of your students to present an informative or explanatory speech on a topic such as "Gaining Confidence and Poise," "How to Select a Topic for a Speech," "How to Develop the Ability to Speak Clearly and Precisely," and "How to Organize a Speech." Examine at least three references in the bibliography at the end of this chapter and design topics on which your students might speak in your class. Then, explain why you would or would not encourage your students to speak on topics drawn from speech content.

(d) The following list of topics consists of some of the topics used by students in a course called "Basic Speech Development" in a high school in a middlewestern university. Study the topics to determine which ones you believe are acceptable for expository speeches by students in grade nine. Be prepared to support your answer in class.

100 Topics Designed to Challenge High School Students

1. Why we bury the dead
2. The antiquity of insects
3. Chief principles of Communism
4. The nature of falsehood
5. Personality—What it is
6. Esperanto
7. The four thermometer scales
8. Modern etiquette
9. Chief tenet of the Moslem religion
10. Causes of earthquakes
11. Methods of gate crashing
12. Why the Great Lakes tilt
13. Training dogs for the blind
14. Positions in fencing
15. Hazards of the home
16. What goes on in a beehive
17. What makes people buy
18. Training dogs for hunting
19. Why we have social strata
20. What determines our hobbies
21. Hunting to hounds
22. How weather is forecast
23. Why we sleep

24. How to bind a book
25. How a cold front develops
26. The sine curve
27. Causes of drought
28. How to convert time in time zones
29. What constitutes literature
30. Sound effects in radio
31. The essence of jazz
32. Sources of superstition
33. How movies are made
34. The interpretation of drums
35. The social value of cheese
36. The antiquity of wedding customs
37. Palmistry—What it is
38. What makes a good novel
39. Allusion, delusion, and illusion
40. Learning to listen
41. Habits of salmon
42. The scientific lie-detector
43. Making an etching
44. Balance and emphasis in pictures
45. Wirephoto—How it is produced
46. Chief causes of suicide
47. Learning to observe
48. The photo-electric cell
49. Products from waste wood
50. How fish see
51. Jefferson's idea of liberty
52. Methods of trick photography
53. The art of cockfighting
54. Setting stones in rings
55. The art and science of speech
56. The benefits of soybeans
57. Considerations in buying an automobile
58. How to tie a bowline knot
59. How to tell a funny story
60. City manager form of government
61. Benefits from reading great books
62. Control of soil erosion
63. How hail is produced
64. Propaganda—bad and good
65. Writing effective letters
66. The significance of fingerprints
67. Balanced diet—What it means
68. What makes clothes dramatic
69. How good pictures are made
70. Why young men grow beards
71. When a house is a home
72. Hidden secrets in a library
73. The handling of telegrams
74. Contributions by Paul Bunyon
75. Advertising—Types and effects
76. What makes a speech effective
77. How to select a good steak
78. How to improve your memory
79. Planning a garden
80. A good golf swing
81. How to apply an arm splint
82. How to play chess
83. How a student should study
84. The forward pass
85. Preparing for an examination
86. Methods of offensive football
87. How tax money is used
88. The importance of the grade-point system
89. The great Chicago fire
90. How to keep score in bowling
91. How not to waste time in reading a newspaper
92. The Nobel Prize—What it means
93. Speech—Its benefits for students
94. How a newspaper is printed
95. How to play the bagpipe
96. Excellent speech—Its benefits for a farmer
97. Security measures in the home
98. Sculpturing at Mount Rushmore
99. How to remember people and their names
100. Why the race in space

(e) Outline a plan for helping your high school students do the desired research in the library to obtain and record sufficient, accurate, and up-to-date information on one to five of the topics in letter *d* above. Be specific in your outline.

(*f*) Distinguish between a topic, title, subject, subject matter, content, developmental details, and ideas of a speech. Examine textbooks in speech education to determine how these terms are used in the literature of speech education. Then, study speeches by well-known speakers to find examples of topics, titles, and so on, and prepare to present to the class your concepts and illustrations of each of these terms that you conclude is different from each of the other terms.

(*g*) Analyze speeches of great speakers and speeches by current speakers to determine the kinds of content which the speakers employed. Evaluate the content of each of some of the speeches.

(*h*) Make a list of "resource" persons who are likely to be available in the high school and community in which you teach. Then, list topics on which these persons could assist high school students who might speak on the topics on your list.

(*i*) Consult teachers of various subject matter areas in a high school to determine the kinds of oral activity in which students in their classes are engaged. Make a list of topics on which the same students in your classes might speak. Explain why teachers in other subject matter areas would or would not welcome the teacher of speech inviting students in his class to speak on such topics as "Preparing and Presenting a Class Report," "Demonstrating an Experiment in Science," "Explaining a Problem in Mathematics," and "Preparing and Presenting a Book Report." Explain what you believe would be the effect of designing a part of a program of speech education to help students with their speech and speech forms employed by them in their classes, courses, and activities in the school.

(*j*) Prepare to define or to explain succinctly what you interpret each of the following terms to mean:

acting	criteria	education
adjustment	criticism	effective speech
adolescence	culture	empathy
articulation	debate	enunciation
attributes of a speaker	democracy	equal rights
beauty	dependability	extemporaneous speak-
behavioral goals	desirable educational	ing
born equal	outcomes	fact
civic competence	developmental details	forensics
civic responsibility	developmental problems	general education
civil rights	of youth	good speech
compulsion for learning	discussion	human rights
content of speeches	dramatic art	humility

ideal	pantomime	speech ability
imagination	poise	speech education
imperative needs of youth	prejudice	speech experience
	privileges	speech situation
impromptu	proficiency	speech need
incentive	professional education	spiritual values
integrity	progressive education	standards
intellectual honesty	pronunciation	subject
judgment	reading	subject matter
justice	reflective thinking	supporting details
learning	respect	teaching
libel	rights	title
liberal education	salable skills	topic
listening	self-direction for the common good	training
logic		trustworthy
maturation	self-discipline	understanding
maturity	self-realization	voice
memorized	slander	well born
moral accountability for ideas expressed	social role	well-furnished mind
	speaking	wisdom
opinion	special education	writing
oral interpretation	speech, a	work
oratory		

(*k*) Invite each of your students to present an expository speech in which he defines or explains succinctly a concept which you would expect him to be able to explain before he completed your course in speech education in a high school. Ponder the terms in letter j above.

(*l*) Select topics which are suitable for the accomplishment of each of the various purposes of speechmaking: to inform, to describe, to explain, to provoke thought, to convince, to actuate, and to entertain.

2. *Organization.* Most speakers, especially beginners, need help in organizing their ideas clearly for their audiences and for themselves. Probably they need more help in arranging their ideas than on any other one fundamental of speech. In fact, ideas and their organization are basic to effective speaking to an audience and are probably basic to improvement by most students in each of the other fundamentals of speech. Of course, most students can profit by stimulation and guidance by a teacher in voice development, use of language, control of bodily action for communication, and so on, but students can hardly succeed in employing the other fundamentals of speech until they have ideas and until the ideas are clearly arranged and developed. This is why students in a beginning course in speech education are apprehensive, hesitant, and incapable of getting a desired reaction from members of the class and the teacher. Conversely, the con-

fident student, with something important to say, who has it clearly organized in his mind, and who wants to say it will likely lead the class in his initial performances, realize satisfaction from his first success, and be much more ready for stimulation and guidance as he seeks to improve himself in all the fundamentals of speech. To succeed in employing the "fundamentals" approach in teaching students to organize their ideas clearly, the teacher will focus on helping his students to get ideas and to organize or outline their ideas before he urges them to attempt significant speaking and speechmaking.

Basic principles of organization are included in most textbooks in speech education designed for use by high school students. In many of these texts, model plans of organization are set forth as examples. Organization is emphasized in these books because their authors recognize that systematic organization of ideas helps both the listener and the speaker. Students need to see the relationship between major ideas in these model outlines, recognize minor ideas and their relationship to the major ideas, interpret the symbols used as guides to help them distinguish more easily the important ideas from the less important ideas, and understand that audiences need help by speakers to understand clearly all of these relationships. However, the teacher and his students will realize how difficult it is to learn to organize ideas without careful application of principles and concepts.

Neither the teacher nor his students can organize ideas clearly and acceptably without knowing the audience and without determining and clarifying the objective for achievement as a result of speaking with members of the audience. Probably unlike his students, the teacher of speech, as he organizes his ideas to teach a class, knows his audience, knows the occasion and the situation, knows his objective, and knows what materials he has in his files and in his head to carry out his purpose. In fact, he knows much more than he can use. As he organizes his ideas, the teacher knows that what he includes is not necessarily more important than what he leaves out. Probably he will decide what his controlling purpose is and he will often find it helpful if he writes his controlling purpose or objective in the form of a complete sentence. A tentative outline of his ideas would be very useful. His objective and his tentative outline can aid him in deciding what materials are best for his objective, in developing the central and controlling ideas which will aid his achievement, and in determining what kind of organization will serve best. But the teacher of speech knows also that it is not easy for him, even with his understanding of principles and procedures of organization, to make a satisfactory outline of each new topic he organizes. Therefore, he should bear in mind that his students do need help in gaining insight and ability in organization.

Students know, usually, that a speech should have an introduction, a body, and a conclusion. Few of them, and not all teachers of speech, place emphasis on an introduction, *a statement of objective,* a body, and a conclusion. The teacher needs to guide his students to gain knowledge, understanding, and ability in organizing their ideas within the framework indicated by the divisions or parts of a speech. Above all, the student should determine the objective for which he is going to talk and should hold firmly to it as he prepares to talk and, of course, as he talks. He should then attempt to formulate a basic plan of organization which will serve best in achieving his objective with his audience. First, the teacher of speech may encourage the student to make a tentative outline based on his own ideas. It is true that making a tentative outline is time consuming and can delay the student's preparation. Yet such an outline can cause the student to take stock of what he already knows about the topic, to avoid too much outside influence on his point of view, to make the final plan of organization his own, to reveal his need for further knowledge, to provide a framework of his own as a guide for gathering materials, and to provide a point of reference and departure for building his outline. Helping students with their outlining can provide excellent opportunities for them to see proper relationships and patterns of their ideas and to determine the soundness of their reasoning and logic. Schmidt[6] suggested the use of individual dittoed outlines to be completed by the students and corrected and returned to them by the teacher. Then, the students and the teacher study and discuss the outlines to learn how to organize ideas for communication.

After the objective is determined and the tentative outline by each student is analyzed, the teacher may guide the student to organize in depth and detail by a plan that seems best for his objective: (1) chronological: beginning at a certain time and moving forward or backward consistently; (2) logical: oriented to subject matter or reasoning from effect to effect, effect to cause, or, usually, cause to effect; (3) psychological: oriented most directly to the audience by setting forth developmental details such as examples, factual illustrations, hypothetical illustrations, or other detail familiar to the audience and leading to a point; (4) problem-solution: oriented to a problem and moving toward a solution or solutions; (5) space-order; (6) definition; (7) topical, or other. Regardless of the pattern of organization of the body of the outline, each point in it should, of course, relate to the objective and, after the point is developed, contribute to the achievement of the objective with the audience.

The conclusion of a speech can contribute importantly to its effectiveness and success. It contains the last words the listeners will hear and is often marked by high attention by the audience. Therefore, students of

---

[6] Ralph N. Schmidt, "The Teaching of Outlining," *The Speech Teacher,* vol. 3, no. 1 (January 1954), pp. 33–35.

speaking and speechmaking should be taught to organize and use it. Depending upon the type of speech, the conclusion may be in the form of a summary, a series of questions, a quotation, a brief anecdote, an appeal for action, or an allusion to history or literature. It should be brief and consistent with the rest of the speech. It should not be abrupt or inconclusive. From beginning to end, it should be designed to let the audience know that the speech is about to end. Therefore, students should be taught to organize it to serve the objective of the speech and to apply it well in the interests of the audience.

The introduction is the part of a speech which should be prepared last. Most writers of textbooks in speech education have indicated that the introduction should be prepared after the body and conclusion are developed, because the speaker should know exactly what he is introducing before he prepares to do so. These writers indicate that an effective introduction will get the attention and goodwill of the audience, lead into and clarify the topic, arouse the interest of the listeners, and either lead to or include a statement of the intended objective. Obviously, the introduction is an important part of a speech and it should be a part of the planning of the speech. Briefly, its object is to make the audience ready to hear the speaker and his speech.

In teaching organization of ideas for communication, the aim is to help students become aware of principles and patterns of organization, types of outlines, and acceptable forms and arrangements of speech outlines. However, the test of students' awareness and understanding of organization is in their demonstrated ability to organize their ideas for communication. Activities which can help students to understand organization and to be able to outline ideas clearly for themselves and others are:

(a) Read at least two or three references at the end of this chapter on organization and prepare to discuss the importance of clear organization of ideas in speaking and in speechmaking.

(b) Analyze the organization of a recent speech by a prominent speaker. Explain to the class the ways you believe the speech to be organized clearly and the ways in which you believe the organization of the speech could be improved. Ponder the parts of the speech and indicate how well you believe each part may have accomplished its purpose.

(c) Prepare to assign specific speeches to students in which each student will concentrate on the total organization of one or more speeches or concentrate on the introduction, objective, body, and conclusion of one or more of the speeches.

(d) Set down jumbled data from which students can construct an outline or outlines which will show the relationship of ideas to an objective suitable for achievement in a speech.

(e) As a class, work out a cooperative outline for some specific speech assignment starting by describing an audience, deciding on the objective of the outline, choosing a topic, and preparing the outline to serve the objective and, in turn, the audience.

(f) Require students to present to the teacher outlines in advance of their own speeches in class. Have selected students outline the main ideas and support as the speech is delivered. Let each speaker check the outlines prepared by the selected students against the outline prepared by him.

(g) Choose from *Vital Speeches of the Day, Representative American Speeches,* or other source of significant speeches a speech which impresses you favorably and which has an introduction, an objective stated or implied, a body, and a conclusion. Leaving out the introduction and the conclusion, read it to the class or mimeograph it and invite your students to read it. After they have listened to the body, or read it, invite each student to state what he believes to be the objective of the speech and compose an effective introduction and conclusion. Then, read the introduction to the class and make a comparison of the speaker's introduction with the introductions prepared by members of the class. Treat the conclusions in the same way.

(h) Choose a topic for each of the following patterns of organization: chronological, logical, psychological, and problem-solution. Then, invite each of your students to state at least three main points for development in the body of a speech on each topic. Compare.

3. *Developmental and Supporting Details.* After knowing the audience, identifying the objective, choosing and narrowing the topic, and making a tentative outline of his ideas on the topic to serve his objective as he communicates with his audience, the student speaker needs to develop his outline or, depending on the kind of objective, support the ideas in his outline. Although developmental details and supporting details are not mutually exclusive, students may find it helpful to think of developmental details as those which tend to amplify and clarify a major idea or a minor idea in his outline and supporting details as those which tend to establish, prove, and uphold an idea. Most high school students will need help in recognizing the various types of developmental and supporting details and in using them effectively.

Developmental and supporting details include hypothetical and factual illustrations, examples, definitions, statistics, evidence of fact, evidence of authority, and testimony. Students of speech should become familiar with all these types of details with which they can develop and support ideas in their outlines, speaking, and speechmaking.

The well-qualified teacher of speech knows that the library is an essential source of ideas and of all kinds of essential developmental and supporting details for developing "well-furnished minds and well-furnished speech, speaking, oral interpretation, acting, and speechmaking." Sometimes a teacher emphasizes that students should use their own experiences in their speech performances. Unfortunately, the teacher is too frequently disappointed with students who seem to him to "talk in a vacuum" and to "talk without anything to say." Possibly the teacher can be challenged by students who have a paucity of ideas and information as much as a physician can be challenged by a patient with a serious illness. Nearly all high school students need to be taught the sources of developmental and supporting details. The teacher of speech, working with a well-qualified librarian, can be of real service to his students in speech education by planning and teaching a unit on "The Location and Use of Developmental and Supporting Details in Speech Education." However, even if the unit lasted three weeks or longer, the teacher should follow it up by showing the students how their use of data from the library has helped them in their speech performances. Also, if the students have learned how to gather information and data and to use it effectively in their speeches, they can apply this knowledge to other courses of study. Most librarians are happy to cooperate with the teacher of speech in helping students become familiar with library sources of developmental and supporting details for use in speech education and in all education. Sources such as the following can be especially useful to students and teachers of speech:

For biographical information, consult: *American Men of Science* in three volumes, beginning with the 9th edition, *The Physical Sciences, The Biological Sciences,* and *The Social Sciences; Current Biography; Dictionary of American Biography of Americans; Directory of American Scholars; International Who's Who; The Dictionary of National Biography* of citizens in the United Kingdom; *Twentieth Century Authors; Webster's Biographical Dictionary; Who's Who; Who's Who in America;* and *Who's Who in the Middle West.*

The Card Catalog presents, alphabetically by author, title, and subject matter, all books available in the library. *The Cumulative Book Index* lists all books printed in the United States since 1928.

The Readers' Guide to Periodical Literature lists alphabetically by author, title, and subject nearly all periodicals in the United States. It is published in monthly installments, the installments are assembled into quarterly volumes, and the quarterly volumes are assembled into yearly volumes. *The International Index to Periodicals* lists articles in magazines and periodicals *outside* of the United States.

The Monthly Catalog of United States Government Publications lists all publications issued by the various agencies and departments of the government. The entries are arranged by subject and title. Although the librarian will probably need to teach students to use it, *The Monthly Catalog of United States Government Publications* is probably the best single source of authoritative government information available in the library.

The New York Times Index lists by subject and author, if the name of the author is available in the newspaper itself, all articles that have appeared in *The New York Times*. Students of speech may profit by knowing that they can obtain the date of an article listed in *The New York Times Index* and find other articles on the same subject in other newspapers in the United States.

The Public Affairs Information Service lists articles in books, documents, pamphlets, and periodicals which treat subjects on public affairs.

John Bartlett's *Familiar Quotations,* Revised, can be most helpful to speakers and speechmakers in their efforts to find ideas and to find their own ideas succinctly expressed.

The Vertical File Service Catalog, issued monthly, lists pamphlets on all sorts of topics published by various organizations.

For an abundance of information on almost all significant topics within the range of human knowledge and for helpful reference lists at the end of each article, consult the encyclopedias: *Collier's Encyclopedia, The National Cyclopedia, Encyclopedia Americana, Encyclopaedia Britannica,* and *The Britannica Book of the Year* which is an annual supplement to the *Encyclopaedia Britannica* since 1938.

For citations of specialized information, consult the *Agricultural Index,* the *Art Index, Dramatic Index,* the *Education Index,* the *Engineering Index,* the *Industrial Index,* and the *Speech Index* which is an index to famous speeches.

The *Monthly Labor Review* makes available reports on costs of living, employment, industrial disputes, payrolls, and retail prices.

The Statesman's Yearbook: Statistical and Historical Annual of the States of the World presents a wealth of information during the period from 1867 to the present.

The *Statistical Abstract of the United States* is a valuable source of statistical information covering the period from 1878 to the present.

The *Survey of Current Business* reports statistics on both domestic and foreign trade including both exports and imports.

Other sources of information which can be helpful to students of speech are: *The Annals of the American Academy of Political and Social Science;* the *Congressional Digest;* the *Encyclopedia of Religion and Ethics,* 1908–1927; the *Encyclopedia of the Social Sciences,* 1930–1935; the *Information Please Almanac,* 1947 to the present; Baird's *Representative American Speeches;* the *Reference Shelf; University Debater's Annual; Vital Speeches of the Day;* and the *World Almanac and Book of Facts,* 1885 to the present.

The teacher of speech can hardly help his students to become familiar with the innumerable sources of developmental and supporting details without teaching his students to use the sources. Therefore, he will want to invite his students to investigate topics by finding out what the related sources have to offer and to teach his students to set up some system for recording and retaining information which they can use. A system employing 3" x 5", 4" x 6", or 5" x 8" cards is best. Such cards can be very convenient for classifying and grouping a student's ideas. Of course, the teacher should help his students work out a system for recording data on each card. If the student learns early how to record data with convenient headings, form, complete identification of source, and limited data on each card, he will have at his fingertips a system and file for use in developing his ideas, outlines, and speeches.

Besides teaching the available sources and types of developmental and supporting details, the teacher must also show students the difference between facts, informed opinion, sound judgment, and emotional bias. Careful checking of ideas and the developmental and their supporting details should become second nature to the student.

The effective use of developmental and supporting materials which give concreteness and vividness to ideas basic to speaking and to a speech results in clear understanding by listeners. These details, usually within the experience of the listeners, help the listeners to learn by making an association between new material and old, between the familiar and the unfamiliar, and between what interests them and what does not. The result of the association is new interest, new knowledge, new understanding, and, above all, learning and a desire for additional learning.

The competent and conscientious teacher of speech will make every reasonable effort to help his students solve their problems in locating and using sources of ideas and data, in determining the best way to record ideas and data in a conveniently usable form, in setting up a system for filing ideas and data as they collect materials, and in applying their information in their development of outlines and in their oral presentations. To these ends, the following activities should prove helpful to the teacher of speech and to his students:

(*a*) Read at least two or three references cited at the end of this chapter to understand various types of developmental and supporting details. Prepare to explain each type and how you would teach high school students to use it.

(*b*) Select speeches in which developmental and supporting details are employed effectively and make a plan for teaching high school students to identify and analyze the various types of details in the speeches.

(*c*) Invite each student to prepare and present at least one speech in which he will make a special effort to demonstrate the use of specific types of developmental and supporting details.

(d) Make a plan for giving each student a general statement for his development with as many developmental details as he can find. Then, do the same thing with a general statement to which he will apply as many supporting details as he can find.

(e) Plan a series of questions which can be answered by students by their consulting the various library sources enumerated in this chapter. Explain how you, as a teacher of speech, plan to have your students record the answers. Indicate how you plan to supervise your students as they seek the answers to your questions.

(f) Devise a plan for teaching your students to start their own personal files of developmental and supporting details, bibliographical data, and ideas for their own use in discussion, debate, oral interpretation, pantomime, speechmaking, and so on. Provide flexibility in your plan to enable individual students to exercise freedom of choice. Explain your own personal file and system and indicate the reasons for your choice.

(g) Invite each of your students to find a clever, short anecdote, give specifically its source, tell it to the class, and explain how and why it might be used in a speech.

(h) Present in class a plan for assigning speeches of definition. Indicate a time limit, perhaps two minutes, for each student to define a technical, slang, or other term.

(i) Explain your procedures, as a teacher of speech, for introducing, showing, and evaluating the Coronet Films on "How to Judge Authorities" and "How to Judge Facts." If possible, preview the films for the purpose already indicated.

4. *Adjustment to the Speech Situation.* Adjustment by each student to speech situations in a course in speech education is essential and basic to his satisfactory speech performance and achievement. His satisfactory speech performance and achievement in all sorts of speech situations are essential and basic to his learning and development of his fundamentals of speech and his desirable speech attributes. These fundamentals and attributes will give him self-confidence, self-control, poise, and desired effectiveness in appropriate, challenging, and worthwhile speech situations, all of which he needs for success, satisfaction, and happiness, now and later, as a speaker, person, and citizen in a democracy. These are the desired outcomes of speech education and of all education. It is to these ends that the teacher of speech is committed and obligated.

Harry G. Barnes' definition of "adjustment to the speaking situation" provides an operational frame of reference for the teacher of speech and his students. It defines the process of adjustment, states the objective of adjustment to be achieved by students of speech, and specifies, both positively and negatively, characteristics of the well-adjusted speaker. Barnes' definition follows:

> The process of adjustment to the speaking situation is the process by which the speaker, in executing the speech act, adjusts, organizes, and controls the functioning of his bodily mechanism in accordance with, and in spite of, conditions within the immediate speaking situation.
> . . . A speaker who is well adjusted to the speaking situation possesses a stable, well integrated bodily mechanism, exhibits poise, balance, ease, naturalness, purposiveness. He is free from inhibitions, bodily tensions, and mannerisms. He speaks coherently, fluently, and emphatically.
> A speaker who is not well adjusted to the speaking situation possesses an unstable, poorly integrated bodily mechanism; he lacks poise, is unbalanced, ill at ease, unnatural, tense, inhibited; his behavior is purposeless; uncontrolled bodily mannerisms are apparent. He is nervous, excited, frightened, hesitant, uncertain, chaotic, and unable to speak coherently, fluently, and emphatically.[7]

Adjustment to the speech situation is obviously essential and basic to all that a speaker does and says. But basic to adjustment itself is the speaker's preparation. The speaker who is well prepared knows his audience and his objective, has his ideas organized and developed, believes in his ideas and their importance for the audience, and is therefore confident.

Speech fright has been cited by students as the chief handicap to their adjustment to speech situations. They seldom cite their lack of either general or specific preparation as a handicap. Speech fright has been variously defined by many different people. It can be apprehension of failure in a speech situation, anxiety, emotional tension, fear, or at least nervousness. As such, it is a handicap; but sometimes speech fright is merely the human organism's preparation for adjustment and success in speech situations. With additional adrenalin in the blood stream, more oxygen in the lungs, increased blood pressure and pulse rate, greater perspiration, extra energy, and greater mental alertness, speech fright, if controlled and used, can be an asset, rather than a liability or handicap.

Experimenters have defined speech fright for the purposes of their experiments. Greenleaf defined it as ". . . an evaluative disability, occurring in social speech situations, and characterized by anticipatory negative reactions of fear, avoidance, and various internal and overt manifestations of

---

[7] Harry G. Barnes, "A Philosophy of Speech Education," Baconian Lecture, State University of Iowa, March 18, 1938, p. 6. Cited by Eugene C. Chenoweth, *The Quarterly Journal of Speech*, vol. 26, no. 4 (December 1940), pp. 585–588.

tension and behavioral maladjustment."[8] Although Greenleaf's definition is helpful in identifying characteristics of speech fright, it gives few clues which can help the teacher to stimulate and guide the speech-frightened student. Gordon Low moved forward in presenting an operational definition of speech fright as:

> ... the emotional disturbance of the physical and mental behavior of the public speaker as it is manifest by the observable characteristics: poor eye contact, nervous hand movements, restless shifting of feet, awkward posture, body quiver, timid voice, embarrassment, and other physical and vocal cues empathically perceived.[9]

Although Low's definition identifies some of the symptoms of speech fright and implies some measures by which teachers of speech may help their students to control their bodies in speech situations, it neither indicates the causes nor gives insight into speech fright and its significant detrimental and beneficial effect on the speaker's behavior.

Experimental studies have been designed to identify and measure symptoms of speech fright. Three approaches to identification and measurement of these symptoms are evident: (1) reports by speakers or introspective reports of their speech fright, (2) reports by observers of speakers in speech situations, and (3) reports by qualified medical personnel of the physiological changes in speakers before, during, and after their speaking. Most of the results of experimental studies were obtained by the use of at least one of these three methods; sometimes all three methods were used. Teachers of speech can be alert to the results of research which has been accomplished and may find the methods useful to them in helping their students of speech understand speech fright and control and use it in speaking situations.

Roback stated, as a result of introspection by students, that 37 percent of 1000 students in extension courses for adults reported self-consciousness as "their greatest personal handicap in life."[10]

Knower reported that 56 percent of one group of 210 students and 61 percent of another group of 277 students, both groups at the University of Minnesota, "listed some form of nervousness as one of their speech problems." Also, in a group of 512 high school students of speech, 74 percent reported that they were "at least somewhat nervous when speaking." In-

---

[8] Floyd I. Greenleaf, "An Experimental Study of Social Speech Fright," Unpublished M.A. Thesis (State University of Iowa, 1947).

[9] Gordon Low, "The Relation of Psychometric Factors to Stage Fright," Unpublished M.A. Thesis (University of Utah, 1950).

[10] A. A. Roback, *Self-Consciousness—Self Treated*. Sci-Art Publishers, 1936. pp. 41-42. (Cited by Franklin H. Knower, "A Study of Speech Attitudes and Adjustments," *Speech Monographs*, vol. 5 (1938), pp. 130-131.

cidentally, eight teachers of speech in eight different schools who rated these same high school students judged only 29 percent of them "to be free from some form of emotional difficulty in speaking situations."[11]

Greenleaf reported the distribution of self-ratings of degree of speech fright by 1173 freshmen and sophomores in Communication Skills classes at the State University of Iowa. Using the method of introspection, as did Knower, Greenleaf reported that in one group of 384 students, 6 percent indicated affliction by a severe degree of speech fright; 45 percent, moderate; 33 percent, mild; and 16 percent, none. In the other group of 789 students, 10 percent of the students indicated severe speech fright; 47 percent, moderate; 32 percent, mild; and 11 percent, none.[12] In response to a questionnaire, the 789 students revealed the following symptoms of their speech fright:

1. Dryness of throat or mouth
2. Forgetting
3. Tension in the abdominal region
4. Inability to produce voice
5. Stuttering or stammering
6. Tremors of knees and hands
7. Weak voice
8. Excessive perspiration
9. Accelerated heart rate
10. Speech rate too fast or too slow
11. Stomach upset.
12. Difficulty in breathing
13. Inability to look at audience
14. Feeling that the audience is disapproving
15. Inability to finish speaking
16. Excessive hesitation
17. Dread before speaking[13]

Gilkinson used the introspective method in obtaining "Personal Reports of Confidence of Speakers" from 420 men and women students of speech at the University of Minnesota. He used a list of 104 questions expressing feelings of confidence and fear to guide each student in his introspection of his feelings in speech situations. Seventy percent of the students indicated that they were in a state of nervous tension before getting up to speak; 57 percent reported that they found it difficult to search the mind calmly for the right word to express their thoughts; 40 percent reported that fear of forgetting caused them to jumble their speech at times; 37 percent indicated that their voices sounded strange to them when they addressed a group; and only 6 percent of the whole group reported that speaking in public was "a pleasurable experience unaccompanied by any doubts or fears."[14]

[11] Franklin H. Knower, "A Study of Speech Attitudes and Adjustments," *Speech Monographs*, vol. 5 (1938), pp. 130–131.
[12] Floyd I. Greenleaf, "An Exploratory Study of Speech Fright," *The Quarterly Journal of Speech*, vol. 38, no. 3 (October 1952), pp. 326–330.
[13] *Ibid.*, p. 329.
[14] Howard Gilkinson, "Social Fears as Reported by Students in College Speech Classes," *Speech Monographs*, vol. 9 (1942), pp. 141–160.

Dickens and his associates completed a study in which reports by observers of speakers were emphasized as a method of measurement of speech fright. These experimenters found evidence that ratings by observers or Judges' Ratings and Personal Reports of Confidence by Speakers or ratings by introspection tended to validate one another. These experimenters reported that

> ... correlation seemed reasonable in view of the fact that Personal Reports of Confidence by Speakers purported to measure how the speakers *felt*, while Judges' Ratings purported to measure how they *looked* and *sounded*.

Among the conclusions which were supported by their experimental study were these:

> 1. The Judges' Rating technique was highly reliable when ratings of as few as five judges were averaged.
> 2. In general, the Judges' Ratings and Personal Reports of Confidence of Speakers techniques tended to validate one another.
> 3. The accuracy of Judges' Ratings scores—'accuracy' defined as agreement with Personal Reports of Confidence of Speakers did not vary significantly in terms of sex differences, distance from speakers, or amount of judges' teaching experience. ...
> 4. There was markedly greater vacillation by judges in rating 'fearful' speakers than 'confident' ones.
> 5. Analysis of individual ratings revealed such gross inaccuracies as to suggest that a speech teacher can place little faith in his unsupported judgment as to the emotions felt by a given student in a given speech.
> 6. Judges tended to underestimate students' fears much more frequently than to overestimate them.[15]

Dickens and Parker gave emphasis to the measurement of physiological changes in speakers in an experimental study of 50 men and 50 women who gave regularly assigned speeches in a course in Fundamentals of Speech at Redlands University. The normal blood pressure and the normal pulse rate of each speaker were determined several days ahead of the beginning of the experiment. Then, each of the 100 students spoke extemporaneously for three to five minutes. Immediately *after* each speech, registered nurses determined the speaker's systolic and diastolic blood pressure and pulse rate. One month later, the same procedure was repeated *except* that each speaker's blood pressure and pulse rate were determined immediately *before*, rather than *after*, his speech. Incidentally, the other

---

[15] Milton Dickens, Francis Gibson, and Caleb Prall, "An Experimental Study of the Overt Manifestations of Stage Fright," *Speech Monographs*, vol. 17, no. 1 (March 1950), pp. 37–47.

two methods of measurement of speech fright, reports by students of their feelings and reports by observers of speakers, were used along with the method of determining the physiological changes in speakers. The conclusions from this study were:

    1. The normal pulse and blood pressure rates of over 90 per cent of the subjects were measurably affected by the speaking situation.

    2. The amounts of circulatory fluctations were marked; mean amounts of fluctuation were: 18.1 for pulse, 10.1 for systolic blood pressure, and 7.3 for diastolic blood pressure.

    3. The direction of fluctuations was predominantly upward although in a substantial minority of instances the rates decreased.

    4. A very significantly larger number of subjects showed greater pulse fluctutation immediately before speaking than immediately after speaking.

    5. Corresponding differences in blood pressure fluctuation before and after speaking were not statistically significant.

    6. Among the male subjects, the physiological scores, and the introspective scores, and the judges' ratings were definitely and positively correlated. . . .

    7. Among the female subjects, although the correlation values showed approximately the same relative relationships among the three types of measurement as for males, theirs were very much smaller, often negative, often not significant. . . .

    8. In general, the judges' ratings and the physiological scores produced higher correlations than the introspective ratings by the students.

    9. The data showed many significant sex differences: women's scores were higher toward the *fear* and for introspective scores and pulse fluctuations; men's scores, for judges' ratings and blood pressure fluctuation.[16]

This study supports several hypotheses, but one in particular is that the anticipation of speaking is more disturbing to students than the act of speaking.

Some teachers of speech seem to believe that it is best to ignore the problem of speech fright as much as possible. These teachers probably assume that talking about a student's fear, reading about it, and demonstrating it will only cause the student to become more concerned than would normally occur. For the student who lacks courage in his initial speech performances and who has not yet learned to adjust himself to speech situations, the teachers concentrate on challenging him to talk frequently. They challenge him to express himself on topics which are important to

---

[16] Milton Dickens and William R. Parker, "An Experimental Study of Certain Physiological, Introspective, and Rating-Scale Techniques for the Measurement of Stage Fright," *Speech Monographs*, vol. 18, no. 4 (November 1951), pp. 251–259.

him and to help him to get his ideas clearly in mind so that he can give attention to what he has to say and to his audience without too much concern about himself and how he talks. They encourage the speech-frightened student by complimenting him at every opportunity on his effort and achievement. They assure him that a degree of speech fright is necessary for his best speech performance and that his problem is to control it rather than to eliminate it. The teacher should tell him that "normal" speech fright is essential during both his preparation and his speaking; that experimental evidence shows that so-called speech fright is a manifestation of preparation by the human organism to meet the "emergency."

Other teachers of speech anticipate their students' concern and questions about speech fright and begin a frank discussion of what it is, of its manifestations and symptoms, of its many possible causes, of its advantages and disadvantages for students who experience it, and of means for controlling and using it. These teachers can tell their students frankly that nothing concerns teachers of speech more than do students who are *not* concerned with the prospects of their success in speech and in speaking. Also, these teachers may assure their students that teachers of speech feel no little anxiety about their own success in helping every student in the class to become a self-confident, self-controlled, poised, and effective speaker who will be able to enjoy much pleasure and satisfaction as he talks efficiently and effectively with people singly and in groups. By teaching a unit which provides for several short speech performances designed to enable students with varying degrees of speech fright to succeed in increasingly complex speech experiences, teachers can help students gain courage and ability, satisfaction and enjoyment from their participation, and learn to control and direct their emotion so that it will be a constructive force rather than a handicap.

Some teachers of speech use another method in helping their students to adjust to speech situations. They tend to treat students gently, especially during the initial meetings of the class, to use teacher-centered methods with the focus on what the teacher says and does; to engage students in group activities such as buzz sessions, discussion, or choral speaking; to encourage the most courageous students in the class to "talk on their feet," and to manage to convey to all the students the idea that speech is easy and that speech is fun. These methods remind us of how some parents entice children to the dentist or little boys to the barber. Although these teachers, like the parents, may succeed in achieving the immediate objective, the method consumes too much time, postpones the day on which students must, sooner or later, realize that speech is not easy and that fun per se is not the objective. The result is small gain in any genuine speech benefits. In fact, these teachers may be guilty of adjusting themselves to the students without giving the students any real help even in their adjustment to speech situations.

Some typical symptoms of speech fright include: (1) withdrawal manifested by the student's absence on the days of his scheduled speech performances, requests for postponement based on a "claim" of illness or unpreparedness, failure to look at the audience, retreating behind the speaker's stand, posture that indicates withdrawing, and actual withdrawal after a rapid finish or before the finish of the speech performance; (2) excessive tension due to muscular reactions involving antagonistic muscle groups which result in trembling, fidgeting, and random movements; (3) physiological reactions such as increased heart beat, faster breathing, dry mouth, and increased perspiration; and (4) voice reactions such as a rise in pitch, decreased or increased loudness level, strain, and tenseness.

Typical causes of speech fright are: (1) conflict between the urge to communicate and the urge to withdraw; (2) fear of failure and fear of not performing; (3) heightened emotion mistaken for fear; (4) unfamiliarity with the speech situation; (5) a speech situation which is too complex for the speaker; (6) lack of objective, motivation, and knowledge of what to do and how to do it; (7) lack of specific preparation; (8) faulty concept of psychological reactions; (9) faulty evaluation of physiological changes; (10) fear of not meeting a standard, real or imaginary; and (11) possible basic personal deviations. Although these are some of the typical causes of speech fright, other causes are too numerous to mention here even if all of them were known. However, the teacher of speech can be alert to detect other causes such as those growing out of a student's relationships with other students especially of the opposite sex, parents, and teachers.

Typical therapies which can be used by teachers of speech to stimulate and guide students to reduce the intensity of speech fright and to learn to control it are: (1) keep physically fit; (2) study your emotions in an effort to understand them; (3) develop habits of relaxation and control bodily action; (4) realistically evaluate yourself as a speaker in the light of attainable objectives; (5) prepare as thoroughly as possible; (6) select topics which interest you, are likely to hold the attention of your audience, and are worthy of your effort in communicating with your listeners; (7) use an outline while speaking to minimize memory lapses; (8) don't take the situation too seriously; (9) use physical activity when first starting to speak in order to rid yourself of muscular tension; (10) practice the speech by talking it aloud to parents, a recorder, or in an empty room in which you imagine your audience to be seated; (11) seek opportunities to speak wherever you can find an audience; (12) use visual aids such as a blackboard, a chart, a map, or an actual object which is related to what you are talking about or which can serve you in talking; (13) don't take yourself too seriously but try to use humor in some form to cause laughter; (14) never give up after you have started but finish your speech no matter what; and (15) engage yourself in speech courses and in extra-class speech activities.

Obviously, no one of these therapies will solve the problem of speech fright or of adjustment to a speech situation for all students. Likewise, all of them together hardly solve the problem for any one student. In fact, much speaking in a variety of increasingly complex speech situations seems to be the best single therapy for learning to adjust to speech situations, to control and use "normal" speech fright, and to develop self-confidence, self-control, poise, and freedom from excessive tension. Great speakers and great performers of all kinds who have developed the greatest self-assurance in speaking and in performing seem to have done it by much speaking and much performing. In fact, they have probably repeated a speech or a performance until it has become routine.

Speech fright is a response which is subject to conditioning. Both adjustment to speech situations and poise in speech situations are subject to teaching and learning. Henrikson did an experimental study involving 205 students in a first course in speech. Based on the results of introspective measurement *before* and *after* these students participated in seven different kinds of speech situations, he reported, in substance, these conclusions:

1. This study agrees with previous investigations in indicating that speech training promotes confidence in the speaking situation.

2. The feelings of confidence resulting from speech training are somewhat general and do not apply only to the types of speaking in which the student has participated during the course.

3. ... feelings of stage fright are in a constant state of flux. Taking the work in speech accelerates a growth in confidence.

4. A variety of factors influence a student's stage fright. As might be expected, *practice, the attitude of the instructor*, and *the attitude of classmates* rank high as causes. *Feelings of having succeeded* or *having failed* and *analysis of the causes of the stage fright*, contrary to what might have been expected, rank low.[17]

Paulson, who used the introspective method of measurement in determining increased self-confidence of 271 students at the University of Minnesota after ten weeks of speech training, reported these conclusions which support and even surpass those by Henrikson: (1) Both men and women showed significant increases in confidence, and (2) After a period of ten weeks of speech training, the mean scores of both men and women showed that improved confidence tended to remain even though they

---

[17] Ernest H. Henrikson, "Some Effects on Stage Fright of a Course in Speech," *The Quarterly Journal of Speech*, vol. 29, no. 4 (December 1943), pp. 490–491.

spoke to an audience composed of strangers.[18] Robinson cited numerous experimental studies, such as those by Eckert, Edwards, Keyes, Moore, and Rose, and concluded that "Almost without exception studies which have tested specific methods for the development of confidence have shown that repeated performances will increase confidence."[19] Robinson recommended adequate preparation which includes (1) thorough understanding and application of the principles of speech arrangement and composition, (2) the development of proper mental attitudes, (3) the selection of appropriate messages for communication, and (4) rehearsal. He advised that:

> ... we can help our students to become more confident speakers by teaching them that: I. A feeling of anticipation is a natural and desirable state. ... II. The appearance of confidence and poise, regardless of inner tensions, can be readily acquired. ... III. Confidence in and of itself is no substitute for good preparation and practice. ....[20]

It would appear that the high school teacher of speech should strive to achieve the following objectives in working with a student on adjustment to the speech situation: (1) help the student understand adjustment, speech fright, and poise; (2) assist the student in identifying and analyzing manifestations and symptoms of speech fright; (3) aid the student in determining the cause or causes of his own speech fright; (4) help the student learn to accept "normal" speech fright and learn to control and use it; and (5) encourage the student to use purposeful bodily action in speaking.

Some suggested activities to accomplish these objectives include:

(*a*) Discuss adjustment, speech fright, poise, and speech effectiveness with the class. Assign appropriate chapters in textbooks in speech education for high school students and utilize the students' personal experiences in the discussion.

(*b*) Prepare to state what you infer from each of the following statements. Then, explain ways in which you, as a teacher of speech, could use such statements in a unit on "Building Confidence and Poise."

1. Gracie Allen, after 34 years of performance: "I've played five and six performances a day on tour and, before each curtain rose, I've had that strange tenseness we call stage fright; and when I'm through my hands are wet."

---

[18] Stanley F. Paulson, "Changes in Confidence during a Period of Speech Training: Transfer of Training and Comparison of Improved and Non-Improved Groups on the Bell Adjustment Inventory," *Speech Monographs*, vol. 18, no. 4 (November 1951), pp. 260–265.

[19] Edward R. Robinson, "What Can the Speech Teacher Do About Students' Stagefright?" *The Speech Teacher*, vol. 8, no. 1 (January 1959), pp. 8–14.

[20] *Ibid.*, p. 14.

2. Henry Ward Beecher, an eloquent pulpit orator who spoke to nearly three thousand people each Sunday morning and evening for forty years at Plymouth Church in New York City: As he entered the church and walked toward the pulpit, he prayed that the Lord would strike him down so that he would not have to preach.

3. William Jennings Bryan, after his famous speech on "The Cross of Gold," said that only his knowledge that he had a good conclusion kept him going.

4. Cicero: "I turn pale at the outset of a speech, and quake in every limb."

5. Winston Churchill, probably the greatest orator of the twentieth century, prepared meticulously many possible lines of thought, so fearful was he, when he was a young member of Parliament, that he might have to debate something which he had not previously studied.

6. After Eva Le Gallienne had finished her thousandth performance, when a reporter asked her if she still had stage fright, said: "Yes, and it gets worse every year."

7. Prime Minister Nehru of India who spoke English eloquently to many different audiences around the world was so fearful of speaking that he regularly paid a fine rather than participate in debate in the famous Cambridge Union at Cambridge University.

8. Mark Twain said that if he were going to be hanged he would know he could make a good showing, but he was not always so confident that he could make a successful speech.

9. Daniel Webster, one of the greatest orators of all time, found his first speechmaking to be agonizing when he was a student at Exeter Academy.

(*c*) Outline procedures by which you would build, during the first meetings of your class of beginners in speech education, an *esprit de corps* favorable for students' adjustment to the initial speech situations in which each student would be called upon to speak.

(*d*) Explain how you could use information from each student's autobiography to help students in your class of beginners to adjust rapidly and well to the initial speech situations in your class. State examples of the kinds of information you would use.

(*e*) Prepare an assignment of an expository speech for which you would encourage each student to select a topic in which he would likely be interested, with which he would likely be familiar, and about which he would likely be eager to communicate with other students in the class. Then, prepare for the same purpose an assignment of an argumentative speech.

(*f*) Detail a plan for your use of the introspective method of measurement of symptoms of speech fright. Explain how you would use the plan and what you would hope to accomplish with it in helping your students.

(g) Suggest specific techniques for controlling tension and emotional reactions to appropriate, challenging, and worthwhile speech experiences. Ponder:

    1. Prepare adequately a well-organized and a well-developed speech.

    2. Avoid the "How Am I Doing" attitude; work for an "Are They Understanding My Message" attitude.

    3. Rehearse aloud, standing up; work to include purposeful bodily action while rehearsing.

    4. Watch your breathing. Make certain that you have an adequate breath supply before starting to speak.

    5. In practice sessions, go through the entire speech each time. This will help avoid psychological blocks at the end of different parts of the speech.

(h) Read *Speech Handicapped School Children,* Revised Edition, pp. 272–283. Explain how the nine specific ways of helping stutterers can be applied to helping speech frightened students.

(i) Read one of the experimental studies cited in the bibliography at the end of this chapter. Be prepared to state its purpose, methodology, findings, conclusions, and your evaluation of the study.

5. *Bodily Action for Purposes of Communication.* The speech code consists of audible symbols and visible bodily action. The code is verbal when it affects the listener by stimulating his ears; it is nonverbal when it stimulates his eyes.

The bodily action of a human infant appears to be purposeless, useless, wasteful, and even ridiculous. Speechwise, the random bodily action of the child appears to be as senseless as the bodily status of a fisherman who persists in sitting without ever getting a bite. But, unlike the bodily status of the luckless fisherman, the aimless bodily action of the child results, sooner or later, in a desired response from its mother and, as if the child had made a mental note of the specific action which stimulated the desired response by its mother, it repeats the same action again and again so long as it gets the same desired response. Similarly, it *learns* to use another specific bodily action to get another desired response; while still some other bodily action gets an undesired response. The child learns by both trial and error and trial and success which bodily action not to use and which to use to get desired responses only. Later, with stimulation and guidance by people whom it observes and imitates, the child learns to control and use its bodily action to feed itself, sit, stand, walk, vocalize, and talk. Thus, the human infant develops its nonverbal, visible, speech code for purposes of communication to satisfy its needs and wants.

The verbal, vocal, and audible speech code, consisting of audible symbols, is an outgrowth of visible bodily action and an integral part of it. The human infant coos and wails purposelessly and wastefully until the random bodily action of cooing and wailing results in rewards and penalties by its mother or other elder person. The child learns the connection between its sounds which result in a satisfying reward and its other sounds which result in a dissatisfying penalty. As the child learns which sounds are rewarding and which ones are penalizing, it continues, through many trials and successes, to manipulate its bodily action to produce rewarding sounds and to avoid penalizing ones; later, words; and, later, simple sentences. Of course, it learns to imitate audible symbols which it hears and to produce those symbols. If it hears symbols of the English language, rather than those of some other language, the child will learn to speak English. Otherwise, it will learn to produce symbols of whatever language is used to stimulate and guide its control, refinement, and use of its verbal, vocal, and audible speech code for purposes of communication to satisfy its needs and wants.

Teachers of speech today recognize in the child's learning of its speech code a number of concepts which are basic to teaching bodily action for purposes of communication:

(a) The bodily action of a speaker for purposes of communication refers to any behavior of his body which stirs up meaning in an audience. It includes his posture, facial expression, gestures, and bodily movement.

(b) The visible speech code is a fundamental of speech which is learned by the development, control, refinement, and use of his bodily action in a variety of speech situations.

(c) The audible speech code is a fundamental of speech which is an outgrowth of a speaker's visible bodily action and an integral part of it.

(d) Visible bodily action, when it is controlled and used purposefully by a speaker, is as much a part of thought as are his audible symbols.

(e) Visible bodily action is motivated by the speaker's objective, his thought and feeling, his desire to speak, and the reactions of members of the audience.

(f) Effective bodily action in speaking, as in everything else, is purposeful, free, spontaneous, natural, well coordinated, varied, unobtrusive, and responsive to meaning.

(g) The visual speech code of a speaker is effective to the extent that his audience responds to it by tending to reflect his expressions and muscular "sets." This process of reflection is, of course, known as empathy.

(*h*) A speaker's adjustment to a speech situation and his confidence and poise in the situation are dependent, in no small measure, on his effective control and use of bodily action for purposes of communication.

(*i*) Although effective bodily action for purposes of communication by a speaker is a natural outgrowth of his many speech experiences, specific instruction, drill, exercise, criticism, and evaluation of the speaker's visible speech code can aid the speaker to control, develop, refine, and use it with increasing effectiveness.

(*j*) The visible speech code, like its audible counterpart, is for communication; not for exhibition. Therefore, the audience should not be aware of the speaker's bodily action or his audible symbols but the attention of both the speaker and the audience should be focused on the speaker's idea or message.

Teachers of speech should, of course, stimulate and guide high school students to develop their capacities for the visible speech code. Students need to know that their nonverbal code will either be effective in their communication with an audience which observes them or it will detract from the effectiveness of their communication by means of their verbal speech code. To make it effective for each student will require patience and skill by the teacher of speech and will call forth effort and courage from each student. Teachers and students can derive inspiration from the achievement of people who study and practice, long and hard, to control, develop, refine, and use bodily action and movement to excel as tennis players, pianists, boxers, typists, basketball and football players, surgeons, actors, dancers, pantomimists, oral interpreters, and speakers. Teachers must realize that speakers who evoke desired responses from audiences succeed through their self-motivated visible bodily action or their self-motivated audible symbols, or both; not through their learning and application of rules of gesture or other bodily action. Likewise, these teachers should help their students to know the benefits which they can derive from their use of visible bodily action for purposes of communication. Some of these benefits are:

(*a*) Bodily action in speaking can help the speaker adjust to the speech situation. It can help him to reduce, control, and use speech fright, rather than either to be "frozen" by his fright or to mark himself as a speech frightened speaker.

(*b*) The use of visible bodily action by a speaker suggests to the audience his readiness for speaking. Of course, the speaker should be neither lethargic, slow, and lazy nor overly tense, excitable, or purposeless as could be suggested by his bodily action or lack of it.

(c) Bodily action in speaking tends to increase the rapidity of the speaker's thinking and to contribute to the fluency with which he uses audible speech symbols.

(d) Well-controlled and well-used bodily action in speaking tends to arouse and maintain confidence of the audience in the speaker and his message.

(e) Skillful use of the visible speech code tends to enable a speaker to command the vim, vigor, and vitality characteristic of the desire and ability to communicate effectively with an audience.

(f) The effective use of visible bodily action can make the speaker's meaning more easily understood and remembered by the audience.

(g) The nonverbal speech code can be used effectively to emphasize ideas, words, phrases, or even whole sentences which express ideas in a climactic order to the point of a strong climax in a speech.

(h) Bodily action in speaking can supplement a speaker's use of his audible symbols and vice versa, and thereby increase the effectiveness of his speaking.

(i) The use of bodily action in speaking, including, of course, the manipulation of the head and shoulders, the eyes and facial expressions, gestures and bodily movements, coupled with the use of audible speech, affords rich and varied means by which to serve the purposes of speaking.

(j) Visual eye contact of a speaker with members of his audience is an essential and especially useful bodily action for adjustment, courtesy, and effective communication.

(k) Visible bodily action by a speaker can tend to afford him empathic responses by members of his audience and thereby afford members of his audience empathic release of muscular and nervous tension.

Once students have recognized the need for purposeful bodily action and the benefits to be derived from it, they can more easily begin to develop effective habits of their own. A program for developing effective habits of bodily action should include:

(a) An analysis and report by each student of his conclusions about the posture, facial expressions, gestures, and bodily movements of others in a variety of speech situations compared to the characteristics and skills of his own bodily action in speech situations in which he finds himself.

(b) An analysis and report on the bodily action of members of audiences, including the bodily action of members of the class as he speaks to them, to determine the bodily responses of listeners and observers to the bodily action of speakers, including himself, and to determine the amount and kind of bodily action which seems to be appropriate and effective for purposes of communication with different kinds and sizes of audiences, including, as examples, high school students, adults, and children.

(c) An evaluation of the effectiveness of each student's own bodily action and bodily movements in helping him to achieve various specific purposes of communication with members of the class, and, if possible, with members of audiences other than the class.

(d) A study of principles of effective use of the body for purposes of communication.

(e) Continuous study of the posture, facial expressions, gestures, and bodily movement of other members of the class to determine the amount and kind of bodily action and movement which they control and use effectively and which they do not control and use effectively.

(f) A continuous analysis of the capacity of each student for using bodily action compared to the ability which he has developed through actual practice in speech situations in the class.

(g) Invitations to each student to speak in speech situations designed to provide opportunities for communication through the use of purposeful bodily action and movement.

The two main objectives to be achieved by the teacher of speech and his students are (1) to help each student understand the effect in speech situations of well controlled, refined, and well used posture, bodily action, and bodily movement, and (2) to help each student control, develop, refine, and use his posture, bodily action, and bodily movement for the purposes of communication with his audience.

Some suggested activities to accomplish these two objectives are:

(a) Outline a plan for your use in leading a discussion on "How can posture, bodily action, and bodily movement best contribute to a speaker's effectiveness in speech situations?" Indicate in your plan specific ways by which you and your students can demonstrate the effectiveness and ineffectiveness of the visible speech code for purposes of communcation. Prepare to present your outline in a meeting of teachers of speech.

(b) Prepare and present in class an assignment designed to help each student analyze the posture, facial expressions, gestures, and bodily movements of speakers and other public performers in a variety of speech situations. Designate situations which you would recommend and outline your instructions to your students. Consider stage and television plays, platform and television speechmaking by which different purposes of communication are served, sales in which an auctioneer is crying, church ceremonies and services, street corner conversations, interschool ball games, political rallies, busloads of people, movies, concerts, variety shows, and so on.

(c) Outline assignments by which each student in your class can analyze his own posture, facial expressions, gestures, and bodily movements in speaking. Consider mirrors, motion picture cameras, closed circuit television, reports by other students and the teacher, and any other devices and media. Present your plan or plans to the class.

(d) Assume that you would divide your students into groups and have each group present a five-minute group pantomime with a plot worked out in detail. Present in class a plan by which you would hope to use group pantomimes to help your students control, refine, and use visible bodily action only for communication with the class and with you. Designate the kinds of plots which you would have each group of students consider for pantomiming. Consider fairy tales, folk tales, nursery rhymes, western stories, community situations, school situations, and so on.

(e) Explain how you could use the following in stimulating and guiding your students to understand and develop to a high level of their individual capacities their individual abilities in the use of the nonverbal speech code: Hamlet's "Advice to the Players"; the "Seven Ages of Man" in Shakespeare's *As You Like It*; Mark Twain's "The Whitewashing of the Fence" in *Tom Sawyer*; Dame Chat, Gammer, and Hodge in "Gammer Gurton's Needle"; "Goldilocks and the Three Bears"; "Jack and the Beanstalk"; stories of Paul Bunyon; "King Arthur and His Court"; "Little Orphan Annie"; *The Last of the Mohicans*; Ebenezer Scrooge and Tiny Tim in "A Christmas Carol"; and "The Last Supper." Of course, you may designate others.

(f) List by name or otherwise a number of advertisements on television which you believe you could use for group pantomimes by students in your class. Consider advertisements such as the following: Coca-Cola, Woodbury's soap, and others. Explain to the class how you would use the advertisements which you select. Indicate the outcomes which you desire your students to realize from their pantomimes.

(g) Assume that a member of your class is to be a narrator and that other members are going to do pantomimes with two to six students in a group. As the narrator tells the story of a picture, the painter, the kind of picture it is, and where it hangs, the small group of students will arrange themselves to represent the characters in the picture. Each of the students will give particular attention to the posture, facial expression, and gestures of each character. Explain to the class pictures which might be used such as "The Last Supper" and "The Dance of the Nymphs."

(h) Compile a list of topics which you believe would be suitable for individual pantomimes by boys and another list suitable for girls. Assume that each pantomime will be about three minutes in length and that each student will present a specific speech situation with a specific sequence of events. Explain to the class how each pantomime will affect the student's posture, facial expression, gestures, and bodily movement.

(*i*) Outline a plan for each student to give a speech in which bodily action and movement are necessary for communication. Assume that the speech will test what each student has learned in group and individual pantomimes. Indicate the kind of speech and topics which you believe would be appropriate.

(*j*) Devise or select practice sentences which require descriptive and emphatic gestures and movements. Explain to the class your philosophy of teaching bodily action and movement.

(*k*) Plan demonstrations of various postures and explain their likely effects on a speaker and on his audience.

(*l*) Plan an assignment designed to stimulate and guide students to control, refine, and use bodily action in playing charades. Indicate titles of books and other ideas which you might use to help your students gain abandon and effectiveness in speaking by use of visible bodily action and movement.

(*m*) Formulate a plan which you might use to stimulate and guide your students to pantomime scenes which prevail in a high school and in a community. Specify the situations in the school and in the community which would lend themselves to group and individual pantomimes.

(*n*) Indicate measures by which you believe you could help your students to apply the desired outcomes of group and individual pantomimes to serve improved bodily action and bodily movement in conversation, discussion, oral interpretation, speechmaking, and acting.

(*o*) Examine at least two of the references in the bibliography at the end of this chapter to help you plan a series of drills and exercises which you would recommend for helping students develop their control and use of bodily action and movement for purposes of communication. Prepare to present to the class your evaluation of the drills and exercises suggested in the references which you examine.

6. *Voice Usage.* Much of what has just been stated about bodily action can be applied to voice usage. In fact, voice production is a bodily act. The development of voice usage in speaking is achieved by the control, direction, and coordination of bodily action to produce voice and to use it as a carrier of audible symbols, spoken words, and, in fact, all spoken language.

Voice production can be an excellent starting point in stimulating and guiding students to control, develop, and use their voices in speaking. Students need to understand what happens in voice production, why and how it happens, its effect on the formulation of audible symbols, and its impact on listeners. Their understanding of voice production can help them to become increasingly self-directive in their control, development, and use of their voices as they realize:

(*a*) the relationships between thought and bodily action, bodily action and voice production, voice production and spoken language, and spoken language and their effectiveness in communication.

(*b*) why and how their voice habits developed, how their voice habits can be changed, and why new and better voice habits may be necessary and desirable for purposes of most effective voice usage in communication.

(*c*) why and how respiration for life only is different than respiration for speaking and how expiration can be controlled and directed for increasingly better voice usage.

(*d*) why the ear is important in voice development and how the ear serves both the listener and the speaker.

(*e*) why the pitch of girls' voices is ordinarily higher than that of boys', and how optimum pitch levels can be achieved and maintained automatically and habitually by both girls and boys in speech situations.

(*f*) why some voices "crack" and "change" during adolescence, how to protect and treat "changing" voices, and why the "changes" can be accepted as "normal" and beneficial.

(*g*) why and how hoarseness can result from "common colds" and from yelling.

(*h*) why the quality of voices differs and how vocal quality can be controlled, directed, and used to achieve desired effects on listeners.

(*i*) why some voices are better than others for purposes of communication by means of audible speech.

(*j*) why and how voices are carriers of audible symbols, spoken words, and, in fact, all spoken language.

(*k*) how to avoid vocal attributes which detract from what a speaker says because the attention of the listener is, at least to a degree, centered on the voice and voice usage of the speaker rather than on his message.

(*l*) how to develop a clear, flexible, well-modulated, and unobtrusive voice responsive to meaning which can serve as an effective stimulus to listeners by holding their attention on the speaker's message and by compelling their interest in it.

Once a student understands why and how he produces his voice and how it affects listeners, he is better able to evaluate his own voice usage, to determine his objective in voice development, to understand how to control and develop his voice as a carrier of spoken language, and to effect desirable changes in his voice usage.

Voice training is, at best, extraordinarily time-consuming. In a class of fifteen to twenty students in a course in basic speech development which meets one hour a day, five days a week, for one school year, or a maximum of 180 clock-hours, finding time for adequate voice training for each student can be an acute problem. If the class meets a maximum of 90 clock-hours during a single semester, which is customary, the problem seems to be insoluble. As a teacher tries to teach ten fundamentals of speech to twenty students during a semester, he realizes that he has less than ten clock hours per fundamental and less than thirty minutes to work with each student on each fundamental of speech. Fortunately, the teacher can plan to stimulate and guide the whole group of students, as one group, to understand much of the information basic to voice training. Likewise, he may turn the class into a laboratory in which he may supervise his students as they, individually, work on their voice problems, provided each student is well aware of his problem, well motivated, and well grounded in his knowledge of procedures for effecting improvement in his voice and voice usage.

Effectiveness of voice training depends on understanding by the teacher and his students of the listening mechanism as well as the speech mechanism. Although a student can learn to listen without detailed knowledge of the ear, he can hardly appreciate the causes and effects of his listening habits or the effects of his voice usage on listeners unless he does understand the ear, its function, its operation, and its relationship to the central nervous system. Likewise, a student can learn to use his voice and to speak without detailed knowledge of the speech mechanism, but he will likely be better motivated and better able to learn if he understands the mechanism and how it is innervated, directed, and coordinated to perform the acts of respiration, phonation, resonation, and enunciation and articulation. Also, it seems to be mandatory that he understand the psychological attributes and variables of voice and their effect on the interest and comprehension by listeners. Every student in voice training needs to be able to recognize:

(*a*) Loudness—too soft, too loud, monotonous in loudness level, lack of acceptable accent on syllables, lack of meaningful stress on words, and lack of emphasis on phrases within sentences to enable listeners to comprehend the meaning.

(*b*) Pitch—too high, too low, sameness of pitch level, pitch patterns, lack of inflection, uncontrolled variation, and lack of optimum pitch range.

(*c*) Quality—breathy, denasal, harsh, hoarse, hoarse-husky, infantile, muffled, nasal, oratund, strident, and thin.

(*d*) Duration—prolonged or slow production of tones, staccato or fast production of tones, monotonous or patterned tones, and uncontrolled variation in length of tones.

Teachers of speech know that the range of acceptability of each vocal attribute is wide. They know that an effective speaker or actor, especially an actor who portrays a character with one or more extreme vocal characteristics, may use one or more of his vocal attributes of loudness, pitch, quality, and duration to stimulate responses which he desires by his listeners. For example, Madame X may vary widely all attributes of her voice as she screams when confronted with danger: excessive loudness, high pitch, strident quality, and prolonged duration of the scream. Mr. Bully may use a harsh quality of voice to impress his audience with his threatening toughness. Miss Blondie may use a soft, low-pitched, breathy voice to accomplish her desired vocal effect. In fact, skilled speakers and actors, on and off platforms and stages, vary their vocal attributes, sometimes to extremes, to achieve their desired effects. Nevertheless, any one of the attributes of voice used in the extreme, especially if it is used consistently, can be a handicap to a speaker. The desired outcome of voice training is a clear, flexible, well-modulated, and unobtrusive voice which is *responsive to meaning*. In responding to meaning, the voice is capable of extreme variation in each of its attributes. Although the voice should, generally, be unobtrusively pleasant, it should be capable of harshness whenever the speaker may want to get a specific response from his audience. Pleasantness of voice may well be cultivated but not at the expense of clarity, flexibility, or responsiveness to meaning.

Bridging the gap between a student's knowledge of voice production and his effective voice usage in speaking is a function of method in speech education. Methods of voice training pose problems which need to be solved by teachers of speech. Some of these problems and their possible solutions follow:

(*a*) To what extent should the teacher of speech be concerned with the development of skill in voice usage by each of his students? Of course, the assumption is that voice usage is a fundamental of speech and that, therefore, the teacher of speech who uses the fundamentals approach in teaching speech is obligated to teach voice usage. As Eisenson indicated:

> . . . an effective voice is one which can be heard without conscious effort or strain. It is consonant with the speaker's message and helps make the message readily audible and intelligible. An effective voice . . . should be as loud as the specific situation demands.[21]

Of course, the teacher of speech is concerned with the development of skill in vocal usage by each student to the extent that he can be heard

---

[21] Jon Eisenson, *The Improvement of Voice and Diction.* New York: The Macmillan Company, 1958. p. 5.

THE "FUNDAMENTALS" APPROACH   153

without strain in speech situations which demand vocal adjustment. But the teacher may well be concerned with development by each of his students of skill in each of the psychological attributes and variables to the point that he establishes in his central nervous system almost automatic control and direction of acceptable voice patterns in speaking. Therefore, before the teacher of speech can be assured that training in voice usage is effective, he must test voice usage by each of his students in a variety of speech situations.[22] This means that the teacher should provide meaningful speech situations in which each student demonstrates almost automatic control and direction of acceptable voice usage in conversation, discussion, oral interpretation, speechmaking, and other speech experiences typical of his school and community. However, the teacher should not concentrate exclusively on his student's development of "skill in voice usage" but also on his "understanding the skill." When the student exercises automatically acceptable voice usage and, at the same time, understands why his voice usage is acceptable, he and his teacher can be confident that his improved audible speech behavior is certain and likely to be lasting in its consequences.

(b) Do students with greater lung capacity than that of other students have any significant advantage in voice usage? Hedde and Brigance, in their book, *The New American Speech,* available in many high schools throughout the United States, advised:

> You need more air to build a volume of voice and to sustain tones. The amount of air used in speech is not large, but you need a reserve to maintain vigor of tone and to prevent running out of breath at the end of a phrase.[23]

They suggested activities for testing and developing control of breathing while speaking, for developing deep inhalation, and for developing controlled exhalation. Likewise, Loren Reid in his book entitled *Teaching Speech* stated in 1960:

> You will need to show that since tone is produced on the exhaled breath stream, a good supply of breath, steadily under control, is essential.[24]

Gray and Wise, as a result of a number of experimental studies, stated:

> Despite the fact that formerly much attention was given to increasing the capacity of the lungs, there is no evidence that the amount of the vital

---

[22] Theodore D. Hanley and Wayne L. Thurman, *Developing Vocal Skills.* New York: Holt, Rinehart and Winston, Inc., 1962. pp. 31–33.
[23] Wilhelmina G. Hedde and William Norwood Brigance, *The New American Speech.* Philadelphia: J. B. Lippincott Company, 1957. pp. 64–65.
[24] Loren Reid, *Teaching Speech.* Columbia, Missouri: Artcraft Press, 1960. p. 117.

capacity is of any significance in the production of voice. There is, moreover, no evidence that either quality of tone, strength of tone, or ability to control the strength is in any way dependent upon the total amount of air that one can draw into the lungs. . . . There is no evidence that those people who use a large amount of *tidal air*, as it is called, either in actual volume or in proportion to vital capacity, have any better voices or are any better speakers than those who use smaller actual or proportionate amounts of breath, the correlations being again too small to be significant. Another interesting fact is that not everyone requires more breath to speak loudly than to speak in a normal voice. In fact, in a study on this subject, almost one-third of the 140 people studied used even less breath in speaking loudly than in speaking normally. Increase in loudness in such cases seems to be achieved by adjustments in resonance, resulting in a greater audibility of the tone without corresponding increase in volume of breath used.[25]

Nevertheless, the teacher of speech may find that an adequate breath reserve, whatever it may be for a student, tends to give him a secure feeling of having enough "air power" to give his voice resonance and vigor, to enable him to relax and relieve the tensions of muscles in his neck and throat, and to make it possible for him to sustain strong tones to the end of his phrases in voice usage. The teacher hardly dares to ignore evidence of lack of relationship between lung capacity and voice usage or to ignore the respiration habits of his students. Of course, he should be aware of further evidence cited on his next problem in teaching voice usage.

(c) Is respiration for life only different from respiration for voice usage in audible speech? In respiration for life only, inspiration and expiration are automatic, continuous, involuntary, quiet, rhythmic, and usually shallow. Any bodily exertion in addition to that necessary for sustaining life only increases the amount of oxygen needed by the body and, in turn, the amount of carbon dioxide which the body needs to discharge. But in respiration for voice usage in audible speech, expiration is controlled and directed to set the vocal folds into vibration, to effect audibility by adjustments in resonance, to sustain vocalization, to build up pressures for articulation, and to give vigor to utterance as necessary to stir up meaning in an audience and evoke the desired response to the speaker's voice usage in audible speech. In fact, the voluntary control and

---

[25] Giles Wilkeson Gray and Claude Merton Wise, *The Bases of Speech*, 3rd ed. New York: Harper & Row, Publishers, 1959. pp. 139–140. (Cited the following studies: Harriett R. Idol, "A Statistical Study of Respiration in Relation to Speech Characteristics," in *Studies in Experimental Phonetics*, Giles Wilkeson Gray, ed., *Louisiana State University Studies*, No. 27. Baton Rouge, Louisiana: Louisiana State University Press, 1936. pp. 79–98; Charles F. Lindsley, "The Psychophysical Determinants of Voice Quality," *Speech Monographs*, vol. 1 (1934), pp. 79–116; and John Barnes, "Vital Capacity and Ability in Oral Reading," *The Quarterly Journal of Speech*, vol. 12, no. 3 (June 1926), pp. 176–182.)

direction of expiration to meet the demands for vigorous utterance results in quick and spaced inspirations, which is the equivalent of controlled and directed inspiration in vigorous utterance. However, evidence again indicates that the presumption of an increase in the rate of respiration or in the depth of inspiration is false. Gray and Wise cited the following experimental evidence which supports the falsity of the presumption:

> The capacity of the lungs varies considerably among different people. A fair average for men is perhaps 225 cubic inches and for women from 50 to 75 cubic inches less. That is the volume of air that can be inhaled and exhaled in a single cycle of respiration, and it is called the *vital capacity*. There is in addition a small volume of air, amounting perhaps to 100 cubic inches, that cannot be entirely expelled. It is called the *residual air*. . . . The average quantity of air which passes into and out of the lungs in a single respiratory cycle is no more than about 30 cubic inches, or about 13 percent of the vital capacity. Furthermore, the amount of air used in uttering a single phrase is generally little if any more than in casual breathing. In fact, more than one-half of a group of 140 subjects breathed more deeply for "life purposes" than for normal speech.[26]

Although the moot question of how much "air capacity" and "air power" are needed for vigorous voice usage in audible speech seems to be answered, the teacher may well conclude that breath control is essential. Whether a sound is voiced or voiceless, air power is always involved. The breath stream needs to be controlled and directed before the desired sounds can be produced. But there is perhaps an even more important problem which needs to be solved by the teacher of speech who would stimulate and guide his students in developing their habits of respiration for phonation and voice usage.

(*d*) Is one type of breathing better than another for voice usage in speaking? Although the problem of respiration for speaking is fraught with controversy, there seems to be widespread agreement recently among teachers of speech and experimenters on some phases of the process of respiration. Some of these agreements are:

1. In speaking, a person inspires quickly but prolongs expiration in an effort to sustain the tone of his voice and his audible speech until he has uttered a word, phrase, sentence, or, in some cases, even more than one sentence. Hanley and Thurman have stated that "the ratio of inhalation time to exhalation time is about 1 to 1 in relaxed life breathing. In breathing for speech, the ratio averages about 1 to 7."[27]

2. Breathing is basic to voice production and audible speech, because, as stated by Hahn and her associates:

[26] *Ibid.*, p. 139.
[27] Theodore D. Hanley and Wayne L. Thurman, *op. cit.*, p. 55.

The breath is now the source of energy which sets the tensed vocal folds into vibration to produce vocal sound. To make this vibration efficient and steady, you must control the breath stream being exhaled.[28]

3. Clavicular breathing is an unacceptable type of breathing for vocal production and audible speech because the elevation of the shoulders and clavicles on inspirations is inefficient, tension in the neck muscles and larynx affects pitch and effects harshness, relaxation of the neck and shoulder muscles make it difficult to control loudness, and lifting the thoracic structure tends to exhaust the speaker.

4. Each student should be helped by the teacher to discover for himself the *type or types of breathing which best suit his voice production and audible speech*, regardless of whether his breathing is diaphragmatic-abdominal, medial, upper thoracic, or, as is most likely, "mixed" or "combined" except for clavicular breathing.

As each teacher of speech searches for his solution to the problem of what type of respiration is best for sustained voice usage in spoken language, he may heed Donald Ecroyd, who stated:

Speech takes place on the exhaled breath. This means, obviously, that breathing is basic to speech, and that exercises designed to improve and develop your breath control will probably help you have a better speaking voice. There has been a lot of nonsense written about this relationship, however, and it would probably be wise to stick to the facts. It takes little or no more breath to speak than it takes to live. . . . Breathing centered in the lower trunk is not necessarily "the best" way to breathe for speech. . . . Breathing for speech is not essentially different from any other kind of breathing—except in terms of rhythm.[29]

(e) What is the significance of drill as a method of voice training? Rita Lee Kramer warned against the use of vocal drill in the case of voices which have not yet matured:

Because some voices have not yet changed and because many are still shaky, drill might be more harmful than useful. The best procedure for the teacher is to present the exercises to the class, demonstrating them herself, carefully explaining the exact purpose of each exercise. If she finds in the class a voice with which she can safely work, she might use pupil demonstration. She should encourage private drill in appropriate exercises.[30]

[28] Elise Hahn, Donald E. Hargis, Charles W. Lomas, and Daniel Vandraegen, *Basic Voice Training for Speech*. New York: McGraw-Hill, Inc., 1957. p. 29.
[29] Donald H. Ecroyd, *Speech in the Classroom*. Englewood Cliffs, N.J.: Prentice-Hall, Inc., 1960. pp. 5–6.
[30] Rita Lee Kramer, "A Voice Training Program for High School Sophomores," *The Speech Teacher*, vol. 3, no. 1 (January 1954), pp. 23–25.

Although the teacher of speech may well heed the caution expressed by Miss Kramer, he should also be alert to the results of any experimental studies which may affirm or deny her warning and its implications. In the meantime, he may use drill judiciously and effectively in stimulating the growth and maturity of voices with which he can safely work and encourage private drill in appropriate exercises. As Evelyn Konigsberg indicated: "Drill need not be dull and dreary. It can be thought provoking, stimulating, and even entertaining."[31] After a student sees clearly what is to be achieved by his drill and practice, reasons for his achieving the objective, why drill and practice constitute the best method for achieving it, and values to be realized by his efforts, he will likely pursue his drill and practice to establish acceptable voice attributes, variables, and patterns. Even though Weaver, Borchers, and Smith warned that "Voice-training will not be successful if attention is centered on voice per se," they went on to state that:

> The students who want to *use* good voices will make more progress than those who want to *have* good voices. This means that students must improve their voices because they want to read literature well, give effective science demonstrations, take part in social studies discussions, clarify mathematics problems, report on the lives of music composers, give physical education directions, describe pictures, act in plays, be masters of ceremonies at dinners, introduce speakers in assemblies, teach Sunday School classes, use the telephone effectively, be interesting in conversation, read for club meetings, or participate in any one or more of hundreds of occasions, when a good voice will help them to be successful.[32]

A teacher of speech appears to be obligated to help each of his students achieve objectives of voice training such as the following in his speaking and reading in various speech situations in the school and community:

(*a*) To recognize the importance of his developing his voice so that it is clearly audible, easily and readily flexible, expressive, unaffected and unobtrusive, vital with continuously adequate reserve strength, well-coordinated with his visible bodily action, well-modulated, and responsive to the meaning of his audible speech.

(*b*) To become sensitive to the vocal attributes and variables such as loudness, pitch, quality, and duration in the voice usage of people other than himself.

(*c*) To learn to evaluate accurately his own voice attributes, limitations, patterns, skills, and variables.

[31] Evelyn Konigsberg, "Making Drill Functional," *The Speech Teacher*, vol. 1, no. 2 (March 1952), pp. 128–130.

[32] Andrew T. Weaver, Gladys L. Borchers, and Donald K. Smith, *The Teaching of Speech*. Englewood Cliffs, N.J.: Prentice-Hall, Inc., 1952. pp. 164–165.

(d) To understand the process of respiration and how he can control and direct it for *adequate breath pressure* to set the whole vibratory system, including the vocal bands and the resonators, into vibration to generate vocal tones and also how he can control and direct his process of respiration for the *greater breath pressure* as required to sustain and project a loud and, of course, voiceless whisper.[33]

(e) To understand the whole vibrating system and how he can control and direct his vocal bands, in coordination with his respiration, to generate vocal sound and how he can control and direct his resonators, including his larynx, pharynx, and mouth, to modify his vocal loudness, pitch, quality, and duration.

(f) To understand the function of his ear and to train it so that he can recognize in his own voice acceptable and unacceptable loudness, pitch, quality, and duration, can discriminate between acceptable and unacceptable voice production, and can evaluate his progress and successes in attaining the desired outcome of his voice training and development.

(g) To develop control of his respiration to insure adequate vocal power in any speech situation in which he might find himself without causing strain in his voice mechanism.

(h) To develop control of his vibratory system to insure the generation of an acceptable and easy flow of vocal sound, adequate and flexible loudness, optimum or at least satisfactory pitch variation to avoid monotony, pleasant and flexible voice quality, and vocal duration in keeping with an acceptable and flexible rate of oral utterance.

(i) To become habituated, by his insight, repetition, and practice, in acceptable vocal attributes and variables to the point that they are automatically, naturally, and spontaneously controlled in his speaking and reading.

(j) To test his vocal efficiency and effectiveness in a variety of types of oral communication typical of the school and community in an effort to assure him that his gains in voice usage are permanent and secure in his speech behavior.

Activities which can help the teacher of speech to prepare in advance for helping each of his students achieve objectives of voice training are:

(a) Prepare to lead a discussion of the attributes and variables of an efficient and effective voice in speaking and reading. As a part of your preparation, draw upon at least three references on voice usage cited at the end of this chapter.

(b) Present a plan for developing the sensitivity of your students to the vocal attributes and variables of people other than themselves. Con-

---

[33] E. Mary Huyck and Kenneth D. A. Allen, "Diaphragmatic Action of Good and Poor Speaking Voices," *Speech Monographs*, vol. 4 (1937), pp. 101–109.

sider their listening to strangers, to people you know, to each other, to recorded voices which you may present in class, and to the voices of actors, announcers, speakers, and readers on radio, television, public platforms, pulpits, stages, and so on. Indicate how you can determine the effect of your plan on your students' sensitivity to the vocal attributes and variables.

(c) Assume that you are going to use a tape recorder to help each of your students learn to evaluate accurately his own vocal attributes, limitations, patterns, skills, and variables. Explain how you would use the tape recorder to accomplish your objective. Consider time limits, what each student would be asked to record, and details of your plan for stimulating and guiding each student in his analysis of his recording.

(d) After consulting references on Voice Usage, prepare to support your affirmation or denial of each of these statements:

1. Attributes of the human voice disclose significant clues concerning an individual's personal attributes.

2. Voice is perceived by a listener's eardrum being set into vibration by oscillations of air pressure generated by a speaker.

3. A teacher of speech is obligated to stimulate and guide each of his students to develop in his central nervous system automatic control and direction of acceptable voice patterns in speaking.

4. Voice training cannot be successful if attention is centered on voice per se.

5. Voice usage is effective, other things being equal, in proportion to the lung capacity of the speaker.

6. A teacher of speech is safe in assuming that a greater amount of breath is needed to speak loudly than to speak softly.

7. "Air power" is basic to relaxation of the throat, voice resonance and vigor, and sustained voice usage.

8. Good respiration in speech depends upon enough "vital capacity" to enable the speaker to complete each of his phrases without his pausing to breathe.

9. A teacher of speech is obligated to help each student to discover the type of respiration which can best serve his voice production and audible speech.

10. A breathy voice, like a loud whisper, utilizes more "vital capacity" than does a clear, flexible, well-modulated, and unobtrusive voice.

11. Breathing exercises to increase the lung capacities of speakers are a waste of effort and time.

12. Breath control by a speaker is basic to his voice production and to his sustained audible speech.

13. Disorders of vocal loudness vary from that of the person who

can generate no vocal sound to that of the person who has a deficiency in hearing.

14. Disagreeable vocal pitch is either too high or too low, calls attention to itself, reduces efficiency of the speech of the speaker, and results in fatigue and strain.

15. Disorders of vocal quality such as breathiness, harshness, hoarseness, and nasality occur among high school students more frequently than do disorders of vocal loudness and vocal pitch.

(e) Present to the class your plan for stimulating and guiding your students to understand what happens in voice production, why and how it happens, its effect on the formulation of their audible symbols, and its impact on listeners. Consult references on voice production such as those cited at the end of this chapter.

(f) Prepare to lead a discussion on the importance and place of voice training in a course in basic speech development.

(g) Prepare to demonstrate to your class, with equipment from the department of physics in your high school, the principles of loudness, pitch, quality, and duration.

(h) Prepare a list of audio-visual aids which you would recommend for use in voice training. Consider actual objects such as the respiration and voice mechanism of an animal or fowl, charts, films, models, and pictures. Explain how each of them can be used to significant advantage in teaching voice usage.

(i) Select from references such as those cited at the end of this chapter drills and exercises designed for use by your students to:

1. Evaluate their vocal skills.
2. Promote relaxation of the neck and throat muscles.
3. Develop control of loudness in accenting syllables, stressing words, and emphasizing phrases in speaking and reading.
4. Develop control of vocal pitch.
5. Develop each of these vocal qualities: breathy, harsh, hoarse, nasal, and the like.
6. Develop vocal duration with appropriate variety.
7. Develop clear, flexible, well-modulated, and unobtrusive voices responsive to the meaning of prose and poetry selected to challenge expressiveness in voice usage.
8. Promote awareness and sensitivity in speaking and reading.

(j) Prepare a list of audio-visual aids which can be used to advantage in ear training. Consider actual objects, charts, films, models, and pictures. Explain how each of them can be used to stimulate and guide students to understand the function of the ear in listening and speaking. Discuss their likely effect on ear and voice training.

THE "FUNDAMENTALS" APPROACH   161

(*k*) Examine references listed under voice usage at the end of Chapter 5 and prepare a list of at least 25 passages which can profitably be read aloud with varying degrees of loudness, pitch, and duration by students who seek improvement in their voice usage. Demonstrate in class how the passages can be used to develop vocal variation.

(*l*) Explain to the class a plan for helping your students to experiment with different kinds of respiration for speaking to determine the kind best suited for each individual.

(*m*) Bring to class a list of selections of poetry and prose with which you can test the effectiveness of vocal usage by your students in reading aloud. Read two of your selections to determine their potentialities for testing vocal effectiveness.

(*n*) Design an assignment of speechmaking by your students to determine their vocal variation in talking with an audience. Suggest topics on which you would ask your students to talk. Explain how and why the topics would likely elicit from the students effective vocal usage.

7. *Enunciation, Articulation, and Pronunciation.* A person may have a clear, flexible, well-modulated, and unobtrusive voice which responds readily and accurately to meaning but have problems with his enunciation or articulation, or both. Or he may form his speech sounds satisfactorily, but have problems with his pronunciation.

A teacher of speech needs to be prepared to help each of his students to identify and solve his problems of enunciation, articulation, and pronunciation. These processes or acts were learned, initially and probably unconsciously, by imitation. Each student in a class in speech education, like the teacher and every other person, learned his audible speech symbols from his parents and other adults around him who were, probably automatically and inadvertently, his teachers of speech. He learned by "trial and error" and by "trial and at least some success" audible speech sounds and symbols as he heard them produced by people around him. He probably was no more aware of the processes by which he formed the sounds than were the people who taught him. Likewise, he may have learned from other children in school and from teachers and others to form additional speech symbols and to improve those which he learned earlier. He probably succeeded, within his first seven years, in "mastering" his speech sound production as it will be "mastered" when he comes to a teacher of speech in a high school. Until the teacher of speech makes him sensitive to his problems in speech sound production, he may not be concerned about it or, even so, he will likely not be able to identify or solve his problem. If his teacher of speech succeeds in helping him to determine specifically and meaningfully his problem, he will likely be ready and willing to effect improvement in his enunciation, articulation, and pronunciation.

Enunciation and articulation are usually used synonomously. In a broad sense, pronunciation includes both enunciation and articulation. But each of these terms may be used by a teacher of speech and his students to specify a different process of speech sound production and to suggest three slightly different objectives and desired outcomes of speech sound production. Enunciation might be defined as the process of forming a vowel or vowel-like sound by using the velum, lower jaw, tongue, and lips to set up resonance conditions necessary to produce the desired vocal characteristics of each of the vowels. Articulation may be defined as the process of forming a consonant sound by using the vocal bands, palates, tongue, lower jaw, teeth, and lips to obstruct and divert the breath stream, as it is expired, and thereby to build and release pressure necessary to produce the desired distinction of each of the consonants. Pronunciation can be defined as the process of *selecting* and forming vowels and consonants into syllables and words which are spoken with accent on appropriate syllables.

Criteria by which to evaluate the enunciation of vowels are *clarity, accuracy, intelligibility,* and *acceptability.* Each vowel is enunciated by a steady, unobstructed, and relatively unmodified expiration of air which sets the vocal bands or cords into vibration. As explained by Hahn, Hargis, Lomas, and Vandraegen,[34] five conditions must be present for enunciation or for the formation of vowels:

> 1. The vocal folds must be in vibration so that the sound is voiced.
> 2. The velum must be raised so that the opening into the nasal cavity is closed and the breath stream is directed through the oral cavity.
> 3. The mouth must be open, with the tongue tip behind the lower front teeth, so that there is a relatively open passageway from the level of the vocal folds through the lips.
> 4. The lower jaw, the tongue, and the lips must move to vary the size and shape of the oral cavity and of the lip opening to differentiate each sound.
> 5. The position of the articulators (or enunciators) must be held momentarily (the time varying with the vowel) for stable production.

Diphthongs are enunciated as vowels and their enunciation can be evaluated by the criteria of vowel formation. Black and Moore explained diphthongs and their production:

> Two vowels are frequently spoken in rapid succession, or, more precisely, as a glide in which the speaker starts with one vowel and ends

[34] Elise Hahn, Donald E. Hargis, Charles W. Lomas, and Daniel Vandraegen, *op. cit.*

with another. The combination occurs within a syllable and often gives an impression of a single sound to a listener. This dual vowel sound that comes with an unimpeded flow of breath is a *diphthong*.

Many students err doubly in their notions about diphthongs. First, they hear these dual sounds as single vowels and, secondly, assume that diphthongs relate in some manner to two letters in spelling. . . . Diphthongs, or combinations of two vowels, are not necessarily represented in writing by two, three, four, or any particular number of letters. The one-letter word "I" contains two vowels and, therefore, a diphthong. The following words both exemplify the six common diphthongs and illustrate further some of the inconsistencies between spelling and pronunciation. The same diphthong appears throughout a row. (1) boy, soy, boil; (2) I, write, pie, aye, eye; (3) cow, house, bough, bow (verb) or bow wow; (4) you, few, new, united, pneumatic, lute; (5) a, mate, fate, weight, wait, veil; and (6) oh, owe, open, though, sew, roam, yeoman.[35]

Criteria for articulation of consonants are *distinctness, accuracy, intelligibility,* and *acceptability*. Distinctness of audible speech is determined primarily by the preciseness with which consonants are articulated. As stated by Andersch and Staats,

> Upon examination, we find that the final product—the pronounced word—is dependent upon two elements: first, upon the accurate production of the sequence of sounds which go to make up the word (articulation); and second, upon the fitting together of these sounds with proper emphasis or accent so that the resulting symbol is easily recognized (pronunciation).[36]

Although carelessness or slovenliness of articulation is a fault of audible speech by many students in high school, pedantic articulation is not to be desired. In fact, elegant, fancy, and highbrow articulation, like a "beautiful" voice or obviously planned gestures, is probably as confusing, distracting, and unacceptable as "lazy" articulation. A teacher of speech is obligated to help each of his students to enunciate clearly and articulate accurately and distinctly the sequence of sounds which compose his audible speech. Also, each student, in order to be well-motivated and self-directive in developing his articulation to a level of acceptability, needs to learn the distinctive features of consonants as set forth in standard books for beginning students in speech education. Many of these books are cited under "Enunciation, Articulation, and Pronunciation" at the end of this chapter. Hanley and Thurman set forth some concepts and distinctive

---

[35] John W. Black and Wilbur E. Moore, *Speech—Code, Meaning, and Communication*. New York: McGraw-Hill, Inc., 1955. pp. 86–87.

[36] Elizabeth G. Andersch and Lorin C. Staats, *Speech for Everyday Use*, rev. ed. New York: Holt, Rinehart and Winston, Inc., 1960. p. 147.

features of consonants which can be most helpful to the teacher and his students:

> The consonants are the dividing units in connected speech; they often separate the vowels and sometimes influence the beginnings and endings of the vowels, modulating the flow of sound. It is interesting to note that vowels so influenced by initiating and terminating consonants are more easily recognized than vowels produced and heard in isolation. . . . Each of the consonants sounds is presented in this text in terms of three descriptive elements: (1) the place of production of the sound, that is, the locus of blockage, constriction, or diverted air stream; (2) the type of sound, that is, the acoustic nature of the sound, whether fricative, plosive, and so on; (3) the voicing of the sound, that is, whether or not vocal cord tone is present.[37]

A teacher of speech will need to recognize both adequacies and inadequacies in all eight processes in the production of the audible speech code of each of his students: innervation, respiration, phonation, resonance, enunciation, articulation, pronunciation, and audition. Problems of enunciation will likely occur most frequently in a class in speech education in high school. Most of the problems of articulation will stem from general carelessness and slovenliness but some problems may stem from specific speech defects due to organic disorders such as abnormalities of the facial muscles, lips, teeth, tongue, palates, throat, and nose. Speech defects due to organic disorders will likely require aid from a specially trained speech correctionist or physician, or both. However, some specific speech defects such as lisping and stuttering may not be due to organic disorders. If a student needs the services of a specialist other than a teacher of speech, the principal of the high school should be informed about the problem and should either arrange for such services or authorize the teacher of speech to do so. Afterward, the teacher of speech is not absolved from his responsibilities for the student and his speech but, in fact, needs to assume the additional obligation to cooperate with the speech correctionist in helping the student correct or compensate for the defect.

A teacher of speech can stimulate and guide each of most of his students to develop distinct, accurate, intelligible, and acceptable articulation. The following pattern should prove to be helpful:

(*a*) Make certain the student can recognize the consonant as he misarticulates it.

(*b*) Make certain the student can recognize the consonant as he hears it articulated distinctly, accurately, intelligibly, and acceptably.

(*c*) Show the student how to articulate the consonant acceptably in isolation.

[37] Theodore D. Hanley and Wayne L. Thurman, *Developing Vocal Skills*. New York: Holt, Rinehart and Winston, Inc., 1962. pp. 70–71.

(*d*) Test the student's ability to articulate the consonant in isolation.

(*e*) Reinforce the student's ability to articulate the consonant acceptably, easily, and readily in isolation.

(*f*) Test the student's ability to alternate readily between his articulation of the consonant and his misarticulation of it.

(*g*) Give the student practice in articulating the consonant in initial, medial, and especially final positions in words, depending, of course, on the positions in which the consonant appears in words and especially on the positions in which the student misarticulated the consonant.

(*h*) Test the student's articulation of the consonant as he reads aloud and speaks.

(*i*) Work to make the student's acceptable articulation of the consonant habitual in his conversational speech.

Acceptable spoken English comprises no fewer than fifteen vowels, five diphthongs, and twenty-two consonants. Also, consonants vary considerably in the manner in which they are articulated acceptably, as stated by Hahn and her associates:

1. The vocal folds may or may not vibrate depending on whether the consonant is voiced or voiceless.

2. The velum [soft palate] must be raised, closing off the nasal passage, for all except the three nasal consonants.

3. The oral cavity must be blocked or narrowed for each sound.

4. The lower jaw, the tongue, and the lips must move to form the narrowing or block.

5. The articulators either hold the position for the consonant or glide through it depending upon the nature of the sound.[38]

Criteria for the evaluation of pronunciation are *clarity, distinctness, accuracy, intelligibility, correctness,* and *acceptability*. In pronunciation vowel sounds in syllables need to be enunciated *clearly;* consonant sounds need to be articulated *distinctly;* and both need to be selected and formed *accurately, intelligibly,* and *acceptably* into syllables and words. In addition and, of course, simultaneously, syllables in words need to be selected and accentuated *correctly* and *acceptably* as words need to be selected and formed correctly and acceptably into phrases with stress on the appropriate word to help the listener attach to the phrase the meaning intended by the speaker. Likewise, phrases need to be selected and formed correctly and acceptably into sentences, either stated explicitly or implicitly, with emphasis on the appropriate phrase or phrases to help the listener attach to each sentence the meaning intended by the speaker.

Lexicographers, linguists, and phoneticians are not agreed on what constitutes "acceptable," "correct," or "standard" pronunciation. An ex-

[38] Elise Hahn, Donald E. Hargis, Charles W. Lomas, and Daniel Vandraegen, *op. cit.* pp. 164–165.

amination of any two different dictionaries to determine the acceptable and correct pronunciation and exact meaning of each of many words can easily result in bafflement. For example, what is the acceptable and correct pronunciation of "adult," "Alma Mater," "amen," "apparatus," "applicable," "biography," "blessed," "comparable," "coupon," and "dictionary?" The *Winston Simplified Dictionary*, Encyclopedic Edition, 1929, presents one "acceptable" and "correct" pronunciation for each of these words. Funk and Wagnalls' *New College Standard Dictionary*, Emphatype Edition, 1956, presents one pronunciation which varies from Winston's for three of the words. *Webster's New International Dictionary*, Second Edition, 1958, presents two "acceptable" and "correct" pronunciations for each of the words. Three different pronunciations for each of at least two of the words are given in all three dictionaries. But these are only a few examples of hundreds of words for which the pronunciation varies in dictionaries.

The exact meaning of many words is difficult to determine by consulting a dictionary. For example, "articulation," "enunciation," and "pronunciation" are hardly defined exactly in any one or in all three of the dictionaries just cited. However, a dictionary is probably the best available guide for acceptable and correct pronunciation by teachers and students of speech. Lexicographers know that the pronunciation of words, except those used infrequently, changes during the course of their conscientious and meticulous preparation and publication of a new edition of a dictionary. Also, most dictionaries do not indicate differences in pronunciation of a word in the major dialect regions of the United States: (1) Eastern—designating especially states along the Atlantic Seaboard; (2) Southern—designating especially the states of Alabama, Georgia, Louisiana, and Mississippi; and (3) General American—designating most states in the Central and Western sections of the country. In fact, most dictionaries reflect the pronunciation in the General American region. However, a teacher of speech may well use his copy of *A Pronouncing Dictionary of American English* by Kenyon and Knott which records the pronunciation of words in each of the three dialect regions as stated by them.

§2. Colloquial pronunciation is here treated as the conversational and familiar utterance of cultivated speakers when speaking in the normal contacts of life and concerned with what they are saying, not how they are saying it. There are, of course, different styles of colloquial, from that of the everyday contacts of family life to the somewhat less familiar contacts of social and business or professional life. The variant pronunciations of the same word frequently shown will often reflect the different styles of the colloquial. In all cases of words that are not formal per se, unstudied everyday speech is the basis. It is of course true that the majority of words in general use are the same for colloquial as for formal language, and are pronounced alike in both styles.

> By permission. From A Pronouncing Dictionary of American English, Copyright 1953 by G. & C. Merriam Co., Publishers of Merriam Webster Dictionaries.

Every teacher of speech would probably be delighted to know that his pronunciation, including his enunciation and articulation, is clear, distinct, accurate, intelligible, correct, and acceptable. But how is he to evaluate the correctness and acceptability of his pronunciation and that of his students? Gray and Wise have offered him counsel as follows.

> Correct pronunciation may be defined as the pronunciation of the educated, careful speakers of the general region in which a person happens to have formed his speech habits.... "Correctness," or acceptability, if one prefers the latter term, is essentially a matter of agreement among speakers as to the particular manner in which they prefer to utter words; different general regions have arrived through linguistic processes at different agreements, any one of which, for its respective region, is entirely acceptable. It follows, then, that there can be no "correct" pronunciation except in terms of its acceptability.
>
> Listening to good speakers will give additional ideas as to current tendencies, for pronunciations are constantly, though slowly, changing. As a general rule, the pronunciation indicated by any good dictionary should be acceptable....[39]

A teacher of speech can "tune his ears" and needs to stimulate and guide his students to tune theirs to pronunciations by educated, careful speakers, including himself, in the school and community, on radio and television networks, on platforms and stages, and on the theater screen.

High school students should understand the workings of an acceptable dictionary. Diacritical marks as well as syllabication may become the responsibility of a teacher of speech. Each student needs help in evaluating his own pronunciation, including his enunciation and articulation, and in setting up standards for his own achievement.

Time spent on helping students to become familiar with the common types of pronunciation errors will be time well spent. These include substitution of one sound for another, adding a sound not needed, omitting a sound that is required, inverting sounds, and misplacing the accent.

Many teachers of speech in high schools are probably missing an opportunity, perhaps because they lack confidence in teaching phonetic symbols, to give their students work in phonetics as a most effective means of helping them to study the sounds of English speech. Rasmussen has reported success with a ten- to fifteen-day unit in a required course in speech education in high school.[40]

Every teacher of speech could probably increase remarkably his efficiency and effectiveness *if he were to teach his students to use the International Phonetic Alphabet.* The ability to use phonetic symbols can

---

[39] Giles W. Gray and Claude M. Wise, *op. cit.* pp. 56–57.

[40] Don Rasmussen, "High School Students Can Take Phonetics—And Like It," *Central States Speech Journal,* Fall 1955, pp. 17–18.

be valuable in the study of audible speech. In fact, phonetics probably embodies the most basic skills in studying speech sounds and in representing the sounds accurately. The alphabet of the International Phonetics Association consists of at least fifty symbols. Each symbol represents a phoneme or family of sounds enough alike to be represented by a single symbol. True, variations within a phoneme, called allophones, do occur; but, for the purpose of teaching speech, each symbol represents one speech sound only and each speech sound is represented by one symbol only. For each student it is, obviously, important that he be able and willing to analyze his sound usage and that of other people, including his teacher's. If a student possesses these basic tools for analyzing speech sound usage, he is likely to be much better motivated and able to detect and correct his audible speech errors, enunciate his vowels clearly, articulate his consonants distinctly, and pronounce his syllables and words accurately, intelligibly, correctly, and acceptably.

The auvitor, or audio-visual tutor, holds promise in teaching articulation, enunciation, and pronunciation as well as other oral and written language skills. It was devised to teach phonetics as a system to be learned habitually and to teach other language skills using phonetics as the medium of intercommunication between a student and the machine. College students and their teachers alike have demonstrated much enthusiasm for the students' mastering each phonetic skill as they worked with the auvitor system. Although college students have learned, by using simulated models of the auvitor, to transcribe messages phonetically with near perfect accuracy after only fifteen hours of instruction, auvitor techniques of instruction are applicable at any educational level. Its portability enables the auvitor to be used by a student for home and school instruction. The machine is versatile in presenting stimuli to a student orally, phonetically, pictorially, printed, or in any combination. A student's response can also be in any or all of these forms. The subject matter may be in the form of a word, a phrase, a sentence, a paragraph, a picture, a sound, a question to be answered, or in any combination. Each student can work at his own pace in developing his skill in comprehending, for example, each of the phonetic symbols and each of the sounds represented by the symbols.[41]

Activities which can help the teacher of speech to prepare in advance for helping each of his students to develop clear enunciation, distinct articulation, and acceptable pronunciation are:

(a) Prepare a test with which to determine the needs of high school

---

[41] For information about the Mast Teaching Machine, Model 1700-L, and the Auvitor Sound Unit, Model 1740, and their Phonetics Program, write to the Mast Development Company, 2212 East Twelfth Street, Davenport, Iowa.

students in their enunciation of vowel and articulation of consonant sounds. Consult references cited under "Enunciation, Articulation, and Pronunciation" at the end of this chapter. Demonstrate the use of your test by administering it to the class.

(b) Explain the relationships between innervation, respiration, phonation, resonance, pronunciation, and audition to enunciation and articulation. What are the differences between vowels and vowel formation and consonants and consonant formation?

(c) Outline procedures for helping each student to recognize any specific inadequacies and defects in his enunciation and articulation. Consider: (1) recording his audible speech in his speaking and reading aloud; (2) using sentences loaded especially with all or most vowel and consonant sounds; (3) using word lists with each vowel sound preceded and succeeded by a combination of consonant sounds and with consonant sounds in initial, medial, and final positions in words; (4) recording his brief conversation with his teacher who stimulates and guides him in answering questions designed to reveal differences, when the recording is reproduced, in his vowel sound formation in conversation from that in his reading aloud and his speechmaking; and (5) using recordings by actors and speakers who are especially agile and competent in speech sound formation.

(d) Construct a chart for each student's use in recording his adequacies and inadequacies in enunciation and articulation. Consider arranging on the chart: (1) vowel, diphthong, and consonant sounds in phonetic symbols; (2) places for rating his clarity, distinctness, accuracy, and intelligibility of each sound; (3) notations of specific causes of his inadequacies and defects of each sound; and (4) suggested procedures for improvement. Consult references at the end of this chapter for your analysis of other such charts.

(e) Explain to the class how a teacher of speech should use projects 1 and 2, pages 246–249, in *General Speech,* First Edition, by A. Craig Baird and Franklin H. Knower. If you choose to revise either or both projects for your use, accomplish the revisions. Then, administer at least a portion of each project to members of the class to demonstrate the practicality of each project in testing the enunciation and articulation of students of speech. You are invited to use both phonetic symbols and diacritical marks in both projects.

(f) Plan reading assignments on enunciation and articulation for high school students. Consult textbooks such as those listed at the end of this chapter. Report to the class an outline of the assignments which you prepare and explain what you believe high school students should know after accomplishing the assignments.

(g) Prepare an outline of considerations and procedures for your use in referring a student with an articulatory or other speech defect to a speech correctionist. Consider: (1) the attitude of the student toward referral and its likely effect on him, (2) the wishes of his parents, (3) the responsibility of the principal, (4) the attitude of other students toward the student with the handicap and the probable effect of their attitude on him, and (5) the attitude of other teachers who have the student with the defect in their classes and who find him to be doing excellent work or mediocre work in their classes.

(*h*) Collect from textbooks in speech education, such as those cited at the end of this chapter, exercises which you recommend for use by students and their teachers in improving students' enunciation and articulation. Consider exercises for developing: (1) relaxation of the neck and throat, (2) control of respiration for speaking, (3) support of vocal tone, (4) control and variation of vocal pitch, (5) relaxation of the lower jaw, (6) control and flexibility of the tongue, (7) function of the palate and uvula, and (8) agility and control of the lips.

(*i*) Report to the class the potential uses of records, such as the following in teaching enunciation and articulation: (1) *The Sounds of English* by W. C. Greet, (2) *Everyday Sentences in Spoken English* by H. E. Palmer, (3) *Poems* recorded by Ogden Nash, (4) *Anthology of English Lyrics* by Cornelia Otis Skinner, (5) *Shakespeare* by John Barrymore, (6) *A Christmas Carol* recorded by Ernest Chappell, and (7) *Bible Stories* recorded by Ronald Colman. You are invited to collect and to report, likewise, on other records which you would recommend.

(*j*) View films such as the following: (1) *Your Tell-Tale Voice*, American Telephone and Telegraph Company; (2) *Mechanics of Breathing and Your Voice*, Encyclopaedia Britannica; and (3) *Using Your Voice*, Young American Films. You are invited to make a list of other available films and to view them. After viewing each film, list items found in it that can be helpful to high school students in improving their (1) respiration for speech, (2) enunciation of vowel sounds, (3) articulation of consonant sounds, (4) vocal pitch variation, (5) control of voice range, and (6) communication of meaning.

(*k*) Present to the class your evaluation of the unit on "Voice and Articulation," pages 41–45, in *Teaching Speech* by Loren D. Reid.

(*l*) Demonstrate in class your teaching of front, central, and back vowel sound production with the aid of a vowel chart.

(*m*) Demonstrate in class your teaching of the articulation of affricatives, fricatives, nasals, plosives, and the semivowel. You may assume that other members of the class are your students for your demonstration. Use the blackboard, a chart, or other visual aids in your demonstration.

(*n*) Compile on 4 x 6 cards tongue twisters and other drills found in most textbooks on speech education for use by high school students in a beginning course in speech. Explain how you could use the collection in teaching enunciation and articulation.

(o) Devise a plan for using phonetic symbols in teaching "correct" and "acceptable" pronunciation. Do likewise in using diacritical marks. Explain the advantages and disadvantages in using each of the two sets of symbols.

(p) Support your affirmation or denial of each of the following statements: (1) Pronunciation of a word is correct if it is used by a sufficient number of the most cultivated speakers in a community; (2) The function of a pronouncing dictionary is to record pronunciations prevailing in the best usage, not to dictate pronunciations; (3) A colloquialism is a localism which should be avoided in speaking; (4) Colloquial pronunciation is the conversational and familiar utterance of cultivated speakers when speaking in the normal contacts of life and concerned with what they are saying, not how they are saying it; (5) To be sure of the correct pronunciation of his name, a person should consult the best available pronouncing dictionary; (6) The student who asks his teacher of speech for the correct way to pronounce a word calls for an answer based on a false assumption; (7) A vowel is an open, unobstructed utterance of voice or whisper without audible friction above the larynx; (8) A consonant is a speech sound characterized by a definite stoppage at some point in the breath passage that modifies the sound and marks its character; (9) A syllable is one or more speech sounds forming an uninterrupted unit of utterance; (10) The first pronunciation given in a dictionary is always the best pronunciation; and (11) A teacher of speech is, of course, concerned with helping his students to achieve the normal speech of educated people.

(q) What are the most plausible causes of differences in English pronunciations? Consider: (1) climate; (2) differences in the speech mechanisms of people; (3) differences in the effort, energy, and time; (4) faulty imitation; (5) faulty listening; (6) mixture of the races; and (7) racial temperament.

(r) Outline and present to the class your plan for helping students to pronounce correctly and acceptably each of these words:

abdomen	bade	creek
advertisement	because	dance
any	blue	data
apparatus	chauffeur	debate
arctic	chocolate	depot
ask	class	details
athletic	column	detour
aunt	coupon	dictionary

dramatist	irrefutable	precedence
drown	irrelevant	presentation
either	just	program
envelope	lamentable	often
finance	larynx	ration
forehead	leisure	research
garage	library	roof
get	literature	schedule
government	luxury	secretive
half	men	stationery
height	mischievous	statistics
humor	Monday	status
hundred	necessary	suite
idea	news	theater
illustrate	pen	toward
infantile	penalize	Tuesday
inquiry	pianist	what

(*s*) Examine at least five textbooks cited at the end of this chapter to find the kinds of methods and materials suggested for teaching correct and acceptable pronunciation. Report your findings to the class.

(*t*) Compile a list of words which are often mispronounced due to (1) additions, (2) distortions, (3) omissions, and (4) substitutions. Map out a plan for helping students to correct each kind of mispronunciation.

8. *Language.* The word "language" has many meanings. In any discussion of oral communication, the definition of language which is generally accepted limits its meaning to the conventional sounds which makes up words and to the use of those words in grammatical relationships. A teacher of speech is concerned, therefore, with language as a study of words and the ways of putting words together acceptably and effectively to evoke the meaning in the listener desired by the speaker.

In speaking the choice of words is, of course, of utmost importance. Without the proper selection of words, the speaker promotes the possibility of a breakdown in the two-way communicative process between the speaker and the listener. Certain words may stir up unfavorable reactions in the minds of the listeners; others may make it difficult for them to understand. A teacher of speech in high school needs to stimulate and guide students to become aware of the importance of their word choice in their efforts to speak purposefully and understandably. Work on vocabulary, emphasis on denotative and connotative meanings of words, the changing meaning of words, problems of semantics, and words in their contextual use are all aspects of language which the teacher of speech can cover with his students to their great advantage.

Basic principles of language usage have been formulated by many writers. Andersch and Staats[42] have indicated the following positive steps which can be taken by a speaker to improve the language of his speaking:

    a. Be exact in your use of words.
    b. Avoid overworked words.
    c. Use vivid and colorful language.
    d. Adapt your language to the situation.
    e. Always use language that is in good taste.
    f. Avoid verbosity.
    g. Make a real effort to build a vocabulary to suit your needs.

Other writers have indicated that the speaker must adapt his language to his purpose, to his audience, to the occasion, and to himself; must be accurate in his use of language; must use concrete words; must use an "oral" style; must use variety and vividness in word choice; must use frequent repetition in speaking; and must include variety in kinds and lengths of sentences.

Suggested means for improving one's oral style of speaking include careful listening to effective speech, speaking, and speechmaking by speakers in person or on magnetic tapes or other means of reproduction. Reading, especially reading aloud, can also be a great help in the use of language. Reading aloud tends to increase the student's speech vocabulary and makes him more aware of sentence patterns and vivid phrasing. Speaking often can also help the student learn to use language well if he is stimulated and guided to correct bad habits of language usage he may have acquired. Writing can also aid a speaker in the development of his language usage. Language growth through reading, speaking, and writing has been illustrated by such author-speakers as Quintilian, Edmund Burke, Benjamin Franklin, Woodrow Wilson, Winston Churchill, and others. Vocabulary study is another important means of improving one's language. All of these means for improving language and language usage can be employed in courses in speech education. In fact, in order to be most effective, they are appropriate for use in every classroom in a high school.

Closely allied to all methods for teaching language usage is the problem of grammar. Brandeis[43] outlined a plan with which he evidently believed the problem could be solved. He stated:

> . . . the speech student in high school and in college should seek to establish speech which meets, within reason, the demands of acceptable grammar. . . . The "within reason" clause above should allow him not only to retain the strengths of his regionalisms, but also to be proud of

[42] Elizabeth G. Andersch and Lorin C. Staats, *op. cit.*, p. 119.
[43] Paul D. Brandeis, "Grammar and Pronunciation in the Speech Classroom," *The Speech Teacher*, vol. 8, no. 3 (September 1959), p. 236.

them as a part of his heritage. The general attitude that language change is an integral part of a dynamic, interesting world should be made clear.

Language has been defined in various ways. Each definition has significance for a teacher of speech and his students. Concerning one important concept of language, Hayakawa wrote:

> When someone shouts at you, "Look out!" and you duck in time to avoid being hit by a thrown ball, you owe your escape from injury to the fundamental cooperative act by which most of the higher animals survive: namely, communication by means of noises. You did not see the ball coming; nevertheless, someone did see it coming, and he made certain *noises to communicate* his alarm to you. . . . Indeed, most of the time when we are listening to the noises that people make or looking at the black marks on paper that stand for such noises, we are drawing upon the experiences of the nervous systems of others in order to make up what our own nervous systems have missed. . . . Human beings use extremely complicated systems of sputtering, hissing, gurgling, clucking, and cooing noises called *language*, with which they express and report what goes on in their nervous systems. . . . When a man says, "I see a river," a second man can say, "He says he sees a river"—which is a statement about a statement. About this statement-about-a-statement, further statements can be made—and about those still more. *Language, in short, can be about language.*
>
> In addition to having developed language, man has also developed means of making, on clay tablets, bits of wood or stone, skins of animals, and paper, more or less permanent marks and scratches which *stand* for language.[44]

Language may, therefore, be interpreted as voiced and unvoiced sounds arranged in various combinations of syllables and words which are pronounced by a speaker to stir up meaning in a listener and to evoke from him a response desired by the speaker. If a teacher of speech accepts this concept as his teaching definition of language, exclusive of all others, and insists that the others merely *stand for* language, he, thereby, indicates that language is not a fundamental of speech but rather it is audible speech itself. He can, of course, support his position by citing the practices of many teachers of speech and testimony by language authorities such as Scott, Carr, and Wilkinson who wrote:

> Since civilized peoples employ written words as well as spoken words in conveying thought and feeling, the form in which language is recorded must be taken into account, as well as the uttered sounds of speech, in any study of what language is and what it has been. In the early history

[44] Samuel I. Hayakawa, *Language in Action.* New York: Harcourt, Brace & World, Inc., 1941. pp. 15–17.

of mankind language was only vocal sound. Today there are persons who read more words in a day than they speak or hear. In no language does the written form attempt to record all the variations in the utterance of the speakers of that language. As a result the educated person recognizes words both by the eye and by the ear, and there is often a striking lack of agreement between the written form and a graphic representation of the spoken word.[45]

But even if spoken language did antedate and does, in each instance, precede written language as is generally accepted, the teaching of both spoken and written language is an important function of a teacher of speech in a high school. Probably an extensive knowledge of the exact meaning of English words and ability to organize them in various meaningful combinations in both speaking and writing accompany outstanding success in this country more than any other single characteristic subject to isolation and measurement.[46] Dewey supported the significance of language, especially when he wrote:

> Three typical views have been maintained regarding the relation of thought and language; first, that they are identical; second, that words are the garb or clothing of thought but only for carrying it; and third, that while language is not thought, it is necessary for thinking as well as for communication.[47]

Neither a teacher of English nor any other teacher in a high school seems to have greater responsibility or authority, except by possible delegation and tradition, than a teacher of speech to teach the English language as a fundamental of listening, reading, speaking, writing, and successful enterprise. Also, other meaningful forms and kinds of language are important, sometimes instantaneously effective, and even crucial, under some circumstances, in communication such as signals at street intersections, signs and signals on highways, railways, and airways, pictorial symbols in oriental writing, ideograph figures in books and periodicals, signals used by members of production staffs in radio and television, sign language by deafmutes, and artistry of actors and speakers. In all such forms and kinds of language, the objective is to communicate *intelligibly, accurately, meaningfully,* and *acceptably* with listeners, observers, and readers who may be removed in space or time, or both, from the communicator.

Mario Pei, in discussing the constituent elements of language, stated:

[45] Harry F. Scott, Wilbur L. Carr, and Gerald T. Wilkinson, *Language and Its Growth—An Introduction to the History of Language.* Chicago: Scott, Foresman and Company, 1935. pp. 1 and 2.
[46] A. R. Bandini, "Words—And Little Else," *Better English*, November 1939, pp. 9–16.
[47] John Dewey, *op. cit.,* p. 230.

... since the main characteristic of language is meaningfulness and since a transfer of meaning can take place without the medium of sound, ... the phonetic aspect of language is secondary to the semantic feature. To the grammarian, language is primarily a series of grammatical forms, roots, and endings. To the literary specialist, language is a series of words so arranged as to produce a harmonious or logical effect. To the lexicographer, language is fundamentally a list of words with their separate derivations, histories, and meanings. To the man in the street, language is what he uses, quite unconsciously, to communicate with his fellow men. Obviously, these partial definitions are all correct. But precisely because they are *all* correct, the sum total of language amounts to something greater than any of them. Sounds in themselves do not constitute language, yet the spoken language consists of sounds. Meaningfulness may be achieved in a number of non-linguistic ways, therefore meaningfulness alone does not constitute language; yet language, to be worthy of the name, must be meaningful. Grammatical forms and grammatical categories, taken by themselves, are dead things ... yet language is characterized by their presence to the extent that there is no language, however primitive, that does not possess some system of grammar. Spoken and written language consists of separate words; but unless these words are arranged in certain sequences, they will not only fail to convey beauty or logic, but will even fail to convey complete meaning. Lastly, a language that does not serve as a medium of communication is a traitor to its function.[48]

The following objectives and implied procedures are suggested for achievement in teaching language:

(a) To help students understand language, its forms, kinds, and usage, and its importance in communication.

(b) To lead students to formulate criteria by which language comprehension, appreciation, and usage can be validly evaluated by them.

(c) To stimulate and guide students to analyze and evaluate their own language comprehension, appreciation, and usage as well as the language of others.

(d) To lead each student to set up goals for his own achievement in his language comprehension, appreciation, and usage.

(e) To stimulate and guide each student to develop, to a high level of his language potential, his will and ability to comprehend and appreciate language and to use it intelligibly, accurately, meaningfully, and acceptably.

(f) To help students develop increasingly the quality and quantity of their vocabularies.

[48] Mario Pei, *The Story of Language*. Philadelphia: J. B. Lippincott Company, 1949. pp. 95–96.

(g) To help students develop their appreciation of language style and its attributes in their listening, reading, speaking, and writing.

(h) To help students develop their understanding and appreciation for semantic changes in language.

Many teachers of speech have made effective use of such activities as the following in teaching a unit on language:

(a) Read about language in references cited under "Language" at the end of this chapter. Present in class your explanation and your outline of procedures for helping students to understand each of the following: (1) Language—Its Meaning and Importance, (2) Theories of the Origin of Language, (3) The Kinds and Causes of Changes in Language, (4) Sources of New Words, (5) Why Obsolescence in Language, (6) Kinds of Semantic Changes, (7) Connotative and Denotative Words, (8) Idioms and Homophones, (9) The Effect of Slang, (10) The Importance of "Correct" Language Usage, (11) The Basis of Authority in Language Usage.

(b) Concepts, experiences, events, and objects to which words refer are called "referents." Explain how you believe high school students could be stimulated and guided to become habituated in distinguishing words from referents.

(c) Explain the differences between connotative and denotative meanings of words. Outline a plan for helping high school students to recognize the differences and to demonstrate both connotative and denotative meanings in their language usage.

(d) Prepare a list of vocabulary tests appropriate for testing the vocabularies of high school students. Explain their merits and demerits and how they could be used in teaching vocabulary.

(e) Discuss differences and likenesses between oral and written language.

(f) Explain how a teacher could use a tape recorder in teaching language usage to high school students.

(g) Select speeches of today and of the past which can be used as excellent examples of effective language usage for analysis by students of language. Make an effort to select speeches which comprise both colloquial and distinguished language usage. Explain how you would use them in your class.

(h) Select paragraphs from six or more speeches and submit in class a plan for stimulating and guiding your students to rewrite each paragraph in an effort by them to substitute more accurate and specific words to achieve better language usage.

(i) Compile a list of topics for speeches of description by your students. Plan an assignment designed to emphasize effective language usage in the speeches and in the analysis of each speech in class. Support your topics and plan in class.

(*j*) Formulate your criteria for the evaluation of language usage. Present in class the criteria and your support.

(*k*) Select one speech and show in class how the language would need to be changed if it were delivered to several different audiences in several different situations.

(*l*) Select one article from a magazine, one article from a newspaper, and one ad and underline all of the connotative terms in each. Come to class prepared to support values to be derived from such an exercise in language usage.

(*m*) Discuss and illustrate "levels of language usage."

(*n*) Come to class prepared to write one general word on the blackboard and then have the class members add ten specific words which could be used in place of it. Explain values to be derived from the exercise.

(*o*) Bring to class a list of at least ten words which illustrate each of three semantic changes in the English language.

(*p*) Present in class the framework of a unit with which you would hope to teach high school students to understand English language usage and to help them to effect improvement in their comprehension, appreciation, and use of the English language.

(*q*) Examine references listed under "Language" at the end of this chapter, especially those designed for use by high school students. Report to the class the kind and extent of treatment of language in the various references.

9. *Adaptation in the Speech Situation.* Success in speaking and speechmaking is dependent upon the speaker's adapting his thought, language, and bodily action to the audience. Such adaptation will be conditioned by the audience and the occasion. Oftentimes, some adaptation must be accomplished prior to the actual speaking or reading; other times, it will have to be done after meeting the audience with little or no prior indication of a need for adaptation. Regardless of when it is accomplished, students need to be alert to the need for adaptation. Skillful and effective adaptation is almost impossible without predictions concerning the characteristics of the prospective audience.

Audience analysis is vital to effective speaking. Knowing as much as possible about the listeners, their interests, cultural level, attitude toward the topic, and attitude toward the speaker will be very helpful. Using this information to adapt to the audience is necessary. Primary questions often asked in audience analysis include: Who will be in the audience? What are they like? What do they know about my topic already? What is their attitude toward my topic and what I intend to say about it? What is likely to be their mood while I am speaking? This type of information and the analysis of it can lead to considerable adaptation to the audience prior to meeting it.

Adaptation may be necessary during the performance. The size, shape, and acoustics of the room may make it vital for a speaker, reader, or other platform or stage performer to adapt his vocal projection. Whether he is the only speaker or one of a series of speakers and the order in which he speaks may make some adaptation necessary. Interruptions such as a door slamming, a fire engine going by, a class dismissal bell, and so on, may call for immediate adaptation to the audience by overcoming such distractions. Often it may be necessary for him to make adaptation in his language usage depending upon the educational level of his audience. Talking to a third grade class is much different from talking on the same topic to a Parent Teachers' Association or a high school faculty. The presence or absence or breakdown of a public address system may call for immediate adaptation. Many experienced speakers have made effective adaptation to the chairman's introduction. These types of adaptations need to be pointed out to students and suggestions given for helping them make changes as needed.

Many teachers of speech believe that adaptation should be taught along with the other fundamentals of speech. However, it can be treated as a separate fundamental and attention should probably be focused on it since it is so vital to speaking and speechmaking, to oral interpretation, and to other forms of speaking. The teacher of speech can work toward helping his students to become acquainted with the need for adaptation in the speech situation, helping them work out suggestions for making necessary adaptations, and providing them with as much experience in speaking as possible to give them opportunities for specific adaptations.

Some suggested activities to help in teaching adaptation in the speech situation are:

(a) Examine references under "Adaptation in the Speech Situation" at the end of this chapter. Explain in class how and why you would teach adaptation. Consider: (1) adaptation of the audience to the speaker and the speaker to the audience, (2) adaptation of the speaker to his objective and subject, and (3) adaptation of the objective and subject to the audience and the audience to the objective and subject.

(b) Prepare to affirm, deny, or modify each: (1) The difference between talking to one person and to a hundred or more people is insignificant, except in the speaker's mind; (2) If a speaker speaks normally at 150 words per minute, on the average, he will need to speak slowly—

perhaps 125 or even 100 words per minute—in talking with a very large audience; (3) Other things being equal, the rate of speaking should be adjusted to the chronological age of the audience; (4) Audiences want to understand speakers' ideas rather than to be impressed with their extraordinary skills and techniques; (5) Adjustment in speech situations is learned only from experience in speaking in a variety of situations; (6) The speech mechanism serves more fundamental functions than speaking and, therefore, can not be relied upon to behave properly when you speak to a large audience; (7) Speech fright can be conquered and need not, therefore, be a deterrent to adjustment in a speech situation; (8) Naturalness of a speaker is the best single criterion of both adjustment and effectiveness; (9) In a speech situation, the audience more than any other factor affects adaptation by the speaker; and (10) When a speaker is at his best in a speech situation, he is most eloquent.

(c) Prepare a list of speeches in each of which the speaker has obviously made an effort to accomplish adaptation in the situation. Explain in class what each of them did and how you could use each of their speeches in teaching students to adapt in speech situations.

(d) Prepare a list of topics appropriate for impromptu speeches by high school students. Explain how the topics could be used in teaching adaptation. What are the advantages and disadvantages of encouraging students to make impromptu speeches in a class in speech education?

(e) During a series of speeches by members of a class, students selected in advance by the teacher may be permitted to heckle each speaker after a certain amount of his speaking time has elapsed. Do you approve? Why? Why not?

(f) Compile a list of questions which you would want answered about a speech situation in which you were anxious to speak effectively and successfully. Consider questions about (1) the audience, (2) the occasion, (3) the purpose, (4) the topic, (5) the desired outcome, and (6) any other factor. Attempt to establish in class your right and obligation to obtain reasonably specific and correct answers to each of your questions. Explain how you believe your questions could be used in teaching students to make adjustments in speech situations.

(g) Assume that students in your class are going to address a group in a neighboring town. Have each of half of the class members write a letter to the chairman of the program asking about the situation. Have each member of the other half of the class reply to one of the letters. Explain the likely effect on students' adjustment during their speechmaking in class.

(h) If, during assigned speeches, the students and the teacher in a class in high school are to evaluate the adaptation by each speaker, what criteria should be used to determine each student's degree of adjustment in the situation?

10. *Listening*. Some teachers may object to the inclusion of "Listening" as a fundamental of speech. They may point to courses in "communication skills" in some colleges or to courses in "language arts" in some high schools and

> ... emphasize that the process of communication is predominantly composed of four skills: reading, writing, speaking, and listening.[49]

They may insist that, whereas speaking is an "expressive art," listening is a "receptive art." However, speaking and "speechmaking" imply listening. Although Wiksell stated in 1946 that "very little recorded effort has been found which attempts to define listening per se,"[50] listening is interpreted here to mean the act of attaching meaning to the audible symbols or visible bodily signals, or both, by a speaker to stir up meaning in an audience and thereby elicit from it the response desired by the speaker. As it is interpreted here, it includes, but is not limited to, auditory and visual reception and perception. In addition, it includes interpretation of what is perceived and, therefore, comprehension, even though only instantaneous, of the meaning intended by the speaker. Preferably, it includes comprehension of the exact meaning intended by the speaker. Because listening is an integral part of the process of speaking and "speechmaking," because a teacher of speech in a high school finds it necessary to give attention to the problem of listening by each student who has much more opportunity to listen than to speak, and because listening by members of each speaker's audience and by himself is important to the speaker, it is included as a fundamental of speech.

In Chapter 6, the reader will find an example of a resource unit on listening. This unit includes much basic information on listening as a fundamental of speech. Teachers of speech know that speakers as well as members of an audience need to listen. Speakers need to comprehend and to retain what is said. Many people have observed that the most effective speakers are those who listen attentively and carefully. Careful listening is almost always revealed in their remarks at the beginning of their speaking and sometimes intermittently throughout their speaking. Their adaptation depends, in part, on their careful listening. The improvement of the personal speech habits of any speaker is dependent on his ability to recognize, interpret, and comprehend the meanings stirred up in his audi-

---

[49] Ralph G. Nichols, "Factors in Listening Comprehension," *Speech Monographs*, vol. 15, no. 2 (1948), pp. 154–163.

[50] Wesley Wiksell, "The Problem of Listening," *The Quarterly Journal of Speech*, vol. 32, no. 4 (December 1946), pp. 505–508.

ence by his voice, enunciation, articulation, pronunciation, language, and visible bodily action. This means also that he needs to listen to the signals by members of his audience.

Sometimes a teacher of speech may indicate by his effort to emphasize the listener's role in the communicative act that the listener has primary responsibility for effective communication in a speech situation. The teacher should guard against giving this impression. The function of the speaker should not be relegated, surely, to a secondary role. On the contrary, each speaker needs to be continuously aware of his responsibilities to his listeners for his speaking to achieve socially worthy objectives, for the significance, soundness, and veracity of what he says, for saying exactly what he means to say, and for eliciting from his listeners socially desirable responses. Freedom of a speaker to speak implies his commensurate responsibilities to his listeners and to himself. Freedom to listen or not to listen implies responsibilities of the listener: (1) to determine his purpose for listening; (2) to listen with altertness, courtesy, patience, and respect for the right of the speaker to speak; (3) to concentrate, depending, of course, on the suitability of his purpose for listening in the situation, on comprehending the meaning intended by the speaker; (4) to retain his ideas long enough to evaluate the purpose of the speaker and his desired outcome, the accuracy and soundness of the ideas, their relevance to the purpose and desired outcome; and (5) to exercise discrimination in what he will accept and what he will reject.

A teacher of speech can work toward these objectives in teaching listening: (1) to stimulate and guide students to understand the significance of listening for both the audience and the speaker; (2) to help students develop their abilities and wills to comprehend the meaning intended as they interpret the audible symbols and visible bodily signals by speakers, actors, discussants, oral interpreters, debaters, and others; and (3) to help students develop their appreciation of speakers' responsibility in aiding their listeners.

Activities which can be helpful in achieving these objectives are:

(*a*) Examine references such as those listed under "Listening" at the end of this chapter to determine (1) the meaning of listening, (2) its importance in communication, (3) factors of effective listening, and (4) factors which hinder effective listening.

(*b*) Read about "Listening," pages 60–65, in *The Bases of Speech*, 3rd ed., by Gray and Wise, and prepare to affirm, deny, or modify in class these assertions: (1) "Auding" holds especial significance for teachers of speech; (2) Auding is related to speaking as reading is to writing; (3) A test of ideas developed in *a speech*, administered to members of a class immediately after the speaker has concluded his speech, is a test of the abilities of the class members to listen; (4) Improvement in listening effects improvement in reading and vice versa; (5) Listening can be taught by teaching speech; (6) Frank questioning by students in a speech class of an inadequately supported conclusion by a speaker effects improvement in the students' listening; (7) Effective speaking is an active process but effective listening is passive; (8) Improvement in language and language usage by a listener effects improvement in his listening; (9) A student's ability to listen to a speech on a topic is closely related to his knowledge and understanding of the topic before he hears the speech; and (10) Motivation by a person to listen is the chief determinant of how well he listens.

(c) Based on your study of references listed under "Listening" at the end of this chapter, explain the relationship of each of the following to a student's effective listening to speeches: (1) ability to detect fallacies in reasoning, (2) ability to draw inferences, (3) ability to outline a speech, (4) audibility of the speaker, (5) emotional adjustment to the speaker, (6) experience in listening to difficult material, (7) high school speech training, (8) intelligence, (9) listening for main ideas rather than for facts, (10) parental occupation, (11) physical fatigue, (12) reading comprehension, (13) rearing as an only child, (14) recognition of correct English language usage, (15) room ventilation and temperature, (16) scholastic achievement in high school, (17) sex of listener, (18) size of listener's vocabulary, (19) speaker's effectiveness, and (20) susceptibility of listener to distraction.

(d) Report to the class on the value of inventories of listening such as the inventory on pages 292–295, *General Speech: An Introduction* by Baird and Knower. Explain the purpose, use, and likely benefits of listening inventories in teaching listening as a fundamental of speech.

(e) Report to the class on the value of the *Brown-Carlsen Listening Comprehension Test* and the *Sequential Tests of Educational Progress: Listening 1A and Listening 1B*. Explain the uses and benefits of these tests in teaching listening as a fundamental of speech.

(f) Make a list of recordings such as "You Can Hear It Now" for use in teaching listening. Devise a plan for using the recordings in effecting improvement in listening comprehension. Present your plan in class.

(g) Examine catalogs of audio-visual aids to determine the films available for use in teaching listening for (1) criticism, (2) enjoyment, (3) knowledge, and (4) understanding. In class report your findings and how the films can be used.

(h) Plan exercises for practice by students in discriminative listening: listening for everyday sounds, contrasting sounds, other people's voices, et cetera.

(i) Make a list of specific instances in each of which listening made a difference to a speaker. Explain in class how such instances could be used by a teacher to effect listening comprehension by students.

(j) Outline a unit for teaching listening as a fundamental of speech.

"Fundamentals" Course of Study

The following outline of a course of study utilizing the fundamentals of speech approach is suggested only as one way of organizing a speech course. The order or sequence of units as presented is not *necessarily* to be followed. The teacher of speech will need to make adjustments according to the interests, needs, and abilities of his students.

The outline is suggested for consideration in a course for one semester, consisting of eighteen weeks:

Orientation and Diagnosis	1 week
Basic Content or Ideas	1 week
Organization of Ideas	2 weeks
Developmental or Supporting Details	2 weeks
Adjustment to the Speech Situation	1 week
Bodily Action for Communication	2 weeks
Voice Usage	1½ weeks
Enunciation, Articulation, and Pronunciation	1½ weeks
Language	2 weeks
Adaptation in the Speech Situation	1 week
Listening	2 weeks
Examinations, Interruptions, etc.	1 week

The "Activities" Approach

The "activities" approach in teaching speech utilizes those speech situations in which people talk. The teacher organizes and builds a course in speech education consisting of projects or units. Each project or unit is centered on students' participation in a speech activity. The students read, discuss, and practice the types of speaking or reading suggested in the activity. This approach takes advantage of the opportunity provided by each of the speech activities for each student to gain knowledge, understanding, and skill of fundamentals of speech and his personal speech attributes as they are applied by him in the activity. The focus by each student and his teacher on the student's success in the activity tends to give the student perspective on each of the fundamentals of speech and its relationship and significance to his successful participation in the activity.

The speech activities which are usually included are: (1) informal speech, (2) public speaking, (3) discussion, (4) debate, (5) parliamentary procedure, (6) oral reading and interpretation, (7) choral speaking, (8) storytelling, (9) dramatics, and (10) acting and speaking on radio and television.

1. *Informal Speech.* Conversation, social introductions, interviews, and telephone usage are sometimes included in a beginning course in speech education in a high school. Their inclusion can help students realize that insight and practice in all types of speech situations can contribute to the development of fundamentals of speech and desirable personal speech attributes.

Many high school students recognize their need for assistance in conversing with others. They realize that they converse with people from whom they want social acceptance. They hardly suspect conversation as their greatest advertisement or self-centeredness as their greatest obstacle to its excellence and effectiveness. They may find "conversing with their friends" as their most enjoyable activity. They are not likely to have recognized conversation as a significant means for making them aware of their togetherness or as giving them a sense of well-being because, as a result of it, they know they are together. Even though they engage extensively in conversation every day for companionship, which few of them do not, they hardly anticipate or recognize values other than companionship per se to be derived from it. A teacher of speech can help them to understand the elements of conversation, such as interest in what the other person talks about, attentive listening, ability to ask questions, ability and willingness to contribute from their own ever increasing knowledge and understanding of a variety of topics, sincerity without affectation or pretense, informality, flexibility in thought and language, courtesy and tact without obvious patronizing, willingness as well as ability to think quickly, and effective speech habits. Also, a teacher of speech can help students to understand and develop criteria by which to evaluate conversations, recognize values to be derived from engaging in conversations with a variety of people at different educational and occupational levels, common faults and what can be done to correct them, and characteristics of excellence in conversing with friends, acquaintances, and strangers. Helping students to understand that an effective conversationalist is one who has a background of knowledge and interests, speaks with enthusiasm and interest, uses interesting details, is courteous, and is tolerant can be valuable for students. They should recognize that effective conversation does not come easily, but must be learned through informed and intelligent practice.[51] Likewise, teaching conversation effectively in a classroom is not easily accomplished, especially

[51] Kraid I. Ashbaugh, "Teaching the Art of Conversation," *The Speech Teacher*, vol. 6, no. 2 (March 1957), pp. 109–111.

if the objective is to help students to develop their conversational abilities and to demonstrate their abilities as conversationalists. A teacher of speech can help students to understand answers to their questions:

(a) Why do people converse?

(b) What constitutes excellent conversation?

(c) What is the difference between conversation and discussion?

(d) What objectives can be served by conversation?

(e) What are ways of starting conversations? With peers? With elders? With younger people? With friends? With strangers?

(f) How can people prepare to engage in conversations? Attitudes? Knowledge? Understandings? Skills?

(g) What are the specific skills of an excellent conversationalist? How are they developed?

(h) What kinds of topics lend themselves well to conversations? What are sources of topics for conversation?

(i) What topics should be avoided? Why should any topics be avoided?

(j) What kinds of situations are appropriate for conversations? Inappropriate? What makes some situations more appropriate than others?

(k) How can a person find topics of interest to another person with whom he wants to converse?

(l) How can a person show consideration for another person in a conversation?

(m) How can a person know when to talk and when not to talk in a conversation?

(n) What are ways of encouraging a quiet person in a group to converse?

(o) What are ways of changing the subject of a conversation? What ways are unacceptable?

(p) How can a person differ with what another person says in a conversation? What should be done if a conflict develops?

(q) What are obstacles to be avoided or overcome in a conversation? How?

(r) What are satisfactions to be gained in conversations?

(s) What are appropriate ways of ending a conversation to the satisfaction of another person or persons who would like to prolong it and who are apparently gaining considerable satisfaction from it?

A teacher of speech may find difficulty in setting up situations in a classroom for developing conversational skills. However, some situations and procedures are suggested at the end of this chapter.

Social introductions concern most high school students. A teacher of speech can discover problems which bother his students and which may cause them to avoid whenever possible social introductions. The teacher can at least help his students to learn accepted principles which govern social introductions. Tests of knowledge of social usage such as the one by Strang, Brown, and Stratton for junior and senior high schools[52] can be utilized to discover students' needs for understanding the amenities of social situations in which they find themselves. After the teacher has gained the respect and confidence of the students, they can tell him many of their problems in social situations. A teacher of speech can, of course, provide opportunities for students to develop their understandings and abilities through practice in social situations by setting up imaginary situations in the classroom or by planning actual extra-class situations in which these amenities can be performed by the students.

Students in high school should know about interviewing, because they are often required to obtain information from other persons. Many of them will have had, or will soon have, interviews for job applications. The teacher of speech can help each student understand that he should be adequately prepared before approaching the interviewer if the student is applying for a job. Likewise, the teacher can help the student to understand that he should be no less well prepared if he is the interviewer seeking information from another person. He should have specific suggestions on how to conduct the interview to get the best results and, of course, the methods for making an appointment for the interview and thanking the interviewee for it. Demonstrations by members of the class can help them in learning acceptable procedures and courtesies. The use of an actual interview with some member of the community or school can be a very valuable experience for students.

Although too little time may be utilized in both the home and the school in teaching telephone usage, correct and acceptable procedures and formalities can well be learned and demonstrated by students, supervised by the teacher. Students become "sophisticated" at an early age in "monopolizing" the telephone. Some of their telephone habits persist into their adulthood. Because of their use and misuse of the telephone for prolonged conversations, they often may not recognize their lack of understanding and lack of acceptable techniques and courtesies in making telephone calls, answering the telephone, and using techniques which are taught each year to thousands of employees of business organizations, including telephone companies. A teacher of speech can help them to recognize the similarities and differences between a telephone conversation and a face-to-face conversation.

With telephonic equipment obtained from a telephone company, a

[52] Ruth Strang, Marion A. Brown, and Dorothy C. Stratton, *Test of Knowledge of Social Usage*. Teachers College, Columbia University, New York: Bureau of Publications, 1942.

teacher of speech can help students to realize that the telephone accentuates imperfections of voice and speech. Such equipment coupled with a tape recorder can be used to help students to develop clear, flexible, well-modulated, and unobtrusive voices "with a smile" which are responsive to meaning instead of monotonous, uncertain, whining, tiny, and shrill voices which are often characteristic of voices heard on the telephone. Students can be taught to speak directly into the mouthpiece with their lips no more than half an inch away, to project their voices firmly as if the listener were six feet away, to enunciate clearly, to articulate distinctly, and to speak slowly enough for the listener to comprehend the meaning and, also, to speak rapidly so as not to waste time. Today, telephone techniques and courtesies require uniform formalities as families, business organizations, and professional people utilize the telephone to order and sell merchandise, make and adjust complaints, reach decisions, give instructions, request reservations, call the doctor, seek fast action by fire departments and police, and maintain good feeling among friends. Of course, a unit on telephone usage can be worthless and perhaps catastrophic or, depending largely on the imagination and industry of the teacher, important and even exciting in teaching telephone usage and some of the fundamentals of speech. Experience indicates to some of us who have taught a unit on "informal speech," including telephone usage, that the instruction and practice have not only had an immediate effect on the procedures and amenities of telephone usage by students but that they have, in turn, made local calls for the purpose of checking the usage by their elders.

Each of these "informal" speech activities may, of course, become formal. Each of them offers opportunities for teaching fundamentals of speech and for helping students to apply the fundamentals in realistic speech situations. Simultaneously, students can be stimulated and guided to gain confidence in using correct and acceptable procedures and courtesies in conversation, social introductions, interviews, and telephone usage.

2. *Public Speaking*. This speech activity is probably the one most used and perhaps best suited for teaching all of the fundamentals of speech because it affords opportunity for experience by students in preparing and delivering many types of speeches which people give in public. A teacher of speech should not be concerned with making "great" orators of students, but rather with helping each student to be as effective as it is possible for him to be when he speaks.

Topics often included in this unit are determining and clarifying the objective of a speech, analyzing the audience and situation, selecting and limiting the topic of the speech, making a tentative outline, gathering materials with which to develop and support ideas in the outline related to the objective, completing the final plan of the speech, practicing the speech with an imaginary or real audience, selecting and arranging visual aids and perhaps audio aids, anticipating questions which may occur to the audience as a result of the speech and planning to answer the questions, and delivering the speech effectively. The types of speeches can be varied to satisfy the speech interests, meet the needs, and develop the abilities of students. They can include autobiographical speeches, expository speeches with or without visual aids, speeches to describe, argumentative speeches, sales talks, speeches to provoke thinking, and such talks which students and adults are called upon to give in the school and community. Providing students opportunities to speak in public can be helpful in motivating them. The use of a Speaker's Bureau for local business and professional meetings, having students speak to other classes, encouraging students to talk in assemblies, and inviting students to speak on special occasions in the school are useful and widely accepted suggestions.

At the beginning of the unit in public speaking, a teacher of speech should stress the importance of an "extemporaneous" delivery that involves an informal, conversational style. By insisting upon extemporaneous speaking from the first, the teacher can minimize the danger of some students reading their speeches from a manuscript, reading their speeches from memory, or resorting to "impromptu" speeches when they are not called for.

The teacher of speech should place emphasis upon careful preparation, clear understanding of the topic, a well-organized and well-supported speech, use of logical reasoning, language appropriate to the audience and speaker, and delivery consistent with the abilities of the student. If the teacher of speech is alert, diligent, patient, tactfully firm, and generous with sincere praise of accomplishment and with helpful suggestions for improvement, students will probably show improvement and gain much satisfaction from it.

3. *Discussion.* Discussion is a process by which people talk together in a cooperative, logical, and objective manner in order to solve a problem, to find answers related to a problem, to reach tentative and seemingly sound conclusions about a problem based on reasoning and analysis of all of the relevant argument, data, evidence, and opinion available to them, or, at least, to share information about a problem. Discussion seems to be used more and more, in one form or another, in our democratic society and, therefore, it is well for high school students to know how to make the most profitable and best use of it.

The discussion process is closely allied by most writers with reflective thinking and the work of John Dewey, the educational philosopher. Both discussion and reflective thinking follow a similar pattern: a felt difficulty, definition and analysis of the problem, citing and consideration of the possible solutions, choice of the most practicable and desirable solution, and determination of means by which the best solution can be put into effect.

Most units on discussion include a consideration of its definition and pattern; its importance in everyday democratic living; its types, such as informal, round table, panel, and symposium; preparation for discussion and for leading it; responsibilities of a discussant; responsibilities of a leader; and criteria and procedures for evaluating a discussion, its discussants, and its leader.

Many teachers of speech motivate discussants and help them to become familiar with the process of discussion by the use of field trips to view actual discussions in progress, films and film strips appropriate to a unit on discussion, discussions on television which students are encouraged to evaluate, readings on discussion and on aspects of it, classroom discussions on problems of interest and value to the students, participation in interscholastic discussion contests in which critics as well as students and teachers evaluate discussions, and presentations of different types of discussion to the student body in school assembly programs.

Effective discussion involves careful preparation by each student in the analysis of the problem, in gathering relevant material, and in organizing material for ready reference during the discussion. The development of group and individual discussion outlines is helpful in teaching discussion.

Since the concepts and procedures of the discussion process are typical, if not identical, to those of reflective thinking and both practicable and desirable in solving problems in everyday living in a democratic society, this speech activity deserves attention and learning by students at the high school level. If a student does reflective thinking on a challenging, appropriate, and worthwhile problem, gathers significant data on the problem, learns to improve his own speech skills in this type of oral communication, and develops his appreciation of the interpersonal relationships of a group of discussants, the work is worthwhile for its impact on his attitude, thinking, speaking, and living.

4. *Debate.* Debate is closely allied with discussion. In solving a problem, conflicts arise which are not resolved by the discussants as a result of their examining the relevant argument and evidence available to them. Debate permits individuals with conflicting points of view to present their cases. It involves speakers who are prepared to argue for the acceptance of a proposition and other speakers who are prepared to argue for its rejection. It can provide accepted rules of procedure which give each side an equal chance to present arguments.

A unit on debate normally includes such topics as definition, purposes and values of debate, selection of debate propositions, determining the issues, preparing the briefs, building the cases, collecting material, using argument and evidence, reasoning, refutation, responsibilities of each speaker, and criteria and procedures for judging the debates.

Relatively simple propositions should be selected for the first debates. Propositions of local school or community interest are often successful ones. For later debates students may undertake the national high school debate proposition or others of a more complex nature. In a course in speech education in a high school devoted to many speech activities, obviously little more than developing some understanding of the procedures of debate can be accomplished. However, debate is an essential speech activity which should be included in a basic speech activities course.

Work in debate can offer excellent opportunities for a teacher of speech to help students develop their skills of research, critical thinking, and extemporaneous speaking. Working up a case for a debate involves intensive and highly motivated research that it is not found in all speech activities. Skill in building arguments, using evidence, reasoning, and detecting flaws in the reasoning of others is basic to debating. Perhaps in no other activity is this opportunity so readily available. Debating makes it necessary for a speaker to think on his feet. This is a skill which is sought by many adults.

Additional information on debate is in Chapter 9.

5. *Parliamentary Procedure.* Much of the speaking in our society is done by groups using parliamentary procedure. These groups may be as large as the United States Congress operating with very formal and highly developed rules, or as small as a drama club in a high school operating according to basic parliamentary procedures. Whatever the size of the group and no matter how important or trivial the topics for consideration, business will proceed more quickly, more fairly, and with the best chance of satisfactory results if the members of the group understand and practice parliamentary law. Most students participate in class and club organizations and can see the practical advantages of studying parliamentary procedure.

In a unit on parliamentary procedure, the teacher should develop an understanding by his students of the basic principles upon which a group operates in using parliamentary law. The concept of majority rule and protection of minorities, understanding of commonly used motions, and familiarity with the order of business and standard references can all be studied to great advantage.

Most units in parliamentary procedure include a consideration of fundamental principles, order of business, making motions, precedence and classification of motions, voting, constitutions, by-laws, standing rules, and nominations and elections.

Much practical drill in as realistic a situation as possible should be utilized. Organizing a class into a club by starting with a meeting to organize and working through the steps necessary to formulate officially a club has often been used as a teaching device. Practice in making, discussing, amending, and voting upon the various motions is vital. All students should get this practice. Chairmen can be rotated. Students can present motions in which they are interested. Friendly competition in drill sessions should be encouraged. A unit on parliamentary procedure can be one of the most interesting, liveliest, and rewarding units taught by a teacher of speech. A teacher of speech should not be deterred by lack of knowledge of the subject. A good way to learn parliamentary procedure is to teach it.

6. *Oral Reading and Interpretation.* Effective oral readers and interpreters at the high school level are not as numerous as a teacher of speech would like. Too often reading aloud becomes just a matter of saying words. Too often a high school student impersonates or acts rather than interprets and speaks his selection. Helping the student to understand just what effective oral reading or oral interpretation is and providing him with opportunities for understanding and applying basic principles are perhaps the key tasks of a teacher of speech.

High school students need to understand clearly that when they *read* aloud they are interested in getting the meaning of the printed page across to the listener. However, when they *interpret* orally they are attempting to re-create for the listener the experience of the author of the selection. In oral interpretation, they want the audience to *feel* as well as understand the meaning. Interpretative reading is that style of reading aloud in which the reader achieves the desired effect primarily through vocal utterance, facial expression, and suggestive bodily action rather than by literal gestures or character posture. The character is *suggested* rather than portrayed *literally*. The material may or may not be memorized, but the interpretative reader usually presents the material from a book or manuscript.

In order for a teacher of speech to help high school students become more effective readers and interpreters, he should make them aware of such basic principles as: the reader's first objective is to communicate an idea to the listener; he should develop a communicative attitude; he must preserve the feeling of spontaneity; and he must work to project both thought and emotion in his reading.

Basic to effective reading aloud is a clear and full understanding of the selection to be read. Coupled with this understanding of the selection is an understanding of the techniques and art of talking with an audience.

The teacher of speech is obligated to plan carefully for both of these emphases.

The "impression" of the selection is achieved through thought analysis, word meanings, word groupings, relationships between word groups, understanding of figures of speech, recognition of the author's attitude, recognition of the author's purpose, and the like. Effective "expression" is concerned with voice usage and its elements of quality, pitch, variety, melody, force, time, pause, emphasis, ryhthm, and so on. Facial expressions and other suggestive physical action are important and should not be ignored by either the teacher or the student. A teacher of speech can likely profit by heeding the advice of Simley[53] on "Hints for the Student Reader."

A typical oral interpretation unit includes an emphasis on the meaning and importance of oral interpretation, differences between oral interpretation and other forms of speech, materials for oral interpretation, grasping the meaning of a selection, techniques of interpretation, projection in talking with an audience, and criteria and procedures for evaluating both interpretation and projection.

Activities which many high school teachers have used in teaching oral interpretation are lecture-discussions on effective and ineffective reading; specific work on phrasing, grouping, and eye contact; assignments on background information and study necessary for understanding a selection; viewing of movies such as "Appreciation and the Study of Literature"; drills and exercises for vocal variety; many performances by students using various types of selections; listening to recordings of effective oral interpretation; and presenting programs to the school assembly or public gatherings by the best readers.

The benefits of effective oral interpretation are many. The student can increase his vocabulary, learn the emotional reactions words can produce as well as understanding of their meanings, become increasingly better acquainted with literature, learn to enjoy the literature he uses, and become more sensitive to meaning and its effect in oral interpretation and reading aloud. His speech skills can improve as he recognizes how flexible and variable his oral utterance can be.

7. *Choral Speaking.* Group interpretation of literature is known by a number of names: group speaking, choral reading, verse speaking, choric speech, and perhaps others. This speech activity involves a group of readers re-creating literature by reading the lines in the melodies and rhythms of speech. The choir is often divided into groups, usually by pitch and resonance differences.

There are several variations of choral speaking: unison, with every-

---

[53] Anne Simley, "Hints for the Student Reader," *The Speech Teacher*, vol. 6, no. 3 (September 1957), pp. 233–236.

one reading in concert; antiphonal, with the choir divided into two groups; refrain, using one or more solo voices with the entire choir supplying the repeated refrain; and line-a-person, with individual members of the choir speaking a single line.

Values of working on choral speaking include greater appreciation of literature, especially poetry; self-confidence; increased speech agility and improved speech; and greater ability to interpret a printed page.

A suggested pattern or procedure is to start with the division of the class into groups. Four groups are used, consisting usually of high and low voices for girls and the same for boys. Simple poems can be used at first. Some teachers of speech give each of the four groups a separate poem to read in unison. From this simple procedure of reading in unison, they move onto antiphonal readings and finally work on refrain readings.

The verse choir director will likely find that he needs to work on the concepts of rhythm, melody, and meter with his students. Articulation exercises are often needed to correct indistinct and blurred articulations. The basic principles of oral interpretation are pertinent in this type of activity. The students must understand the literature which they speak and they will therefore likely need help in interpreting it effectively.

8. *Storytelling.* Storytelling is older than reading and is as popular today as ever. It has an advantage of providing the student with a situation in which audience contact and communication with the audience are brought forcibly home to him much more than in reading from the printed page. It has personal advantages to the student too. Authorities agree that storytelling helps to acquaint students with good literature, helps to develop poise and other desirable personal attributes, increases his understanding of people, and helps him to organize and unify a series of events.

The storyteller should be aware of the many kinds of stories available for telling: fables, myths, mystery stories, fairy tales, legends, folk tales, biographical events, Bible stories, adventure stories, and others which even the students, if given the opportunity, will bring to the attention of the teacher. Selecting a story worth telling is important and should probably be the starting point for work in this speech activity. The story should have an interesting plot, believable characters, suspense, vivid setting, contrast, vivid language, and unity of theme. The student should be stimulated and guided to choose a story which he can enjoy and that is appropriate for the audience and the occasion.

Suggestions for "working up" the story should be given to the student. They can include: (1) read the story you've selected through silently a few times to fix the plot and main characters, (2) tell the story aloud as often as needed to feel secure about the general plan, use your own words, remember the plot as you tell the story, but don't memorize it, and

(3) use an extemporaneous style of delivery but stay close to the author's original mood and intention.

The student should recognize the importance of the voice in storytelling and remember that he can succeed largely by his work with spoken language and the words in the language.

Some common dangers to be avoided lie in altering the story to suit special occasions, introducing words unfamiliar to the audience, over-illustration, obscuring the point of the story by too many details, overexplanation, and getting side-tracked on nonessentials.

The telling of a story is an excellent means by which to help students to learn to interpret audience reactions. Students can profit by many opportunities for them to test their own storytelling skills and to analyze the reactions of their audience.

9. *Dramatics*. The interest of most high school students in putting on a play is great. The wise teacher of speech will likely use this interest to promote development in the fundamentals of speech as well as to acquaint students with the practical and esthetic aspects of the theater.

In a basic course in speech education, it is impossible to go into much detail in a unit on dramatics. Many high schools offer advanced courses in dramatics for especially interested and talented students. However, it can be advantageous to utilize this speech activity in a basic course so that high school students become aware of the problems and the values of producing a play.

Objectives of such a unit should include helping students to appreciate plays as good literature, to become familiar with the many facets of dramatic production, to improve in speech skills, to help them in their development of desirable personal attributes, and to provide criteria by which to evaluate drama on radio, television, motion picture, and stage.

Among the topics for inclusion in a unit on dramatics are the history of the theater, interpretation and acting, and play production including scenery, lighting, costuming, make-up, properties, house management, publicity, ticket sales and accounting, and directing. Playwrighting can be stimulating and exciting, educationally profitable, and satisfying.

Specific classroom activities can revolve naturally around the producing of one-act plays or of scenes and cuttings from longer plays. These may be performed eventually for the student body during an assembly program or possibly used as programs for enjoyment, learning, and satisfaction by peers, parents, and friends of the students. Often, however, they should remain as classroom projects as are other classroom projects.

Detailed help in play production is to be found in Chapter 9.

10. *Radio and Television Acting and Speaking*. Americans are said to be afraid of a moment of silence. Perhaps the accusation is, to some

extent, supported by the fact that we have millions of radio and television sets. On the other hand, the development of radio and television may be the most significant technical advance in human communication since the invention of movable type. Since radio and television have become so much a part of our everyday life and probably influence us more than we realize, it would seem wise to include a unit on radio and television acting and speaking in a course in speech education in the high school. Not only can a teacher of speech help students to recognize the great influence of radio and television and help them develop standards by which to judge programs they hear and see, but the teacher can utilize the media for helping students to develop their speech proficiency.

Most teachers of speech in high schools have access to a public address system or a tape recorder, or both. These items are useful in working on radio speech and drama. Most students in high schools are interested in radio-type speech activities since they listen to radio. Often the school's public address system is located in or near the speech classroom and students in the class are asked to make the daily announcements over it. Many high schools utilize local radio and television stations as outlets for special programs.

Although most units on radio and television speaking and acting focus on producing various types of radio and television programs including plays, many teachers of speech include work on the scientific background of broadcasting and telecasting. Visits to radio and television studios are most helpful in making clear to students explanations of the equipment and its uses.

Students will likely want to know the specific requirements of radio speech, radio drama, television speech, and television drama. They will likely want to become familiar with the terminology used, the equipment needed, and the limitations of the activities. Mock-ups of television cameras can be made and utilized effectively in the classroom. Specific assignments of radio commercials, interviews, and plays can be taped and played back to the rest of the class for analysis. Television commercials, quiz programs, and dramatic presentations can be utilized effectively.

The individual student's speech proficiency is the teacher's first concern, but the teacher should not lose sight of the tremendous opportunities for helping the student make more effective choices in his own listening and viewing and providing him a basis for increasingly better attitudes toward these media and the use which he can make of them.

"Activities" Course of Study. The following is a suggested course of study utilizing the speech activities approach in a basic course in speech education. It is not to be inferred that the units must be taught in the order indicated. Each teacher of speech should conclude what activities

THE "ACTIVITIES" APPROACH 197

will do the best job according to the objectives he sets up and according to the interests, needs, and abilities of his students. It is surely obvious that including all the activities in a one-semester course in speech education is hardly feasible. A year's course of study, 36 weeks, is indicated. A teacher of speech can select those activities most appropriate for a one-semester, 18 weeks, course.

First Semester

Orientation and Diagnosis	1 week
Informal Speech Activities	2 weeks
Public Speaking	5 weeks
Discussion	3 weeks
Debate	3 weeks
Parliamentary Procedure	3 weeks
Examinations, etc.	1 week

Second Semester

Oral Reading and Interpretation	3 weeks
Choral Speaking	2 weeks
Storytelling	2 weeks
Dramatics	6 weeks
Radio and Television Speech and Drama	4 weeks
Examinations, etc.	1 week

An actual example of the activities approach is found in "A Guide for the Teaching of a One-Year Course in Speech Fundamentals in High School: Learning to Speak and to Listen" prepared by Mrs. Mary E. Adams and used by her in the Detroit Lakes, Minnesota, High School.[54]

The units she uses include:

Orientation	3 weeks
Listening	2 weeks
Basic Speeches	12 weeks
Oral Reading	3 weeks
The Interview	1 week
Parliamentary Procedure	1 week
Discussion	3 weeks
Drama	4 weeks
Special Occasion Speeches	2 weeks
Radio Speech and Acting	4 weeks

Fundamentals-Activities Course of Study. Probably the approach utilized most frequently by teachers of speech in high schools is the approach in which selected speech activities and selected fundamentals of

[54] "A Guide for the Teaching of a One-Year Course in Speech Fundamentals in High School: Learning to Speak and to Listen." 60 pages.

speech are chosen for the course of study. The course constructed by the "Speech in the Secondary School" Interest Group of the Speech Association of America in 1959[55] is an example. It includes these units:

Introduction	1 week
Bodily Action	2 weeks
Informal Speech	1 week
Voice and Diction	2 weeks
Listening and Speaker-Audience Relationships	1 week
Preparation and Delivery of Talks	3 weeks
Parliamentary Procedure	2 weeks
Oral Reading and Interpretation	3 weeks
Discussion	3 weeks

Another example of this combination approach is the curriculum guide entitled "Basic Speech for High Schools," published in 1958 by the Michigan Speech Association.[56] These units are suggested:

Orientation	1 week
Conversations	1 week
Listening	no time indicated
Discussion	no time indicated
Preparing to Speak	no time indicated
Our Bodies Speak	4 weeks
Gathering Information	3 weeks
Voice	no time indicated
Parliamentary Procedure	1 week
Critical Thinking	no time indicated

The "Subject Matter" Approach

The subject matter approach refers to the teacher's directing the attention and effort of students to their *knowing* about speech and *understanding* its meaning, nature, role, and significance in learning, human relationships, and communication. Rather than sustained emphasis on guided *practice* and *demonstration* by students of their use of basic speech skills in "delivery" or their speech abilities in speech activities, the teacher places emphasis on their mastery of speech subject matter. Obviously, students' acquisition of knowledge about speech and understanding it as

---

[55] Secondary School Interest Group, "Fundamentals of Speech: A Basic Course for High Schools," *The Speech Teacher*, vol. 8, no. 2 (March 1959), pp. 93–113. (Copies may be obtained from the Executive Secretary, Speech Association of America, Statler Hilton Hotel, New York, New York 10001. 20¢ each.)

[56] Michigan Speech Association, *Curriculum Guide: Basic Speech for High Schools*. Ann Arbor, Michigan: Department of the Michigan Education Association, 1958.

a form of behavior give no assurance that they will develop proficiency in the ten fundamentals of speech or effectiveness in the ten speech activities presented earlier in this chapter. But neither do students who are proficient in their use of speech skills and effective in speech activities such as dramatics or forensics, or both, give assurance of their knowledge or understanding of audible symbols or visible bodily action employed by themselves and others for purposes of adaptation, cooperation, influence, and control in speech situations. Furthermore, these students seldom show much, if any, interest in speech behavior, its origins, its development, its effect and impact, or its manifestations in private or public affairs.

Whether speech subject matter, proficient use of speech skills, or effective speech performance in speech activities is most important to teach and learn is not the issue. Balcer, Seabury, and most, if not all, students and teachers of speech will probably agree that every student should, insofar as possible, know and understand all he can about speech behavior and develop his speech skills and effectiveness of his participation in speech activities. The effect and success of the subject matter approach to teaching speech depend, partly, on the validity of such assumptions as the following:

1. That speech is not merely a skill, a vehicle, or a means to a utilitarian end to be developed by students who concern themselves with the improvement of their voices, bodily action, enunciation and articulation, poise, and oral utterance or who concern themselves with the improvement of their speech abilities and attributes in speech activities with the stimulation and guidance of a teacher who is well qualified to coach them to attain superior ratings on their performances in the activities.

2. That speech, recognized as a subject for study, teaching, and learning by scholars and teachers in the ancient world of Greece and Rome and in modern colleges and universities, comprises an abundant and increasing body of knowledge significant and essential for study by students in high schools and colleges.

3. That knowledge about speech and its meaning, bases, elements, development, effect, and manifestations is basic to an understanding of fundamentals of speech, its forms, its theories, its principles, and practices.

4. That understanding of speech and all of its phases, interrelationships, and extrarelationships are basic to insightful speech practices and performances and to growth in ability and desirable personal speech attributes.

5. That speech, as a subject for study, learning, and research, should provide opportunities for students to apply their knowledge and understanding in a series of carefully planned speech performances consisting of drills, exercises, activities, and tests designed to reveal increased knowl-

edge and understanding or lack of it, as well as skill in speech fundamentals and effectiveness of speech performances in speech activities.

6. That students' achievement, improvement, and development, resulting partly and basically from their knowledge and understanding of speech, are basic to their speech abilities and desirable personal speech attributes as communicators in the school and in everyday speech activities outside of the school as well as in interscholastic speech activities.

7. That the primary function of a teacher of speech is to stimulate, instruct, guide, and evaluate students' acquisition of knowledge about speech, their understanding of the subject matter comprised by speech, their mastery of fundamentals and forms of speech, and their abilities and attributes in performances as conversationalists, discussants, oral interpreters, actors, speakers, debaters, communicators, students, persons, and citizens.

In the subject matter approach, a teacher of speech organizes units of subject matter to be read, studied, discussed, and applied by students in their preparation, their practice and rehearsal, and their performance in speech drills and activities in many areas of academic instruction in speech. Although the teacher directs the attention and effort of students, initially, to the study of appropriate, challenging, and worthwhile subject matter, the curiosity, interests, and needs of students can direct the attention of the teacher and study by students of many concepts, theories, topics, and problems in speech textbooks and speech references. Examples of such cooperation and procedure by the teacher and students are prevalent in speech correction, in the production of a play, and in preparation for interscholastic debating and participation in individual speech events. The teacher prepares to clarify the objective and desired outcomes of students' reading and study, plans questions to bring out salient points of students' oral reports and to assure accuracy, prepares to lead discussions and conduct recitations to help students answer questions and solve problems posed by the materials, and designs tests, written and oral, with which to evaluate students' knowledge and understanding of speech subject matter. Attention and effort can be focused on the study of speakers as communicators, on the subjects and messages of the speakers, and on the reactions by members of the audience to the speaker, his message, and his speaking. The teacher needs, obviously, to make crystal clear to the students that their grasp of the meaning of speech principles and procedures is basic to their successful achievement, development, and improvement as students of speech and to any lasting benefit. The teacher needs to stimulate and guide students to apply what they know and understand about speech in their preparation and practice, otherwise teacher and students are often disappointed with students' application of what they know and understand about speech to effect informed, insightful, improved, and effective speech performance. Although a teacher of speech usually finds it easier to "teach" speech by use of the activities approach or the fundamentals approach, he correctly anticipates that students want to know about speech and to understand concepts, principles, procedures, and theories of it. Oftentimes, they want to know and understand criteria and standards by which to evaluate their successes in learning what they can in a course in basic speech development, in essential speech experiences, in oral interpretation and acting, in discussion and debate, in drama, and in public address. Likewise, they want to know how to evaluate their own speech, speaking, and speech performances. Their attention and effort can be readily directed by a qualified teacher of speech to their study of such topics as the following:

1. What is speech? "Good" speech? Effective speech? Differences between "good" and effective speech? Fundamentals of speech? Why and for what specific purposes do we speak? In what kinds of speech experiences and situations do we participate? Why do we need to study speech? How can our study of speech benefit us and others in courses and activities in and out of school? How can we identify our speech needs? Speech abilities? Speech potential? How can we know that our study of speech is beneficial?

2. How does speech develop? Why is it not a physical inheritance like eyes, ears, hands, and feet? If we are born without speech ability, how do most of us accomplish the tremendous feat of learning it by the age of six? Why is speech considered to be complicated? How does speech develop in the lower animals? How did the human race learn to speak? What is to be learned by our understanding theories of speech development such as the interjection, onomatopoeia, gesture, yo-he-ho, and social control? What is the significance of the concept of speech as a secondary function of bodily organs acting in unison? What is the relationship of language, thinking, and speech? What is the significance of speech in gaining social acceptance and success? How does speech serve us in social adaptation, cooperation, influence, and control in social situations?

3. What is the significance to students of their knowledge and understanding of anatomy, fine arts, literature, physics, physiology, political science, psychology, and so on? Is it desirable to develop speech skills without knowledge and understanding of speech and its relationship to these areas of study? Do students of speech who know and understand most about speech and areas of study related to it demonstrate excellence of speech in speaking compared to students who are only skillful in factors of delivery? What are the bases of speech? Why is it physical? Physiological? Neurological? Phonetic? Psychological? Social? What can be the

effect of an understanding of the bases of speech on a student's skills in speaking? What is the basis of distrust of the person who exercises exceptional skill in speaking? Why do some people seem to be gifted with confidence and others seem to be lacking it in speech situations?

4. What is the importance of speech in listening and learning and in human relationships? What is the significance of attitudes of speakers and listeners? How is speaker-audience adjustment accomplished? Speaker-subject adjustment? Audience-subject adjustment? What are the purposes and desired outcomes of speaking? What is the meaning of "logical divisions" and "patterns of organization" of ideas in communication? What is the substance with which ideas are developed and supported? What is involved in the comprehension and use of language in speech and speaking? How can control and use of bodily action and voice by a speaker contribute to the effectiveness of his speech and speaking? What is the significance of clear enunciation, distinct articulation, and acceptable pronunciation for speech effectiveness? What is the relationship and significance of analytical and discriminating listening?

5. Why is an understanding of speech forms helpful or necessary for effective participation in speech activities? What are the differences between conversation, discussion, oral interpretation, acting, extemporaneous speaking, oratory, and debate? In what ways are they similar? What conventions, rules, and traditions govern each of these forms? Is an actor a speaker? Is a speaker an actor? Why are conversers, platform speakers, and debaters expected to talk extemporaneously and actors and orators expected to speak from memory? Why are oral interpreters of literature expected to read from a manuscript? Why are oral interpreters expected to refrain from acting, impersonation, or speaking as the poet or author of the selection? Why do we expect actors to appear on a stage and to play persons other than themselves? Why are debaters expected to support only one side of the proposition, clash with the opposition, and display enthusiasm for debating without exceeding a time limit, without scouting, and too often without an audience? Why is an orator expected to inspire and persuade his audience without speaking extemporaneously?

6. Phonetics, diacritics, spelling, and standards of pronunciation embrace subject matter which, if it is taught by a teacher who is prepared and interested in stimulating and guiding students to learn it, can lead to their awareness of speech sound distinctions in listening and in their own utterance. Without insight gained from their acquisition and mastery of the subject matter of these topics, are students likely to improve both significantly and lastingly in their awareness of speech sound distinctions in listening and in utterance?

7. The subject matter approach can be used by a teacher of speech to help students develop their understanding and appreciation of public

addresses by speakers recognized for the impact of their expository, persuasive, and inspirational speeches and speaking on our social, economic, educational, political and personal problems, and courses of action; our beliefs, imagination, and language; and our speaking, writing, listening, and reading. Students can be challenged successfully to analyze and discuss speakers and their speeches and speaking if their attention and effort are directed to such speakers and speeches as Susan B. Anthony, "Are Women Persons?"; Bruce Barton, "Which Knew Not Joseph"; William Jennings Bryan, "The Cross of Gold"; Vannever Bush, "The Gentlemen of Culture"; Nicholas Murray Butler, "Five Evidences of an Education"; Winston Churchill, "Blood, Sweat, and Tears"; Lionel Crocker, "Leadership and the Spoken Word"; William O. Douglas, "The Function of Democracy"; Virgil M. Hancher, "The Art of Contemplation"; Thomas Henry Huxley, "The Method of Scientific Investigation"; Sir James Jeans, "Why the Sky Is Blue"; Pericles, "Funeral Oration"; William Lyon Phelps, "Owning Books"; Franklin D. Roosevelt, "Eight Common Principles for a Better World"; Theodore Roosevelt, "The Strenuous Life"; Carl Sandburg, "Abraham Lincoln"; Alfred E. Smith, "The Cooing Dove"; Adlai E. Stevenson, "The Educated Citizen"; Robert A. Taft, "Forward, America— Which Way and What Speed"; Harry S. Truman, "Powers of the President"; Henry Van Dyke, "Salt"; Booker T. Washington, "Atlanta Address"; Daniel Webster, "Bunker Hill Address"; Woodrow Wilson, "The League of Nations"; and other speakers and speeches selected by the students and the teacher. A unit on the criteria of rhetorical criticism, based on the writings of Plato, Aristotle, Cicero, Quintilian, and modern theorists may be included in their study of public address. Recordings, platform and television speakers, oral reports, and substantial research papers may augment lectures and discussion.

8. Likewise, a teacher of speech can use the subject matter approach to help students develop their understanding and enjoyment of plays recognized by critics in drama and dramaturgy for their quality and impact on our insight, interests, outlook, imagination, and language, and on social, economic, political, and personal problems and issues. Students can be challenged profitably to read, interpret, and analyze plays by famous playwrights, among them Sophocles, Shakespeare, Chekhov, Ibsen, Moliere, Barrie, Galsworthy, Giraudoux, Coward, Eliot, Fry, Shaw, Anouilh, Anderson, Chase, Miller, O'Neill, Sherwood, Williams, and others. A unit on dramaturgy and on dramatic criticism can furnish worthwhile subject matter for analysis by students, with stimulation and guidance by the teacher. Films, recordings, acting of scenes, legitimate and television drama, oral reports, and substantial research papers may augment lectures and discussion to enable students to evolve standards by which they can select other playwrights and plays for their study and enjoyment.

Projects

1. Discuss the advantages and disadvantages of the "fundamentals" approach, the "activities" approach, and the "subject matter" approach in teaching speech. Which one is the most popular? Why?

2. Prepare a unit on one of the ten fundamentals of speech. Develop appropriate readings, assignments, study guides, and handouts.

3. Assume that you as a teacher of speech are responsible for what students talk about and what they say about it in your class. Prepare to explain procedures which you would use.

4. Prepare a list of procedures which could be used to teach each of the fundamentals of speech. Submit the list to your instructor for evaluation. Be prepared to report to the class one of your lists of procedures and to solicit from members of the class their reactions.

5. Record the voices of the members of your class in methods of teaching speech. Have the members analyze each one on an appropriate form devised by you.

6. Prepare a bulletin board display which would indicate the importance of a specific speech fundamental or speech activity.

7. Bring to class at least one poem suitable for choral speaking. Each member of the class contribute at least one selection to a complete set which may be duplicated for future use by all members of the class.

8. Bring to class an annotated log of good educational radio and television programs for high school students. Explain to the class how one of the programs could be used in teaching speech.

9. With the class divided by the instructor into two-student teams, let each team present an effective and an ineffective example of a specific informal speech activity such as social conversation, telephoning, interviewing, et cetera. Analyze each example presented by a two-student team and prepare a statement of suggestions for improvement of each example which needs improvement.

10. Make a list of each of the kinds of stories available for telling. Prepare to present to the class a plan for using one of the stories in the teaching of speech. Indicate its values in acquainting students with good literature and how you would use it to effect improvement by students in one or more fundamentals of speech. Be prepared to answer questions about your procedures.

11. Select at least three one-act plays which you believe would be excellent for performance by high school students in a class in basic speech development. Indicate desirable outcomes for students as a result of their participation in the one-act play unit. Be ready to lead a class discussion

on the values and procedures for achieving objectives of a unit on dramatics.

12. Collect courses of study in speech from various state departments of education. Compare and evaluate them for members of the class.

13. Explain to the class the various types of group discussion. Use appropriate diagrams on the blackboard to make clear differences between the various types.

14. Investigate the American Tape Exchange Service sponsored by the Speech Association of America. Present the results of your investigation, including the kinds of tapes which are available, to members of the class.

15. Present in class a plan for surveying high schools to discover the curricular patterns which are used in the teaching of speech. Indicate the various patterns which you would expect to find in the high schools.

16. Discuss with your classmates the possible methods for handling speech fright in a class of high school students. Supplement the discussion by reading about speech fright in books identified at the end of this chapter. Prepare to explain to the class which methods you believe to be best. Tell why.

17. Compile a list of words, sentences, and paragraphs which would be suitable for use by a teacher of speech as articulation drills. Demonstrate in class how you would conduct the drills.

18. Find examples of public speeches that you feel would be good models to use in your class in speech education in high school. Prepare a letter with which to seek permission to duplicate the speeches for exchange with your classmates.

19. "The beginning course in speech in high school should be a public speaking course." State your position on this statement and present the reasons for your position.

20. "The beginning course in speech in high school should be a course in oral interpretation and dramatics." State your position on this statement and the reasons for your belief.

21. Prepare to explain to the class why discussion and debate are complementary to each other.

22. Demonstrate to the class the differences between interpretation, impersonation, and acting. Choose material which will enable you to do the demonstration.

23. Survey students in high school or college to find out what they believe to be values of their participation in dramatics. Compare the results of your survey with those of other surveys.

Selected Bibliography

Fundamentals of Speech

1. *Basic Content or Ideas*

BAIRD, A. CRAIG, and FRANKLIN H. KNOWER, *General Speech*, 2nd ed. New York: McGraw-Hill, Inc., 1957.

BRIGANCE, W. N., *Speech: Its Techniques and Disciplines in a Free Society*. New York: Appleton-Century-Crofts, Inc., 1952.

BRYANT, DONALD C., and KARL R. WALLACE, *Fundamentals of Public Speaking*, 3rd ed. New York: Appleton-Century-Crofts, Inc., 1960.

MUDD, CHARLES S., and MALCOLM O. SILLARS, *Speech: Content and Communication*. San Francisco: Chandler Publishing Company, 1962.

ST. ONGE, KEITH R., *Creative Speech*. Belmont, California: Wadsworth Publishing Company, Inc., 1964.

SOPER, PAUL L., *Basic Public Speaking*. New York: Oxford University Press, 1956.

STROUD, JAMES B., *Psychology of Education*. New York: David McKay Company, Inc., 1956.

THOMAS, CHARLES KENNETH, *Handbook of Speech Improvement*. New York: McGraw-Hill, Inc., 1953.

WEAVER, ANDREW T., and ORDEAN G. NESS, *The Fundamentals and Forms of Speech*. New York: The Odyssey Press, Inc., 1957.

2. *Organization*

BARNES, HARRY G., and LORETTA WAGNER SMITH, *Speech Fundamentals*. Englewood Cliffs, N.J.: Prentice-Hall, Inc., 1953.

BRYANT, DONALD C., and KARL R. WALLACE, *Fundamentals of Public Speaking*, 3rd ed. New York: Appleton-Century-Crofts, Inc., 1960.

GILMAN, WILBUR E., BOWER ALY, and LOREN D. REID, *The Fundamentals of Speaking*. New York: The Macmillan Company, 1951.

MCBURNEY, JAMES H., and ERNEST J. WRAGE, *The Art of Good Speech*. Englewood Cliffs, N.J.: Prentice-Hall, Inc., 1953.

MONROE, ALAN H., *Principles and Types of Speech*. Chicago: Scott, Foresman and Company, 1955.

OLIVER, ROBERT T., DALLAS C. DICKEY, and HAROLD P. ZELKO, *Communicative Speech*. New York: Holt, Rinehart and Winston, Inc., 1955.

THOMPSON, WAYNE N., *Fundamentals of Communication*. New York: McGraw-Hill, Inc., 1957.

WHITE, EUGENE E., and CLAIR R. HENDERLIDER, *Practical Public Speaking*. New York: The Macmillan Company, 1954.

3. *Developmental and Supporting Details*

ANDERSCH, ELIZABETH G., and LORIN C. STAATS, *Speech for Everyday Use*, rev. ed. New York: Holt, Rinehart and Winston, 1960.

BAIRD, A. CRAIG, and FRANKLIN H. KNOWER, *Essentials of General Speech.*
New York: McGraw-Hill, Inc., 1960.
BARNES, HARRY G., and LORETTA W. SMITH, *Speech Fundamentals.* Englewood Cliffs, N.J.: Prentice-Hall, Inc., 1953.
BRYANT, DONALD C., and KARL R. WALLACE, *Fundamentals of Public Speaking,* 3rd ed. New York: Appleton-Century-Crofts, Inc., 1960.
HEDDE, WILHELMINA G., and WILLIAM N. BRIGANCE, *The New American Speech.* Philadelphia: J. B. Lippincott Company, 1957.
MCBURNEY, JAMES H., and ERNEST J. WRAGE, *Guide to Good Speech,* 2nd ed. Englewood Cliffs, N.J.: Prentice-Hall, Inc., 1960.
MONROE, ALAN H., *Principles and Types of Speech.* Chicago: Scott, Foresman and Company, 1955.
WHITE, EUGENE E., and CLAIR R. HENDERLIDER, *Practical Public Speaking.* New York: The Macmillan Company, 1954.

4. *Adjustment to the Speech Situation*

BAIRD, A. CRAIG, and FRANKLIN H. KNOWER, *General Speech,* 2nd ed. New York: McGraw-Hill, Inc., 1957.
CLEVENGER, THEODORE, JR., and GREGG PHIFER, "What Do Beginning College Speech Texts Say About Stage Fright?" *Speech Teacher,* vol. 8, no. 1 (January 1959), pp. 1–7.
FRIEDERICH, WILLARD J., and RUTH A. WILCOX, *Teaching Speech in High School.* New York: The Macmillan Company, 1953.
LOMAS, CHARLES, "The Psychology of Stage Fright," *Quarterly Journal of Speech,* vol. 23, no. 1 (February 1937), pp. 35–44.
REID, LOREN D., *Teaching Speech,* 3rd ed. Columbia, Missouri: Artcraft Press, 1960.

5. *Bodily Action for Purposes of Communication*

ADAMS, HARLEN M., and THOMAS C. POLLOCK, *Speak Up!* New York: The Macmillan Company, 1956.
BAIRD, A. CRAIG, and FRANKLIN H. KNOWER, *General Speech.* New York: McGraw-Hill, Inc., 1957.
BRADEN, WALDO W., and ASSOCIATES, *Speech Methods and Resources.* New York: Harper & Row, Publishers, 1961.
BRYANT, DONALD C., and KARL R. WALLACE, *Fundamentals of Public Speaking,* 3rd ed. New York: Appleton-Century-Crofts, Inc., 1960.
CROCKER, LIONEL, *Public Speaking for College Students,* 3rd ed. New York: American Book Company, 1956.
DENSMORE, G. E., "The Teaching of Speech Delivery," *Quarterly Journal of Speech,* vol. 32, no. 1 (February 1946), pp. 67–71.
DRUSHAL, J. GARVER, "An Objective Analysis of Two Techniques of Teaching Delivery in Public Speaking," *Quarterly Journal of Speech,* vol. 35, no. 4 (December 1939), pp. 561–569.
GRAY, GILES W., and WALDO W. BRADEN, *Public Speaking: Principles and Practice.* New York: Harper & Row, Publishers, 1951.

Griffith, Francis, Catherine Nelson, and Edward Stasheff, *Your Speech*. New York: Harcourt, Brace & World, 1960.
Hedde, Wilhelmina G., and William N. Brigance, *The New American Speech*. Philadelphia: J. B. Lippincott Company, 1957.
Irwin, John V., and Marjorie Rosenberger, *Modern Speech*. New York: Holt, Rinehart and Winston, Inc., 1961.
McBurney, James H., and Ernest J. Wrage, *Guide to Good Speech*. Englewood Cliffs, N.J.: Prentice-Hall, Inc., 1960.
Monroe, Alan H., *Principles and Types of Speech*, 3rd ed. Chicago: Scott, Foresman and Company, 1955.
Parrish, Wayland Maxfield, "Elocution: A Definition and a Challenge," *Quarterly Journal of Speech*, vol. 43, no. 1 (February 1957), pp. 1–11.
———, "The Concept of 'Naturalness,'" *Quarterly Journal of Speech*, vol. 37, no. 4 (December 1951), pp. 448–454.
Robinson, Karl F., and E. J. Kerikas, *Teaching Speech Methods and Materials*. New York: David McKay Company, Inc., 1963.
Sarett, Lew, W. T. Foster, and James H. McBurney, *Speech: A High School Course*. Boston: Houghton Mifflin Company, 1956.
Weaver, Andrew T., Gladys L. Borchers, and Donald K. Smith, *The Teaching of Speech*. Englewood Cliffs, N.J.: Prentice-Hall, Inc., 1952.
———, and Ordean Gerhard Ness, *The Fundamentals and Forms of Speech*. New York: The Odyssey Press, 1957.

6. *Voice Usage*

Akin, Johnnye, *And So We Speak: Voice and Articulation*. Englewood Cliffs, N.J.: Prentice-Hall, Inc., 1958.
Barnes, John, "Vital Capacity and Ability in Oral Reading," *Quarterly Journal of Speech*, vol. 12, no. 3 (June 1926), pp. 176–182.
Brown, Hazel P., *American Speech Sounds and Rhythm—Elementary-Intermediate-Advanced*. New York: I.C.R. Corporation, 1959.
Bryant, Donald C., and Karl R. Wallace, *Fundamentals of Public Speaking*, 3rd ed. New York: Appleton-Century-Crofts, Inc., 1960.
Cartier, F. A., *The Phonetic Alphabet*. Dubuque, Iowa: William C. Brown Company, Publishers, 1954.
Cotton, Jack C., "Tongue Movements and Vocal Quality," *Speech Monographs*, vol. 4 (1937), pp. 38–43.
Ecroyd, Donald H., "A Rationale for the Teaching of Voice and Diction," *Speech Teacher*, vol. 8, no. 3 (September 1959), pp. 256–259.
Fairbanks, Grant, *Practical Voice Practice*. New York: Harper & Row, Publishers, 1944.
———, *Voice and Articulation Drillbook*, 2nd ed. New York: Harper & Row, Publishers, 1960.
Grim, Harriet Elizabeth, *Practical Voice Training*. New York: Appleton-Century-Crofts, Inc., 1948.
Hauth, Lus, "Voice Improvement: The Speech Teacher's Responsibility," *Speech Teacher*, vol. 10, no. 1 (January 1961), pp. 48–52.

LINDSLEY, CHARLES F., "Psycho-Physical Determinants of Voice Quality," *Speech Monographs*, vol. 1 (1934), pp. 79–116.
MANSER, RUTH B., and LEONARD FINLAN, *The Speaking Voice*. New York: David McKay Company, Inc., 1950.
MCCURDY, FRANCES LEA, "Speech Improvement and the High School Speech Class," *Central States Speech Journal*, Spring, 1958, pp. 43–46.
MOORE, PAUL, "Vocal Fold Movement during Vocalization," *Speech Monographs*, vol. 4 (1937), pp. 44–55.
OGILVIE, MARDEL, *Teaching Speech in the High School*. New York: Appleton-Century-Crofts, Inc., 1961.
THOMAS, CHARLES KENNETH, *Handbook of Speech Improvement*. New York: McGraw-Hill, Inc., 1953.
VAN DUSEN, C. RAYMOND, *Training the Voice for Speech*, 2nd ed. New York: McGraw-Hill, Inc., 1953.

7. *Enunciation, Articulation, and Pronunciation*

AKIN, JOHNNYE, *And So We Speak: Voice and Articulation*. Englewood Cliffs, N.J.: Prentice-Hall, Inc., 1958.
ANDERSON, VIRGIL A., *Improving the Child's Speech*. New York: Oxford University Press, Inc., 1953.
BACKUS, OLLIE, and JANE E. BEASLEY, *Speech Therapy with Children*. Boston: Houghton Mifflin Company, 1951.
BAIRD, A. CRAIG, and FRANKLIN H. KNOWER, *Essentials of General Speech*, 2nd ed. New York: McGraw-Hill, Inc., 1960.
BERRY, MILDRED F., and JON EISENSON, *Speech Disorders: Principles and Practices of Therapy*. New York: Appleton-Century-Crofts, Inc., 1956.
DODD, CELESTE VARNELL, and HUGH F. SEABURY, *Our Speech*. Austin, Texas: The Steck Company, 1940.
FAIRBANKS, GRANT, *Practical Voice Practice*. New York: Harper & Row, Publishers, 1944.
———, *Voice and Articulation Drillbook*. New York: Harper & Row, Publishers, 1960.
GRASHAM, JOHN A., and GLENN G. GOODER, *Improving Your Speech*. New York: Harcourt, Brace & World, 1960.
GRIFFITH, FRANCIS, CATHERINE NELSON, and EDWARD STASHEFF, *Your Speech*. New York: Harcourt, Brace & World, 1955.
HEDDE, WILHELMINA G., and WILLIAM N. BRIGANCE, *The New American Speech*. Philadelphia: J. B. Lippincott Company, 1957.
HICKS, HELEN GERTRUDE, *Voice and Speech for Effective Communication*. Dubuque, Iowa: William C. Brown Company, Publishers, 1963.
———, *Voice and Speech for Effective Communication—A Reading Book*. Dubuque, Iowa: William C. Brown Company, Publishers, 1963.
JOHNSON, WENDELL, FREDERICK L. DARLEY, and D. C. SPRIESTERSBACH, *Diagnostic Manual in Speech Correction*. New York: Harper & Row, Publishers, 1963.
———, SPENCER F. BROWN, JAMES F. CURTIS, CLARENCE W. EDNEY, and

Jacqueline Keaster, *Speech Handicapped School Children*, rev. ed. New York: Harper & Row, Publishers, 1956.

Kelley, J. C., "The Classroom Communication Test in Voice and Articulation Course," *Speech Teacher*, vol. 4, no. 2 (March 1955), pp. 89–97.

Konigsberg, Evelyn, and Mildred Windecker, "Speech Correction in the High School," *Speech Teacher*, vol. 4, no. 4 (November 1955), pp. 247–252.

Lorberg, M. G. Jr., "The Classroom Teacher and the Speech Correction Program," *Speech Teacher*, vol. 4, no. 1 (January 1955), p. 42.

Mulgrave, Dorothy, *Speech for the Classroom Teacher*, 3rd ed. Englewood Cliffs, N.J.: Prentice-Hall, Inc., 1955.

Pronovost, Wilbert L., "Methods of Developing the Speaking Voice in the Elementary School," *Boston University Journal of Education*, October, 1956.

Raubicheck, Letitia, *Your Voice and Speech*. Englewood Cliffs, N.J.: Prentice-Hall, Inc., 1953.

Thomas, C. K., *An Introduction to the Phonetics of American English*, 2nd ed. New York: The Ronald Press, 1958.

Van Riper, Charles, and John Irwin, *Voice and Articulation*. Englewood Cliffs, N.J.: Prentice-Hall, Inc., 1958.

Wise, Claude M., *Applied Phonetics*. Englewood Cliffs, N.J.: Prentice-Hall, Inc., 1957.

8. Language

Baird, A. Craig, and Franklin H. Knower, *Essentials of General Speech*, 2nd ed. New York: McGraw-Hill, Inc., 1960.

Black, John W., and Wilbur C. Moore, *Speech: Code, Meaning, and Communication*. New York: McGraw-Hill, Inc., 1955.

Borchers, Gladys L., "An Approach to the Problem of Oral Style," *Quarterly Journal of Speech*, vol. 22, no. 1 (February 1936), pp. 114–117.

Bryant, Donald C., and Karl R. Wallace, *Fundamentals of Public Speaking*, 3rd ed. New York: Appleton-Century-Crofts, Inc., 1960.

Hayakawa, S. I., *Language in Action*. New York: Harcourt, Brace & World, 1941.

———, *Language in Thought and Action*. New York: Harcourt, Brace & World, 1949.

———, *Language: Meaning and Maturity*. New York: Harper & Row, Publishers, 1959.

Johnson, Wendell, *People in Quandaries*. New York: Harper & Row, Publishers, 1946.

Lee, Irving J., "Four Ways of Looking at a Speech," *Quarterly Journal of Speech*, vol. 28, no. 2 (April 1942), pp. 148–155.

———, *Language Habits in Human Affairs: An Introduction to General Semantics*. New York: Harper & Row, Publishers, 1941.

Murphy, Richard, "The Speech as Literary Genre," *Quarterly Journal of Speech*, vol. 44, no. 2 (April 1958), pp. 117–127.

ROBINSON, KARL F., and E. J. KERIKAS, *Teaching Speech Methods and Materials*. New York: David McKay Company, Inc., 1963.
THOMAS, GORDON L., "Oral Style and Intelligibility," *Speech Monographs*, vol. 23, no. 1 (March 1956), pp. 46–54.
THONSSEN, LESTER, and A. CRAIG BAIRD, *Speech Criticism*. New York: Ronald Press Company, 1948.
———, and HOWARD GILKINSON, *Basic Training in Speech*. Boston: D. C. Heath and Company, 1953.
WEAVER, ANDREW T., GLADYS L. BORCHERS, and DONALD K. SMITH, *The Teaching of Speech*. Englewood Cliffs, N.J.: Prentice-Hall, Inc., 1952.

9. *Adaptation in the Speaking Situation*

ANDERSCH, ELIZABETH G., and LORIN C. STAATS, *Speech for Everyday Use*, rev. ed. New York: Holt, Rinehart and Winston, Inc., 1960.
BAIRD, A. CRAIG, and FRANKLIN H. KNOWER, *Essentials of General Speech*, 2nd ed. New York: McGraw-Hill, Inc., 1960.
BRIGANCE, WILLIAM NORWOOD, *Speech*. New York: Appleton-Century-Crofts, Inc., 1952.
GILMAN, WILBUR E., BOWER ALY, and LOREN D. REID, *The Fundamentals of Speaking*. New York: The Macmillan Company, 1951.
GRAY, GILES W., and WALDO W. BRADEN, *Public Speaking: Principles and Practice*, 2nd ed. New York: Harper & Row, Publishers, 1963.
MCBURNEY, JAMES H., and ERNEST J. WRAGE, *The Art of Good Speech*. Englewood Cliffs, N.J.: Prentice-Hall, Inc., 1953.
SANDFORD, WILLIAM P., and W. HAYES YEAGER, *Principles of Effective Speaking*. New York: The Ronald Press Company, 1950.

10. *Listening*

ANDERSCH, ELIZABETH G., and LORIN C. STAATS, *Speech for Everyday Use*, rev. ed. New York: Holt, Rinehart and Winston, Inc., 1960.
BAIRD, A. CRAIG, and FRANKLIN H. KNOWER, *Essentials of General Speech*, 2nd ed. New York; McGraw-Hill, Inc., 1960.
BARRETT, HAROLD, *Practical Methods in Speech*. New York: Holt, Rinehart and Winston, Inc., 1959.
BROWN, CHARLES T., "Studies in Listening Comprehension," *Speech Monographs*, vol. 26, no. 4 (November 1959), pp. 288–294.
DUKER, SAM, *Listening Bibliography*. New York: The Scarecrow Press, Inc., 1964.
GRIFFITH, FRANCIS, CATHERINE NELSON, and EDWARD STASHEFF, *Your Speech*. New York: Harcourt, Brace & World, 1955.
HACKETT, HERBERT, MARTIN ANDERSEN, SETH FESSENDEN, and LESSIE LEE HAGEN, *Understanding and Being Understood*. New York: David McKay Company, Inc., 1957.
HEDDE, WILHELMINA G., and WILLIAM NORWOOD BRIGANCE, *The New American Speech*. Philadelphia: J. B. Lippincott Company, 1957.

JOHNSON, WENDELL, *Your Most Enchanted Listener*. New York: Harper & Row, Publishers, 1956.

MCCLENDON, PAUL I., "An Experimental Study of the Relationship Between the Note-Taking Practices and Listening Comprehension of College Freshmen during Expository Lectures," *Speech Monographs*, vol. 25, no. 3 (August 1958), pp. 222–228.

RENWICK, RALPH, JR., "A Listening Course for High School Seniors," *Speech Teacher*, vol. 6, no. 1 (January 1957), pp. 59–62.

ROBINSON, KARL F., "Teaching Listening through Evaluation and Criticism," *Speech Teacher*, vol. 2, no. 3 (September 1953), pp. 178–180.

———, and E. J. KERIKAS, *Teaching Speech Methods and Materials*. New York: David McKay Company, Inc., 1963.

WEAVER, ANDREW T., GLADYS L. BORCHERS, and DONALD K. SMITH, *The Teaching of Speech*. New York: Prentice-Hall, Inc., 1952.

WHITE, WILLIAM H., JR., *Is Anybody Listening?* New York: Simon and Schuster, Inc., 1952.

Selected Bibliography

Speech Activities

1. *Informal Speech*

DODD, CELESTE VARNELL, and HUGH F. SEABURY, *Our Speech*. Austin, Texas: The Steck Company, 1940.

ELSON, E. F., and ALBERTA PECK, *The Art of Speaking*. Boston: Ginn & Company, 1952.

GRIFFITH, FRANCIS, CATHERINE NELSON, and EDWARD STASHEFF, *Your Speech*. New York: Harcourt, Brace & World, 1955.

MAWHINNEY, CLARA KREFTING, "Speech in Informal Social Activities," *Bulletin of the National Association of Secondary School Principals*, November, 1945, pp. 47–50.

OGILVIE, MARDEL, *Teaching Speech in the High School*. New York: Appleton-Century-Crofts, Inc., 1961.

REID, LOREN, *Teaching Speech*, 3rd. ed. Columbia, Missouri: Artcraft Press, 1960.

WEAVER, ANDREW T., GLADYS L. BORCHERS, and DONALD K. SMITH, *The Teaching of Speech*. Englewood Cliffs, N.J.: Prentice-Hall, Inc., 1952.

———, and ORDEAN G. NESS, *The Fundamentals and Forms of Speech*. New York: The Odyssey Press, 1957.

YOUNGBLOOD, DOROTHY, "Informal and Business Speech," *Bulletin of the National Association of Secondary School Principals*, January, 1948, pp. 98–101.

2. *Public Speaking*

ANDERSCH, ELIZABETH G., and LORIN C. STAATS, *Speech for Everyday Use*, rev. ed. New York: Holt, Rinehart and Winston, Inc., 1960.

BAIRD, A. CRAIG, and FRANKLIN H. KNOWER, *General Speech*, 2nd ed. New York: McGraw-Hill, Inc., 1957.
BRADEN, WALDO W., and MARY LOUISE GEHRING, *Speech Practices: A Resource Book for the Student of Public Speaking*. New York: Harper & Row, Publishers, 1958.
BRYANT, DONALD C., and KARL R. WALLACE, *Fundamentals of Public Speaking*, 3rd ed. New York: Appleton-Century-Crofts, Inc., 1960.
GRAY, GILES W., and WALDO W. BRADEN, *Public Speaking: Principles and Practice*, 2nd ed. New York: Harper & Row, Publishers, 1963.
MONROE, ALAN H., *Principles and Types of Speech*, 5th ed. Chicago: Scott, Foresman and Company, 1962.
NICHOLS, MARIE HOCHMUTH, *Rhetoric and Criticism*. Baton Rouge, Louisiana: Louisiana State University Press, 1963.
OLIVER, ROBERT T., and RUPERT L. CORTRIGHT, *Effective Speech*, 4th ed. New York: Holt, Rinehart and Winston, Inc., 1962.
REID, LOREN D., *First Principles of Public Speaking*, 2nd ed. Columbia, Missouri: Artcraft Press, 1962.
SARETT, LEW, W. T. FOSTER, and ALMA SARETT, *Basic Principles of Speech*, 3rd ed. Boston: Houghton Mifflin Company, 1958.
WHITE, EUGENE E., *Practical Public Speaking*, 2nd ed. New York: The Macmillan Company, 1964.

3. *Discussion and Debate*

BAIRD, A. CRAIG, *Argumentation, Discussion, and Debate*. New York: McGraw-Hill, Inc., 1950.
———, *Public Discussion and Debate*. Boston: Ginn and Company, 1928.
BRADEN, WALDO W., and EARNEST BRANDENBURG, *Oral Decision-Making: Principles of Discussion and Debate*. New York: Harper & Row, Publishers, 1955.
CHENOWETH, EUGENE C., *Discussion and Debate*. Dubuque, Iowa: William C. Brown Company, Publishers, 1951.
———, *Discussion and Debate Project Book*. Dubuque, Iowa: William C. Brown Company, Publishers, 1952.
CROWELL, LAURA, *Discussion: Method of Democracy*. Chicago: Scott, Foresman and Company, 1963.
EHNINGER, DOUGLAS, and WAYNE BROCKRIEDE, *Decision by Debate*. New York: Dodd, Mead & Company, Inc., 1963.
EWBANK, HENRY LEE, and J. JEFFERY AUER, *Discussion and Debate: Tools of a Democracy*, 2nd ed. New York: Appleton-Century-Crofts, Inc., 1951.
FREELEY, AUSTIN J., *Argumentation and Debate*. Belmont, California: Wadsworth Publishing Company, Inc., 1961.
GULLY, HALBERT E., *Essentials of Discussion and Debate*. New York: Holt, Rinehart and Winston, Inc., 1955.
HUBER, ROBERT B., *Influencing Through Argumentation*. New York: David McKay Company, Inc., 1963.

Kruger, Arthur N., *Modern Debate: Its Logic and Strategy.* New York: McGraw-Hill, Inc., 1960.

———, *A Classified Bibliography of Argumentation and Debate.* New York: The Scarecrow Press, Inc., 1964.

McBath, James H., ed., and Contributing Authors, *Argumentation and Debate: Principles and Practices,* rev. ed. New York: Holt, Rinehart and Winston, Inc., 1963.

McBurney, J. H., and Kenneth G. Hance, *Discussion in Human Affairs.* New York: Harper & Row, Publishers, 1950.

Musgrave, George M., *Competitive Debate: Rules and Techniques,* 3rd ed. New York: The H. W. Wilson Company, 1957.

Potter, David, and Martin P. Anderson, *Discussion: A Guide to Effective Practice.* Belmont, California: Wadsworth Publishing Company, Inc., 1963.

Summers, Harrison B., Forest L. Whan, and Thomas A. Rousse, *How to Debate: A Textbook for Beginners.* New York: The H. W. Wilson Company, 1950.

Utterback, William E., *Group Thinking and Conference Leadership,* rev. ed. New York: Holt, Rinehart and Winston, Inc., 1964.

Wagner, Russell H., and Carroll C. Arnold, *Handbook of Group Discussion.* Boston: Houghton Mifflin Company, 1950.

4. Parliamentary Procedure

Auer, J. Jeffery, *Essentials of Parliamentary Procedure,* 3rd. ed. New York: Appleton-Century-Crofts, Inc., 1959.

Davidson, Henry A., *Handbook of Parliamentary Procedure.* New York: The Ronald Press Company, 1955.

Gray, Giles W., "Points of Emphasis in Teaching Parliamentary Procedure," *Speech Teacher,* vol. 13, no. 1 (January 1964), pp. 10–15.

Gray, John W., and Richard G. Rea, "Teaching Parliamentary Procedure through Programmed Instruction," *Speech Teacher,* vol. 13, no. 1 (January 1964), pp. 21–24.

Menderson, Melanie F., *Parliamentary Procedure Simplified.* Cincinnati, Ohio: The Dale Press, 1959.

O'Brien, Joseph F., *Parliamentary Law for the Layman: Procedure and Strategy for Meetings.* New York: Harper & Row, Publishers, Inc., 1952.

Ralph, David C., "The Flannel Board as an Aid in Teaching Parliamentary Procedure," *Speech Teacher,* vol. 8, no. 1 (January 1959), pp. 15–21.

Robert, H. M., *Robert's Rules of Order,* 75th Anniversary Edition. Chicago: Scott, Foresman and Company, 1959.

Sturgis, Alice F., *Learning Parliamentary Procedure.* Boston: Houghton Mifflin Company, 1953.

5. Oral Reading and Interpretation

Aggertt, Otis J., and Elbert R. Bowen, *Communicative Reading.* New York: The Macmillan Company, 1956.

Armstrong, Chloe, and Paul D. Brandeis, *The Oral Interpretation of Literature.* New York: McGraw-Hill, Inc., 1963.

BACON, WALLACE A., and ROBERT S. BREEN, *Literature as Experience.* New York. McGraw-Hill, Inc., 1959.
COBIN, MARTIN, *Theory and Technique of Interpretation.* Englewood Cliffs, N.J.: Prentice-Hall, Inc., 1959.
COGER, LESLIE IRENE, and MELVIN R. WHITE, *Studies in Readers' Theatre.* New York: S and F Press, 1963.
COMPERE, MOIREE, *Living Literature for Oral Interpretation.* New York: Appleton-Century-Crofts, Inc., 1949.
CROCKER, LIONEL G., and LOUIS M. EICH, *Oral Reading,* 2nd ed. Englewood Cliffs, N.J.: Prentice-Hall, Inc., 1955.
DOLMAN, JOHN, JR., *The Art of Reading Aloud.* New York: Harper and Row, Publishers, 1956.
HILE, FREDRICK W., and JOSEPH A. WIGLEY, *Oral Interpretation Workbook.* Dubuque, Iowa: William C. Brown Company, 1958.
LOWREY, SARA, and GERTRUDE JOHNSON, *Interpretative Reading,* rev. ed. New York: Appleton-Century-Crofts, Inc., 1953.
LYNCH, GLADYS E., and HAROLD C. CRAIN, *Projects in Oral Interpretation.* New York: Holt, Rinehart and Winston, Inc., 1959.
PARRISH, WAYLAND M., *Reading Aloud,* 3rd ed. New York: The Ronald Press Company, 1953.
SMITH, JOSEPH, and JAMES LINN, *Oral Reading Skills.* New York: Harper & Row, Publishers, 1960.
WOOLBERT, CHARLES H., and SEVERINA E. NELSON, *The Art of Interpretative Speech,* 4th ed. New York: Appleton-Century-Crofts, Inc., 1956.

6. Choral Speaking

ABNEY, LOUISE, *Choral Speaking Arrangements for the Junior High.* Magnolia, Mass.: Expression Company, 1959.
BROWN, HELEN A., and HARRY J. HELTMAN, *Choral Reading for Fun and Recreation.* Philadelphia: The Westminster Press, 1956.
GARRISON, GERALDINE, "Bibliography of Choral Speaking in the Elementary School," *Speech Teacher,* vol. 3, no. 2 (March 1954), pp. 107–111.
GULLAN, MAJORIE, *The Speech Choir: With American Poetry and English Ballads for Choral Reading.* New York: Harper & Row, Publishers, 1937.
HAMM, AGNES C., *Choral Speaking Techniques,* 3rd ed. Tower Press, 1951.
HEDDE, WILHELMINA G., and WILLIAM N. BRIGANCE, *The New American Speech.* Philadelphia: J. B. Lippincott Company, 1957.
RAUBICHECK, LETITIA, *Choral Speaking Is Fun—Book I.* New York: Noble & Noble, Inc., 1955.
———, *Choral Speaking Is Fun—Book II.* New York: Noble and Noble, Inc., 1958.

7. Storytelling

ARBUTHNOT, MAY HILL, *Children and Books,* rev. ed. Chicago: Scott, Foresman and Company, 1957.
BONES, WOUTRINA A., *Children's Stories and How to Tell Them.* New York: Harcourt, Brace & World, 1949.

Dodd, Celeste Varnell, and Hugh F. Seabury, *Our Speech*. Austin, Texas: The Steck Company, 1940.

Hedde, Wilhelmina G., and William N. Brigance, *The New American Speech*. Philadelphia: J. B. Lippincott Company, 1957.

Sawyer, Ruth, *The Way of the Story Teller*. New York: The Viking Press, 1945.

Shedlock, Marie, *Art of the Story-Teller*, 3rd ed. New York: Dover Publications, 1951.

Weaver, Andrew T., Gladys L. Borchers, and Donald K. Smith, *The Teaching of Speech*. Englewood Cliffs, N.J.: Prentice-Hall, Inc., 1952.

8. Dramatics

Albright, H. D., *Working Up a Part*, 2nd ed. Boston: Houghton Mifflin Company, 1959.

Barnes, Grace, and M. J. Sutcliffe, *On Stage, Everyone*. New York: The Macmillan Company, 1954.

Bierman, Judah, James Hart, and Stanley Johnson, *The Dramatic Experience*. Englewood Cliffs, N.J.: Prentice-Hall, Inc., 1958.

Boleslavsky, Richard, *Acting: The First Six Lessons*. New York: Theatre Arts Books, 1959.

Brockett, Oscar G., *The Theatre: An Introduction*. New York: Holt, Rinehart and Winston, Inc., 1964.

Canfield, Curtis, *The Craft of Play Directing*. New York: Holt, Rinehart and Winston, Inc., 1963.

Cole, Toby, and Helen Kirch Chinoy, *Directors on Directing: A Source Book of the Modern Theatre*. Indianapolis: The Bobbs-Merrill Company, Inc., 1963.

Corson, Richard, *Stage Makeup*, 3rd ed. New York: Appleton-Century-Crofts, Inc., 1960.

Dean, Alexander, and Lawrence Carra, *Fundamentals of Play Directing*, rev. ed. New York: Holt, Rinehart and Winston, Inc., 1965.

Dietrich, John E., *Play Direction*. Englewood Cliffs, N.J.: Prentice-Hall, Inc., 1953.

Dolman, John, *The Art of Play Production*, rev. ed. New York: Harper & Row, Publishers, 1946.

———, *The Art of Acting*. New York: Harper & Row, Publishers, 1949.

Friederich, Willard J., *The High School Drama Course*. Cincinnati, Ohio: The National Thespian Society, 1956.

Gassner, John, *Producing the Play*, rev. enl. New York: Holt, Rinehart and Winston, Inc., 1953.

Gillette, A. S., *Stage Scenery: Its Construction and Rigging*. New York: Harper & Row, Publishers, 1959.

Hatlan, Theodore W., *Orientation to the Theatre*. New York: Appleton-Century-Crofts, Inc., 1962.

Heffner, Hubert C., Samuel Selden, and Hunton D. Sellman, *Modern Theatre Practice*, 4th ed. New York: Appleton-Century-Crofts, Inc., 1959.

McCandless, Stanley, *A Method of Lighting the Stage*, 4th ed. New York: Theatre Arts Books, 1958.
Ommanney, Katherine A., and Pierce A. Ommanney, *The Stage and the School*, rev. ed. New York: Harper & Row, Publishers, 1950.
Rice, Elmer, *The Living Theatre*. New York: Harper & Row, Publishers, 1959.
Selden, Samuel, *First Steps in Acting*. New York: Appleton-Century-Crofts, Inc., 1947.
———, and Hunton D. Sellman, *Stage Scenery and Lighting*, 3rd ed. New York: Appleton-Century-Crofts, Inc., 1959.
Whiting, Frank M., *Introduction to the Theatre*, rev. ed. New York: Harper & Row, Publishers, 1954.
Wright, Edward A., *A Primer for Playgoers*. Englewood Cliffs, N.J.: Prentice-Hall, Inc., 1958.

9. *Radio and Television*

Becker, Samuel L., and H. Clay Harshbarger, *Television: Techniques for Planning and Performance*. New York: Holt, Rinehart and Winston, Inc., 1958.
Chester, Giraud, and Garnet R. Garrison, *Television and Radio: An Introduction*, 2nd ed. New York: Appleton-Century-Crofts, Inc., 1956.
Duerr, Edwin, *Radio and Television Acting*. New York: Holt, Rinehart and Winston, Inc., 1950.
Henneke, Ben Fraf, and Edward S. Dumit, *The Announcer's Handbook*. New York: Holt, Rinehart and Winston, Inc., 1959.
Hilliard, Robert L., *Understanding Television*. New York: Hastings House, Publishers, Inc., 1964.
Kingson, Walter K., and Rome Cowgill, *Television Acting and Directing: A Handbook*. New York: Holt, Rinehart and Winston, Inc., 1965.
Lawton, Sherman P., *Introduction to Modern Broadcasting: A Manual for Students*. New York: Harper & Row, Publishers, 1964.
Robinson, Karl F., and Stanley T. Donner, "Suggested Units in Radio for the Secondary School," *Quarterly Journal of Speech*, vol. 33, no. 2 (April 1947), pp. 225–228.
Roe, Yale, *Television Station Management*. New York: Hastings House, Publishers, Inc., 1964.
Turnbull, Robert B., *Radio and Television Sound Effects*. New York: Holt, Rinehart and Winston, Inc., 1951.
Wylie, Max, *Radio and Television Writing*, rev. ed. New York: Holt, Rinehart and Winston, Inc., 1950.
Zettl, Herbert, *Television Production Handbook*. Belmont, California: Wadsworth Publishing Company, Inc., 1961.

Collections of Speeches and Speech Criticism

Arnold, Carroll C., Douglas Ehninger, and John C. Gerber, *The Speaker's Resource Book*. Chicago: Scott, Foresman and Company, 1961.

Bach, Robert O., ed., *Communication: The Art of Understanding and Being Understood*. New York: Hastings House, Publishers, Inc., 1963.

Baird, A. Craig, *American Public Addresses: 1740–1952*. New York: McGraw-Hill, Inc., 1956.

———, *Representative American Speeches*. New York: H. W. Wilson Company, annually since 1937–1938.

Black, John W., and Wilbur E. Moore, *Speech: Code, Meaning, and Communication*. New York: McGraw-Hill, Inc., 1955.

Brembeck, Winston L., and William Smiley Howell, *Persuasion: A Means of Social Control*. Englewood Cliffs, N. J.: Prentice-Hall, Inc., 1952.

Brigance, W. N., comp., *Classified Speech Models*. New York: F. S. Crofts and Company, 1930.

———, ed., *History and Criticism of American Public Address*. New York: McGraw-Hill, Inc., 1943. 2 vols.

Dunlap, Orrin E., Jr., *Communications in Space*. New York: Harper and Row, Publishers, 1962.

Eisenson, Jon, Jeffery Auer, and John V. Irwin, *The Psychology of Communication*. New York: Appleton-Century-Crofts, Inc., 1963.

Goodrich, Chauncey A., *Select British Eloquence*. Indianapolis: The Bobbs-Merrill Company, Inc., 1963.

Gordon, George N., Irving Falk, and William Hodapp, *The Idea Invaders: International Propaganda and Mass Communication*. New York: Hastings House, Publishers, Inc., 1963.

Gray, Giles W., and Claude M. Wise, *The Bases of Speech*, 3rd ed. New York: Harper & Row, Publishers, 1959.

Hochmuth, Marie, Donald Bryant, Karl Wallace, and W. N. Brigance, *History and Criticism of American Public Address*. Englewood Cliffs, N.J.: Prentice-Hall, Inc., 1956. 3 vols.

Lee, Irving J., and Laura L. Lee, *Conferee's Handbook for Handling Barriers in Communication*. New York: Harper & Row, Publishers, 1957.

Nichols, Marie Hochmuth, *Rhetoric and Criticism*. Baton Rouge, Louisiana: Louisiana State University Press, 1963.

Parrish, W. M., and Marie Hochmuth, *American Speeches*. New York: David McKay Company, Inc., 1954.

Peterson, Houston, ed., *A Treasury of the World's Great Speeches*. New York: Simon and Schuster, Inc., 1954.

Redding, W. Charles, and George A. Sanborn, *Business and Industrial Communication: A Source Book*. New York: Harper & Row, Publishers, 1964.

Schramm, Wilbur, *Responsibility in Mass Communication*. New York: Harper & Row, Publishers, 1957.

Sutton, Roberta, *Speech Index*. New York: The H. W. Wilson Company, 1935.

Thompson, Wayne N., *Fundamentals of Communication: An Integrated Approach*. New York: McGraw-Hill, Inc., 1963.

Thonssen, Lester, and William L. Finkel, *Ideas That Matter*. New York: The Ronald Press Company, 1961.

THORP, WILLARD, MERLE CURTIS, and CARLOS BAKER, *American Issues*. Philadelphia: J. B. Lippincott Company, 1941.
WOOLBERT, CHARLES HENRY, *Fundamentals of Speech*, 3rd ed. New York: Harper & Row, Publishers, 1934.
WRAGE, ERNEST J., and BARNET BASKERVILLE, *American Forum: Speeches on Historical Issues, 1788–1900*. New York: Harper & Row, Publishers, 1960.

Collections of Drama and Dramatic Criticism

ANDERSON, MAXWELL, *The Essence of Tragedy and Other Footnotes and Papers*. Washington, D.C.: Anderson House, Publisher, 1939.
BAKER, BLANCHE, *Dramatic Bibliography*. New York: The H. W. Wilson Company, 1933.
BUTCHER, S. H., *Aristotle's Theory of Poetry and Fine Art*. New York: Dover Publications, 1951.
CLARK, BARRETT H., *European Theories of Drama*. New York: Crown Publishers, Inc., 1947.
DOWNER, ALAN S., *Fifty Years of American Drama, 1900–1950*. Chicago: Henry Regnery Company, 1951.
———, *The British Drama: A Handbook in Brief Chronicle*. New York: Appleton-Century-Crofts, Inc., 1950.
FITZGERALD, BURDETTE S., *World Tales: For Creative Dramatics and Storytelling*. Englewood Cliffs, N.J.: Prentice-Hall, Inc., 1962.
GASSNER, JOHN, *Masters of the Drama*. New York: Random House, Inc., 1947.
———, *Masters of the Drama*, rev. ed. New York: Dover Publications, 1954.
GILBERT, ALLAN H., *Literary Criticism: Plato to Dryden*. New York: American Book Company, 1940.
GRANVILLE, WILFRED, *Theatre Dictionary: British and American Terms in the Drama, Opera, and Ballet*. New York: Philosophical Library, 1952.
HEWITT, BERNARD, *Theatre, U.S.A., 1668–1957*. New York: McGraw-Hill, Inc., 1959.
JONES, ROBERT E., *Dramatic Imagination*. New York: Duell, Sloan & Pearce, Inc., 1941.
MACGOWAN, KENNETH, and WILLIAM MELNITZ, *The Living Stage: A History of the World Theatre*. Englewood Cliffs, N.J.: Prentice-Hall, Inc., 1955.
MATTHEWS, BRANDER, *The Development of the Drama*. New York: Charles Scribner's Sons, 1934.
MAYORGA, MARGARET, ed., *Best One-Act Plays*. New York: Dodd, Mead & Company, Inc., annually since 1937.
MILLET, FRED B., and GERALD E. BENTLEY, *The Art of the Drama*. New York: Appleton-Century-Crofts, Inc., 1952.
NICOLL, ALLARDYCE, *The Theory of Drama*. London: George G. Harrap & Co., Ltd., 1931.
———, *World Drama: From Aeschylus to Anouilh*. New York: Harcourt, Brace & World, 1950.

OTTEMILLER, JOHN H., *Index to Play Collections*. New York: The H. W. Wilson Company, 1943.

QUINN, ARTHUR H., *A History of American Drama from the Beginning to the Civil War*. New York: Appleton-Century-Crofts, Inc., 1946.

———, *A History of American Drama from the Civil War to the Present Day*. New York: Appleton-Century-Crofts, Inc., 1945.

RICE, ELMER, *The Living Theatre*. New York: Harper & Row, Publishers, 1959.

WARD, ALFRED C., *Specimens of English Dramatic Criticism, 17th to 20th Centuries*. London: Milford, Publishers, 1945.

WATSON, E. BRADLEE, and BENFIELD PRESSEY, ed., *Contemporary Drama: American, English, and European*. New York: Charles Scribner's Sons, 1956.

———, *Contemporary Drama: American, English, Irish, and European*. New York: Charles Scribner's Sons, 1959.

WRIGHT, EDWARD A., *A Primer for Playgoers*. Englewood Cliffs, N.J.: Prentice-Hall, Inc., 1958.

CHAPTER

6

The Resource Unit in Teaching Speech

The basic problem of planning and developing learning experiences involves preplanning by the teacher, which concerns designing, selecting, and organizing learning experiences for the student who wants to attain educational objectives.

Saylor and Alexander listed the following characteristics of desirable learning experiences:

1. Directly related to goals.
2. Meaningful to learners.
3. Appropriate to maturity of learners.
4. Satisfying to learners.
5. Flexible in development.
6. Related to other experiences.[1]

Of particular importance to the teacher is the principle that learning experiences which are most effective, longer retained, and seemingly most significant are those that are well organized. The "unit" is a term that has come into use to signify an organization of related learning experiences.

One of the most effective ways of planning by teachers in recent years has been by their use of "resource" units. Of the states which have published curriculum guides in English, for example, 57 percent have included one or more sample units of the resource type.[2]

[1] J. Galen Saylor and William M. Alexander, *Curriculum Planning for Better Teaching and Learning*. New York: Holt, Rinehart and Winston, Inc., 1954. pp. 391–396.
[2] Arno Jewett, *English Language Arts in American High Schools*. United States Department of Health, Education, and Welfare Bulletin, No. 13, 1958. p. 53.

Resource units have been variously defined. The National Council of Social Studies defined resource units as "rich resources from which the individual teacher can extract procedures which will help him teach most effectively."[3]

Alberty defined a resource unit as a "systematic and comprehensive survey, analysis, and organization of the possible resources [e.g., problems, issues, activities, bibliographies, and so on] which a teacher might utilize in planning, developing, and evaluating a learning unit."[4]

Klohr's detailed study of resource units used the following definition: "The resource unit is defined in this study as a carefully planned series of suggestions centered in some broad problem, topic, or area of experience and organized to serve as a source of ideas, materials, and procedures to help a teacher in preplanning a learning unit."[5]

Elements of a Resource Unit

In actual practice there appears to be no set formula or one accepted form for the production of a resource unit. However, Klohr's investigation revealed a number of common elements in resource units adjudged to be effective. A well-organized and effective resource unit for use in the secondary school seems to incorporate:

1. A wealth of suggested learning experiences.
2. A survey of possible ways to evaluate the suggested learning experiences.
3. A carefully selected bibliography and list of teaching aids.
4. A stimulating presentation of the scope of the problem area with which the unit deals.
5. A formulation of the philosophy underlying the resource unit and a statement of the specific objectives.
6. Suggestions for the use of the resource unit.[6]

Typical resource units have the following characteristics: (1) they are prepared by a teacher or teachers; (2) they are not given to the students; (3) they are each organized around a central problem or topic; (4) they each contain more materials than any one teacher can use; and (5) they

---

[3] John M. Haefner and others, *Housing America: A Source Unit for the Social Studies.* Washington, D.C.: National Council for Social Studies, Bulletin No. 14, 1940. p. 11.

[4] Harold Alberty, *Reorganizing the High School Curriculum.* New York: The Macmillan Company, 1947. p. 250.

[5] Paul Robert Klohr, "A Study of the Role of the Resource Unit in the Curriculum Reorganization of Selected Secondary Schools," Unpublished Doctoral Dissertation (Ohio State University, 1948).

[6] Paul R. Klohr, "The Resource Unit in Curriculum Reorganization," *National Association of Secondary School Principals Bulletin,* May 1950, pp. 74–77.

each contain suggestions for aims, activities, bibliography, and other classroom activities.

The following outline is suggested as a workable pattern for a resource unit:

Descriptive Title of the Unit   GRADE LEVEL———

I. THE PROBLEM.   What is the nature of the problem as it relates to one or more of the following:
   A. *The prospective students?*   Explain why you believe this problem is a personal problem for the students, whether or not they realize it, drawing from your knowledge of adolescent psychology. Describe the nature of their needs as revealed by their test scores, writings, actions, comments, et cetera.
   B. *The community and larger social environment?*   Explain why you believe this is a social problem whether or not you think society recognizes it as a problem, and why citizens need to recognize the problem, understand it, and seek solutions for it.
   C. *Other factors?*   Include here any other factors which indicate that students need to know and understand the problem such as the will of the school administration, content of a curriculum, philosophy of a textbook, or acceptance of traditional subject matter. Personal judgments of needs might fall into this category.

II. THE OBJECTIVES.   State here what it is that you wish your students to achieve by the end of the unit. All of the subject matter, activities, and materials should be selected to help students achieve these objectives, directly or indirectly. Keep this section brief, realistic, and, above all, clear.
   A. Knowledge.
   B. Understandings.
   C. Skills.
   D. Attitudes or appreciations.

III. SUBJECT MATTER.   Outline here in some detail the knowledge which your students will need in order to clarify the nature of the problem, to understand possible solutions, and to test the solutions. Some of the knowledge may be needed for the students to gain understandings, needed skills, and desirable attitudes or appreciations. You should include more subject matter than you will use in any specific situation. Indicate parts of the subject matter that may be omitted if the students have more background on the problem than you anticipate.

IV. LEARNING ACTIVITIES.   Include here the activities which the students may undertake in order to achieve the objectives of the unit. Since this is a resource unit, you should include more activities than you would likely use with any specific group of students or in any specific situation. You may, for example, include a field trip to a play, even though that might not be possible in a given situation. Include activities for the whole class, for groups within the class, and for individual students.

A. *Initiatory activities.* List here the activities which will introduce students to the problem and arouse their interest in it.
B. *Developmental activities.* List the activities which will help students to clarify the problem, understand the possible solutions to it, and decide upon the best hypothetical solution. It is in these activities that the bulk of the knowledge, skills, and attitudes or appreciations may be learned.
C. *Culminating activities.* These activities should clarify, summarize, and open the students' eyes to new problems or new possibilities for further study.

V. MATERIALS. List the materials which can be useful in learning the subject matter, in carrying out the activities, and in achieving the objectives. Be specific; give full bibliographic information including sources, publisher, film rental library, et cetera. Place an asterisk (*) before materials which are within the easy reach and comprehension of all students, and a plus sign (+) before materials which only the faster or otherwise well-equipped students can likely use.
A. *Student reading materials.* Books, pamphlets, periodicals, dittoed sheets, tests, and the like belong here. If dittoed sheets are to be used for study guides, teacher-constructed tests, et cetera, include an example of each if practicable.
B. *Bulletin board materials.*
C. *Demonstration materials.* Student writing, pictures, newspaper articles, or other materials for opaque projection, direct demonstration, or display; films and filmstrips; and recordings.
D. *Teacher references.*

VI. EVALUATION. Explain how you intend to evaluate the success with which the students achieve the objectives. Note any procedures you may use to test the effectiveness of any of the methods or materials which you use. If the evaluation includes original or written tests, include copies. If the evaluation includes standardized or other printed tests, include the source and price of each test.

Sample Resource Unit

The following illustrative resource unit on "Listening for Pleasure and Profit" is presented to indicate to the teacher of speech the possible utility of resource units. Also, it is presented in anticipation of the student who is a potential teacher in the field of speech communication, especially in the more limited field of listening. It illustrates the variety of learning experiences and resource materials which may be included in a resource unit.

SAMPLE RESOURCE UNIT

LISTENING FOR PLEASURE AND PROFIT
Senior High School Speech Classes

I. THE PROBLEM

   A. *The prospective students:* Speaking is only half of the communication cycle; listening completes it. In the span of one's lifetime, and especially during the school years, more time is spent on the listening phase than on the speaking phase of the cycle. During these formative years, students are in the process of forming the ethical standards, political and social concepts, and attitudes and appreciations which will determine largely the success and happiness of their personal lives. Since the importance of the spoken word in developing these characteristics is understood and accepted, students have a need for developing their listening abilities. They should understand that listening is a medium of learning and that it can be improved through training.

   B. *The community and larger social environment:* A good citizen is a good listener. The spoken word keeps gaining more and more importance in our modern society. The extensive use of the telephone, movies, radio, and television has resulted in an increasing importance of the spoken word. Our democratic form of government is based upon a well-informed public. Most of our information about vital public matters comes through the medium of the spoken word.

   C. *Other factors:* In many professions and occupations effective speaking and listening are important. Social relationships depend heavily upon conversation in which good listening habits are necessary. Modern entertainment, in many ways, depends upon good listening. Much college work is based upon lectures and discussions which make specific demands upon effective listening skills.

II. OBJECTIVES

   A. *General.* The broad objective of the unit is to help the students to prepare for effective listening in any speaking situation. Growing from this general and central aim are the following enabling goals:
   1. To develop a respect for listening as a medium of learning.
   2. To gain an appreciation of the role of the listener in contributing to the speaking situation.
   3. To work toward the elimination of poor listening habits already acquired.
   4. To develop the basic skills, concepts, and attitudes essential to good listening habits.
   5. To give the student experience in listening to informative speech by coordinating specific listening assignments with related assignments in speech, reading, and writing.

   B. *Specific.*
   1. Knowledge.
      a. Good listening is as difficult a task as good speaking, and should be studied as such.

b. Communication is a two-way cycle involving both speaking and listening.
c. Listening is an "active" process.
d. Concentration is essential to good listening and can be improved by the use and training of definite techniques.
e. Listening differs from hearing; listening can be classified into three types.
f. An effective listener understands something of the devices used by speakers to mislead listeners.
g. An effective listener realizes the sources of difficulty in good listening and knows methods for correcting them.
h. Good listening habits help one to explore the social world, secure new information, and discover new interests.

2. Skills.
   a. To be able to listen with a definite purpose in mind.
   b. To be able to listen accurately despite distractions caused by the situation or the speaker.
   c. To be able to reconcile thought speed to speech speed.
   d. To be able to pick out the central ideas of a speech.
   e. To be able to make mental associations as he listens, relating what he hears to his experience.
   f. To evaluate that to which he listens.
   g. To analyze, summarize, and structuralize the presentation.
   h. To maintain an awareness of his own motives in listening and to learn to exercise emotional control in all listening situations.

3. Attitudes and appreciations.
   a. Recognition of the importance of standards of judgment in evaluating speaking.
   b. Awareness of the importance of good listening habits.
   c. Awareness of the personal benefit to be derived from efficient and effective listening.
   d. Awareness of the responsibility of the listener in the communicative situation.
   e. Awareness of the value of delaying reactions and judging objectively what is said by others with whom the listener disagrees.

III. SUBJECT MATTER OUTLINE
  A. *The nature of listening.*
    1. Listening and hearing are not identical.
       a. Hearing is the physical perception of sound.
       b. Listening is the attachment of meaning to aural symbols perceived.
    2. Effective listening is an active, not a passive process.
    3. Some types of listening are:
       a. Appreciative listening.
          (1) It can increase enjoyment of life.
          (2) It can enlarge our experience.

(3) It can expand the range of what we enjoy.
(4) It can improve our use of language.
(5) It can decrease the tension of daily life.
    b. Informative listening.
       (1) It is listening for an answer to a definite problem or question.
       (2) It is listening for directions.
       (3) It is listening for news of current or past interest.
       (4) It is listening for general information.
    c. Critical listening.
       (1) It makes us aware of prejudice in ourselves and others.
       (2) It makes us judge on the basis of facts and information rather than emotions and falsehoods.
       (3) It counteracts the danger of propaganda by making us aware of the methods of the propagandist such as:
           (a) Name-calling.
           (b) Glittering generalities.
           (c) Transfer.
           (d) Testimonial.
           (e) Plain folks.
           (f) Card stacking.
           (g) Band wagon.
       (4) It makes us ask questions to test statements.
           (a) What is the date and origin of the evidence?
           (b) What is the competency of the source?
           (c) Is the source neutral and unprejudiced?
B. *The importance of listening.*
   1. Frequency of listening.
      a. Rankin's study: "Forty-two percent of the communication time of an adult is spent in listening which is more time proportionately than is spent in speaking, reading, or writing."
   2. Importance of listening in conversation.
      a. In the give-and-take of conversation, listening is imperative and courteous.
      b. Listening is what makes conversation effective and harmonious.
   3. Importance of listening to the speaker.
      a. Listening stimulates the speaker and gives him clues to his communicative effectiveness.
   4. Importance of listening in industry.
      a. Improvement of listening skills increases production and efficiency in business and industry.
   5. Importance of listening in learning.
      a. The Commission on the English Curriculum indicated that "pupils from pre-school through college learn more frequently by listening than by any other means."
      b. The majority of pupil and teacher time in school is spent in listening.
      c. Donald E. Bird reported that three separate studies indicated that

listening is more important than reading for success in 38 to 42 percent of college courses taken by freshmen.
  6. Importance of listening in a democracy.
     a. Our political, economic, ethical, and religious ideas are largely determined by the spoken word.
     b. In this age of radio and television, we are in danger of being "led by the ears."
C. *Problems encountered in listening comprehension.*
  1. A basic problem is the reconciling of thought speed to speech speed.
     a. We are able to think much faster than the speaker can verbalize.
     b. The speaker is limited in this respect; the listener can use this "excess time" wisely or unwisely.
  2. External physical situations may make listening difficult.
     a. Uncomfortable position, inadequate ventilation, or crowded conditions may affect listening.
     b. Outside distractions such as noise, weather, or people make listening difficult.
  3. The speaker may fail to communicate effectively.
     a. Poor enunciation and articulation, low volume, or too rapid speech may obscure meaning.
     b. Mispronunciation, unfamiliar vocabulary, or unclear sentences may detract from content.
     c. Lack of enthusiasm, organization, or purpose may invite boredom or mental departure.
  4. The listener may fail because of personal factors.
     a. Intelligence, experience, emotional maturity, and prejudice may affect interpretation.
        (1) What the listener wants, expects, or hopes to hear can affect meaning.
        (2) Antagonism or personal friendship can cause difficulty.
     b. Words may produce different mental impressions than those intended by the speaker.
        (1) Some words have different meanings for different people.
        (2) Emotion-laden words or ideas cause "blocking" in the listener.
     c. Lack of interest or previous experience with the topic at hand can cause listening difficulty.
     d. Common listening habits which cause ineffectiveness were reported by Ralph G. Nichols:
        (1) Calling the subject uninteresting.
        (2) Criticizing the speaker's delivery.
        (3) Getting overstimulated by some point within the speech.
        (4) Listening only for facts.
        (5) Trying to take all notes in outline form.
        (6) Faking attention to the speaker.
        (7) Tolerating or creating distractions.
        (8) Avoiding difficult expository material.

(9) Letting emotion-laden words arouse personal antagonism.
(10) Wasting the advantage of thought speed over speech speed.
D. *Essentials of good listening habits; techniques of improvement.*
  1. Concentration is the answer to the problem of reconciling speech speed to thought speed.
     a. Excess time of the listener should be used to absorb the meaning of the speech.
     b. Four techniques to aid concentration are:
        (1) Anticipate the speaker's next point.
        (2) Identify the kinds of supporting or developmental materials used.
        (3) Recapitulate what has been covered.
        (4) Search for hidden meanings.
     c. "Structuralizing" the speech also helps.
        (1) Each speech has a specific purpose. Identify it.
        (2) The general structure of the organized speech is: introduction, thesis, body, and conclusion.
  2. The listener should arrange favorable conditions or adjust to unfavorable physical conditions.
     a. Bad ventilation or uncomfortable positions, including inability to see the speaker, should be corrected as one enters the situation or becomes aware of it.
     b. Noise, whispering, shuffling, and the like should not be tolerated by good listeners.
  3. The listener should adjust to the speech and to the speaker.
     a. Peculiarities of the speaker should not be used as an excuse to end concentration.
     b. Faults or defects in the speech presentation require greater, rather than less, attention.
     c. Listeners should behave courteously in order to facilitate the speaker's performance.
  4. Personal factors should be made conducive to effective listening.
     a. Inexperience with the material at hand can be overcome only through personal effort.
        (1) Study technical terms involved.
        (2) Obtain help from others.
        (3) Read pertinent material.
     b. To help eliminate lack of interest, the listener should seek a personal purpose to which the topic can contribute.
     c. Objectivity should be maintained in the face of emotion-laden words or ideas.
     d. Good listeners look for the central ideas of a speech.
        (1) Use a good system of note-taking to aid memory.
  5. You can improve your listening while conversing.
     a. In daily conversation, cultivate the art of give-and-take.
        (1) Do not monopolize the conversation.
        (2) Conversation is not a talk-fest for one star performer.

b. Exhibit conscious attention to the speaker.
c. Try to learn something from the conversation.
d. Watch the speaker as well as listen.
e. Observe your own conversation and create a will to improve it.

IV. LEARNING ACTIVITIES
   A. *Initiatory activities.*
      1. Begin the unit by reading a short prose selection. Dictate five or more questions. Discuss and analyze the reasons for wrong answers.
      2. Conduct a listening poll to see how much time the students think they spend listening each day and the situations in which they listen most. Compare these results with the findings of research.
      3. Ask the students in a quiz to list the names of three radio and television programs, giving also the names of the announcers, stars, band leaders, sponsors, products, and so on. Class discussions should follow to point out how well or how poorly they listen and why.
      4. Give each student a mimeographed copy of the first half of a speech to read. Then play the recording of the last half of the speech. Follow this with a quiz on the factual material of the speech. Discuss the difference in the amount of retention between the read and the heard parts of the speech.
      5. Discuss the difference between hearing and listening and from this point branch out into such related topics as types of listening, how to listen, and so on.
      6. After an assembly period which features a speaker or a movie, use the speaker or movie to focus on listening.
      7. Use a standardized listening test.
   B. *Developmental activities.*
      1. Assembly programs, radio and television programs at home and at school, debates, forum discussions, classroom talks by visitors, speeches and arguments read aloud by the teacher, class talks on current problems, motion pictures fostering American ideas and ideals, and newscasts can be used to develop efficient listening habits.
      2. Schedule a speech assignment so that after a student has spoken you will have at least ten minutes class time remaining. Without prior warning, announce to the class after the talk that each student is to write immediately a summary of the talk just heard.
      3. Have students take class notes on student speeches. Compare and evaluate the results to find out the weaknesses in note-taking practices.
      4. Invite students to formulate a chart on which to record the results of their analyses of their listening habits. Have each of them complete a copy of the chart on his own listening habits. Lead them in a discussion of the results and of their listening abilities and needs.
      5. Play a recording of a poorly organized and poorly presented speech. After listening to the speech, ask why the students had trouble listening to it. Have them write down the central ideas, et cetera. Replay the recording after the discussion to re-enforce the point.

6. Have students relate examples from their own experience to indicate that we usually hear what we want to hear.
7. Make a recording of a radio or television speech. Begin playing the recording with the students listening carefully. Stop the recording at the appropriate place and ask the students to write down what they think the speaker's next point will be.
8. Invite members of the class to list distractions present in listening situations. If the opportunity presents itself for you to listen with them, you list distractions in the same listening situations. Construct a "code of listening manners" and then discuss reasons why they are important.
9. Use the same recording as in number 7 and have the students select "emotional" words used in the recording. Evaluate their use and the effect of such use.
10. Play the recording of a short speech. Ask the students to guess the speaker's age, nationality, race, personality, occupation. Discuss whether the guesses reveal their prejudices.
11. Have the class prepare and use "out-of-class listening report" forms for assembly speakers, radio and television speeches, et cetera. Analyze in class the results of the use of the forms by the students in listening to speakers and speeches.
12. Appoint three or four students to prepare short and simple sets of directions or recipes for making or assembling something, or for going somewhere. After each short speech, call on each of the other students to explain in his own words the directions or recipe presented by the speaker.
13. Invite each student in the class to "make" a speech. During each of a number of the speeches, stop the speaker and ask each member of the class to:
    a. Anticipate the next point of the speaker.
    b. Write out the main points already covered.
    c. Write out any hidden meanings found.
    d. Evaluate types of support used.
    e. Indicate what seems to be the central idea.
    f. Turn in notes taken so far.
14. Have students prepare short quizzes covering main points, supporting materials, et cetera, of their speeches. After his speech, a student gives his quiz to the rest of the class. Use the results to reveal listening faults of listeners and to help the speaker see his strengths and weaknesses as a speaker.
15. Have the students listen to a humorous program on radio or television. Record it and play it later in the class. Have students listen for different kinds of humor: exaggeration or understatement; peculiarities of language; play on words, especially parodies and puns; unexpected endings; satire; irony; ridiculous situations. Lead the students in their analysis and discussion of the program.

16. Have an out-of-class assignment in which students listen for propaganda techniques used in speaking situations. Invite each student to report the techniques to which he listened and present his analysis of the techniques.
17. Read a poem to the class. Preceding the reading of the poem, present to the class facts of the life of the poet that have no bearing on the poem's content. Have each member of the class summarize the content of the poem. Check each summary on the ability of the student who wrote it to give the content of the poem rather than on his ability to give factual information about the poet's life. Lead the class in a discussion of the results.

C. *Culminating activities.*
1. Review and summarize the materials covered. Find out if the students believe they have been able to use efficient and effective listening techniques in other classes and situations.
2. Have students prepare a speech or write a paper on the general topic of "listening" or "how I improved my listening."
3. Use another form of the standardized test given at the beginning of the unit, and compare the results.
4. Give a test over the "subject-matter" of listening.
5. If the students are interested, help them to organize a "Radio-Television Appreciation Club" or some similar organization designed to continue or promote their interest in efficient and effective listening.
6. Have students write and act scenes in which they depict such aspects of the unit as "poor listening habits can get one into trouble," "the difference between a good and poor listener," "efficient listening is hard work," and so on.
7. Invite students to participate in small group discussions in class on problems related to listening efficiency. Have each of the students who do not participate in a given discussion present a summary of the findings of the discussion.

V. MATERIALS
A. *Reading materials.*
Anderson, Harold M., "Teaching the Art of Listening," *School Review*, vol. 32 (February 1949), p. 631.
Andersch, Elizabeth G., and Lorin C. Staats, *Speech for Everyday Use*, rev. ed. New York: Holt, Rinehart and Winston, Inc., 1960. pp. 162–196.
Baird, A. Craig, and Franklin Knower, *General Speech*. New York: McGraw-Hill, Inc., 1949, ch. 16.
Bird, Donald E., "Bibliography of Selected Materials about Listening," *Education*, January, 1955, pp. 1–7.
Borchers, Gladys L., and Claude M. Wise, *Modern Speech: An Introduction to Speaking and Understanding*. New York: Harcourt, Brace and Company, 1948. pp. 284–299.
Brown, James I., "Why Not Teach Listening?" *School and Society*, vol. 69 (February 1, 1949), pp. 141–153, 168.

Chase, Stuart, "Learning to Listen," *The Power of Words*. New York: Harcourt, Brace and Company, 1954. pp. 165–173.

Elson, E. F., and Alberta Peck, *The Art of Speaking*. Boston: Ginn & Company, 1952. pp. 66–94.

Gray, Giles W., and Claude M. Wise, *The Bases of Speech*, 3rd. ed. New York: Harper & Row, Publishers, 1959, pp. 60–65.

Griffith, Francis, Catherine Nelson, and Edward Stasheff, *Your Speech*. New York: Harcourt, Brace & World, 1955. pp. 188–212.

Hedde, Wilhelmina G., and William N. Brigance, *The New American Speech*. Philadelphia: J. B. Lippincott Company, 1957. pp. 115–126.

Hook, J. N., "Developing Good Listeners," *Journal of Education*, vol. 132 (April 1949), pp. 110–114.

Johnson, Wendell, "The Fateful Process of Mr. A Talking to Mr. B," *Harvard Business Review*, vol. 31 (1953), pp. 49–56.

Lee, Irving J., *How to Talk with People*. New York: Harper & Row, Publishers, 1952. pp. 17–21.

Nichols, Ralph G., "Factors in Listening Comprehension," *Speech Monographs*, vol. 15 (1948), pp. 154–163.

―――, "Listening: Questions and Problems," *Quarterly Journal of Speech*, vol. 33, no. 1 (February 1947), pp. 83–86.

―――, and Leonard A. Stevens, *Are You Listening?* New York: McGraw-Hill, Inc., 1957.

―――, and Thomas R. Lewis, *Listening and Speaking*. Dubuque, Iowa: William C. Brown Company, 1954.

Niles, Doris, "Teaching Listening in the Speech Fundamentals Course," *Speech Teacher*, vol. 6, no. 4 (November 1957), pp. 300–304.

Pronovost, Wilbert, *The Teaching of Speaking and Listening in the Elementary School*. New York: David McKay Company, Inc., 1959.

Robinson, Karl F., and E. J. Kerikas, *Teaching Speech: Methods and Materials*. New York: David McKay Company, Inc., 1963. pp. 261–279.

Sarett, Lew, William T. Foster, and Alma J. Sarett, *Basic Principles of Speech*, 3rd ed. Boston: Houghton Mifflin Company, 1958, pp. 152–183.

St. Onge, Keith R., *Creative Speech*. Belmont, California: Wadsworth Publishing Company, Inc., 1964. pp. 47–54.

Sterner, Alice, K. M. Saunders, and M. A. Kaplan, *Skill in Listening*. Chicago: National Council of Teachers of English, 1946.

Weaver, Andrew T., and Ordean G. Ness, *The Fundamentals and Forms of Speech*. New York: The Odyssey Press, 1957. pp. 86–109.

―――, Gladys L. Borchers, and Donald K. Smith, *The Teaching of Speech*. Englewood Cliffs, N. J.: Prentice-Hall, Inc., 1952. pp. 248–267.

B. Demonstration materials.
1. Movie: *Taking Notes in Class*. Shows the best method for taking classroom notes which will serve effectively as a basis for study and review. Black and white. $3.50 rental. Jam Handy Organization, 2821 East Grand Boulevard, Detroit, Michigan.

2. Filmstrip: *How to Listen*, series. Society for Visual Education, Inc., 1345 West Diversey Parkway, Chicago, Illinois. Black and white with captions. Set, $12.00. Cartoon drawings offer criteria to determine the quality of listening and make suggestions for improving listening. Titles are: "How to Tell the Differences between Essentials and Details," 48 frames; "How to Discover the Purpose of a Speaker," 53 frames; "How to Tell the Difference between Facts and Opinions," 47 frames; and "Information, Persuasion, and Propaganda," 52 frames.
3. Movie: *Learning from Class Discussion.* Coronet, 1950. 10 minutes. Sound. Black and white. This film attempts to show the value of discussion as a learning tool in the classroom.
4. Records: *Our Common Heritage.* Great poems celebrating milestones in the history of America, edited with notes, by Louis Untermeyer. Decca Album No. A-536, 78 RPM, complete on eight 10-inch records. $10.50 plus tax. Sixteen poems, very familiar ones for the most part, have been arranged.
5. Sound Filmstrips: *Speaking of Safety.* A series of six sound filmstrips prepared by Irving J. Lee and produced by Sarra, Inc., Chicago, for the National Council, 425 North Michigan Avenue, Chicago, Illinois. Price, $115.00; rental, $7.50. Titles are: "The Power of Speech," 12:15 minutes; "Butterflies in Your Stomach," 14:10 minutes; "The Key to Good Speaking," 10:15 minutes; "On Your Feet," 11:05 minutes; "Now You're Talking," 10:10 minutes; and "Ring the Bell," 13:45 minutes.
6. Filmstrip: *How to Converse.* Society for Visual Education, Inc., 1950. 44 frames. Black and white. Price, $3.25.
7. Movie: *Listen Well, Learn Well.* Coronet Instructional Films. 11 minutes. Sound. Sale price, $50.00. Deals with auditory habits. Suitable for use at all levels.
8. Timely radio and television shows.
9. Tape recordings. There are a variety of tapes available from many State University Tape Recording Services. One merely sends in a roll of tape and the cost of return mailing.

VI. EVALUATIVE PROCEDURES
  A. *Informational summaries in response to such questions as:*
    1. Is listening important?
    2. Can listening be improved?
    3. What is the difference between a good and poor listener?
    4. What are your listening habits that cause you trouble?
    5. What can you do to reconcile thought speed and speech speed?
  B. Lead a class discussion on what students think they have learned.
  C. Teacher evaluation of individual listening tests given during the unit and throughout the remainder of the school year.
  D. Indications of improved listening in the classroom: What are they?
  E. *Use of standardized tests:*

1. *Brown-Carlsen Test of Listening Comprehension* which may be obtained from the World Book Company.
2. "The Dow Test," *Speech Monographs*, vol. 20, no. 2 (June 1953), p. 120.
3. Sequential Tests of Educational Programs (STEP). Cooperative Tests Division, Educational Testing Service, 20 Nassau Street, Princeton, New Jersey.

F. Teacher-made tests over material in the unit.

Sample Teaching Unit

The planning of specific teaching units is also a task of the individual teacher of speech. A teaching unit differs from a resource unit in at least two respects: (1) The teaching unit is prepared specifically for one class and includes only those activities and materials which seem necessary, appropriate, and feasible for helping members of the class to achieve objectives of the unit. (2) A teaching unit involves a special arrangement of activities and materials including plans for a specific introduction of the specific unit, for the development of understanding and ability by the students, and for culminating activities to help the students and the teacher to evaluate the achievement, progress, and growth of students as a result of effective teaching of the unit.

An experienced teacher of speech who has prepared a resource unit need only check appropriate sections for use in the teaching unit. However, often a brief outline is found desirable as a guide for the teacher in teaching a unit. Which learning activities the teacher selects depends upon the individual speech class, its needs, and its abilities determined by the students in the class. The following skeleton outlines of a teaching unit on "Listening" illustrate how the teacher may use materials from the resource unit. The first unit which follows might be suitable for a class which has had no previous contact with listening as a subject for study.

I. Initiatory Activity. Use a standardized listening test to determine the listening efficiency of the students. The results of the test will become a basis for class discussion of listening, its importance, and its components.

II. Subject Matter. Draw upon or use all of the subject matter presented in the resource unit.

III. Developmental Activities. Select activities in the resource unit. If an activity not in the resource unit occurs to you and seems to be needed by students in the class, use it in the teaching unit and add it to your resource unit. The activities indicated below are not necessarily used in the sequence in which they are presented.

    A. Stimulate and guide class discussions on the importance of listening, how listening differs from hearing, and factors which interfere with effective listening.

B. Have the students use an assembly program as a "listening experience." At the next class period following the program, check with the students to help them share their listening experiences in the assembly and analyze the experiences. Help them to become alert to differences in their individual listening experiences.
C. Stimulate and guide the students to formulate a chart entitled "Analysis of Poor Listening Habits." Invite each student to complete a copy of the chart by recording his conclusions about his own listening habits after he has had an opportunity to study his own listening.
D. Assign a series of student speeches. During the delivery of these speeches, have students do one or more of the following:
1. Make outlines of a speech and compare the outlines with the original outline by the speaker.
2. Ask each student to jot down what he believes to be the central idea of each speech. Compare and analyze the results.
3. Invite students to present to the class their individual evaluations of the type of supporting materials used in one or more of the speeches.
4. Have each student write out any "hidden meanings" detected in one or more of the speeches. Analyze.
5. Have each student indicate factors which influenced his listening efficiency. Lead the students in a comparison of the factors indicated by them.
E. Arrange for all members of the class to do an out-of-class listening assignment. Possibly the teacher will make a point to be present in the situation in which the students listen to a program as a basis for the accomplishment of the listening assignment. Then, the teacher can lead members of the class in an evaluation of the results of their assignment.
IV. Culminating Activity. Administer Form B of the standardized listening test and compare the results with Form A of the same test which was administered to the group early in the unit.

For a class which has had work on listening in a previous class such as in English or speech, the following instructional unit might work well.

I. Initiatory Activity. Ask the students in a quiz to list the names of radio or television programs, or both, giving also the names of the stars, announcers, band leaders, sponsors, products, and so on, of the programs. Use this device to start discussion on the topic that we hear what we want to hear and listen to what we want to listen.
II. Subject Matter. If a quick review seems to be in order, it might be well to cover the meaning and nature of listening, the types of listening, why we listen clearly, and so on. With an advanced group, the teacher may find it wise to concentrate on the techniques of improving listening efficiency: concentration, favorable environmental conditions, adjustment of the listener to the immediate situation including the speech and speaker, and ways of eliminating the personal factors which cause trouble.

III. Developmental Activities.
  A. Have student speeches in which you emphasize concentration techniques such as:
    1. Anticipate the speaker's next point.
    2. Identify kinds of development or support.
    3. Recapitulate what has been covered.
    4. Search for hidden meanings.
  B. Provide opportunities for your students to "structuralize" speeches.
  C. Play a recording of a poorly organized speech. Discuss it and methods for improving it.
  D. Play recordings of short conversations. Ask students to guess the speaker's age, nationality, race, personality, occupation, and so on. Discuss how prejudice interferes with efficient listening.
  E. Have an out-of-class assignment in which students listen for propaganda techniques used in speaking.
IV. Culminating Activity. Organize the class into discussion groups with each group responsible for discussing some selected aspect of the general problem of "Improving Listening Efficiency." Use each group's discussion as a listening exercise for the other students in the class.

Sample Lesson Plan

The final step for the teacher, after having selected from his resource unit objectives, methods, and materials suitable for his teaching unit, is the preparation of daily lesson plans for the periods to be used.

Many experienced teachers find that the making of daily lesson plans becomes almost second nature after some years; others find it a "must" for all their teaching. Inexperienced teachers need to organize each lesson, to know specifically what the objective is or what the objectives are, and to keep each day's lesson plan in mind as a flexible guide in teaching.

The following outline is typical of the form used by many teachers for a daily lesson plan. All but item number V is completed prior to teaching the lesson.

NAME: UNIT:
DATE: HOUR   GRADE LEVEL:

  I. *Objectives.* (All objectives for this particular day, including attitude, knowledge, understandings, and skills.)
  II. *Outline of Content.* (Textbook material and pages, supplementary texts and materials, and audio-visual aids.)
  III. *Activities to Accomplish Objectives.* (Describe in detail. If you are using discussion, list specifically your main questions.)
  IV. *Time Budget.* (Allotment for each activity.)
  V. *Self-Appraisal.* (How well did you accomplish your objectives? Was disci-

pline successful? Your attitude toward the class? Class response? Would you add, change, or omit your lesson plan for today?)

An example of a daily lesson plan follows.[7] It follows the pattern indicated and is intended to introduce the members of a class in speech education to listening.

NAME: Mrs. Nanette Davis UNIT: Listening
DATE: September 25, 19— HOURS: 9:45-10:45 GRADE LEVEL: 11th and 12th

I. *Objectives.* The objective for this day is the introduction of the unit on listening. The students will practice listening, writing central ideas, implications, and personal impressions of the material which they read. The readings will begin with the simple material and move to the complex for practice in the listening skill. In some cases, knowledge of the material will greatly aid listening comprehension, and lack of knowledge (as in the more difficult material) will obviously hinder the students' abilities to listen responsively. Because this is the introduction to the unit, the inductive method will be used with the hope that the attitudes and understandings which the students develop will result from their use and involvement, rather than from their rote memorization of stock phrases delivered by the teacher. The specific objectives for the day include a general *introduction* to the complexities of listening and an *appreciation* of the many requirements that go into listening comprehension. Because the students are participating in a panel discussion, some basic understandings should be gained also by the students.

II. *Outline of Content.*
   A. Materials: maps of Africa and Europe, chalkboard, chalk, tape recorder, paper, and pencil.
   B. Tape of the following excerpts:
      1. *The Hemingway Reader,* "The Sun Also Rises," pp. 266 and 267. 3 minutes.
      2. *Inside Africa* by John Gunther, "The Union of South Africa," pp. 478 and 479. 2 minutes.
      3. *A History of Political Theory* by Professor George H. Sabine, "Modern Absolutism," p. 335. (Difficult expository material) 3 minutes.
      4. *Jabberwocky* by Lewis Carroll, pp. 467 and 468. 2 minutes.

III. *Activities to Accomplish Objectives.*
   A. From the recordings, students are to (1) write the central idea in one sentence, (2) state the inferences the material makes including implied meaning behind the ideas, (3) state their personal impressions of each reading: if they did or did not like it, what purpose they saw in it, why, and so on.
   B. Five students will then go to the board, singly, and each will write down his central idea, inferences, and impressions in one sentence, and the

[7] Included by permission of Mrs. Nanette Davis, Saint Cloud State College.

class shall observe different interpretations and how well the students understood the material which was read. Five-minute discussion on this aspect will then ensue.
- C. A panel of five students will be chosen to discuss and call on the class for participation on the problem, "What Do We Hear," with the class secretary writing an outline of the class discussion on the board. Some of the points in the discussion should be: sounds, ideas, implications, purpose, main points, emotionalisms of speaker, value judgments, facts, attitudes, and personal impressions of the listener.
- D. The panel and class discussion is preliminary for tomorrow's discussion on "How to Improve Listening" and "Characteristics of the Good and Bad Listener." Four minutes of the discussion should be devoted to how effective the readings from the tape recorder were in testing their listening comprehension. This allows the students to be the judge of the teacher and to make the teaching situation a two-way street.

IV. *Time Budget.*
- A. Outline of Content: readings and setting up maps to illuminate two of the readings. Time, 15 minutes.
- B. Students writing five sentences on the blackboard and class discussion. Time, 10 minutes.
- C. Panel discussion on "What Do We Hear?" Time, 20 minutes.
- D. Remainder of discussion period devoted to evaluation of how effective the recordings were in teaching listening. Time, 4 minutes.

V. *Self-Appraisal.* Objectives, discipline, attitude, class response to be evaluated at time of operation.

Suggestions for Resource Units

A resource unit can be built around any of the fundamentals of speech, speech activities, or speech subject matter mentioned in Chapter 5. Successful units have been formulated on such fundamentals as content or ideas, organization of ideas, developmental or supporting details, adjustment to the speech situation, effective use of bodily action, effective use of voice, comprehension and use of language, and so on. Speech activities such as discussion, oral interpretation, debate, one-act plays, parliamentary procedure, speaking on radio and television, and so on have been used as topics for resource units. Phases of speech subject matter have been used in helping students to gain knowledge and understanding of speech, each of the fundamentals of knowledge, acoustics, the origin and development of speech, speech forms, parliamentary law, procedures in discussion leadership, playwrights and their dramas, speakers and their speeches, and the like.

Many teachers, some of whom may not know that they are using it, employ the resource unit plan in teaching speech. If a teacher of speech is to do his best teaching, a well-organized plan must be made and used by him in his classroom and in his work with students in extra-class and interscholastic speech activities. His achievement in formulating resource units can serve him well in his designing teaching units. Likewise, teaching units can be helpful to him and his students as he prepares and uses daily lesson plans.

Projects

1. Formulate a "resource unit" on one of the fundamentals of speech, on a speech activity, and on a topic which embraces a body of speech content necessary for increased knowledge and understanding by students of speech.

2. Study your state course of study in speech or language arts to discover if resource units are included.

3. Observe a teacher in a classroom who is using the unit method of teaching. Note carefully the initiatory, developmental, and culminating activities used.

4. Construct a lesson plan for a 50-minute class period using the outline suggested in this chapter.

5. Obtain copies of courses of study in schools in your area and study them for illustrative resource units, teaching units, and lesson plans.

Selected Bibliography

BURTON, WILLIAM H., *The Guidance of Learning Activities*, 2nd ed. New York: Appleton-Century-Crofts, Inc., 1952.

Commission on the English Curriculum of the National Council of Teachers of English, *The English Language Arts*. New York: Appleton-Century-Crofts, Inc., 1952.

———, *The English Language Arts in the Secondary School*. New York: Appleton-Century-Crofts, Inc., 1956.

DRAPER, E. M., and G. GARDNER, "How to Construct a Resource Unit," *Clearing House*, vol. 26 (January 1952), pp. 267–270.

JONES, ARTHUR J., et al., *Principles of Unit Construction*. New York: McGraw-Hill, Inc., 1939.

LEESE, J., "Developing Units in the Modern Secondary School," *High School Journal*, vol. 28 (November 1945), pp. 259–262.

ROBINSON, KARL F., and E. J. KERIKAS, *Teaching Speech: Methods and Materials*. New York: David McKay Company, Inc., 1963.

WEAVER, ANDREW T., GLADYS L. BORCHERS, and DONALD K. SMITH, *The Teaching of Speech*. Englewood Cliffs, N.J.: Prentice-Hall, Inc., 1952.

ZOLLINGER, MARIAN, "Five Units and How They Grow," *English Journal*, vol. 39 (October 1950), pp. 423–429.

CHAPTER

7

Evaluating, Testing and Grading in Speech Education

Evaluation of achievement, development, and improvement of students in speech situations is a major activity and responsibility of a teacher of speech. As the class periods roll by, the teacher is plunged headlong into the task of evaluating the speech, speaking, and speech attributes of his students in a variety of circumstances. His evaluation of a student should not be a deep-guarded secret, kept until the end of a grading period, to be revealed, finally, as if it were a part of some "teacher versus student" plot. Rather, the importance of constructive evaluation comes from telling each student *what* and *how* to improve. This information should be given as soon and as often as possible. Constructive evaluation begun early can bring a teacher to the realization that being a critic is one of his foremost and most difficult tasks.

Critical judgment involves a thorough understanding of the thing being criticized, the formulation of acceptable criteria or standards of judgment, and the application of these criteria or standards to the object, idea, or event for the purpose of evaluation.[1] This means that the teacher of speech needs a basic understanding of the communication process involving a speaker, his speech and speaking, and his listener. In addition, the most effective teacher will have arrived, somehow, at standards which he can apply to the students in their speech performances, whether in acting, discussing, speaking, reading aloud, debating, or speechmaking. As Basker-

[1] Barnet Baskerville, "The Critical Method in Speech," *Central States Speech Journal,* July, 1950, p. 1.

ville pointed out, "It is the function of criticism to render intelligent and relevant judgments, and in so doing ultimately to elevate standards and improve practice."[2] By his evaluations and grading practices, the teacher can make the class hours in speech education lasting educational experiences for the students. Uninformed, unsound, unfair, and too infrequent evaluations and grading practices can be meaningless or harmful. Careful, thoughtful evaluations and grading practices should not be omitted or neglected.

Role of the Teacher in Evaluation

The most important aspect in evaluation is the evaluator or critic. The manner and method of the teacher influence the effectiveness of his evaluations. Sincere interest in the individual student, awareness of the student's interests, needs, and abilities, a realization that growth may come slowly, and recognition of the potential of the individual are all vital considerations. A teacher of speech needs to keep constantly in mind that his purpose is to give the individual student a clear, valid, and "objective" appraisal of his speech and speaking. Periodic judgments of the speech abilities and needs and personal speech attributes of the student, coupled with sincere praise and helpful suggestions, can stimulate interest, give direction to his efforts, and bring him successful achievement, growth, and satisfaction.

Growth in Desirable Attitudes

Since evaluation is primary to effective teaching, the teacher faces the task of helping his students develop good attitudes toward evaluation and criticism. Students must be made aware of the standards used in evaluation, and of the relationship between the standards and achievement, improvement, and growth.

The teacher can point out to students early in the course how constant evaluation is necessary to all learning. Using examples from other classes, especially from school activities such as basketball, track, football, dramatics, journalism, and cheerleading, and from out-of-school activities such as driving a car, on-the-job training, and so on, the teacher can show that we improve by having someone point out our strengths and weaknesses. We learn from others, both from their comments and from observing them. Realization of this need for constant evaluation helps to promote a desirable attitude toward evaluation in the classroom in speech education.

[2] *Ibid.*, p. 5.

The teacher can do much by giving students a voice in setting up goals to be attained in their study and other performance. The goals can easily imply standards by which to evaluate study and performance by the students. Too often the teacher of speech acts much like the father who takes the family out for a Sunday drive. The youngsters ask, "Where are we going, Dad?" and the answer may be "Just for a ride." Could it be that teachers of speech, like the father, take their students "for a ride"? The teacher *must* know where he and the class are going, but does the teacher of speech always know? The students also *must* have a clear understanding of their own speech needs and abilities, the relationship and impact of teaching and learning to their needs and abilities, and their achievements and potentialities for achievement. One method for helping them is to discuss effective speech communication and thereby enable students to arrive, inductively, at a list of the elements inherent in effective communication.

At the time the teacher plans with his students what they are expected to learn, they can work together to formulate criteria to be used in evaluation.

Evaluation must be done by those concerned with the planning of the lesson. To be effective, it needs to be continuous. Students develop by knowing and understanding why they are doing what they are doing, by setting up new goals or objectives, and by evaluating their efforts in achieving them.

A third important aspect in gaining a desirable attitude toward evaluation in a class is the teacher's role. His attitude, manner, and tone should help build an atmosphere which will encourage students to welcome evaluation as a part of the learning experience. Uncomplimentary and blunt criticism is apt to arouse antagonism rather than a desire to improve.

The Art of Criticism

One of the first problems facing a speech critic is to determine the standards by which to judge his student speakers. Since we are concerned with oral communication, the standards which we use to judge a specific speaking performance are largely conditioned by the student's goal or purpose. If his aim is to entertain his classmates, the basic question is, "Did he entertain them?" But another influence in determining standards will be the speech teacher's own ideas of what is effective oral communication, which depend on his personal experiences, the speech courses he has taken, his speaking experiences, and by evaluating speakers he has heard. The teacher should ask himself what the basis is for his evaluations and check himself periodically on his philosophy of teaching speech.

In criticizing, we are concerned with being "objective" in a very "subjective" situation. The whole process of criticism and evaluation of speech and speaking is complicated, especially for the beginning teacher. Surely there are basic criteria we can use, which will likely meet with general agreement by most critics. A speech should contain a variety of supporting materials, so we can probably reach agreement as to whether the speech contains these materials, and whether the materials support the speech. Similarly, critical audiences can also agree on whether a speaker contradicts himself, whether his eye-contact is satisfactory, and whether his vocal projection is well adjusted to the audience.

Holtzman[3] has called our attention to three basic principles of criticism: (1) The degree to which the response desired by the speaker is the primary guide for the critic in speech communication. What can the critic say or write which will improve the student's ability in communication? (2) Criticism must have a focus on one main idea. Don't overwhelm your students by a barrage of suggestions. Help each of them to concentrate on one thing at a time. (3) Criticism should be progressive. It should involve a general scheme through a semester or year.

Another helpful suggestion was made by Seiger who wrote that

> ... a certain degree of empathy is the best tool a teacher can use in helping his students to solve their problems in public speaking. How well he listens to his students, how closely he can identify their speech problems with his own determines, to a large extent, a speech teacher's success. Criticism based on understanding the individual is the key to the teacher's approach.[4]

He outlined the following program as a starting point in the training of a listener-critic:

> 1. The teacher of public speaking should regularly subject himself to an analysis of his own abilities as a speaker before a committee of his colleagues. After a series of speeches, the members of the committee should acquaint him with their evaluation of his limitations, needs, assets, and potentialities.
>
> 2. He should follow a strict program of attempted improvement as a public speaker. In so doing, he should work to understand his own capacities and, even more important, strive to gain insight into the problem of the speaker attempting to develop his skill.
>
> 3. The teacher of public speaking should discard our conventional terminology as a means of helping students to understand themselves and their difficulties and get rid of the latter. Instead, he should be able to

---

[3] Paul D. Holtzman, "Speech Criticism and Evaluation as Communication," *Speech Teacher*, vol. 9, no. 1 (January 1960), pp. 1–7.

[4] Marvin L. Seiger, "The Speech Teacher: Listener and Critic," *Speech Teacher*, vol. 5, no. 4 (November 1956), p. 260.

THE ART OF CRITICISM

communicate with the student via his own individual pathway of comprehension.[5]

The following suggestions for making effective class criticism will be helpful:

1. Consider substituting the word "evaluation" for criticism. Many students as well as some adults interpret criticism as a destructive or tearing-down process. By asking for an "evaluation" the teacher may avoid eliciting negative comments from the students during student-evaluation periods.

2. Focus on one type of error or weakness in your comments sometimes instead of evaluating the total effect of the performance. Keep your evaluation purposeful and specific.

3. Avoid the use of ridicule, sarcasm, and imitation of a fault unless it is done in the right spirit and accepted in the same spirit.

4. Attempt to give equal time to all students in your class. Don't concentrate on one or two speakers and tend to exclude the others from your consideration.

5. Always remember that you are evaluating *individuals*. Study the student you are evaluating. Remember that some students will be much more sensitive than others. What may work for one student may cause antagonism in another. The teen-age girl may respond well to comment on the way she failed to develop a point in her speech, but resent any reference to her posture or appearance.

6. Recognize that in speech the whole may be more than the sum of its parts. A speech can succeed despite weaknesses that are evident, or it can fail despite excellence in all of its aspects. This means that the teacher should turn his attention to specific aspects after he has reacted to the speech as a whole. This implies also that the teacher should listen to each part of the speech in as normal a manner as possible and as if it were presented in a non-classroom situation.

7. Avoid the repetition of the same "old" critical comments for speaker after speaker. Treat each speech as a new experience, both for the benefit of each student and for focusing attention by all students.

8. Accentuate the positive! Praise is easier "to take" than blame. Don't withhold praise and compliments if they are deserved, but don't use praise indiscriminately. High school students are quick to detect the "phony" or the "exaggerated" compliment. Be honest, sincere, and fair. By balancing frequently sincere praise of a student's good points with helpful suggestions on points which need improvement, a teacher can make much headway in maintaining rapport with his students and, at the same time, effect improvement of speech behavior by each student.

[5] *Ibid.*, p. 261.

9. Keep your evaluation on the important aspects of speaking. Watch any tendency to overemphasize minor, easily detectable points. Delivery factors are, for many people, much easier to comment on than are factors of content, organization, or language. Probably most teachers of speech feel that they are more qualified to comment on factors of delivery than on any other factors of speaking. Remember that your students will get a sense of what is important in speaking by what you select to evaluate. In your evaluation, work for a balance of easily recognizable aspects and those hidden ones which are just as important.

10. Remember that the language of criticism is important. Guard against the use of terminology that is not understood by the student or that has been used so much that it means nothing. The building of a vocabulary of speech, speaking, and speechmaking is an important aspect and function of evaluation. Such terms as pitch, volume, rhythm, and quality are easily understood. Such phrases as "be natural," "use a conversational delivery," and "watch your projection" may mean different things to different students. The teacher should be alert to the language he uses. He should check, from time to time, with his students to determine whether his language is getting the desired response and is, therefore, communicative in his evaluation of their speech behavior.

In evaluating and criticizing his students and their speech performances, the teacher has a great responsibility. He must make sure, to the utmost extent, that he does it carefully, accurately, and clearly—indicating strengths as well as weaknesses, with specific suggestions for improvement, and thus motivate each student to develop his best abilities.

Methods of Evaluation

The two basic types of evaluation used by teachers of speech are (1) oral and (2) written. A balance in the use of the two methods is usual in most classes. Each method has its advantages as well as its disadvantages. Oral evaluation of a speech performance not only helps the individual student but provides help for the whole class. Oral evaluation is a means by which speech concepts and vocabulary can be taught to the group. Specific performances can be tied in closely and evaluated by the standards set up by the class and teacher. However, oral comments are time-consuming and often center on one student's performance more than that of another. Written evaluation can provide splendid opportunities for individual criticism which is not always desirable or possible in oral evaluation. Through written criticism, the teacher can provide for the individual speech needs and abilities of his students and so recognize their individual differences, better than through oral evaluation when the teacher talks to all the class.

Written evaluations provide opportunity for the teacher to give equal attention and time to each of his students which, if one can judge from experience, is not likely to occur in oral evaluations of speech behavior by students.

Oral evaluation must be presented in a clear and effective manner if the teacher is to serve as a model of communication. Obviously, he is expected to serve as a model. This means that his oral evaluations should be well organized, well supported, and well delivered. It means that the teacher of speech should be concrete and specific in presenting his compliments and suggestions. He may use the exact words of the speaker, when possible, which can add much to the effectiveness of the evaluation as the teacher shows what was said and what might have been said.

Three possible times present themselves for offering oral evaluations of speech, speaking, and speechmaking. No one time has been demonstrated to be better than another. Perhaps the best advice is for the teacher to vary the time. Oral evaluation may be presented at the completion of each individual performance. This places some premium on the teacher's being able to present his evaluation immediately after a performance. In this way all students and the teacher have fresh in their minds the performance to be evaluated.

Evaluation may be accomplished after a series of speeches or readings, at which time the teacher can evaluate three, four, or more performances together. In this case, the teacher can compare and contrast the performances and generalize from his observations of all of them.

Evaluation of speech performances by students may wait until the last ten or fifteen minutes of the class session. The teacher can then present his evaluation of the speaking done during the earlier part of the class hour. This type of evaluation is usually of a composite nature in which the strengths and weaknesses of the speech performances by the group are pointed out, with suggestions for improvement.

Some teachers have succeeded in making effective evaluation of factors of delivery by a student during his performance. Seated in the back of the room, a teacher has used flash cards or signals to the speaker to increase his loudness or softness, to look at his audience, to stand or to move, to decrease or increase his rate of speaking, and so on. This method seems to have merit insofar as the student reacts well to the teacher's on-the-spot evaluation. After a student is well enough adjusted in the class to respond easily and effectively to signals, the method affords the student immediate opportunity to apply the evaluation of his speaking.

Finally, oral evaluation may be presented by the teacher immediately before the student begins his preparation for a speech performance in class. Obviously, a student is more likely to give attention to evaluations at a time when he needs help in preparing a speech or reading than just after a performance, when he cannot apply the lessons.

Written evaluation must be clear, easy to read, and meaningful. It, too, should be well organized, written in appropriate penmanship, and well supported. Its language should be carefully chosen to communicate to the reader as accurately as possible the ideas of the evaluator.

Written evaluations may take many forms. Blank sheets of paper may be used. Check lists and rating scales are often employed. Profile charts are sometimes constructed. A blank sheet of paper offers a critic the advantage of focusing upon the individual speaker and identifying *in him, his speech,* and *his speaking* points which merit praise and which call for suggestions if the evaluation is to be most helpful to the student. However, a blank sheet of paper can hardly prevent the critic's overlooking aspects of the speech performance which are subject to evaluation. One or more of the aspects which may be overlooked can be very important. At any rate, a highly competent, impartial, and well-qualified critic and evaluator of speech behavior has little need for a check list. A specific check list or rating scale can remind the teacher of important items to be evaluated. The use of carbon sheets to supply the teacher with a copy of his evaluation of each speech performance can be useful and, in turn, helpful to students if the teacher uses the carbons to check, stimulate, and guide the student's progress. A file of each student's evaluation sheets is an efficient way of helping both students and the teacher to note progress and continued needs. Sample copies of typical rating forms are presented at the end of this chapter.

Student Evaluation

Evaluation in a class in speech education is not the sole responsibility of the teacher. It is a function and responsibility of the entire class. Only through the individual student's evaluation do we discover, oftentimes, his grasp of standards by which to evaluate speaking and whether he is progressing toward goals established by the class and the teacher. If a written comment by a student disagrees with those by the other members of the class, it may indicate the individual student's failure to see clearly some basic concept. Often the use of class evaluation points out a weakness in the teacher's own evaluation of a performance, or reveals his overemphasis on a minor point. Students should realize that a variety of reactions is possible and, in fact, usual. Given the opportunity and encouraged to evaluate their own performances, half the class may decide that one of their number spoke with "nice, direct eye contact" and the rest may say that "no real contact was established." Or they may find that some of them indicate "clear organization" regarding a speech performance whereas other students indicate "lack of clear organization." Students are not likely to learn how to make valid evaluations of speeches, speaking, or speechmaking until they have exercised themselves and their own judgment. However, it may be unwise for the teacher to encourage students to evaluate speech performances by their peers early in the school year. The teacher ought first to be confident that they know the standards to be used. Evaluation by members of the class is dangerous when no standards have been formed or when they are not well understood or accepted.

Evaluation by students can be either oral or written. Both kinds are worth practicing.

Many possibilities for variation in oral student evaluation are practicable and desirable:

1. Call for volunteers after a performance.
2. Call on students without notice and thereby encourage all students to be prepared to make constructive comments.
3. Select in advance of a performance a specific evaluator.
4. Have one student comment on ideas and their organization, a second on developmental or supporting details, a third on bodily action, a fourth on voice, a fifth on enunciation and articulation, a sixth on poise and preparation, et cetera.
5. Use a panel of evaluators to discuss performances during the latter part of the class period.
6. Have students rate the speakers of the day. Call on individual students to justify their ratings with specific reasons.
7. Have students rank the speakers of the day. Call on individuals to justify their rankings with specific reasons.

Written evaluation also has merit. The following methods have been used by high school speech teachers:

1. Give each student a rating blank for each student who is going to speak during the class period and have the completed rating blanks handed to the speaker. They may or may not be signed as the teacher and students elect.
2. Give students blank sheets of paper and have them write whatever comments they believe to be appropriate about the speech performance.
3. Have students rate speakers for the day and post the ratings on the bulletin board.
4. Have students rank speakers of the day and post the rankings on the bulletin board.
5. Have students each write one important compliment, one important suggestion, one rating, and one rank for each performance in a series of speech performances and have these papers handed to the teacher. Ask

each student to sign his paper. The teacher can study the work of each evaluator and, after removing the name of the evaluator from each paper, hand the papers to the speaker.

Many teachers of speech have found it wise to collect all completed rating forms and paragraphs of compliments and suggestions at the end of a class period, keeping them until the next class period. In the interim the teacher can sort and assemble each student's evaluations and carefully analyze the ratings, ranks, and remarks by members of the class for each student. Any rating or remark which is "way out of line" may be removed from the assortment and destroyed, if it does not benefit the student speaker. Then, the evaluations can be returned to the students at the following class period. This close scrutiny can also aid the teacher in discovering weaknesses in the evaluation standards and in discovering individual students who need counsel in applying standards.

The Importance of Self-Criticism

Evaluation is aimed at helping the student to do his best in speech achievement, improvement, and development, and since improvement comes only after the student recognizes his needs, the teacher should regard as important each student's self-evaluation. The student should, through his analysis of evaluations by the teacher and by his peers, learn to "know himself" and recognize his own problems and accept them for his solution. Frequently the teacher of speech should invite students to write their own reactions to their improvement or lack of it. They should be encouraged to answer such questions as "What did you think of your performance today?" and to ask themselves such questions as "Why did I fail to do as well as I thought I would?" Also, they need to be encouraged to answer such questions as "What seemed to be the reactions of other students and of the teacher to my performance today?" and "What specific reactions by students and the teacher did I identify during my performance today?"

The Personal Conference

Teachers of speech should be aware of the effect of a private, personal conference on the student and the teacher as a method of evaluation. Being evaluated in one's own peer group may be distracting, confusing, and even frustrating to some high school students. In a private, personal conference, a teacher has the opportunity, as does the student, for frank and detailed analysis and evaluation of aspects of speech behavior, needs, abilities, and interests which may not be dealt with in the classroom situation or in a written evaluation. Obviously, such private, personal conferences between each student and the teacher take time, often hard to find. However, some students may be "reached" only by this personal approach. Sometimes, it may seem to be the ideal way—and the only way—to establish excellent rapport.

Testing

Testing students' achievement is essential in successful teaching. However, any testing must apply to the specific situation, in trying to measure what is being taught. In fact, progress can hardly be determined without testing. Douglas pointed out that:

> It is generally assumed that the object of measurement in a speech class is a speech. If we are teaching speech behavior, however, not simply public speaking, we will want to measure the whole range of the student's oral communication as it alternates between speaking and listening in formal and in informal situations. So we must also measure his listening ability and development, including his critical and appreciative powers, and his skills in the various speech activities, provided, of course, that we seek to teach these.[6]

Logically, the person best prepared to test students in a class in speech education is the teacher. He is presumed to know what the objectives are, what basic facts and information have been considered by students in the class and in their study outside of the class, what understandings have been developed, and what speech skills have been stressed, and so he *should be* the one person most interested in knowing and in finding out what the students have learned. Of the factors that should be tested, these appear to be essential:

1. The basic body of facts and theory necessary for the student to progress. Such information ought to be secured by the students from lectures, discussions, textbooks, outside readings, and other experiences including speech performances and analyses of speech performances.

2. The growth of the student in his critical appraisal and evaluation of his own speech performances and those by other students and the teacher.

3. The concepts, principles, fundamentals, forms, activities, and practices which students are presumed to understand as a result of their work with the stimulation and guidance by a teacher of speech.

4. The skills in specific speech fundamentals and the integration of these skills in the total speech process and in their speech behavior.

5. The growth of the student in desirable personal speech attributes

---

[6] Jack Douglas, "The Measurement of Speech in the Classroom," *Speech Teacher*, vol. 7, no. 4 (November 1958), p. 314.

such as initiative and industry, imagination, resourcefulness, and purposeful self-direction in his study of speech behavior, in his preparation for participation in speech activities, and in realizing benefits and satisfactions from his participation.

The specific measuring instruments which may be used by a teacher of speech include objective-type tests, essay or subjective-type tests, and observations of speech performances. Since most teachers of speech are concerned with testing knowledge and understanding, attitudes, skills, and attributes, the type of test utilized should, of course, be the one that will measure most effectively what is being tested.

Factual knowledge can usually be measured best by the traditional "objective" test such as true-false, multiple choice, completion, and specific answer. Of course, an objective-type test can be constructed to measure understanding of concepts, principles, procedures, practices, and desired outcomes of speech behavior. However, essay or subjective-type tests are generally accepted as effective measures of the acquisition of understandings developed by students. These tests give students the opportunity to organize, develop, and apply through verbalization specific knowledge to a problem and situation. But in speech education there seems to be no substitute for the trained observer in testing speech skills. Anecdotal records of happenings in the class, rating scales and evaluation forms, and comparison of ratings of an early tape recording with more recent recordings are typical methods used by the observer. Basic to the testing of speech skill are the knowledge and understanding of speech communication acquired by the teacher of speech as a result of his education, experience, and training, especially of his training acquired through teaching.

Most teachers of speech have been bothered by feeling that their observational measurements lack validity and reliability. This feeling is understandable as we think of the complexity of a speech act and especially as we think of the knowledge, understanding, skills, and attributes of a speaker involved in his speech behavior. However, reluctant as a teacher may be to pass judgment on a speaker, there seems to be no acceptable substitute for testing a speaker's behavior in speech situations. Paper-and-pencil tests seem to be no alternative to observation of the student in speech situations. Although paper-and-pencil tests are helpful in testing certain aspects of speech education, they are not helpful in testing speech skills. What a teacher of speech may lack in objectivity, he may compensate for by his selection of significant factors which he can evaluate with confidence, validity, and reliability. Also, he can observe each of his students in a number of speech performances without making up his mind about a student's behavior in a speech situation based on a single performance. He may base his judgment on a number of speech performances or supplement it by the judgment of an increased number of raters of the student's speech behavior in a single speech performance, or, preferably, both.

Probably one of the most helpful lists of procedures for improving measurement is the one provided by Douglas:[7]

1. Begin with the thing to be measured. Tests, like assignments, must be directly related to objectives. Goal, activity, and evaluation must be a closely knit unit.

2. Use tests to generate learning. Keep grading secondary.

3. Do not be concerned with reliability until you have first checked validity. What does the test actually measure?

4. Make your own tests and rating scales. No one else can possibly know as well what you wish to measure.

5. Use a variety of types of tests, selecting them to fit the thing to be measured. Use good published tests when they do fit the purpose. The most thorough type of measurement, to be used in special cases, is the case study with the results of many tests and observations expertly evaluated.

6. When you have no adequate data, refuse to judge. Avoid jumping to conclusions about students; refrain from characterizing and labeling them. Every student is unique and no one will ever know all there is to know about any of them.

7. Review fundamental statistics, know these basic concepts: central tendency, dispersion, distribution, normal curve, sampling, validity, and reliability.

8. Check periodically on your standards and your philosophy of speech education. Review the four historical theories of rhetorical criticism.

9. Learn to accept, emotionally, the necessity of using your own judgment, and to rely on it humbly. Expect to make mistakes occasionally.

10. Depend on your trained and experienced observation as the primary tool of measurement. Continually improve it by (a) learning to listen closely, to concentrate, to keep mentally alert, and to extend the attention span, (b) keeping your mind open, (c) checking your judgment, now and then, against the judgments of other teachers, contest judges, and student judges, (d) formulating the criteria for each assignment clearly, both for yourself and the students, (e) not letting grading interfere with criticism, (f) not concentrating on the easily observed and easily quantified at the expense of the more significant and fundamental matters, and (g) remembering that the whole need not equal the sum of its parts but that the whole exceeds the sum.

[7] *Ibid.*, pp. 317–318.

Teachers tend to agree that the results of teaching speech can be measured. If a teacher knows the objectives of his instruction and if he employs a variety of measuring instruments, he should be able to secure the data necessary to form a basis for sound judgments of the students' speeches and speech behavior.

Grading

Grading is an inherent part of the American school system and is firmly entrenched in modern secondary education. It provides a significant basis upon which credits are earned, honors won, diplomas awarded, and scholarships presented. It is a device used to give a student and his parents some idea of the achievement level of the student in various subjects. Determining a grade for an individual student is no easy task. The beginning teacher of speech often finds himself in a very perplexing situation. Nevertheless, he is obligated to compute a grade at the end of six or nine weeks of the semester and a final grade at the end of the semester or, if it is a full-year course, at the end of one year. Therefore, he should plan frequent tests and evaluations of his students' work and achievement, including their individual performances.

In grading students' achievement, improvement, and development, some standard for grading is essential. Three of the most widely used standards are (1) a teacher-made standard of a "superior" performance against which each student is measured, (2) a standard arrived at by comparing each student with the other students in the particular speech class, and (3) a standard of each student's own achievement and progress in the class. Teachers will often use a combination of the three, consciously or unconsciously.

Each teacher of speech should check to see if the school system in which he teaches has any concept or interpretation of grading with which he should be familiar. He may need to adjust his own standards to the extent that they are compatible with the policy of the school. Administrators are, of course, concerned with the grading standards of each teacher and, likewise, with the way he applies the standards.

One source of assistance for the beginning teacher of speech is the utilization of the experience of other teachers. Comparing his grade on a set of speech performances with the grades by his colleagues on the same, or some of the same, performances may help him. As a teacher arrives at the standards he will utilize in grading, he recognizes specific bases which he will use.

Achievement will likely be a most important basis of grading. Probably the teacher will find, sooner or later, that achievement is the underlying basis of all other factors in his grading. Achievement in acquiring knowledge about speech, in understanding speech behavior, in performances in speech activities, in completing items on a test, and in doing whatever students are invited to do and whatever they volunteer to do in the class may largely determine the grade for each student. In the light of all factors of achievement and based upon the teacher's best judgment of each student's successful achievement or lack of it, the teacher may assign to the student a grade. The teacher may focus on answers to two questions: (a) Can the student communicate well with his fellow men? (b) At what level of effectiveness does he communicate?

Improvement during the grading period is another basis for determining a grade for a student. Since speech is an individualized matter, the teacher will have to resolve the problem of individual *ability* and *improvement*. Most teachers of speech attempt during their diagnostic period at the beginning of the school year to assess each student's interests, needs, and abilities as well as his potential and present level of effectiveness. Determining where a student is and how far he can go with what he has to work with is no easy task. This factor of individual capacity or potentiality will need to be kept in mind during the entire school term. A teacher can go too far in crediting a student with much improvement when the end result is unsatisfactory. Likewise, a teacher can go too far in crediting a student with excellent achievement and ability when the actual improvement is far from the level of his capacity. Obviously, each student should know that the teacher, from the beginning of the course, expects the student to work up to his capacity and that the teacher will be happy with nothing less.

Some teachers consider a student's *attitude* and *effort* in the class as bases for grading. They justify, at least in their own minds, these bases in the same manner that they justify native capacity and commensurate ability as bases for grading. Willingness to accept responsibility, dependability, consideration of the rights and opinions of others, self-control and poise, and work and study habits are often considered as bases in awarding a grade to the student. Again, each teacher of speech must arrive at his own conclusion relative to the importance of these bases of grading. He will likely end up by using all of them or a combination of most of them.

The specific suggestions which follow will help a teacher in the necessary but sometimes confusing task of assigning grades:

1. Explain to your class early in the school year the bases you will use for grading. If you are interested solely in achievement, they should know it. If you plan on grading on achievement plus improvement, they deserve to know. If you will be concerned with their attitude, effort, and promptness in meeting assignment deadlines, they have a right to know.

You may lead the class in a discussion of bases of grading and, thereby, stimulate and guide them to arrive at a statement of criteria by which their grades will be determined. You can, of course, tell them what the criteria will be. If you choose to give them a voice in analyzing the bases and determining the criteria, you need not be surprised if they arrive at the same criteria which you propose. At any rate, your basis for grading should not be a deep, dark secret until report cards are distributed.

2. During the first few performances by your students, it may be wise to omit grades and to concentrate on sincere praise and on your suggestions to them for their improving their speech performances. Students can focus too much on grades and not enough on achievement, improvement, and development.

3. Utilize two grades for each speech performance. Assign one grade for content and organization and another for delivery. Do not average the two grades. Rather, make the student see that both are important and that he must work to improve in both aspects of speech so that his achievement will reflect the level of speaking he is capable of doing.

4. Set up in writing standards for an "A" speech, a "B" speech, a "C" speech, and so on. Oliver, in reporting on the attempt at Pennsylvania State University to help all faculty members in the Department of Speech in this matter, indicated the following criteria:[8]

    I. Normally, an "average" speech (C) should meet the following standards:
       A. Conform to type assigned (expository, persuasive, et cetera).
       B. Conform reasonably to the time limit.
       C. Exhibit sound organization; a clear purpose supported adequately by main ideas that are easily identified.
       D. Fulfill any special requirements of the assignment such as: to use three illustrations, or statistics, or authority.
       E. Be intellectually sound in developing a topic of worth and adequate and dependable evidence.
       F. Exhibit reasonable directness and communicativeness in delivery.
       G. Be correct grammatically and in pronunciation and articulation.
       H. Be ready for presentation on date assigned.
    II. The "better than average" speech (B) should meet the foregoing tests and also:
       A. Contain elements of vividness and special interest in its style.
       B. Be sure of more than average stimulative quality in challenging the audience to think or in arousing depth of response.
       C. Demonstrate skill in winning understanding of unusually difficult concepts or processes; or in winning agreement from auditors initially inclined to disagree with the speaker's purpose.

[8] Robert T. Oliver, "The Eternal (and Infernal) Problem of Grades," *Speech Teacher*, vol. 9, no. 1 (January 1960), pp. 9–10.

D. Establish rapport of a high order through style and delivery which achieve a genuinely communicative circular response.
III. The "superior" speech (A) not only meets the foregoing standards but also:
  A. Constitutes a genuinely individual contribution by the speaker to the thinking of the audience.
  B. Achieves a variety and flexibility of mood and manner suited to the multiple differentiation of thinking and feeling demanded by the subject matter and by the speaker-audience relations.
  C. Achieves a demonstrable progression from the initial uncertainty [of knowledge or belief] held by the audience toward the subject and, by orderly processes, toward a final resolution of the uncertainty in a conclusion that evolves naturally from the materials used by the speaker.
  D. Illustrates skillful mastery of internal transitions and of emphasis in presentation of the speaker's ideas.
IV. Speeches which must be classified as "below average" (D or F) are deficient in some or several of the factors required for the "C" speech.

5. Use the entire grading system. Watch a tendency to become either an "easy" grader or a "tough" grader. If you neglect either the "A" or the "F" of the system, you are really penalizing the students in your classes and students in other classes where the entire range is used.

6. In deciding how much weight to assign to written work and to oral work, consider the ratio of $\frac{1}{3}$–$\frac{2}{3}$ of written to oral, or $\frac{1}{4}$ written and $\frac{3}{4}$ oral.

7. In computing the final grades for the course, consider the suggestion given in number 6 as it pertains to grading. In computing final grades, consider that the usual practice is to allow the final examination to count about as much as a six-week or nine-week grade. If the final examination consists of both a written part and an oral part, use the same ratio of written-oral as suggested in number 6.

A single grade as an indication of a student's achievement in a class in speech can easily be misunderstood unless it is explained clearly by the person giving the grade to those who need to understand it. Many teachers of speech have devised their own report to parents in an attempt to help them see the progress their son or daughter is making or is not making. The "Report Card" on page 259 was prepared for use in a required course in speech at the ninth grade level at the State University of Iowa High School.

In the final analysis, no grading system is better than the teacher who employs it. By securing evidence during each grading period and by analyzing it carefully, by employing sound evaluative techniques, and by keeping an accurate record of marks assigned during each grading period, the teacher can probably answer with confidence questions about the grades which he assigns to students.

Likewise, no rating form, profile chart, or system for rating and ranking students in their speech performances is any better than the teacher-critic who employs it. Presumably every teacher of speech should be capable of using such forms as are presented at the end of this chapter. Also, students in a class in speech education, even in grade nine, should become increasingly capable of analyzing speech performances with and without such forms as those presented for consideration by teachers of speech. The forms vary from a simple form which permits the teacher, and the student, to contribute the criteria used in analyzing speech performances, to a complex form on which many of the criteria for speech performance analysis are designated.

Projects

1. Prepare a paper in which you explain the bases which you would recommend for grading students in a course in basic speech development. Support your recommendation. Be prepared to present your paper to the instructor and to the class.

2. Present to your instructor a rating scale which you recommend for use in evaluating the effectiveness of your instructor of methods and materials in teaching speech.

3. Formulate a statement of your philosophy of evaluating a speech performance by a student in a first course in fundamentals of speech. Consider: objectives, compliments, praise, suggestions, criticism, and evaluation. Support your philosophy.

4. Construct an objective test over this chapter, discuss the test items with your classmates, present your test to your instructor, and be prepared to discuss with the class factors which you considered as you prepared the test.

5. Set up the standards which you would recommend for use in determining an A, B, C, D, and F speech.

6. Formulate a rating form which you would recommend for use in evaluating speech performances. Consider such forms as you can find at the end of this chapter and in other sources available to you.

7. Explain from your personal experience how important it is, or is not, for a teacher of speech to remember that he is evaluating *individuals* and that he must study the student he is evaluating.

8. Discuss the advantages and disadvantages of oral versus written evaluation by the teacher and students.

9. Prepare to explain in class your philosophy on encouraging stu-

ACHIEVEMENT RATINGS

Key: A—Excellent; B—Good; C—Average; D—Fair
F—Unsatisfactory; I—Incomplete

Reporting Periods	I	II	III	IV	Final

FUNDAMENTALS OF SPEECH

	I	II	III	IV	Final
Adjustment to speech situations.					
Quality and integrity of ideas expressed.					
Clarity of organization of ideas.					
Control and use of bodily action.					
Control and use of voice.					
Comprehension and use of language.					
Pronunciation and articulation.					
Courteous and analytical listening and observing.					

PERSONALYSIS

Key: S—Satisfactory; N—Needs Improvement
I—Insufficient Evidence

PERSONAL SPEECH ATTRIBUTES

Willingness to accept responsibility.		

Reporting Periods	I	II	III	IV	Final
Can be depended upon to discharge responsibilities.					
Is considerate of the rights, opinions, and property of others.					
Accepts constructive criticisms and suggestions of teachers and classmates.					
Influences, in a desirable way, the actions of associates.					
Is poised and exercises self-control.					

WORK AND STUDY HABITS

Uses time wisely and efficiently.					
Is prompt with assignments.					
Demonstrates ingenuity and initiative.					
Follows directions carefully.					
Shows neatness and pride in work.					

Prepared by Hugh F. Seabury

dents in a course in basic speech development or in essential speech experiences to criticize, rate, rank, and evaluate each other in speech performances and activites in the class.

10. In a role-playing situation, demonstrate the proper way of carrying on a personal conference with a student who is in a class in speech. You play the role of the teacher. Then, demonstrate an ineffective personal conference.

11. Investigate any established policies affecting grading practices of teachers in a local high school or in one or more high schools which you can visit. Explain to the class what policies, if any, govern the grading practices and why the policies are, or are not, sound and desirable.

12. Examine each of the forms on the succeeding pages and prepare to present to the class your statement of the differences between the forms. Consider: the objective, format, suggested evaluative procedure, criteria, and value of each form for the teacher and students.

ORAL COMMUNICATION CRITIQUE

STUDENT _____ COURSE _____

Directions: Check specific weaknesses (sub-items) and if you choose to do so, evaluate the oral communication of the student in each assignment by the five main items using the following scale: 5—Superior (A); 4—Excellent (B); 3—Average (C); 2—Below Average (D); 1—Unsatisfactory (F).

	ASSIGNMENTS
	1 2 3 4 5 6 7 8 9 10 11 12 13 14 15 16 17 18
I. PREPARATION	
*A. Introduction	
B. Organization	
C. Choice of Material	
D. Supporting Material	
E. Relevancy	
*F. Integrity	
*G. Time Limit	
H. Conclusion	
II. VISIBLE SKILLS	
*A. Approach	
B. Vocal Pause	
C. Eye Contact	
*D. Facial Animation	

	Assignments
	1|2|3|4|5|6|7|8|9|10|11|12|13|14|15|16|17|18
*E. Bodily Action	
*F. Adapting to Audience	
*G. Terminal Pause	
III. Oral Skills	
*A. Loudness	
*B. Pitch	
*C. Quality	
*D. Duration	
*E. Inflection	
*F. Enunciation	
*G. Articulation	
IV. Language Skills	
A. Vocabulary	
*B. Pronunciation	
*C. Correctness	
*D. Effectiveness	
V. General Skills	
*A. Appearance	
*B. Desire to Communicate	
C. Courtesy	
(The following plus the items above marked * apply to oral reading)	
1. Understanding of Meaning	
2. Understanding of Feeling	
3. Familiarity with Material	
4. Effective Subordination	
5. Effective Emphasis	
6. Characterization	
Composite Rating:	
Comment:	

Prepared by Department of Speech of Saint Cloud State College

CRITERIA FOR ORAL COMMUNICATION CRITIQUE

PREPARATION
1. Is the introduction attention-getting? (I-A)
2. Does the introduction lead into the topic for consideration? (I-A)
3. Does the introduction establish in the minds of the members of the audience the importance of the subject? (I-A)
4. Does the introduction result in audience-speaker adjustment, speaker-subject adjustment, and subject-audience adjustment? (I-A)
5. Is the objective clearly stated or implied? (I-B)
6. Is the pattern of organization of ideas clear? (I-B)
7. Are the speaker's main points related well to his objective? (I-B)
8. Is the speech material audience-centered? (I-C)
9. Is the material interesting? (I-C)
10. Is the material fresh, vital, compelling? (I-C)
11. Is the material well motivated? (I-C, D, E)
12. Does the speaker contribute efficiently to the development of his objective? (I-B, D, E, F)
13. Does the speaker summarize when necessary? (I-C, H)
14. Does the speaker use key words for main ideas? (I-B, IV-A, D)
15. Does the speaker stay within the time limitations? (I-G)
16. Is the speaker ethical in his approach and development of the subject? (I-F)
17. Does the speaker use effective illustrations, examples, analogies, and visual aids when applicable? (I-D)

VISIBLE SKILLS
1. Does the speaker look directly at the audience? (II-C)
2. Is the speaker physically animated? (II-D, E)
3. Does the speaker appear to be well-adjusted before he speaks? (II-A, B, C, D, E)
4. Does the speaker use varied bodily action when appropriate? (II-E)
5. Does the bodily action of the speaker indicate that he is sufficiently dynamic? (II-C, D, E)
6. Does the speaker stand easily erect and poised? (II-E, F)
7. Does the speaker adjust to audience attitudes? (II-F)
8. Does the speaker move purposefully? (II-E)
9. Does the speaker reflect physical vitality? (II-C, D, E; V-A, B)
10. Does the speaker utilize vocal and terminal pauses? (II-B, G)

ORAL SKILLS
1. Does speaker use loudness for intelligibility and variety? (III-A, D)
2. Is the speaker's vocal pitch medium low and varied effectively? (III-B)
3. Is the voice quality appealing and varied effectively? (III-C)
4. Is the duration of the voice conducive to variety and clarity in speech tempo? (III-D)
5. Is the voice pattern or inflection varied and interesting? (III-E)
6. Are vowels and vowel-like sounds clearly enunciated? (III-F)
7. Are consonants and consonant-like sounds distinctly articulated? (III-G)

LANGUAGE SKILLS
1. Does the speaker use a dynamic and varied vocabulary? (IV-A)

2. Does the speaker refrain from verbosity? (IV-D)
3. Does the speaker use effectively the question technique? (IV-D)
4. Is there a wise use of repetition? (IV-D)
5. Are sentences effectively balanced? (IV-D)
6. Are words pronounced correctly and acceptably? (IV-B)
7. Does the speaker use acceptable pronunciation? (IV-B)
8. Does the speaker avoid annoying habits, i.e., throat-clearing, "er," "ah," "oh," filler? (IV-D)

GENERAL SKILLS
1. Does the speaker give evidence of his desire to communicate? (V-B)
2. Is the speaker neatly dressed and well-groomed? (V-A)
3. Does the speaker acknowledge courteously his introduction when appropriate? (V-C)
4. Does the speaker adjust with courtesy to interruptions? (V-C)
5. Does the speaker meet the audience with genuine warmth and courtesy? (V-A, B, C)

Prepared by Department of Speech at Saint Cloud State College

State University of Iowa
University High School
Iowa City, Iowa

SPEECH RATING FORM

SPEAKER _____ DATE _____
TOPIC _____ TEACHER _____

INSTRUCTIONS: Please *complete* one of these forms for each speaker, during and/or immediately after his speech. Rate him on each of the five criteria listed, using the following RATING SCALE: 5—Excellent; 4—Above Average; 3—Average; 2—Below Average; 1—Unsatisfactory. After rating him on each of the five criteria, write the sum of the five ratings after TOTAL. Record your comments that explain your rating.

CRITERIA	COMMENTS	RATING
TOPIC: Adapted to interests and background of speaker and audience? Appropriate for occasion? Properly narrowed? Of significance?		
CONTENT: Ideas interesting? Significant? Related to topic? Specific? Valid? Varied? Sufficient? Adapted to purpose and audience?		
ORGANIZATION: Introduction, purpose, body, and conclusion apparent? Division of significant ideas clear and logical? Transitions clear?		

Criteria	Comments	Rating
DELIVERY: Communicative, conversational, direct, fluent, varied? Voice clear and used well? Enunciation clear? Articulation distinct? Pronunciations acceptable? Language clear, intelligible, accurate, varied, vivid, appropriate?		
GENERAL EFFECTIVENESS: Speaker purposeful, easily understood, attention holding? Speaker's purpose realized?		

(Continue comments on back as desired.) TOTAL: _____

JUDGE _____
(Signature)

Prepared by Hugh F. Seabury

A Profile Rating

ACHIEVEMENT IN SPEECH MAKING

STUDENT _____ SECTION _____

TOPIC _____

	5	4	3	2	1	Comments
Choice of Topic						
Choice of Thought						
Choice of Material						
Organization of Material						
Use of Language						
Projection to the Audience						
Use of Bodily Action						
Voice Usage						
Pronunciation						
Enunciation						
Articulation						
Audience Response						

TOTAL SCORE: _____

Composite rating is the Total Score divided by 12: _____
RATING SCALE: 5—Superior; 4—Above Average; 3—Average;
2—Below Average; 1—Unsatisfactory

Prepared by Hugh F. Seabury

SPEECH MAKING

Name _____ Date _____

Topic _____ Assignment _____

Items	High: 9 Low: 1	Comments
Topic: Of interest, significance; properly narrowed; adapted to speaker, audience, occasion?		
Ideas: Clear, sound, original? Is analysis complete, valid?		
Supporting Material: Valid, relevant, sufficient, properly distributed?		
Interest-getting devices: Are ideas and material so handled that interest is caught and held?		
Language: Clear, vivid, appropriate, correct, in conversational mode?		
Organization: Clear, unified, coherent, properly proportioned? Thesis, introduction, conclusion?		
Adaptation of Speech to Audience: Is this speech for this audience on this occasion?		
Bodily Action: Is speaker animated? Does action contribute to expression of ideas, help hold interest?		
Voice: Quality? Attributes properly used to express meaning, hold interest?		
Articulation and Pronunciation: Articulation clear, correct? Pronunciation according to accepted standards?		
Fluency: Is speaker extemporaneous, direct? Does speech keep moving?		

SPEECH MAKING (*Continued*)

Items	High: 9 Low; 1	Comments
Platform Personality: Does speaker "get over the footlights," "sell" himself to audience?		
General Effectiveness: What is the over-all effect of the speech?		
TOTAL		

9, 8, and 7 scores are above average.
6, 5, and 4 scores are adequate.
3, 2, and 1 scores are below average.

_____ Critic

SPEECH RATING BLANK

Name _____ Date _____

Topic _____

Items	High: 9 Low: 1	Comments

Topic and Ideas
   Choice
   Ideas
   Supporting
     Materials		

Organization
   Introduction
   Subject Sentence
   Body-Arrangement
   Conclusion
   Transitions		

Voice Usage
   Flexibility
   Articulation
   Pronunciation
   Basic Quality		

Bodily Action
   Position
   Movement		

SPEECH RATING BLANK (*Continued*)

ITEMS	High: 9 Low: 1	COMMENTS

LANGUAGE
  Grammar
  Vocabulary		

AUDIENCE ADAPTATION
  Eye Contact
  Desire to Communicate		

GENERAL EFFECT		

REMARKS

9, 8, and 7 are above average
6, 5, and 4 are adequate
3, 2, and 1 are below average

                                                          Critic
                                          Prepared by Hugh F. Seabury

State University of Iowa
Department of Speech and Dramatic Art
Iowa City, Iowa
(Used in Course Entitled "Speech for Educators")

NAME OF INTRODUCER _____
Compliments   *Suggestions*

SPEAKER _____
TOPIC _____
Compliments   *Suggestions*

DATE _____ CRITIC _____
                                        Prepared by Hugh F. Seabury

Selected Bibliography

Douglas, Jack, "The Measurement of Speech in the Classroom," *Speech Teacher*, vol. 7, no. 4 (November 1958), pp. 309–319.

Friederich, Willard J., and Ruth A. Wilcox, *Teaching Speech in High School*. New York: The Macmillan Company, 1953.

Holtzman, Paul D., "Speech Criticism and Evaluation Communication," *Speech Teacher*, vol. 9, no. 1 (January 1960), pp. 1–7.

Knower, Franklin H., "What Is a Speech Test?" *Quarterly Journal of Speech*, vol. 30, no. 4 (December 1944), pp. 485–493.

Monroe, Alan, "Testing Speech Performance," *The Bulletin of the National Association of Secondary School Principals* (November 1935), pp. 156–164.

Montgomery, Keith E., "How to Criticize Student Speeches," *Speech Teacher*, vol. 6, no. 3 (September 1957), pp. 200–204.

Oliver, Robert T., "The Eternal (and Infernal) Problem of Grades," *Speech Teacher*, vol. 9, no. 1 (January 1960), pp. 8–11.

Reid, Loren D., *Teaching Speech*, 3rd ed. Columbia, Missouri: Artcraft Press, 1960.

Robinson, Karl F., and E. J. Kerikas, *Teaching Speech: Methods and Materials*. New York: David McKay Company, Inc., 1963.

Sawyer, Thomas M., Jr., "A Grading System for Speech Classes," *Speech Teacher*, vol. 9, no. 1 (January 1960), pp. 12–15.

Weaver, Andrew T., Gladys L. Borchers, and Donald K. Smith, *The Teaching of Speech*. Englewood Cliffs, N. J.: Prentice-Hall, Inc., 1952.

Wiksell, Wesley, "New Methods of Evaluating Instruction and Student Achievement in a Speech Class," *Speech Teacher*, vol. 9, no. 1 (January 1960), pp. 16–19.

CHAPTER 8

Facilities, Equipment, Teaching Aids, and Textbooks

Some administrators and teachers seem to believe that speech can be taught creditably merely with students and a classroom. Perhaps so; but, obviously, much better work can be done by teachers and students of speech who have available modern facilities, special equipment, well-selected teaching aids, and many books at hand. Career teachers of speech who are dedicated to stimulating and guiding students in their achievement, development, and improvement have an inner compulsion to seek the best resources available to effect maximum learning.

The Speech Classroom

There is widespread belief that speech can be taught as creditably in one kind of classroom as in another. In many of our new and very modern school buildings, little or no provision has been made for the special needs of a classroom in which speech can be taught best. School planners recognize the need for classrooms designed especially for effective teaching of such subjects as household arts, science, music, and health and physical education. School principals assign teachers of these subjects to classrooms designed to serve their special teaching needs. School planners and principals are recognizing increasingly, even if slowly, the kind of classroom which can serve the teaching of speech most effectively. Teachers who are assigned to classrooms unsuitable for teaching speech are sometimes inclined to blame school planners or school principals for their plight. In some cases, these complaints may be justified, but the teacher needs to answer some questions about himself and his fellow speech educators before he blames school planners and administrators, who probably desire the best possible conditions. Some teachers of speech are asked to recommend to school planners and administrators the kinds of facilities, equipment, aids, and textbooks which can serve best the teaching of speech. Often, teachers seem unable to make well-informed recommendations which reflect appropriate, challenging, and worthwhile objectives, programs, and desired outcomes of speech education. Every teacher needs to know and to be able to explain his philosophy of teaching speech, significant objectives to be served by a classroom program in speech education, the program itself, desirable outcomes to be realized by his students, and the location and characteristics of a good speech classroom.

The *location* of a speech classroom is important. It should be free from distractions such as street noises, the banging of pipes, the clamor from playgrounds; disturbances from other classrooms or from the school cafeteria. Proximity to the auditorium, or the little theatre in some schools, is advantageous especially if members of a class may move to that room for special practice and performances. If it is feasible, the speech classroom should be located near the school library or, better yet, located so that library materials can at times be conveniently brought into the speech classroom for study supervised by the teacher. Often it is wise for the teacher of speech to take the entire class to the library for special work and to send class committees to the library to carry out assignments in preparing for discussions; for collecting materials for briefs and outlines; for reading prose and poetry for oral interpretation; for reading plays and speeches, and for studying references as an aid in speechmaking. If the school has a central audio-visual room where classes can be taken to see films, filmstrips, kinescopes, and slides, the speech classroom should be located near enough to it. All classrooms cannot, obviously, be immediately adjacent to the school library and the audio-visual room. Nevertheless, the teacher of speech should encourage his students to master the use of library facilities and to rely on the library as a source of content and stimulation.

The *characteristics* of a speech classroom make a greater difference in the outcomes derived from teaching speech than are yet even imagined. Practical working space which provides suitable speaker-listener relationships is very necessary. The speech classroom is, in a very distinct manner, a "laboratory" in which adequate space should be provided for students to work in group performance activities as well as in speaker-audience performances. The "closet" type of room is poor because it does not provide the needed working space, minimizes the need for vocal projection, and makes unlikely the development of habitual vocal variation in loudness of voice. Science rooms, home economics rooms, gymnasiums, and libraries pose problems for a teacher of speech because these situations contain equipment which is unrelated to teaching speech and which detracts seriously from the achievement of speech objectives. Even if this were not true, these rooms do not enable a teacher of speech to place the proper equipment and materials before his students. No matter how acceptable and effective the setting and atmosphere of these rooms for their purposes, they do not suit the particular demands of teaching speech. Long, narrow rooms present problems in audience contact and in the establishment of effective communicative rapport with listeners. Although no specific size of speech classroom is recommended as ideal, the speech classroom should provide (1) a minimum of twenty-five square feet of floor space for each student; (2) good sight lines from each position in the room to each of the other positions; (3) flexibility in arrangement of chairs and tables for students; (4) a speaker's platform or, preferably a stage, consisting of at least 300 square feet and width of twice the depth; (5) a conference room adjacent to the speech classroom and separated from it by glass panels; (6) a light projection and control room, preferably at the opposite end from the stage, connected with small practice-observation rooms; and (7) a recording room or radio studio adjacent to the speech classroom and connected with all of the facilities of the classroom.

Two or more special features of any speech classroom deserve special mention: a speech platform or stage and a conference room. No speech classroom should be without a platform or stage. A stage is more desirable, but a platform which is either permanent or portable is acceptable. A stage can give students the experience and feeling of auditorium-type speech, dramatic, and forensic performances and permit all members of the class to see what is going on. A conference room is also very necessary and may double as a projection and control room, a practice and recording room, and perhaps as a radio studio. Much of the speech work with students requires individual conferences. Student committee groups need facilities to work without disturbing others in the classroom. It should be possible for a teacher of speech in a speech classroom to see what is going on in the speech conference room. Also, when the teacher is in the conference room, he should be able to supervise the activity of students in the speech classroom.

All school classrooms need to be *acoustically* treated, the speech classroom especially. The wall composition should be acoustical tile or other soundproof material. Likewise, the ceiling should be soundproof. Students should be able to participate in voice work and in speech performances of all kinds without disturbing students and faculty members outside of the classroom.

Since the speech classroom is a laboratory, some special *furnishings* are needed: (1) ample chalkboard for the teacher's use in explanations and demonstrations and the students' use in outlining, tabulating, and diagramming; (2) bulletin board space of ample size for displaying motivational type material such as posters, clippings, pictures, assignments, and announcements; (3) a large wall mirror as an aid to the teacher and the students in studying visual aspects of speaking; and (4) cabinets and cases for displaying a variety of books, periodicals, and other special materials desirable and necessary for students' use in their preparation for participation in various speech activities. Pictures of actors and actresses in scenes from plays and of famous orators and speakers in historical settings can all add atmosphere to the speech classroom. Pictures of play casts, forensic squads, and individual students who have been recognized over the years for excellence of speech performances have been used to motivate students. Certificates of achievement, banners, plaques, and trophies can also be used in stimulating and guiding students to achieve, improve, and grow, provided that the awards are not overemphasized.

Other factors of the speech classroom are (1) a window area which gives light without glare and without excessive exposure to sunlight; (2) appropriately painted walls on which pastel colors are often used; (3) a type of floor which permits students to walk noiselessly; (4) adequate indirect artificial lighting; (5) two entrances with one from the hall to the back of the classroom and the other from the hall onto the stage but out of the sight of students in the classroom; (6) even heat with avoidance of extremes in temperature and with individual room adjustment; and (7) special esthetic features including attractive draperies and floor coverings, concealed storage, an unabridged and up-to-date dictionary, and shelves and cabinets for rating sheets and ballots, playscripts, and reference books.

Two sketches of recently constructed speech classrooms are set forth on the next page to indicate what has been done in schools in which the need for a special speech classroom has been recognized.

Equipment

Not only should the teacher be concerned about the classroom, but about basic equipment necessary for excellence of teaching. However, just as the ideal classroom is not available in most schools, neither are all items of equipment immediately available. A well-prepared and dedicated teacher of speech can work effectively and at the same time exercise initiative in cooperating with his adminstrator to get the necessary items of equipment.

EQUIPMENT 273

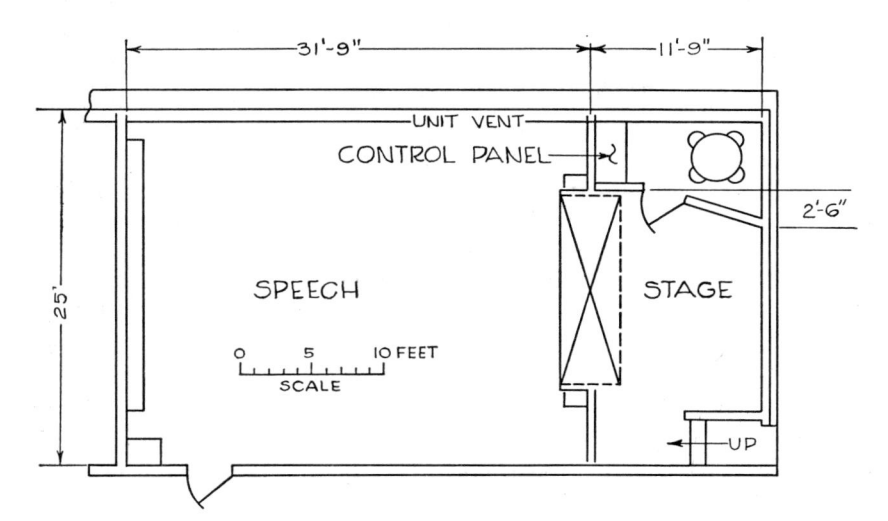

Detroit Lakes, Minnesota, High School. Traynor and Hermanson, Saint Cloud, Minnesota, architects.

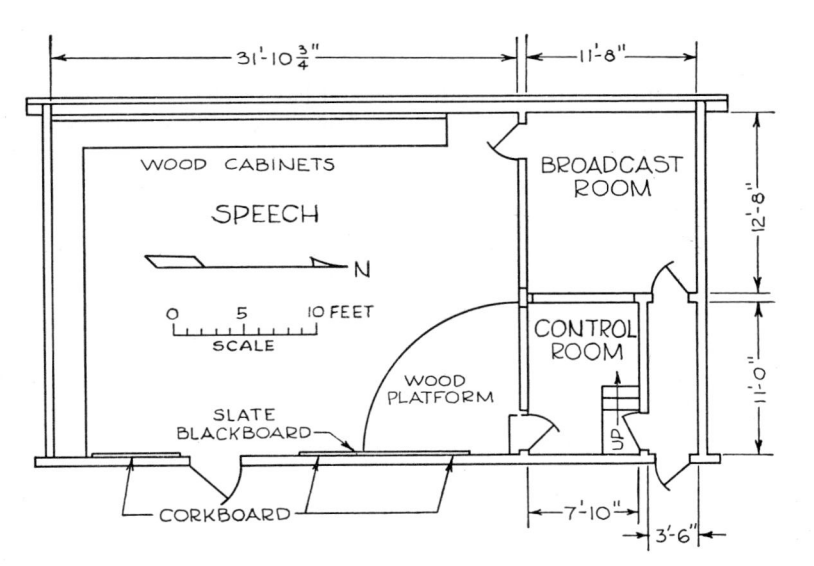

Cathedral High School, Saint Cloud, Minnesota. Pinault and Truszinksi, Saint Cloud, Minnesota, architects.

SPEECH CLASSROOMS

In a modern school, the old-fashioned, fixed seat and desk are rarely seen. Today, movable chairs and desks serve best in classrooms. They are needed in the speech classroom. They provide flexible seating arrangements for special types of speaking such as discussions, interviewing, play rehearsals and productions, and speechmaking. The modern speech classroom should include a number of tables and straight-back chairs which are desirable for panel discussions, paper-and-pencil work during supervised study, outlining, and written examinations which appear to be too much neglected in speech classrooms today.

A lectern or speaker's stand can aid the student in mastering his use of it in speaking, reading aloud, and presiding. Many teachers of speech have obtained such a piece of equipment as a result of an individual or class project in the industrial arts department of the high school.

If the school does not have an audio-visual room in which classes can view films and filmstrips, the speech classroom should include dark shades for darkening the room, plus a screen, preferably permanent, for use in showing films obtained from audio-visual centers.

Adequate filing cabinets are needed for student records, cumulative files, teaching materials, and the enormous amount of supplementary materials such as readings, speeches, pictures, tapes, announcements, and schedules which an effective teacher of speech will accumulate and find useful. Although some filing cabinets should be open to the students under the supervision of the teacher, others should have locks.

Much shelving is needed in a speech classroom. This may be in the form of bookcases to be utilized for a classroom speech library, magazine racks for the display of appropriate periodicals and pamphlets, and shelves for supplementary books, magazines, films, and records.

Appropriate wall charts and models can be used to motivate students and to demonstrate various aspects of speech. The speech classroom should provide adequate facilities for hanging maps, charts, globes, and models.

A wall clock with a second hand can aid the teacher and students in timing speeches and performances. Stop watches, time cards, and timers can facilitate development in each student of a sense of time in speaking and can aid the progression of speech performances.

Few schools today do not possess a tape recorder. This teaching device is a *must* for effective teaching of speech. Because much speech work is diagnostic and analytical, because it is well to let the student hear himself, because each student should be helped to analyze his verbal utterance as he hears it, and because each student should have an opportunity to hear himself after his speech improvement, a recorder should be kept in the speech classroom and used solely by the teacher of speech.

Other items of audio-visual equipment which a teacher of speech can utilize to great advantage include a three-speed record player, a public address system, a radio, a television set, a movie projector, an opaque projector, and filmstrip projector. Actually the day may come when a sound motion picture camera or two, especially when films can be processed in seconds, will be a valuable part of speech classroom equipment.

Teaching Aids

Teaching aids for the teacher of speech can be classified into six types: (1) motion pictures, (2) recordings and transcriptions, (3) filmstrips and slides, (4) charts and models, (5) pictures and printed plays, readings, and speeches, and (6) professional publications.

Many motion pictures which deal directly with dramatics, forensics, and speech have only recently become available. The wise teacher of speech will be selective in the films he chooses and will preview the films and prepare his class for viewing them. The *Educational Film Index*, published annually by the H. W. Wilson Company, provides invaluable information on films and film distributors. Audio-visual aid departments in larger high schools and in colleges and universities provide valuable sources of films. Teachers of speech should become acquainted with the publications available from the United States Office of Education, Washington 25, D.C.

During recent years, recordings of public speeches, debates, discussions, oral readings, plays, and radio programs have been used increasingly by teachers of speech to supplement classroom reading by students. Tape recordings have become a significant part of the speech library in many schools. Several universities provide a "tapes for teaching" service available through their audio-visual education departments whereby a teacher can send a blank tape and have a recording made from a list of tapes available in the audio-visual center of a university. For many years, for example, the State University of Iowa has recorded the championship debates, extemporaneous speeches, oral interpretations, and original orations in the State Finals of the Iowa High School Forensic League. Tapes of each of the debates and individual events have been made available to high schools. Recordings of various speech performances in the speech classroom can be utilized by a teacher of speech for teacher-led student evaluation. Many of these recordings can be used as models.

Filmstrips and slides can be used to clarify and give vividness to points of instruction. Also, they can be used effectively in promoting class discussions and in affording opportunity for the teacher to ask questions and to lead members of the class in critical analyses of elements of speech, speaking, and speechmaking. Of course, the Encyclopaedia Britannica

Films, Inc., has a complete series of filmstrips which are worth investigating by a teacher of speech who wishes to miss no opportunity to make his teaching most effective.

Charts and models, especially of the speech mechanism, are often helpful in explaining how voice is produced, how speech sounds are formed, and how problems result from the ineffective use of the speech mechanism. The departments of biology, health, and physical education in the school have such charts and models which a teacher of speech may borrow. Other charts such as those which present diagrams of debate organization and procedure, arrangements for panel discussions and symposiums, tables of motions in parliamentary procedure, and diagrams of stage areas can be used to clarify such aspects of speech education.

The teacher can show the practicality of speech work by using pictures of actual speakers in action, discussions and debates, interviews, plays, and radio and television productions. These afford opportunity to show applications of speech concepts and theories to real-life situations. A clipping and picture file often becomes one of the best assets of the experienced teacher of speech who is continually on the alert for suitable materials.

One of the best sources for aid in teaching speech is found in the professional publications of dramatic, forensic, and speech organizations. The teacher should be acquainted with the three publications of the Speech Association of America: the *Speech Teacher,* the *Quarterly Journal of Speech,* and *Speech Monographs.* Likewise, he should know all such journals as *Theatre Arts, Players' Magazine, Dramatics,* the *American Educational Theatre Association Journal,* the *Journal of Speech and Hearing Disorders,* the *Journal of Speech and Hearing Research,* and the three English journals, all known as the *English Journal.* The regional speech associations also publish magazines: the Speech Association of the Eastern States publishes *Today's Speech;* the Western Speech Association, *Western Speech;* the Southern Speech Association, the *Southern Speech Journal;* and the Central States Speech Association, *Central States Speech Journal.* Not only do these periodicals publish articles designed to help teachers in teaching speech but they carry advertisements by manufacturers, publishers, and distributors of aids and materials to increase the effectiveness of teaching. Many carry reports of the results of research accomplished in universities, annotated bibliographies of books and periodicals, book reviews, descriptions of audio-visual aids, and reports of speech programs and activities in high schools and colleges across the nation. Every professionally minded and dedicated teacher of speech is likely to be a member of one or more educational and speech organizations and a subscriber to one or more professional publications of his choice.

Several catalogues of free and inexpensive materials have been published.[1] Alert teachers of speech will become acquainted with all such compilations.

Textbooks

Teachers have often stated that the only acceptable speech text is one "that you write yourself!" This statement indicates, perhaps, the basic drawback of any single text: its failure to cover adequately everything that a particular teacher of speech may wish to have included. This makes it difficult to suggest that any single text be considered the end-and-all for a high school speech course. It does suggest, however, that many high school teachers of speech rely heavily on either a single textbook or a limited number of textbooks for help in teaching their courses. Therefore, it is desirable that every teacher of speech be familiar with the available texts and have some notion of how to select one or more textbooks to meet specific needs as they arise.

People expect a teacher to know the literature of his field. Teachers of speech are expected to keep up with what is being written, investigated, subjected to experimentation, and published. They are often asked, even in their initial interviews for positions, to indicate their choice of speech texts. Also, textbooks can become outdated rapidly. Teachers are asked to choose new ones. If a teacher selects a text without a careful evaluation of the available textbooks, he will suffer because of such hasty action. The teacher should obtain and carefully examine, chapter by chapter if not page by page, the textbooks available for use by his students. He will find a wide variety of philosophies, approaches, treatment of various aspects of speech, suggested activities, means for evaluation of students' progress, and suggested outcomes of teaching speech. One suggested solution to this problem is to utilize a check list, or a series of questions, which can help the teacher see the strengths and weaknesses of each textbook. His selection can then be made on the basis of which books meet his needs on the greatest number of items on his checklist. The following is a sample list of questions which could well be utilized:

FACTORS FOR ANALYSIS AND REVIEW OF SPEECH TEXTS
TITLE:
AUTHOR:
PUBLISHER: COPYRIGHT DATE: PRICE:
  Answer each question with a *yes* or *no*; or with *none, poor, fair, good,* or *excellent*; and add a brief comment when clarification seems to be needed.
  1. Is the cover attractive and colorful?
  2. Does the binding seem strong and durable?

[1] Florence M. Santiago, comp., *Inexpensive or Free Materials Useful for Teaching Speech: A Source List for Secondary Schools.* Ann Arbor, Michigan: Braun-Brumfield, Inc., 1959.

3. Is the paper of proper size, quality, and color?
4. Is the type clean-looking and attractive?
5. Is the index complete and usable?
6. Are there illustrations or drawings?   If so,
    a. Are they artistically done?
    b. Are they merely illustrative or provocative of imagination, feeling, and thought?
7. Is there a definite philosophy of speech education set forth in the preface?   In the book itself?   Does it follow one of the following philosophies?
    a. Personality development of the individual?
    b. Functional speech activities?
    c. Fundamentals of speech?
    d. Public speaking?
    e. Speech arts?
    f. Survey course?
    g. Other?
8. For what student groups is the book most appropriate?
    a. For what age?
    b. For what grade level?
    c. For students with speech defects?
    d. For students with interest and ability in speech?
    e. For beginners or advanced students?
    f. For the "average" student?
9. Does the book contain a systematic and balanced treatment of the content of the various areas of speech?
    a. Are the fundamentals of speech adequately presented?
    b. Are speech activities included and adequately developed?
    c. Is basic "voice and phonetics" included?
    d. Are the various purposes of speech considered?
    e. Is listening included and adequately treated?
10. Is the book easy to read by the students for whom it is intended?
    a. Is the style appropriate for high school students?
    b. Are the basic principles and facts clearly presented?
    c. Is the application of the principles clear and significant?
    d. Is there a logical arrangement of sequence of units or chapters, or both?
11. Does the book contain adequate diagnostic and testing methods and materials?
    a. Are self-evaluation forms included?
    b. Are questionnaires included for student use?
    c. Are tests presented?   Are they suitable?
    d. Are critic evaluation forms presented?   Audience evaluation forms?
12. Are there exercises for in-class and out-of-class use?
    a. Do they conform to basic principles of effective learning?
    b. Do they meet the following standards?

(1) Worthwhile?
(2) Functional?
(3) Clear?
(4) Challenging?
(5) Adequate in number?
(6) Adaptable to individual interests, needs, and abilities?
13. What teaching aids are included in the book?
  a. Table of contents?
  b. Suggested plan for course organization?
  c. Bibliographies and student-teacher references?
  d. Suggested audio-visual aids, including sources and suggested ways of utilizing the aids effectively?
  e. Appendices?
  f. Specimen speeches?
14. Does the book make any special contributions to your understanding of the field of speech?
15. Does this text seem to be adaptable to the approach you will use in teaching speech?

No one textbook is likely to be entirely satisfactory. The wise teacher will plan on supplementing the textbook to meet the needs of his students with guidesheets, handouts, and study guides. Having four or five copies of four or more high school textbooks in the speech classroom library for student use, to supplement the regular text, is not an uncommon procedure. One of the best sources for keeping up to date on new books available is the book review section of publications such as the *Speech Teacher,* the *Quarterly Journal of Speech,* the *American Educational Theatre Association Journal,* the *English Journal,* and the *Directory of the Speech Association of America.*

The following list of speech textbooks for use by students in a high school is presented as a basic source of textbook citations for a teacher of speech in a high school. Only textbooks which have been published since 1950 are included. The order of arrangement is alphabetical rather than preferential.

Recent Textbooks in Speech Education

ANDERSCH, ELIZABETH G., and LORIN C. STAATS, *Speech for Everyday Use,* rev. ed. New York: Holt, Rinehart and Winston, Inc., 1960.

BAIRD, A. CRAIG, and FRANKLIN H. KNOWER, *Essentials of General Speech,* 2nd ed. New York: McGraw-Hill, Inc., 1960.

CRANDELL, S. JUDSON, GERALD PHILLIPS, and JOSEPH WIGLEY, *Speech: A Course in Fundamentals.* Chicago: Scott, Foresman and Company, 1964.

ELSON, E. F., and ALBERTA PECK, *The Art of Speaking.* New York: Ginn and Company, 1952.

GRIFFITH, FRANCIS, CATHERINE NELSON, and EDWARD STASHEFF, *Your Speech.* New York: Harcourt, Brace & World, Inc., 1955.

HACKETT, HERBERT, MARTIN ANDERSEN, SETH FESSENDEN, and LESSIE LEE HAGEN, *Understanding and Being Understood.* New York: Longmans, Green and Company, 1957.

HEDDE, WILHELMINA G., and WILLIAM N. BRIGANCE, *The New American Speech.* Philadelphia: J. B. Lippincott Company, 1957.

IRWIN, JOHN V., and MARJORIE ROSENBERGER, *Modern Speech.* New York: Holt, Rinehart and Winston, Inc., 1961.

JONES, E. WINSTON, *A Guide to Effective Speech.* New York: Longmans, Green and Company, 1961.

McBURNEY, JAMES H., and ERNEST J. WRAGE, *Guide to Good Speech*, 2nd ed. Englewood Cliffs, N.J.: Prentice-Hall, Inc., 1960.

———, and ———, *The Art of Good Speech.* Englewood Cliffs, N.J.: Prentice-Hall, Inc., 1953.

MUDD, CHARLES S., and MALCOLM O. SILLARS, *Speech: Content and Communication.* San Francisco: Chandler Publishing Company, 1962.

SARETT, LEW, WILLIAM T. FOSTER, and JAMES H. McBURNEY, *Speech: A High School Course.* Boston: Houghton Mifflin Company, 1956.

ST. ONGE, KEITH R., *Creative Speech.* Belmont, Calif.: Wadsworth Publishing Company, 1964.

WEAVER, ANDREW T., GLADYS L. BORCHERS, and DONALD K. SMITH, *Speaking and Listening.* Englewood Cliffs, N.J.: Prentice-Hall, Inc., 1956.

———, and ORDEAN G. NESS, *The Fundamentals and Forms of Speech.* New York: The Odyssey Press, 1957.

Record Distributors

Audio Book Company, 501 Main Street, Saint Joseph, Michigan.
Caedmon Sales Corporation, 227 Fifth Avenue, New York, New York.
Gloria Chandler Recordings, Inc., 227 West 12th Street, New York 14, New York.
Columbia Records, Educational Division, 779 Seventh Avenue, New York 19, New York.
Decca Distributing Corporation, 50 West 57th Street, New York 19, New York.
Encyclopaedia Britannica Films, 1144 Wilmette Avenue, Wilmette, Illinois.
Enrichment Records, 246 Fifth Avenue, New York, New York.
Folkways Records and Service Corporation, 117 West 46th Street, New York 36, New York.
Lexington Records, Educational Audio-Visual, Inc., 6 East 39th Street, New York 16, New York.
Linguaphone Institute, 30 Rockefeller Plaza, New York 20, New York.
National Council of Teachers of English, 704 South Sixth Street, Champaign, Illinois.
Poetry Records, 475 Fifth Avenue, New York 17, New York.
RCA Victor, Camden, New Jersey. (Order from nearest RCA Victor dealer.)
The Sound Book Press Society, Inc., Scarsdale, New York.

Stanley Bowmar Company, 12 Cleveland Street, Valhalla, New York.
Westminster Recording Sales Corporation, 275 Seventh Avenue, New York, New York.

Film Distributors

Academic Film Company, 516 Fifth Avenue, New York, New York.
American Film Company, 1329 Vine Street, Philadelphia, Pennsylvania.
Astor Pictures Corporation, 130 West 46th Street, New York 19, New York.
Audio Film Center, 2138 East 75th Street, Chicago 49, Illinois.
Arthur Barr Productions, 1265 Brescoe Avenue, Pasadena, California.
Brandon Films, Inc., 200 West 57th Street, New York 19, New York.
Byron, Inc., 1226 Wisconsin Avenue, N.W., Washington 7, D.C.
Colonial Williamsburg Films, Distribution Section, Box 516, Williamsburg, Virginia.
Coronet Instructional Films, Inc., 1150 Wilmette Avenue, Wilmette, Illinois.
Dynamic Films, Inc., 112 West 89th Street, New York 19, New York.
Encyclopaedia Britannica Films, Inc., 1150 Wilmette Avenue, Wilmette, Illinois.
Esso Standard Oil Company, 15 West 51st Street, New York 19, New York.
Films, Inc., 1150 Wilmette Avenue, Wilmette, Illinois.
Gateway Productions, Inc., 1859 Powell Street, San Francisco 11, California.
Goodyear Tire and Rubber Company, Inc., Motion Picture Department, 1144 East Market Street, Akron 16, Ohio.
Harmon Foundation, Division of Visual Experiment, 1040 Nassau Street, New York 38, New York.
Institutional Cinema Service, Inc., 165 West 46th Street, New York 36, New York.
International Film Bureau, 57 East Jackson Boulevard, Chicago 4, Illinois.
McGraw-Hill, Inc., Text-Film Department, 330 West 42nd Street, New York 36, New York.
Minneapolis-Moline Company, Minneapolis 1, Minnesota.
E. L. Marthole, 8855 Lincolnwood Drive, Evanston, Illinois.
National Association of Manufacturers, Film Bureau, 2 East 48th Street, New York 17, New York.
Nu-Art Films, Inc., 227 West 46th Street, New York 36, New York.
Perry Mansfield School of the Theater and Dance, 135 Corona Avenue, Pelham 65, New York. (June 1—October 1, Steamboat Springs, Colorado.)
Teaching Film Custodians, Inc., 25 West 43rd Street, New York 36, New York.
United Nations, Films and Visual Information Division, New York, New York.
Young America Films, Inc., 18 East 41st Street, New York 17, New York.

Projects

1. Sketch what you believe to be "the ideal speech classroom." Assume that you can have as much money as you desire and that you may

equip your ideal speech classroom as you choose. Tell how you would equip it.

2. Evaluate the teaching aids available to the teacher of speech in a high school which you can visit. If possible, confer with the teacher of speech about the training aids. Report to the class the results of your evaluation.

3. Present to the class your plan for furnishing your ideal classroom for teaching speech. Prepare to use the blackboard to clarify your plan and your description of the furnishings.

4. List all of the teaching aids which you believe you could use in teaching speech in your ideal classroom. Then, place the equipment in three classifications: (1) urgently necessary, (2) necessary, and (3) desirable. Be prepared to defend your classification in class.

5. Construct a specific teaching aid and plan a lesson in which you can make effective use of your teaching aid. Prepare to teach the lesson in the class in methods of teaching speech. Lead the class in an evaluation of your use of the teaching aid.

6. Visit an audio-visual center in a large high school or university. Examine a catalog or list of the audio-visual aids available in the center which you visit. Confer with the teacher in charge of the center. Come to class prepared to indicate the audio-visual aids in the center which you would recommend for use by a teacher of speech. Support your recommendation.

7. Choose any five recordings or transcriptions which you would recommend for use by a teacher of speech in his classroom. Explain why you would recommend the recordings, how you believe they could be used, and the desired outcomes which you would hope to realize as a result of their use.

8. Examine at least three recent issues of professional publications such as the *Speech Teacher*, the *Quarterly Journal of Speech*, and *Speech Monographs*. Report to the class your findings which you believe to be significant for increasing the effectiveness of teaching speech in a high school.

9. Study one book review of a recent textbook in the *Speech Teacher*. Then, examine the book and compare your reaction to the book with the reaction of the reviewer in the *Speech Teacher*.

10. Using the guide provided in this chapter, analyze and review one or more of the high school speech texts listed. Present your analysis and review to your instructor and be prepared to present to the class your oral review.

11. Examine at least three recent issues of the *American Educational Theatre Association Journal*. Describe the kinds of materials you find in

the publication and give one detailed report of one article in one of the issues.

Selected Bibliography

BRADEN, WALDO W., ed., *Speech Methods and Resources*. New York: Harper & Row, Publishers, 1961.

DALE, EDGAR, *Audio-Visual Methods in Teaching*. New York: Holt, Rinehart & Winston, 1946.

REID, LOREN D., *Teaching Speech*, 3rd ed. Columbia, Missouri: Artcraft Press, 1960.

ROBINSON, KARL F., and E. J. KERIKAS, *Teaching Speech: Methods and Materials*. New York: David McKay Company, Inc., 1963.

WEAVER, ANDREW T., GLADYS L. BORCHERS, and DONALD K. SMITH, *The Teaching of Speech*. Englewood Cliffs, N.J.: Prentice-Hall, Inc., 1952.

CHAPTER 9

Directing a Co-curricular Speech Program

The student activity program in our American secondary schools is an established part of the total school program. It can hardly be classified as "extra" as it was a few years ago. School administrators are concerned with assuming responsibility for all student activities and for organizing and supervising them on the same basis as that underlying the traditional curricular program of studies in the school. The co-curricular school program is interpreted as a part of the school program which grows out of its curricular program, parallels it, and contributes significantly to objectives which are identical or similar to those of the school itself. In contrast, an extracurricular program does not grow out of the curriculum, may be imposed upon it as is too often true, and may or may not contribute to achieving the objectives of the school. These extracurricular programs and activities are sometimes sponsored and promoted by non-school groups and organizations to serve objectives and to realize outcomes which are not, in both emphasis and kind, completely compatible with the objectives and desired outcomes of the school. Although neither all phases of the curricular program nor all co-curricular activities which are solidly based in the curriculum are necessarily successful and effective, extra-curricular programs and activities are even less likely to be successful and effective in serving the goals of the school.

In 1952, Johnston listed weaknesses of many school activity programs which are still prevalent in high schools today:[1]

[1] Edgar G. Johnston, "Critical Problems in the Administration of Student Activities," *The Bulletin of the National Association of Secondary School Principals*, February, 1952, pp. 1–12.

1. Adoption of an activity program without any real understanding by teachers and pupils of the function it should perform.
2. Failure to allow students to plan, to make intelligent decisions, and to accept responsibility.
3. Participation limited to too few pupils.
4. Over-emphasis on competitive aspects of the program.
5. Devotion of energy to promotion of national organizations with lost sight of most inclusive objectives.
6. Failure to keep the program vitally related to the curriculum.
7. No consistent effort to evaluate the activities in terms of fundamental objectives.
8. Inadequate recognition of duties of teachers in the activity program in considering teachers' load.

Directors of co-curricular speech activities need to be aware of the adverse criticisms directed at their programs. Much of their time and energy is devoted to this aspect of the speech program. In many of the smaller high schools, the co-curricular speech program may be, and too often is, *the speech program.* Although the number of speech courses being introduced into high schools is increasing noticeably, hardly any secondary school in the United States provides no co-curricular speech activity, either of a dramatic or forensic nature. Most of the adverse criticism of speech education in our high schools is directed at out-of-class speech activities. Specifically, complaints are lodged against alleged overconcern about "winning," the loss of regular school time, overemphasis on speech activities for too few students as compared to the number of students participating in other school activities, artificial motivation of students, expense out of proportion to the number of students who receive significant benefits, loss of teacher effectiveness in the classroom as the teacher's interest and effort are directed to the out-of-class speech activities, and inadequate supervision of students who participate in these activities.

Perhaps the role of the co-curricular speech activities program was most clearly defined by the Contest Committee of the North Central Association in its report on "A Program of Speech Education":

> The chief educational goal of extra-class and interscholastic activities in speech must be clearly comprehended. Such activities give the pupil of special aptitude an opportunity for more intensive and extended experience than is possible either in formal courses or in the general education program. In the small school they may provide the only training in speech.
>
> Principals and teachers should, therefore, treat the interscholastic speech activities as having educational values identical with those that govern classroom instruction in speech. Accordingly, these recommendations are offered:
>
> 1. That extra-class events be regarded as the counterpart of curricular instruction.

2. That extra-class events be integrated as closely as possible with class instruction.

3. That extra-class speech activities be taught by a person whose qualifications are in every sense equal to those of persons teaching speech in courses.

4. That the person teaching speech activities be given every right and privilege of other teachers, including the right to have the extra-class teaching counted in the teaching load.[2]

If each director of speech activities approaches this phase of the program of speech education with the idea that the program provides an opportunity to achieve the same educational values he strives for in his classroom work in speech, the critics of this type of activity can easily be silenced. Certainly it is well for each director to ask himself certain questions concerning his own attitude toward co-curricular speech activities and toward his students who participate in the activities. Such questions as the following might help direct one's thinking toward an educationally sound philosophy of co-curricular speech activities:

1. Does my co-curricular speech activities program teach my students a code of ethics?

2. Does my speech activities program help my students understand and use the reflective process in arriving at conclusions?

3. Does my speech activities program give my students knowledge about the communicative process and understanding of it?

4. Does my speech activities program result in an opportunity for my students to receive a realistic evaluation of their own speech performances in comparison with others?

5. Does my co-curricular speech program grow out of a curricular speech program? If not, am I working toward the inclusion of a course in speech education in the school's curriculum?

6. Do I consider thoughtfully suggestions which I seek from my own state and national speech organizations?

7. Do I maintain a sound and proper perspective on winning in relationship to the educational values which can be derived by students in my program?

8. Is my program financed on a sound basis?

9. Do I limit participation in my co-curricular speech program, including interscholastic activities, to a few students or am I clearly giving evidence of my desire to help many students in my school?

10. Have I adequately taken stock of the students' speech interests, needs, abilities, and capacities in my school?

[2] "A Program of Speech Education—The North Central Association," *Quarterly Journal of Speech*, vol. 37, no. 3 (October 1951), pp. 347–358.

11. Is my program respected in the school and in the community?

12. Does my program succeed in teaching social responsibility?

13. Does my program call for systematic evaluation by me as to what I am accomplishing and as to what I want to accomplish?

14. Do I take advantage of enough opportunities in my community to give my students real and meaningful speech experiences?

15. When I present awards, do I carefully examine the type of awards, the criteria by which I decide to whom awards will be presented, and the manner of presenting awards in the light of educational and psychological implications of the awards?

Directors of speech activities in high schools can obtain helpful and sound suggestions from the annual bulletins of state forensic and speech organizations for immediate application in directing co-curricular programs. They include such ideas and suggestions as:

1. Enroll your school in [your association or league] in September by completing a membership card and mailing it with the fee to [your association or league] office.

2. Familiarize yourself with the bulletins, free copy of the NUEA Discussion and Debate Manual, and other publications of [your association or league].

3. Survey your school library and your own library to see what texts and reference books are available to you and your students on fundamentals of speech, discussion and debate, public speaking, oral interpretation, radio and television, parliamentary procedure, acting and play production, and other speech events.

4. Carry on and develop a curricular and co-curricular program of speech education with *fundamentals of speech* as basic to your dramatics, speech, and forensic program.

5. Begin early to appraise the speech interests, needs, abilities, and potentialities of your students and make plans to stimulate their interests, meet their needs, and develop their abilities to a high level of their capacities through a basic and increasingly complex and diversified program of speech education.

6. Organize at an early date a public speaking bureau and a forensic squad.

7. Organize or cooperate with school and local forums for the discussion of current problems and of the official problem for discussion and the proposition for debate. Speech experiences based on adequate preparation and critiques enable students to develop their speech abilities.

8. Advertise your program. Let community organizations, clubs, and groups know that you have students who are prepared to offer interesting, appropriate, and worthwhile programs: discussions, extemporaneous speeches, readings, skits, original orations, debates, et cetera. Have posters made by students. Report activities and accomplishments of your

students to the home and other newspapers. Get the school and community behind the program in dramatics, forensics, and speech.

9. Secure from your school or from other interested citizens, club, or organization an award or scholarship for your meritorius students. Some high schools offer annually to an outstanding student in forensics or dramatics a scholarship to a summer workshop in speech and dramatic art. Some schools provide hundred dollar scholarships to the Summer Workshop at the State University of Iowa. Books can be used as awards to students who do superior work in speech.

10. Get in touch with the chairman of [your state association or league] concerning some of your problems and accomplishments. He will attempt to interpret rules and regulations, supply sample ballots, rating forms, and instructions, and help to put on exhibition discussions and debates. He will also be glad to recommend students for critic judges of speech events. Expenses of these student critic judges must, of course, be paid by the school.

11. Get in touch with your district director and learn from him details concerning the time and place for the district finals and the names of schools that may be interested in interschool programs in: oral interpretation, one-act plays, split-team debate, conventional debate, open forum discussion, direct clash debate, cross-examination debate, and the like.

12. Request your district director to help arrange a speech festival, a speech and forensic clinic, a forensic meet, a student senate, et cetera, for schools within your district.

13. We are all concerned with economy in the administration of [your association or league]. If the schools will hold a weekend clinic or festival at some central point, participate in invitational festivals, exercise leniency in permitting local judges to serve the festival at nominal pay and lodging expenses in relationship to distance and perhaps other considerations, the expenses may be materially reduced.

14. Supervise most carefully all details of district finals, such as providing schedules, instructions for critics, instructions for chairmen and timekeepers, rating sheets, responsible personnel with authority to conduct the events, rooms, et cetera. Careful organization and supervision make for efficiency and satisfaction in providing speech experiences for high school students.

15. Observe some of the following procedures in developing students in forensics: Get as many on the squad as you can direct and supervise; check school records and check with other teachers to get students who have potential for development; collect available material and see that the students get systematic notes on the chief topics; analyze the subject systematically in accordance with outlines given in various texts in speech and debate; be sure to define terms accurately and organize discussion about three or four chief problems or issues; be sure to have each debater

organize the material into a complete brief or argumentative outline; let the brief include the evidence; organize rebuttal speeches according to suggestions as given in texts; have frequent practice in rebuttal; invite neighboring schools to bring students for early practice; accept invitations from neighboring schools for practice; let your students participate rather than merely observe others.

16. Students develop their speech abilities through well-planned and supervised speech experiences.[3]

A practical suggestion for keeping a record of the participation of your students in invitational and other speech contests and festivals is the composite results form on the ensuing page. Since the director of co-curricular forensic activities will need specific information for publicity purposes, for keeping a record of his budget, for presenting awards at an "awards assembly" in the spring, and so on, a composite reporting form on which to compile such information should prove to be invaluable.

The co-curricular speech activities in a high school and in interscholastic speech associations and leagues comprise (1) one-act plays, (2) discussion, (3) debate, (4) extemporaneous speaking, (5) original oratory, (6) non-original oratory, (7) student senate, (8) oral interpretation, (9) speaking on radio, and (10) speaking on television. Although the following suggestions concerning the direction and supervision of these co-curricular and interscholastic speech activities are aimed primarily at the inexperienced director of these activities, possibly teachers who have been "in the field" may benefit from their consideration of the information presented.

NAME OF TOURNAMENT OR FESTIVAL   HOST SCHOOL

Date	Number of Students	Cost	With/Without School Car

DEBATE

	Decision-Ratings				Award Rank-Rating	
	Round I	Round II	Round III	Round IV	Average Total	Total W-L
Team I (Decision-Ratings)	___ side	___ side	___ side	___ side		
1. _____	_____	_____	_____	_____	_____	_____
2. _____	_____	_____	_____	_____	_____	_____

[3] "Iowa High School Forensic League Events, 1959–1960," *State University of Iowa Extension Bulletin No. 758*, September 1, 1959, pp. 19–23.

290 DIRECTING A CO-CURRICULAR SPEECH PROGRAM

Team II   ____ side ____ side ____ side ____ side
(Decision-
Ratings)   _____ _____ _____ _____ _____ _____
1. _____   _____ _____ _____ _____ _____ _____

2. _____   _____ _____ _____ _____ _____ _____

Team III   ____ side ____ side ____ side ____ side
(Decision-
Ratings)   _____ _____ _____ _____ _____ _____
1. _____   _____ _____ _____ _____ _____ _____

2. _____   _____ _____ _____ _____ _____ _____

Team IV   ____ side ____ side ____ side ____ side
(Decision-
Ratings)   _____ _____ _____ _____ _____ _____
1. _____   _____ _____ _____ _____ _____ _____

2. _____   _____ _____ _____ _____ _____ _____

DISCUSSION

	Round I	Round II	Round III	Round IV	Other	Aver. and Final Rank, Rating, Award
1.	_____	_____	_____	_____	_____	_____
2.	_____	_____	_____	_____	_____	_____
3.	_____	_____	_____	_____	_____	_____
4.	_____	_____	_____	_____	_____	_____

EXTEMPORANEOUS SPEAKING

1. _____ _____ _____ _____ _____ _____
2. _____ _____ _____ _____ _____ _____

ORATORY

1. _____ _____ _____ _____ _____ _____
2. _____ _____ _____ _____ _____ _____

OTHER SPEECH EVENTS

1. _____ _____ _____ _____ _____ _____
2. _____ _____ _____ _____ _____ _____
3. _____ _____ _____ _____ _____ _____
4. _____ _____ _____ _____ _____ _____

Formulated by Donald Dedmon, Chairman, Department of Speech Arts, Colorado State University.

One-Act Plays

Perhaps the most popular speech activity in high schools today is the one-act play. It is a forgone conclusion in many communities that, during the fall semester, the junior class will present its play and that, during the spring semester, the seniors will produce theirs. In many schools, the all-school dramatic production has replaced these class plays. Schools with ambitious programs aimed at serving well the speech interests and needs of a large number of students present three or more "major dramatic productions" and six or more one-act plays. Many state high school associations and leagues include the one-act plays in their contests and festivals as an annual part of their sponsored programs.

Directing a play with its aim of producing an effective, artistic production is no easy task. Often, in spite of everything the director may do, the end result is not what he anticipated. The following suggestions are offered with the hope that they will help promote worthwhile educational and, at the same time, artistic dramatic performances. The one-act play has been chosen for emphasis because it is the length of play most frequently used in both co-curricular and interscholastic speech contests and festivals. However, almost all of the suggestions concerned with the production and performance of one-act plays apply equally well to the longer plays.

Choosing a Play. The selection of a play is a difficult task. The number of plays, many of them below the standards the well-meaning director should hold, is only one of the complicating factors. Few books concerned with play production include lists of plays because tastes change so quickly and it is difficult to prescribe a play without knowing the factors in a school which necessarily have a bearing on play selection.

Some years ago, Ernest Bavely, executive secretary of the National Thespian Society, reported that directors of plays in high schools indicated what they considered to be a desirable and workable list of play standards:

> 1. The high school play should have a worthwhile theme, be sincere and true in its interpretation of life, and accurate in its reflection of customs and manners.
>
> 2. It should have literary value. That is, it should be written in acceptable language and in accordance with accepted standards of playwriting, and, as such, it should be emotionally and intellectually stimulating.
>
> 3. It should be within the capabilities of the high school pupil to understand and appreciate, taking into consideration the influence of vicarious experience and the pupil's natural interests.
>
> 4. It should challenge the highest creative and artistic abilities of all

who are associated with its production, thereby affording rich opportunities for study, analysis, and experimentation.

    5. It should be good theatre, affording opportunities for sincere acting, and be satisfying as entertainment. It should lead rather than follow the community standards of entertainment and appreciation.

    6. It should be free of highly sophisticated or advanced roles, vulgarity or profanity, objectionable matter, and sordid, unwholesome presentations of characters and scenes.[4]

    The use of the word "theme" may cause some misunderstanding. High school students and directors may not agree on just what the "theme" of a play is and sometimes fruitless intellectualization takes place between a director and actors over this matter. Perhaps a director of a play in a high school can more fruitfully concern himself and his students with "thought" or "ideas" provoked by the play and, thereby, be better able to judge plays against the standard of "a worthwhile theme."

    Standard number six can provoke fruitful controversy. It should not be interpreted narrowly and thereby eliminate from consideration each and every play that contains some of the elements indicated. The application of a narrow interpretation of play selection standard number six would mean automatic elimination of such longer plays as *Teahouse of the August Moon, The Man Who Came to Dinner,* and many other plays which have been successfully produced and well accepted in many high schools and communities. This whole aspect of play selection should be considered seriously in the light of factors operating in the local school and community. Obviously, the teacher who directs play in a high school is responsible for choosing the plays which will be produced and presented in his high school and he should, likewise, have authority commensurate with his responsibility. But the wise director, especially if he is either a neophyte as a director or new as a teacher in the community, or both, will seek advice and cooperation from his colleagues, his administrator, and people in his community. After all, he will want the support of all of these people, including the support of his administrators, for the play which he directs and for the production directed by him. Therefore, he will give his principal an opportunity to advise him on his selection of plays until he knows that the principal can depend on the director to select and direct plays which meet at least a reasonably high standard. Sometimes a play to which considerable objection would be offered meets no objection from anybody in the community because the director exercises judgment and skill in handling such elements in the play. Also, the wise director can

[4] Roberta D. Sheets, "Selecting the Play," *Bulletin of the National Association of Secondary School Principals,* December, 1949, pp. 106–107.

utilize "the voice of his students" in his play selection. A few directors have discovered that the interests and abilities of his students, including members of the play cast and crews, can make a difference in play production and presentation. These directors have gone to great length in selecting a number of plays, making the scripts available for reading and study by students, and giving students an opportunity to discuss the plays and to make known to him information which proved valuable in his making a choice of a play for production. All of these suggestions can be summarized by saying that the wise director works at the job of building rapport with his students, his fellow teachers, administrators, and, either directly or indirectly, with people in the community.

Often the director of one-act plays for production in interscholastic contests and festivals will obtain assistance from the state high school speech association or league in his state. In some states, a specific category of drama is prescribed for a particular year; in others, a list of acceptable plays is sent out and schools must select from the list. Before selecting a play for a festival or contest, it is well to check with the state association or league to learn the requirements. Teachers interested in producing noncontest plays may often find helpful suggestions from contest play lists.

Even if the state association or league does indicate a list from which to select a play, the director's task is only somewhat eased. Wide reading of many plays is the only way a director can learn to recognize plays which are worth doing. The following questions may be helpful in selecting a specific play for a specific purpose in a specific school:

1. Is the play worth doing? The play should have some literary merit. It should contain interesting characterizations that are "real" and convincing. Its theme should be worthwhile. Is the play sincere and true in the way it interprets life? Is it accurate in its reflections of the people and customs it is portraying? Is it likely to challenge the audience and the students?

2. Is the play well written? Any play should be carefully studied to determine whether it has a well developed plot, suspense, a well placed climax, a convincing ending, and educational value for members of the audience and especially for students. Is the language of the play consistent with other elements in it? Does it sound like people talking as they would and should in the situations in which they are involved? Is it current, timely, and, preferably, timeless?

3. Is the play suited to the available talent? Obviously, the play should be within the capacity of the high school student. If a student is unable to comprehend the role, he will never be able to portray accurately the role for others. *Peer Gynt* is a good play in the dramatic sense, but a cutting of it would be a very poor choice for the school without a Peer.

The number of characters may restrict the choice of play. A clear understanding of the basic principles of casting is necessary to handle adequately this basic question.

4. Can the play be staged with the facilities available? Any director of a play should carefully consider the basic technical requirements of the play and its production and performance. If the play is to be presented in a contest or festival, attention should be given by the director to the potential stage on which the play will be presented. A director's imagination, however, can often simplify stage requirements. Since, in many contests and festivals, the critic judges are not allowed to consider "sets" in their evaluations, this aspect of staging may not be as important as the lighting, sound effects, costumes, and so on.

5. Is the play suited to the budget? Play directors who operate on an adequate budget at the high school level seem to be few and far between. The play's royalty may become an important factor in the consideration of a play for production in a high school. Likewise, costumes are often expensive to rent and to make. Special set pieces and properties may involve considerable cash.

6. Is the play within the experience and limitations of the director to direct? For a director with minimum or total lack of experience in directing, the problems posed in some plays may be insurmountable even though other plays may pose problems which can be overcome with effort, imagination, and persistence. Any director should be honest with himself and not attempt to direct a play which holds little possibility for his success. One young high school theater director decided during his first year of teaching to do a cutting of Ibsen's *Peer Gynt* for an interscholastic one-act play contest. In writing to a chairman of a department of speech and dramatic art, he mentioned his intention to produce this play. The older, experienced man replied, "How bold you are! I have never felt able in all my years of directing to handle that particular play." However, even a neophyte director should not settle for a play which offers little challenge or merit; but he should be willing to settle for a lesser challenge at first and until he has gained insight through his experience. Nearly every director can more readily achieve success as he goes on.

The practical problems of play selection are perennial ones. After a play is selected, the wise director continues to read plays with a view to selecting additional plays for future production and performance by his students. Inexperienced directors should take courage from the fact that many plays will meet his standards if he reads a great number of plays and reads each one carefully with a view to its production. Finally, one should be reminded to avoid a *poor* cutting of a *good* play and make certain that both he and his cast really like the play they are doing because three to five weeks is too long a time to work on something they don't especially like.

Casting the Play. Once the play has been selected, the next problem facing the director is casting. The importance of careful casting can not be overemphasized. It must be a period of thoughtful consideration of all possibilities before final decisions are made. It is a time-consuming process, but most experienced directors probably agree that it is at least sixty percent of the total job; some directors will go as high as eighty percent! This is one process where mistakes are irreparable and damaging to the entire production and often to the students if the director does not do his job well.

The tryouts, for many directors, are a necessary but unpleasant facet of the whole play production system. Each director tends to work out the system that best suits him, but all of them are involved in giving interested students the opportunity to read and the director opportunity to listen and observe. Whatever system is used, it should be clear to the students that every effort is being made to conduct the tryouts fairly and efficiently.

Proper pre-tryout organization is important. The selection of suitable cuttings by the director typed from the playscript itself, eliminating stage directions, makes the job of sight-reading less complicated. Having copies of the playscript in the school library on a special reserve shelf can do much to have interested students aware of the play prior to actual tryouts. The cuttings should reflect the tone and mood of the play and be typical of the major dramatic moments of it.

Many directors of plays in high schools have discovered the advantages of using a prepared tryout form which is filled out by the student when he appears. A typical tryout blank includes name, address, telephone number, age, height, weight, color of hair, complexion, previous experience in dramatic activities, schedule of classes and out-of-school commitments, special talents, et cetera. This information can prove to be invaluable to the director in future plays as well as in the one being cast. A sample blank on a 4″ by 6″ or 6″ by 8″ card follows:

THE THEATER
(Name of the high school)

NAME (Please print) _____
HOME ADDRESS _____
PARENT'S NAME _____
(Specify Mr. and/or Mrs.)
TELEPHONE NUMBER _____
BIRTHDAY _____ HEIGHT _____ WEIGHT _____
COLOR OF HAIR _____ COLOR OF EYES _____ COMPLEXION _____

	Dramatic Experience			Class Schedule	
Role		Play	Period		Days
					M T W Th F
			1		
			2		
			3		
			4		
			5		
			6		

Tech. Experience (lighting, costuming, construction, and so on.)

Out-of-School Commitments

Type   Hours—Days

The procedure followed by most directors in tryouts is to cut down the total number of students to a smaller number. This smaller number of students includes those who are called back for rereading until a final cast is selected. Most directors seem to favor the general open tryout where any interested person may come and read for any part he desires. This procedure takes time, but it does help foster the encouragement of each student to try again and again for future plays since he is in open competition for a part with all other students interested in that part. Some directors make use of special techniques such as pantomimes, improvisations, and so on to help give them additional information about the capabilities and potential of students.

Since the task of the director in tryouts is to attempt to determine which person best fits each role, he must have a clear idea of the requirements of each role and then must assess the ability of each actor to fulfill that role. Naturally, he should concern himself with such aspects of the individual student-actor as voice quality and usage, ability to project voice, intelligence and maturity necessary to understand adequately another's role and to portray it effectively, interest and enthusiasm, physical characteristics necessary for certain roles, physical expressiveness, and ability to respond quickly and accurately to directions, and so on.[5]

A wise procedure is to announce the entire cast and crews at one designated time and place. The student actors and actresses can then report to the director and sign out playbooks prior to the first rehearsal.

Play Rehearsals. Once the play has been cast, the director enters into his rehearsal. An excellent play and a potentially capable cast can be all for nought if this period is not handled carefully and efficiently. The wise director will prepare his rehearsal schedule and see that all cast members, technical crew members, parents, and the office of the principal have copies bearing the approval of both the director and the principal. Copies

---

[5] An excellent consideration of this aspect of play production is found in John E. Dietrich's book, *Play Direction.* Englewood Cliffs, N.J.: Prentice-Hall, Inc., 1953. ch. 15.

should be placed on bulletin boards and made available to members of the faculty. The number of rehearsals needed will vary depending upon the director's experience, the experience of the cast, the play itself, the size of the cast, and other factors which the director can learn to anticipate. Typically, a one-act play will require from 15 to 25 rehearsals. The length of a rehearsal will vary, but experienced directors agree that one to two hours is suitable for most play rehearsals.

The first rehearsal of the play cast, including crews and committees, is very important. It is here that the director should underscore the principle that the rehearsal period is a time for cooperative effort on the part of all students with the aim of putting on a polished final performance. The director's philosophy, procedures, rules and regulations, duties of the crews and committees, and so on, should all be explained clearly. Questions should be answered concerning production problems, interpretation, and related topics that seem to be bothering the cast and crews. A clear, definite explanation at this first rehearsal period can eliminate many of the problems and the need for many time-consuming interruptions later to consider minor points.

Directors need to consider four types of rehearsals: reading, blocking, polishing, and mounting. On the next page is a rehearsal schedule prepared by a graduate student in theater which might serve well as a pattern for working out a schedule for a one-act play. The director is fortunate if, after he has publicized the rehearsal schedule for a one-act play production, no problems or emergencies arise to make it necessary for him to change the timetable of the rehearsals and the production. Some directors supplement the complete schedule with weekly schedules distributed each Friday for the succeeding week. However, the director should make every effort to anticipate all problems barring emergencies and hope that he and his students can maintain the over-all schedule without changes being necessary.

Performance. After the rehearsals, the first performance is at hand. The director's work is done. He must resist any attempt to make last minute changes or to issue new instructions. He should set the proper example for his students by his own behavior. He should appear to be cool, collected, and confident. If he goes backstage before the performance, he should exert a calming influence and not need to perform any other function. His place is in the audience during the performance. He should pay close attention to the audience's reactions. If he should feel the need for an adult backstage even if it is because he underestimates high school thespians, he should have some person other than himself perform whatever function he might serve.

SCHEDULE FOR A ONE-ACT PLAY PRODUCTION

First Week

DAY	CAST	CREW	COSTUMES AND PROPS
Monday	Tryouts	Design sets	
Tuesday	Tryouts		
Wednesday	Post cast and distribute scripts		
Thursday	First reading		
Friday	Interpretation rehearsal		

Second Week

DAY	CAST	CREW	COSTUMES AND PROPS
Monday	Block first half	Recruit crew (appoint stage manager, sound technician, etc.)	Listing of needed props and costumes
Tuesday	Individual work		
Wednesday	Block second half		
Thursday	Individual work	Start construction	Start construction of needed props and costumes
Friday	Open		

Third Week

DAY	CAST	CREW	COSTUMES AND PROPS
Monday	Polish first half	Construction	Construction
Tuesday	Individual problems		
Wednesday	Polish second half		
Thursday	Individual problems		
Friday	Complete run	Assign production duties	

Fourth Week

DAY	CAST	CREW	COSTUMES AND PROPS
Monday	Technical rehearsal	Crew rehearsal	Clean up problems and new difficulties
Tuesday	Open	Open	
Wednesday	Dress rehearsal		
Thursday	Dress rehearsal		Commitee act as makeup crew Thursday and Friday
Friday	Final performance		

Used by permission of Mr. Arthur Przybilla, graduate student in theater

Directing a play takes time and effort but the results are usually well worth it. The one-act play seems to be simple to produce; it isn't. True, anyone can produce a one-act play, but it requires much hard work and inspiration to produce one well. Whether a director and his students are preparing a one-act play for a school assembly, a play festival or contest, or for some other public performance, the director can do well to keep in mind that the production of a play is a challenge as is any other significant undertaking.

Analysis and Criticism. Every director and his students will have some kinds of standards by which they analyze and criticize the play, its production, and its performance. Otherwise, they are hardly entitled to pass judgment on the degree of success of a rehearsal or final performance. Suggested criteria are set forth on the next two pages of this chapter in the hope that each group will work together in setting standards by which to evaluate the results of their efforts.

Discussion

Several forensic associations and leagues include discussion as an interscholastic event. Although discussion is generally accepted as a noncompetitive activity in which unselfish cooperation by discussants is essential for its effectiveness and success, many state associations and leagues sponsor it as a competitive activity. Critic judges are encouraged to rate the individual discussants, the leader, and the discussion itself which is the equivalent of rating each group of discussants as a whole or as a "team."

Although procedure in these discussion contests varies, schools enter individual students. These students from all schools are grouped, often by lot, into discussion groups of no more than eight students in each group. The groups discuss the same problem, which may vary from state to state or from contest to contest within a state. For example, in the Minnesota State High School League, a problem of state or local concern is selected by a Board of Control for discussion by high school students. In 1960, the problem was "How can stable economic growth in Minnesota be assured?" In October of 1960, a bulletin was presented to the schools by the League in which a discussion outline was provided for use in the contests. The outline was divided into two major sub-problems: one for use in sub-district and district contests in the state of Minnesota and the other for use in the regional contests. The entire problem was discussed at the Minnesota State Contest level. However, students in high schools in many of the fifty states discuss a single problem area and three sub-problems during a school year. For example, in 1963–1964 the national problem area for discussion by high school students was "What should be the role of the federal government in providing medical care to citizens of the United States?" The three specific sub-problems were "What should be the role of the federal government in providing medical care for the aged? . . . for the indigent? . . . in providing health insurance?" Likewise, a single problem area and

CRITIC SHEET FOR DRAMA

TITLE _____

CRITIC JUDGE _____

_____ Strengths and Weaknesses

1. *Choice of play*

2. *Projection of play's meaning*

   Plot

   Tone (comic, serious, satire, etc.)

   Style (realistic, poetic, fantastic, etc.)

   Theme (central idea)

3. *Stage arrangement (ground plan)*

4. *Blocking, movement, groupings, and stage business*

5. *Pacing and climax*

6. *Costume and make-up*

7. *Each actor's performance*

   Characterization

   Spontaneity

   Clarity

Total effectiveness of the production   5 4 3 2 1
(5—Superior; 4—Above Average; 3—Average;
2—Below Average; 1—Unsatisfactory)

(Use reverse side for additional comments)

CRITIC

Adaptation of Critic Sheet used by the Minnesota High School League

JUDGE'S EVALUATION FORM
Oklahoma Speech League
ONE-ACT PLAY

Festival _____ Site _____ Date _____

Name of Play _____ School _____ Class _____
(A, B, or C)

Factors Considered	Evaluation	Comments
1. *Choice of play*		
2. *Acting*		
3. *Voice and diction*		
4. *Vocal interpretation*		
5. *Casting and directing*		
Total Effect	Evaluation Scale I—Superior; II—Excellent; III—Good; IV—Fair; V—Poor	

Criteria for Evaluation

1. *Choice of Play*: Is it really a play? If a cutting from a long play, is it a complete and understandable unit, without jarring transitions? Is it well written? If frivolous, does it have charm? Is it in good taste? Is it one in which at least one character "enlists" the sympathy of the audience?
2. *Acting*: Does all visible behavior appear to be motivated, spontaneous, coordinated, integrated; have vitality and spirit; not overdone; appropriate to the character? Do the actors listen and react effectively? Do they engage in such distracting behavior as shifting from foot to foot, pacing, and so on.
3. *Voice and Diction*: Is pronunciation acceptable (considering the characters)? Is enunciation distinct without being pedantic?
4. *Vocal Interpretation*: Does there appear to be effective vitality and ease in speaking, i.e., the appearance of genuine conversation while making certain that every syllable is projected appropriately? Is the reading effective in terms of meaning, i.e., the correct kind and degrees of emphasis, proper subordination, effective pausing, and so on? Does there appear to be effective emotional motivation of lines, a proper balance in terms of maturity, dominance, appeal to audience sympathy, and so on?
5. *Casting and Directing*: Is the play well cast? Is style of the production appropriate to the script? Are blocking of stage movement and grouping in keeping with the principles of interest, attention, good composition, emphasis, motivation, and so on? Is the tempo appropriate to the mood and type of play? Are climax, suspense, pauses, and so on, developed effectively?

Judge _____

By James Robinson, Director, Oklahoma Speech and Drama Services three sub-problems have been discussed by students in high schools in many of the states during each school year since 1953–1954 when the problem area was "How should we select the President of the United States?" Each of the problem areas and the sub-problems for each area for discussion have been selected by a national referendum of the affiliates and members of the National University Extension Association through its national committee on discussion and debate. Each high school in each of the states has, annually, an opportunity to participate in the national referendum through its state association or league, provided the state office exercises its function of soliciting a vote by each member school upon the many problem areas and discussion problems which are suggested by the state associations and leagues.

In a discussion contest, one hour is usually the time limit for each discussion. This period is divided approximately as follows: introduction of the problem by a chairman, 3 minutes; discussion by participants, 32 minutes; summation, 16 minutes with each person allowed 2 minutes of uninterrupted time to summarize the discussion or any aspect of it; concluding remarks by the chairman, 2 minutes. The chairman is *not* a student, but may be any qualified faculty member, citizen of the community, or judge.

Four common errors found in high school discussion contests which hinder effective discussion have been pointed out by Shepard:

1. In the majority of discussions, the students had apparently failed to exercise reasonable selection in their reading.
2. They had not evaluated their material.
3. They did not evaluate the contributions of other panel members.
4. As a result of these three mistakes, the students were unable to follow the basic steps of discussion.[6]

Other writers have pointed out the weaknesses of the failure of establishing discussion *groups* with bonds which unite individuals into a group relationship and the distortion of the relationship between members of the discussion group by the competitive element in the discussion contest.[7]

These criticisms may be valid. If so, teachers of speech need, obviously, to help their students by stimulating and guiding them to "exercise reasonable selection in their reading," "evaluate their material," "evaluate the contributions of other panel members," and "follow the basic steps of discussion."

The use of "group action" tournaments has been suggested to provide

[6] David W. Shepard, "Some Observations on High School Discussion," *Speech Teacher*, vol. 4, no. 3 (September 1955), pp. 191–195.

[7] Wayne E. Brockriede and Kim Giffin, "Discussion Contests versus Group Action Tournaments," *Quarterly Journal of Speech*, vol. 45, no. 1 (February 1959), pp. 59–64.

an approach to discussion contests which utilizes the motivational force of competition. In these tournaments, the competition is between discussion groups rather than between discussants in each group. In fact, the competition may be between both the groups and between discussants within each group. In any case, the question of competition in discussion is one which needs study and investigation. Probably the goal of the teacher is to help discussants and leaders to "compete" with each other on performing the functions of discussants and leaders from the time of their initial preparation until the time alloted to a discussion has expired. In a sense, each discussant and the leader may be encouraged to excel in discussion and in leadership. If, somehow, the teacher can cause his students to focus on their individual and collective pursuits of answers to questions and solutions to the problem for discussion, the four common errors found in high school discussion contests may be eliminated or, at worst, minimized.

Despite all criticisms, group discussion seems to have a place in forensic activities. The success of discussions seems to be based on their effectiveness in promoting thorough research, sound analysis, logical thinking, and effective oral communication. Of course, discussions, in or out of interscholastic contests, must be properly conducted to effect desirable outcomes. Each teacher of speech is obligated to see that discussion merits a different approach from debate, that it requires the same careful preparation and training as debate, and that students and critics evaluate the results with just as much consideration and care as in any other speech activity.

In helping students to enter a discussion, the teacher is obligated to involve his students in careful preparation in background, analysis, information, evidence, opinions, and reactions to the problem at hand. The construction of outlines by each individual and by each group is useful. The students should read and discuss with the teacher and other discussants the attributes of an effective discussion, the responsibilities of each discussant, and what the leader must do.

Participation in a number of practice discussions is paramount. The inexperienced student who enters a discussion or a discussion contest usually cannot cope with the activity in which other students are well prepared. These practice exercises should be conducted like contest discussions. The teacher should evaluate critically the discussion, the work of each discussant, the leadership of the discussion, and the results of the individual and group efforts. Tape recordings can aid students in evaluating their own discussion. A study of representative rating forms can also be helpful.

Criteria and Ballot for Discussion. Criteria such as the following can help students and teachers of speech in analyzing discussion leaders, discussants, and a group of discussants stimulated and guided by a leader:

I. Evaluate the discussion leader on his:
   A. ability to introduce satisfactorily the problem and to start the discussion.
   B. ability to stimulate spontaneous participation.
   C. ability to equalize the participation by discussants.
   D. ability to summarize the discussion when a summary is necessary.
   E. ability to clarify the discussion and individual contributions when necessary.
   F. ability to move the discussion forward.
   G. ability to maintain coherence of the discussion.
   H. ability to exercise objectivity and fairness.
II. Evaluate the discussant on his:
   A. analysis of the problem.
   B. information on the problem.
   C. use of evidence and forms of support.
   D. organization of material.
   E. reasoning ability.
   F. frequency, quality, and relevancy of contributions.
   G. effective use of language.
   H. bodily action, voice, enunciation, and articulation in speaking.
   I. cooperation with and attitude towards the group.
III. Evaluate the group on:
   A. its overall discussional attitude.
   B. group cooperativeness.
   C. its analysis of the problem.
   D. its use of evidence.
   E. its progression towards a solution.

The three discussion ballots on the next four pages can be helpful to all participants. Of course, students who take part in discussions should understand the objectives and desired outcome of discussion, criteria by which their efforts and achievements are analyzed, and the bases for determining ratings of discussions, discussants, and leaders in discussion contests. Each teacher will want to work with his students to determine criteria by which their success, or lack of it, will be indicated.

CRITIC SHEET FOR DISCUSSION

Participant: _____

Judge: _____

Strengths: 5—Superior; 4—Above Average;
                               3—Average; 2—Below Average;
                               1—Unsatisfactory

DISCUSSION   *305*

	1. Information	5 4 3 2 1
	2. Thinking	5 4 3 2 1
Weaknesses:	3. Cooperation	5 4 3 2 1
	4. Speech Skills	5 4 3 2 1
	5. Participation	5 4 3 2 1
	6. Total Effectiveness	5 4 3 2 1

Suggestions for Improvement:

Judge _____

Adaptation of Critic Sheet used by the Minnesota High School League

OFFICIAL DISCUSSION BALLOT

Group _____ Round _____ Room _____ Time _____

Rate each participant as Superior (5), Excellent (4), Adequate (3), Fair (2), or Unsatisfactory (1).

Individual Ratings

1. _____ _____ _____
   (name of leader)   (school)   (rating)
2. _____ _____ _____
   (discussant)   (school)   (rating)
3. _____ _____ _____
4. _____ _____ _____
5. _____ _____ _____
6. _____ _____ _____
7. _____ _____ _____
8. _____ _____ _____
9. _____ _____ _____
10. _____ _____ _____
11. _____ _____ _____
12. _____ _____ _____

Group Rating

In my opinion the group should be rated as: Superior (5) _____, Excellent (4) _____, Adequate (3) _____, Fair (2) _____, Unsatisfactory (1) _____.

Signed _____
                    (Critic)

Formulated by Hugh F. Seabury

DIAGNOSTIC EVALUATION OF DISCUSSION LEADER AND LEADERSHIP

Scale	
5—Outstanding	Discussion Leader _____
4—Above Average	Problem _____
3—Average	_____
2—Below Average	Observer _____
1—Ineffective	Date _____

INSTRUCTIONS: Check all appropriate adjectives and assign a rating to the leader on each of the major categories. Then, after weighing all of his strengths and weaknesses, assign a composite rating.

Appearance

Approach:	Indifferent ____	Uncertain ____	Purposeful ____
Dress:	Untidy ____	Careless ____	Neat ____
Posture:	Slouching ____	Stiff ____	Acceptable ____
Eye-contact:	Seldom ____	Insufficient ____	Sufficient ____
Self-control:	Lacking ____	Ill at ease ____	Poised ____

REMARKS:

Introduction

Motivation:	Omitted ____	Barely adequate ____	Effective ____
Statement of problem:	Omitted ____	Not clear ____	Clear ____
Scope of problem:	Omitted ____	Vague ____	Clear ____
Definition of terms:	Omitted ____	Vague ____	Clear ____
Basic assumptions:	Not evident ____	Not clear ____	Clear ____
	Not accepted ____	Partially accepted ____	Accepted ____

REMARKS:

Objective

Vague ____	Clear ____	Sharp ____
Unreasonable ____	Questionable ____	Reasonable ____

REMARKS:

Organization and Development of Discussion

Plan:	None evident ____	Faulty ____	Clearly evident ____
Stimulation of spontaneous participation:	Seldom ____	Frequently ____	Always ____
Directing discussion:	Overbearingly ____	Obviously ____	Tactfully ____
Leading the group:	Weakly ____	Autocratically ____	Tactfully ____
Participation of group:	Few members ____	Some members ____	All ____
Entertainment of different viewpoints:	Overlooked ____	Refused ____	Encouraged ____

Clarifying and summar-
   izing: Infrequently ___ Too Often _____ Just right _____
Resolution of conflicts: Weakly _____ Adequately ____ Skillfully _____
Handling aggressive
   members: Weakly _____ Dominatingly ___ Tactfully _____
Achievement of objec-
   tive: Barely _____ Partially _____ Accomplished __
REMARKS:

   KNOWLEDGE AND
   MASTERY OF PROBLEM

                                                                                              Comprehen-
Breadth: Limited _____ Adequate _____ sive _____
Depth: Shallow _____ Adequate _____ Deep _____
REMARKS:

   INSTRUCTIONAL MATER-
   IALS (when appropriate)
Blackboard: Ineffectively   Effectively
               Not used _____ used _____ used _____
                                                                      Effectively em-
Maps and charts: Lacking _____ Displayed _____ ployed _____
Printed materials: None _____ Adequate _____ Effective _____
REMARKS:

   MANNERISMS (Enter below any excessive repetition of peculiarities)
_____
_____

   CONCLUSION
Summary: Too brief _____ Too long _____ Just right _____
Content: Reflects group consensus: No _____ Partially _____ Yes _____
         Includes minority viewpoints: No ____ Partially _____ Yes _____
REMARKS:

   CLASS RESPONSE IN TERMS OF OBJECTIVE AND PROBLEM
Participation: Forced _____ Polite _____ Enthusiastic ____
Attitude: Antagonistic ____ Indifferent _____ Cooperative ____
                                               Barely
Accomplishment: Inadequate _____ adequate _____ Desired _____
REMARKS:

   COMPOSITE RATING (in terms of above categories)
Major strengths:
Major weaknesses:
Other remarks:

                                                            Prepared by Hugh F. Seabury

Debate

Students of debate have noted an increase in interest and participation in argumentation and debate since 1900. Today, all or nearly all fifty states have state-wide associations and leagues which are affiliated with the national office of discussion and debate at the University of Oregon. This office in the National University Extension Association cooperates with the state organizations in soliciting problems and propositions for debate from thousands of high schools, conducts annually at least one national referendum to determine the problem area, discussion problems, and debate propositions of interest to directors of debate and students, and prepares and solicits from governmental, philanthropic, and private sources free and low-cost materials for distribution to high schools. Each state organization, with few exceptions, offers stimulation and guidance to forensic programs in the individual high schools and conducts sub-district, district, regional, and state contests in debating. Many high schools, colleges, and universities also conduct invitational contests in debating. High school students are showing their eagerness to take part, as is evident from the emphasis on discussion and debate in summer workshops sponsored by educational institutions in at least thirty-five states.[8]

"Why have argumentation and debate programs developed so extensively since 1900?" one might ask. Why the increased number of interscholastic associations and leagues? Why do high school students persist in joining summer workshops featuring discussion, argumentation, and debate? Why did medieval syllogistic disputation give way to forensic disputation at Harvard University and elsewhere? Why did forensic disputation develop into literary society debating in educational institutions across the nation? And why did literary society debating give way to our highly developed courses and extra-class and interscholastic programs of discussion, argumentation, and debate? The answer may lie in the belief by students, parents, and progressive educators that well-developed forensic programs provide learning experiences most valid and rewarding for both lower and higher education.

Democracy cannot endure without discussion and debate because these are the basic problem-solving tools of our way of life. Work in debate, as in discussion, is aimed at helping individuals become effective problem-solving members of society. In the twentieth century, when world travel is measured in hours, when inter-hemispheric communication is measured in minutes, when warfare is measured in seconds, and when the pressure of civil, military, and political problems and propositions crowd upon us,

[8] Herman H. Brockhaus, "Summer High School Speech Institutes," *Speech Teacher*, vol. 13, no. 2 (March 1964), pp. 133–138.

is it any wonder that students, parents, and teachers want to prepare themselves through study and discussion to take positions on propositions like those selected by national referendum for 1964–1965, "Resolved: That nuclear weapons should be controlled by an international organization," "Resolved: That conventional weapons should be controlled by an international organization," and "Resolved: That space weapons systems should be controlled by an international organization." Such training can certainly be a part of a student's preparation for his assumption of political responsibilities. This training offers ample opportunity for emphasis on preparation for ethical and moral responsibilities by potential adult citizens.

Forensic training offers other kinds of values to high school students who participate successfully in discussion, argumentation, and debate. First, there are personal values to be gained. Students can learn to know their limitations and their potentialities by seeking solutions to baffling problems for discussion and by participating in rigorous programs of argumentation and debate. Also, personal values accrue from their learning to compete *intellectually* even when the logic of interscholastic debating may falsely emphasize that the better team always wins. Fortunately, this training makes ample provision for teams which excel in debate and lose. A student *cannot lose* who participates in interscholastic debate for two years, has the experience of five tournaments per year, and receives critiques of his ability and performance from thirty to fifty critics. Intellectual competition, not limited to debating but characteristic of excellent debate, is a dynamic, broadening, and deepening experience which is bound to nourish and invigorate the mind. Probably no other high school enterprise exceeds or equals the potential of a rigorous program of discussion, argumentation, and debate for enabling students to evaluate the deluge of information and propaganda coming daily from the mass media of communication. Every day scores of books are printed; hundreds of magazines and newspapers are published; and an incalculable number of words are uttered on the radio, telephone, and television. From this outpouring of ideas, careful selection is necessary. Selection presupposes criteria by which choices can be made. What other phase of secondary education challenges intensive pursuit by students in the formulation of criteria and their application to the analysis of problems and propositions presented by this mass communication deluge? The personal values which students can derive from successful participation in forensic enterprise include self-confidence, poise, and other desirable attributes.

And what about the social values? Although desirable personal values and attributes are inseparable from social values, the success and effectiveness of democratic processes depend primarily on an interested, informed, and active populace. What courses and activities other than forensics instill in students awareness, interest, knowledge, understanding, and intense concentration on social problems and propositions as successfully and everlastingly as is done in forensic enterprise? Address searching questions about civil rights, social security, medicare, common market, United Nations, and other current social and political topics to any students who have participated in forensic activities. Then, address the same questions to students who have taken no part in these activities. From the results of your experiment, supplemented as desired by case studies, and form your own conclusions as to the value of successful participation in discussion, argumentation, and debate. Ask both sets of random samples of students questions designed to reveal their knowledge of library resources and to test their understanding of procedures in locating information relevant to such problems for discussion and propositions for debate as those suggested by the topics already listed. Then answer for yourself whether courses and activities in discussion, argumentation, and debate seem to provide learning experiences most valid for education in the twentieth century.

A director of debate should keep clearly in mind the close connection between discussion and debate. By discussion we mean a cooperative attempt by two or more individuals, with stimulation and guidance by a leader, to find the best solution to a problem. Like reflection by a single individual, discussion is essential and basic to debate and, in a narrow sense, is an integral part of it. Presumably a teacher is obligated to provoke thinking by his students and to stimulate and guide them to acquire an understanding of the best answers to questions and solutions to problems. Likewise, a director of debate should persist in provoking thinking by his students and in stimulating and guiding them to dig up arguments and evidence on all sides of a problem and on both sides of a proposition for debate. Through diligent and persistent preparation and reflection, students can be stimulated and guided in their analysis of arguments and the assumptions underlying the arguments, in weighing evidence, in detecting fallacies in reasoning which lead to unsound and wrong conclusions, and in exercising sound reasoning from available evidence to best conclusions. Thus each student, through his own effort and in the light of his own experience, can formulate his own position on any question.

The wise director of debate will seek opportunities for each of his students to gain experience through well-stocked libraries, understanding of discussion and debate processes, participation in many rounds of discussion, and practice in both direct clash and cross examination as well as traditional debate. Students achieve excellence in debate in proportion to the extent to which they share with one another argument, evidence, and the product of their reflective thinking and experience on all phases of their proposition for debate. But the understanding director does not conclude that discussion should cease when debate begins. Rather, he considers that debate is, in a larger sense, an essential, integral part of the discussion process. He recognizes that a group of individuals can pursue, through investigation and discussion, the best solution to a problem and, after they have examined all the relevant argument, evidence, and information, disagree on what the best solution is. He is aware that the time comes, much too soon, when discussants who disagree on the best solution to a problem must present their case to a third individual or group. In a very real sense, the third party, be he judge or audience, is in the position of the discussant who hopes to find the best solution to the problem. However, the competent and "impartial" judge is presumed to listen carefully to both affirmative and negative debaters present honestly and skillfully argument and evidence which establish the proposition as true or false or as embodying a policy or course of action which should be adopted or rejected. Ordinarily he is requested to render his decision to the team which did the better debating rather than to the team which argued the better side of the proposition. But at this point, students and the director of debate may be tempted to resort to "cases designed to win," questionable strategy, "tricks of delivery," misinterpretation of evidence and argument, and departure from their ethical and moral responsibility to support what they really believe to be the right and best position. Actually, a director of debate recognizes the inseparability of the merits of debating, the merits of the proposition, and the merits of oral presentation by debaters. He may put the emphasis on excellence of debating including assumption by his debaters of their ethical and moral responsibilities, thorough preparation for constructive argument and refutation, and excellence of presentation. He may praise the judge, as directors of debate often do, who is informed, insightful, astute, impartial, highly competent, and courageous and wise in rendering decisions to debaters who demonstrate integrity, responsibilty, and skill in debating rather than to debaters who show greater skill but some lack of integrity and less respect for responsible debating. Every director of debate has a right and an obligation to stimulate and guide his students to develop excellence enabling them to achieve high individual and team ratings and to win debates based on preparation and performance. He has every right to be happy with debaters who advocate successfully positions on a proposition which each of them believes to be sound and just. He and his debaters can then see that debate is an integral part of the total discussion process whereby people take opposite viewpoints and strive to make their viewpoints prevail.

The attitude of a director of debate toward debating and its role in society will naturally influence the program which he promotes. If mere winning of debates, medals, trophies, and publicity is what he wants, he and his debaters are likely to see debating as nothing more than tournament situations on weekends during the school year. If his primary concern is student growth in understanding and ability to discuss public problems and to debate public propositions, he and his students will not fail to see the value of forensic activity in the school, home, church, and community. Although the competitive aspect of debating can be a great stimulus to student preparation and performance in speech activities and can aid students in judging their own competencies as compared with their peers, it seems wise for all concerned to keep the idea of winning in a proper perspective.

Other basic principles of a sound forensic program include (1) providing opportunities for all students who are interested and willing to work; (2) being an integral part of the total educational program of the high school; (3) tying the program in as closely as possible with the curricular offerings of the school; and (4) providing as many opportunities as feasible for discussants and debaters to appear before live audiences provided by school assemblies, civic groups, church groups, exchange programs between schools, and radio and television programs.

To many directors, debate is an opportunity for the gifted student and should be restricted to that group of students. Encouraging all students who are interested and willing to work need not mean that each and every student is capable of representing the high school in interscholastic competition. But every program in discussion, argumentation, and debate ought to make room for students capable of doing the work and capable of profiting from the experience.

The national high school debate proposition. The National University Extension Association through its Committee on Discussion and Debate handles the work of selecting national discussion problems and debate propositions and prepares and solicits the *Forensic Quarterly* and many other materials on the national problem area. This committee usually meets in December with its advisory council consisting of a representative from each, or almost all, of the fifty states. In a three- or four-day meeting, the council studies the results of at least one national referendum on problem areas and three discussion problems and three debate propositions within the scope of each area suggested by the high schools through their respective state organizations. The advisory council recommends to the Committee on Discussion and Debate three problem areas which, after the areas, problems, and propositions are put in final form by a wording committee, are accepted by the Committee on Discussion and Debate for submission to a national referendum of the state organizations. The state associations and leagues submit to their member high schools the areas, problems, and propositions for their study, vote, and return to the state offices. The state associations and leagues across the nation tally the results of the referendum in each of the states and submit the results of the tallies to the national office. After the national office of the Committee on Discussion and Debate tabulates the results of the balloting by the various state organizations, the committee submits to the state associations and leagues the final results of the referendum. The problem area chosen by national referendum is announced by April of each year. Typical is the 1964–1965 selection:

Problem Area for 1964–1965

What policy for control of weapons systems would best insure the prospects for world peace?

Problems for Discussion

1. How can world disarmament best be achieved?
2. What should be the policy of the United States with regard to nuclear weapons?
3. What kind of international organization should control space weapons systems?

Propositions for Debate

1. Resolved: That nuclear weapons should be controlled by an international organization.
2. Resolved: that conventional weapons should be controlled by an international organization.
3. Resolved: That space weapons systems should be controlled by an international organization.

One of the three debate propositions is voted the National High School Debate Proposition by the directors of debate within each of the state associations and leagues by December 1 of each calendar year. However, some states do not use this National Proposition, but choose one of the three propositions by their own state vote prior to the opening of school. Some states formulate their own proposition. For example, the Minnesota High School League members voted in April, 1960, to use the proposition on strengthening significantly the United Nations for debate by high school students during the school year of 1960–1961.

The rationale behind the selection of a problem area and three discussion problems and the delay of a specific debate proposition until January 1 of each year is to encourage directors of debate to start their students with the discussion problem, to lead them through the problem-solving steps, and to get students thoroughly grounded in basic background material in the problem area and thus to stimulate and guide them to prepare for one of the three debate propositions beginning in January.[9] This procedure has much to recommend it. In fact, the program of speech education recommended jointly by the Speech Association of America and the North Central Association should be given careful consideration by each director of debate. Working on the problem area and the three discussion problems can aid students in their analysis of the three debate propositions in preparation for debating one of the three propositions beginning each January.

Every debate program needs to be tailored for the specific school and student body the program is designed to serve. Every director of debate can find practices and techniques which work well for him and which may not work for another director in a neighboring school. However, for the neophyte director of debate, the following suggestions may serve as a flexible guide.

Starting the program. In a school with a long and well-established debate tradition, the problem is usually not to attract students into the program but to select those students to represent the school on specific occasions in interscholastic debate. To build a program from its beginning requires much hard work. Some successful directors of debate have found the following ideas to be useful:

1. Secure recommendations of students from other teachers in the school. Most teachers are happy to cooperate in this matter.

2. Study carefully the permanent record files of the school noting the students with apparent capacity, ability, interest in speech activities, and interest in professions that either require or lend themselves to persuasive speaking such as theology, law, and teaching.

3. Don't overlook the recommendations of students who show an interest in debating and who have friends or acquaintances who ought to be involved in the forensic program.

4. Provide for adequate publicity in the school paper, in the local community paper, on the school bulletin boards, in the school announcements, and over the school public address system which can be vital in arousing interest in your first meetings.

5. Prior to your first meeting with students who are interested, prepare yourself with information about your state forensic league and the materials available from the league office. Survey your school and local libraries to see what texts and reference books are available on debating and on the problem area, problems for discussion, and propositions for debate.

6. Plan carefully your first meeting with students who indicate an

[9] "A Program of Speech Education—The North Central Association," *op. cit.*

interest. About the third week works well in many schools. Do not call your first meeting too early in the school year. Many schools use a "mixer" to start off the school year. Such mixers usually combine entertainment and information about the proposed plans in discussion, argumentation, and debate. At the first meeting, students are asked to fill in an information sheet or interest card. Simple refreshments may top off the evening.

Following is a sample information sheet which can be used or adapted for use at the first meeting of the school year.

Name _____

Class _____ Address _____

Telephone Number _____

Please indicate your experience in the following public address activities:

	Years (circle)
Debate	1 2 3
Discussion	1 2 3
Extemporaneous Speaking	1 2 3
Original Oratory	1 2 3

What other high school have you attended? _____

Please indicate your present schedule of classes and out-of-school commitments:

	Monday	Tuesday	Wednesday	Thursday	Friday
8:00					
9:00					
10:00					
11:00					
12:00					
1:00					
2:00					
3:00					
4:00					
5:00					

Organizing the Program. Once your initial meeting has been held and you have some idea of the interest in debating and have determined a satisfactory time and place for meeting each week, you can get to work. Factors in your local situation will need to be considered in determining whether you can meet for one-hour or two-hour afternoon or evening sessions once, twice, or three times per week. During the early weeks, regular meetings should be scheduled no less than once per week, with individual work scheduled whenever possible.

Several practices are used for getting the group underway. Some directors prefer to have students present speeches on some phase of the debate proposition as quickly as possible. Others may use veteran debaters to present a model debate. A tape recording of a state championship debate may be used for orientation purposes. A symposium with students presenting five- to ten-minute speeches on related aspects of the proposition can work well. The cooperative group discussion approach is a popular procedure whereby the entire debate group discusses the problem area, a problem for discussion, or perhaps a debate proposition. In any event, the problem-solving attitude and method should prevail. With an inexperienced group of students, the director may wish to prepare an outline or analysis of the proposition as a guide for research and discussion. He may have the entire group cooperate in preparing a bibliography.

Whatever introductory method or methods a director of debate uses, a well-organized and systematic schedule is necessary for the remainder of the debate year. Phifer suggested the following schedule which seeks to bring out answers to questions as a possible method of arousing interest and understanding, assuming that you plan for your first interscholastic debating in early December.

>FIRST WEEK: What does the proposition mean?
>
>SECOND AND THIRD WEEKS: What is the problem situation that led to the formulation of this proposition? What are its symptoms, causes, and potential future developments?
>
>FOURTH WEEK: What different specific actions come within the scope of the debate resolution? What other courses of action are proposed for solution of the problem?
>
>FIFTH WEEK: By what criteria should any proposed course of action be evaluated? Toward what goals are intelligent citizens aiming in the given problem situation?
>
>SIXTH AND SEVENTH WEEKS: For each alternative in turn, how well do its probable consequences measure up to the criteria listed earlier? What are its probable costs, dangers, and possible benefits? Do potential benefits outweigh possible disadvantages?
>
>EIGHTH WEEK: Practice debates in preparation for interscholastic competition.[10]

In the early weeks of your group's investigations, you should not overlook the use of a talk by an expert in the community or in the school such as a teacher of economics, political science, history, and so on, on the history and background of the problem. A talk by your school librarian on the available materials will save students much time and effort and may develop their interest in proceeding to the library immediately to investigate the materials.

[10] Gregg Phifer, "Organizing Forensic Programs," *Argumentation and Debate—Principles and Practices*, ed. by David Potter, and prepared under the auspices of Tau Kappa Alpha. New York: Holt, Rinehart and Winston, Inc., 1954. pp. 356–357.

A more detailed program for seven weeks is suggested by Smith:

First Week:
1. Introduction of objectives and values.
2. Get students into a questioning frame of mind about current problems.
3. Suggest sources of material to guide reading and research.
4. Discuss what is involved in debating, that is, techniques, order of speaking, et cetera.
5. Have each student prepare a three-minute speech on some phase of the debate proposition. This can give the coach an opportunity to diagnose the student's speech needs.

Second Week:
1. More specific search for evidence.
2. Round table discussions on the topic.
3. Divide squad into affirmative and negative groups.
4. Round table discussions to develop briefs and outlines.
5. Each side should prepare its own outline and brief.
6. Practice debates for veterans; keep them from loafing while beginners get started and allow beginners an opportunity to hear a practice debate.

Third Week:
1. Specific instructions as to affirmative and negative duties.
2. Lots of practice debates.
3. Tentative cases formed and judged.
4. Judge merits of relative arguments.
5. Follow every debate by thorough criticism phrased so as to benefit the entire squad.

Fourth Week:
1. Cases should be definitely formed and debaters should have a fairly good outline of their speeches.
2. Work on refutation drills.

Fifth and Sixth Weeks:
1. More practice debates and intensive work on speeches.
2. Attention to delivery: poise, directness, vocal variety, platform movement, gestures, et cetera.
3. Develop the individuality of each speaker.
4. Practice debates.
5. Speakers debate on both sides and all four positions if this seems to be practical.

Seventh Week:
1. If there is a tournament to which varsity speakers are to be sent, they should be polishing.
2. Continue practice debates.
3. Work on specific drills and rebuttals.

4. Attention should be paid to choice of words. Speakers should not talk "over the heads" of members of the audience.

5. Speeches should be well organized and reach the point promptly and logically.

6. Have practice in tying up each point to the case as a whole.

7. Debaters should be cautioned not to try to cover too much ground.

8. Learn to divide the responsibility with colleague.

9. In rebuttal pick out only the important arguments.

10. Focus on running rebuttal throughout the debate, not just in rebuttal speeches.[11]

Once a director of debate has worked hard in getting his debaters ready for their first tournament, his responsibility is far from discharged. Perhaps one of the most important debate meetings of your year will be the one immediately following their first debating experience with teams from another school. The results of their experience at the tournament should be evaluated objectively. Be careful not to allow yourself or your students always to blame the judge. Look for evidence of where you need to improve. If you have cautioned your debaters to keep their notes on these first debates, you can always analyze the opposition's cases and work out answers to arguments presented by your opposition. A good tournament will impress upon your debaters the need to keep searching for new argument and evidence and up-to-date notes on their reading. Cases will need to be revised as the season progresses.

As you begin to approach the time for the state competition in your high school association, league, or debate conference, you will do well to schedule many practice debates and attend contests and festivals. Use the tape recorder to let your students hear themselves. Work at developing a suitable philosophy for competitive debating.

One procedure that many directors use is the "running rebuttal" exercise. Start the meeting with one affirmative speaker giving a 2-minute development of an affirmative argument. Following the speech, call on a negative debater, at random, to answer that argument and present a negative argument with a 3-minute time limit. Continue alternating sides in this impromptu manner until all students have been involved at least once and then evaluate the results. Another procedure suitable for later meetings is especially helpful in giving students who may have become "cocky" a proper perspective. This is known as the "heckling" session when you, the director, interrupt and point out inconsistencies, poor reasoning, lack of evidence, insignificant or otherwise deficient arguments presented, and other weaknesses. Obviously, this should be used when the situation is

---

[11] Carney C. Smith, "Practical Procedures in Coaching High School Debate," *Quarterly Journal of Speech*, vol. 29, no. 2 (April 1943), pp. 222–234.

right for such tactics and when it will be a meaningful experience for the debaters.

Types of debate. Although most high school debating is conducted on a "traditional" plan, there are variations which are often used in debate tournaments or may be used for special occasions such as school assemblies, programs for civic organizations, and so on.

Traditional plan. This pattern consists of two affirmative speakers and two negative speakers. The first affirmative speaker presents a 10-minute constructive speech. This is followed by the first negative's 10-minute constructive speech. The second affirmative speaker speaks next for 10 minutes and the second negative speaker concludes the constructive speeches with a 10-minute speech. In the 5-minute "rebuttal" speeches, the order of presentation is: first negative, first affirmative, second negative, and second affirmative.

Since traditional debating is the most popular and since much of the information regarding the individual speeches in traditional debating apply to speeches in other types of debate, the following suggestions are in order to indicate the responsibility of each side:

Affirmative responsibility. The main duties of the affirmative in most debates are to define the terms of the proposition, show a need for a change based upon a thorough understanding of the status quo, present a plan to meet the need, show specifically how the plan could remedy the evils of the present system, show that the plan will not result in new evils, and show that the plan is practicable.

Negative responsibility. The duties of the negative are to respond to the affirmative interpretation and analysis. If it is reasonable, adapt to the affirmative's "case," and make clear what their approach to the proposition is. This approach may be (1) straight refutation of the affirmative's issues, (2) a defense of the status quo, (3) upholding the status quo with repairs, or (4) the offering of a counterplan or a solution which is better than the one proposed by the affirmative.

The materials and methods which each side uses to carry out its responsibility becomes its "case." The affirmative case can be those arguments and the evidence used to support the proposition; the negative case, those arguments and that evidence used to argue against it. The points that each team will try to establish in a debate become the "issues" of the debate. One of the tests of an effective debate team is the cooperation or lack of it between the two members. Cooperation between colleagues on a team can be greatly aided if each has a clear understanding of his responsibilities.

First affirmative. This speaker introduces the proposition by indicating the importance of debating the proposition, by developing briefly the history of the proposition, by defining the terms, by stating the main or major arguments in the affirmative case, and by developing the first or second main argument, or both, with adequate supporting evidence. Finally, the first affirmative speaker should summarize clearly and concisely his presentation. This speech is the only one in the debate which is "set" before the debate begins. This does not imply necessarily that the speech is memorized but it does imply that it should be well organized, developed, and supported. After each main point, an effective transition and the use of internal summarizing will aid the speaker in communicating his ideas. After the first speaker finishes his constructive speech, the audience and judge should be favorably impressed by the excellent presentation of solid, well developed, and well-supported arguments.

First negative. This speaker has several choices depending upon the negative plan of attack. Unless the negative offers a counterplan, however, the first negative speaker is obligated to meet the affirmative in direct clash. He must either refute or show that the arguments of the first affirmative are not inherent in the proposition. This first negative speaker may choose any item in the previous speech that will advance the negative cause: definition of the terms, analysis of the status quo, and so forth. In refutation of an affirmative point, the first negative speaker must state clearly the point to be refuted, make adequate refutation, and show the importance of the refutation of the point to the affirmative's case. The effective first negative speaker will close with a summary and leave the audience with a good picture of the weaknesses of the affirmative position presented so far.

Second affirmative. This speaker's primary task is the continuance of the affirmative case by presenting the plan and showing how the plan eliminates present evils pointed out by the first affirmative speaker. However, he must not overlook the need to rebuild the case of the first affirmative. Many judges prefer that this be done in the first part of the constructive speech, reviewing the issues of his colleague one by one and indicating those arguments the negative ignored and rebuilding those which the first negative attacked. Once this has been done, the speaker, who watches his time carefully so as not to spend too much time on this aspect of the debate, should present the affirmative's plan and indicate how it meets the need. An effective summary should always be included.

Second negative. The second negative speaker continues to attack the affirmative case, to rebuild those arguments advanced by his colleague, and to advance new negative arguments. The second negative speaker will be wise to start with a clear summary of the affirmative case and then center his attack on the major weaknesses. He should concentrate on the affirmative's plan and close his speech with a summary of the negative's stand.

Although there is no set pattern for rebuttal speeches, each debater should have a clear understanding of his obligations in rebuttal.

First negative rebuttal. The first negative rebuttal speaker is in a very advantageous position to analyze and summarize the two cases and select those issues which have become paramount in this particular debate. He should show that he realizes the damage his colleague has done in the immediately preceding speech and not waste time in repeating arguments that have been well established. He should keep in mind always the necessity for showing the listener the relationship of his refutation to the issues and to the cases involved.

First affirmative rebuttal. The first affirmative rebuttal speaker has a different job since he must, in five minutes, try to overcome fifteen minutes of negative attack in one constructive speech and one rebuttal speech. A wise speaker in this position will use the affirmative case for an organizational pattern and be selective in the arguments he chooses to answer or rebuild. He will use evidence to refute the alleged disadvantages of the affirmative case as stated by the negative; he will point out fallacies in the negative arguments; and he will summarize.

Second negative rebuttal. The second negative rebuttal speaker will, also, be selective in the arguments he chooses to attack and to establish. Depending upon the debate, he may review the weaknesses of the affirmative's need, indicate the disadvantages of the affirmative plan, point out inconsistencies in the affirmative case, show the superiority of the negative's argument and evidence, or summarize what the affirmative failed to do. A summary which includes a persuasive appeal to reject the affirmative proposal and accept the negative viewpoint should conclude this final negative speech.

Second affirmative rebuttal. The second affirmative rebuttal speaker should become very selective so as to utilize his time most wisely. Choosing those major points with which the negative has been effective and repairing the damage caused by them is essential. Refutation of the major negative contentions should follow. He must guard against sweeping generalizations or accusations which the negative had no chance to answer, and thus be guilty of taking advantage of his position as the final speaker. A well-phrased summary and plea to adopt the affirmative proposition should conclude his rebuttal speech.

Oregon plan. This type of debating is often referred to as "cross-examination" debate. The speaking order is first affirmative, cross-examined by the second negative; first negative, cross-examined by the first affirmative; second affirmative, cross-examined by the first negative; second negative, cross-examined by the second affirmative; negative rebuttal and summary; and affirmative rebuttal and summary. The final speaker for each side may be either of the two members of a team, or a third affirmative and a third negative speaker may be added for this responsibility. Time limits may vary, but a typical debate would have each constructive speech eight minutes long; each cross-examination, four minutes; and each rebuttal and summary, eight minutes.

Direct clash. This type of debate attempts to bring the two teams to a quick determination of the basic issues by eliminating discussion of non-essentials such as minor points, irrelevant points, and fallacious reasoning. The judge becomes an active member of the debate. Teams may be composed of from two to five debaters. There is no fixed order of speaking, but no speaker is allowed to speak twice in any one clash or allowed to initiate two successive clashes. The debate proceeds as follows:

1. An affirmative opening with a speech of 5 to 8 minutes in which terms are defined, affirmative arguments are outlined, and the affirmative "plan" is presented.

2. A negative speech of 5 to 8 minutes follows in which terms are accepted or rejected, specific issues on which the negative proposes to clash are indicated, additional basic issues are advanced, a counterplan is proposed if one is to be offered, and the points on which there is no disagreement by the negative are indicated.

3. Each side has an additional period of 3 minutes for further clarification.

4. The judge rules on the inclusion or exclusion of protested issues and indicates the order in which the clashes are to be debated.

5. The first clash is opened by an affirmative speaker in a 4-minute presentation in which he indicates his team's position with clear, specific, and well-documented arguments.

6. The negative has a 2-minute speech to deal directly with the argument advanced by the affirmative.

7. The affirmative and negative follow with alternating 2-minute speeches until each side has spoken three times.

8. Unless the clash is then halted by the judge, it is terminated with a 2-minute summary by the affirmative.

9. At the conclusion of the clash, the judge awards the clash to the side which he deems to have been more effective.

10. The same procedure is followed for the second clash, except that the negative opens the clash with a 4-minute speech.

11. This alternating procedure is followed for successive clashes.

12. When one side has been awarded three clashes, it is awarded the decision.

Heckling plan. This is an informal type of cross-examination debate, except that the speaker is subjected to interruptions rather than a set direct questioning period. Speeches are 10 minutes long: first affirmative, first negative, second negative, and second affirmative. There are no rebuttal speeches. The heckling is done by a specific member of the opposition assigned to a member of the other team. No heckling is allowed during the first three minutes or last two minutes of each speech. A timekeeper indicates when the heckling may begin and when it must stop. The heckler may ask questions, interrupt, and make pertinent observations. The heckler is not permitted to demonstrate any intention to waste time, embarrass the speaker, or interject irrelevant remarks. The heckler is to be judged on the relevancy and significance of his questions and observations and the speaker is to be judged on the relevancy and significance of his responses.

Problem-solving debate. This is a combination of discussion and traditional debate. The proposition is stated in the form of a problem or question. Teams are either two or three members and are designated as "A" and "B," not affirmative or negative. The order of speaking is: members of the "A" team speak first, third, and sixth; members of the "B" team speak second, fourth, and fifth. Each team presents three speeches: (1) an analysis speech, (2) a solution speech, and (3) an evaluation speech. Each analysis speech is usually 10 minutes in length; each solution speech, 12 minutes; and each evaluation speech, 8 minutes. Each team's analysis speech should be an unbiased analysis of the problem. The second speaker presents his side's solution based on his team-mate's analysis, and the third speaker weighs the solutions presented by both sides. The third speaker may question the opposition whereupon the members of the opposition are expected to answer briefly and to the point. Thus, the emphasis in this type of problem-solving debate is upon an effort to arrive cooperatively at a logical solution to a problem in an honest effort to seek the truth by applying the problem-solving approach.

Organizing and Conducting a Debate Tournament

Most experience in debate by high school debaters is gained through their participation in debate tournaments. Whether this is good or not is debatable but it is an actuality. Since a local debate tournament provides an opportunity for students to gain experience without traveling, many directors of debate are interested in sponsoring a debate tournament for high school students in their area. In a sense, this is to be commended. The following suggestions are presented with the hope that such an endeavor will prove to be most valuable for all of the students involved in the tournament and that it will run smoothly and effectively. The "magic" words in organizing and conducting a debate tournament are "anticipation" and "planning." The wise tournament manager will start early and be prepared for almost anything!

Announcement and invitation. A suitable date on which there will be few conflicts with other activities should be determined early and invitations sent two or three months in advance. The invitation, or announcement, should include such information as the date of the tournament, a statement of the objective, a statement of requirements of eligibility, a tentative schedule, information concerning recognition and awards, information concerning housing and dining accommodations, and an emphasis on the deadline for entries. A registration form and other materials such as a sample ballot, a list of criteria to be used by the judges, and a statement of rules or regulations which will govern the debates should be included in the first mailing to enable each director of debate to give the tournament manager a prompt indication of the number and names and addresses of schools which are likely to be represented in the tournament. These materials should be designed to enable the director of debate and his students to become acquainted with the procedures and regulations of the tournament and, at the same time, to help him to decide whether he will enter students in the tournament and, if he decides to enter them, to inform the tournament manager of the names of students and judges who will participate.

The way in which fees are to be collected is important for the tournament manager to consider before invitations are mailed. If the fees are to be paid when the registration form is completed and returned, both the letter of invitation and the registration form should carry a statement which makes the point. This procedure is probably best, because it tells the tournament manager exactly how much money he can count on to finance the tournament, it permits him to maintain a record of receipts and expenditures by his use of an accurate bookkeeping system, it minimizes the problem of inadvertent nonpayment of fees, and it frees the tournament manager and the directors to concentrate on the tournament, its objectives, and procedures. Of course, payment of fees in advance has a psychological effect on the directors of debate who commit themselves definitely to entering their students, and on the tournament manager who, because of the commitment, can go ahead with his plans. All fees should be refundable if the manager is notified by a time specified in the letter of invitation and on the registration form. At some tournaments, however, fees are paid at the time of registration on the day of the tournament. If this procedure is to be utilized, this point should be made on both the invitation and registration form. Regardless of which procedure is used, the important thing for the tournament manager to keep in mind is that an efficient system of bookkeeping is a necessity in organizing and conducting a debate tournament.

A sample invitation and registration form appear on the next two pages.

LETTER OF INVITATION

Midtown High School
Midtown, _____
September 20, 19___

Dear Director of Debate:

Midtown High School invites you and your debaters to participate in an invitational debate tournament to be held at Midtown High School on Saturday, December 7, 19___.

The purpose of this tournament is to provide an opportunity for students in the (indicate the geographical area) of the State Forensic League to become increasingly responsible and effective debaters through their participation and achievement in challenging, well-organized, and guided debating. The proposition to be debated in this tournament is:

Resolved: (Insert one of three propositions for debate recommended by the Committee on Discussion and Debate for the current year.)

Constructive speeches will be ten minutes in length and rebuttals, five minutes in length.

Each school may be represented by as many teams as it desires, provided it is represented by the same number of affirmative and negative teams, each with two speakers on a team. Alternate debaters may be substituted between rounds on each team. Each school will furnish one competent and impartial judge for each two teams it enters. Extra judges will be furnished by the local tournament manager upon request and payment of a fee of $5.00 per debate.

The schedule for the day will be as follows:

9:30 – 10:30 A.M.	Registration
10:45 – 11:45	Round I
11:45 – 1:00 P.M.	Lunch
1:00 – 2:00	Round II
2:30 – 3:30	Round III
4:00 –	Results announced.

Lunch will be served in the school cafeteria at $1.00 per person. Paid reservations must be made by each school in advance of the beginning of the tournament.

Please complete and return the enclosed registration form together with fees and payment for luncheon reservations on or before *November 19*. Fees will be refundable in cases of emergency and until December 4.

We look forward to greeting you and your debaters here on the morning of December 7 and trust that you are looking forward to a pleasant and educationally profitable forensic enterprise at Midtown High School.

                                                        Tournament Manager

Invitational Debate Tournament
Midtown High School
December 7, 19___

REGISTRATION FORM

_____ High School will enter _____ teams of two speakers each and will furnish a competent judge for each set of affirmative and negative teams.

Teams   *Affirmative*   *Negative*

1. _____   _____
   Name of Speaker   Name of Speaker

   _____   _____
   Name of Speaker   Name of Speaker
2. _____   _____
   _____   _____

3. _____   _____
   _____   _____

4. _____   _____
   _____   _____

Judges

1. _____   3. _____
        Name of Judge
2. _____   4. _____

We wish to request _____ judges at fee of $5.00 each per debate.
                    Number

Please make reservations for _____ luncheons at $1.00 each.
                              Number

All fees, including payment for luncheon reservations, *are enclosed* with this registration form.

We understand that the deadline for entry is November 19, 19___. Also, we understand that the fees are refundable in case of emergency and in case of withdrawal by December 4.

_____   _____
         Date   Director of Debate

                                  _____
                                          Address

Pre-planning. Everything should be ready when the visiting debaters and their teachers arrive. This means that much pre-planning and organizing will have been accomplished between the day invitations are mailed and the day of the tournament: committees appointed, registration materials prepared, personnel ready, housing and luncheon arrangements completed, chairman-timekeepers available, judging assignments set, and mimeographed material made ready such as schedules, ballots, instructions to judges and timekeepers, time cards, maps as necessary, signs, tabulation forms, and so on.

Nothing can complicate an otherwise efficient debate tournament more than poor scheduling. Ample time should be provided between debates so that debaters and judges are not rushing from debate to debate, especially in a large tournament, and so that personnel in the tabulation room have enough time to tabulate results accurately and completely. A "break" or recess between debates should be considered. One insurance measure is to have a longer recess between rounds one and two in the schedule to permit possible delay in starting round one in case of inclement weather, car trouble, or other calamities.

Pairings in a debate tournament and the assignment of judges can also present problems to the tournament manager. In making pairings, the manager of a tournament should make every reasonable effort to guard against:

1. A team meeting another team twice.

2. A team scheduled against all strong or all weak teams only, except by chance.

3. A team from a school meeting a team from its neighbor school so long as it can have opportunity to meet teams from schools which it has had no opportunity to meet.

4. A director of debate judging his own team.

5. A director judging a team which his team will meet during an immediately succeeding round.

6. A judge listening to a team twice.

The following method for making pairings and assigning judges takes into account each of these factors.

This method includes four steps which are illustrated in worksheet forms below.

Step One

Schools Entered	Estimated Strength	Judge from School
Midtown	Average	Brown
Central City, West High	Strong	Gordon
Central City, East High	Weak	Cohen
Pleasantville	Weak	Johnson
Lakeville	Strong	Lane
Benton	Average	Rodriguez
Riverview	Strong	O'Brien
Easton	Weak	Martin
Millersburg	Average	Jensen

The first step involves a simple listing of the names of schools which are to be represented in the tournament, a recording of the manager's own estimate of the strength of the debate squad of each school derived from his knowledge and best judgment of its previous tournament experience, and a list of judges which the schools are furnishing to make sure that he knows which judge is from which school.

Step Two

Pairings Pattern	Team Numbers Aff. Neg.	Assignment by Strength
Strong	1 – 2	Central City, West
Weak	3 – 4	Easton
Average	5 – 6	Benton
Strong	7 – 8	Lakeville
Weak	9 – 10	Central City, East
Average	11 – 12	Midtown
Strong	13 – 14	Riverview
Weak	15 – 16	Pleasantville
Average	17 – 18	Millersburg

The second step consists of devising a pairings pattern which will allow schools to debate schools of all or different degrees of strength. Although the pairings worksheet has been completed for a tournament which has only nine schools participating in it, three weak, three average, and three strong, a suitable pattern can be worked out by trial and error and hope for success for any number of schools with any number falling under each degree of strength. Code numbers are then assigned to each position in the pattern as illustrated immediately above. Each set of affirmative and negative teams receives two consecutive numbers with each affirmative team assigned an odd number beginning with 1, and each negative team assigned an even number beginning with 2. The final part of step two is the assignment of schools, according to their estimated strength only, to the pattern of numbers.

Step Three

Round I			*Round II*			*Round III*		
Aff.	Neg.	Judge	Aff.	Neg.	Judge	Aff.	Neg.	Judge
1	4		1	6		1	8	
3	6		3	8		3	10	
5	8		5	10		5	12	
7	10		7	12		7	14	
9	12		9	14		9	16	
11	14		11	16		11	18	
13	16		13	18		13	2	
15	18		15	2		15	4	
17	2		17	4		17	6	

The third step is the making of a pairings schedule like the one above and the actual pairing of odd and even numbers. The pairings schedule should include columns in which to make the pairings for each round and later, after step four is completed, to record the names of judges. The affirmative team numbers should be listed beginning with team 1 through as many odd numbers as there are affirmative teams in each round. The negative team numbers move up one place in each round so that in round I, for example, team 1 debates team 4; in round II, team 1 debates team 6; and, in round III, team 1 debates team 8; et cetera. Team 2 always debates the bottommost number in round I; the second from the bottom number in round II; and so on.

Step Four

School Numbers	Judge from School	Other Teams Which He Should Not Judge in Rounds I and II — Aff.	Neg.	Assignment by Round I	II	III
1 – 2	Gordon	15, 13	6, 8	7–10	11–16	17– 6
3 – 4	Martin	17, 15	8, 10	9–12	13–18	1– 8
5 – 6	Rodriguez	1, 17	10, 12	11–14	15– 2	3–10
7 – 8	Lane	3, 1	12, 14	13–16	17– 4	5–12
9 – 10	Cohen	5, 3	14, 16	15–18	1– 6	7–14
11 – 12	Brown	7, 5	16, 18	17– 2	3– 8	9–16
13 – 14	O'Brien	9, 7	18, 2	1– 4	5–10	11–18
15 – 16	Johnson	11, 9	2, 4	3– 6	7–12	13– 2
17 – 18	Jensen	13, 11	4, 6	5– 8	9–14	15– 4

The fourth step is the assignment of judges. A judge's name should be listed beside the code numbers of the teams of the school which is bringing him and also with the code numbers of teams which those from his school will meet in succeeding rounds after round I. He should not be assigned to judge his own team or teams which his teams will meet in succeeding rounds. In assigning him to judge round I, scan the pairings on the pairings schedule to find a point where the judge with code numbers 1 and 2 will not judge any of these teams. Assign that debate to him and then continue assigning the succeeding debates in that round to the succeeding judges. In round II and in all other rounds follow the same procedure until judges have been assigned to all debates in every round. Finally, write in the name of the judge who has been assigned to a debate beside that debate in your pairings schedule which you prepared in the third step. When the pairings schedule is complete as illustrated below, be sure to check it to make certain that it is in accord with the safeguards listed earlier in this chapter.

Pairings Schedule

| Round I ||| Round II ||| Round III |||
Aff.	Neg.	Judge	Aff.	Neg.	Judge	Aff.	Neg.	Judge
1	4	O'Brien	1	6	Cohen	1	8	Martin
3	6	Johnson	3	8	Brown	3	10	Rodriguez
5	8	Jensen	5	10	O'Brien	5	12	Lane
7	10	Gordon	7	12	Johnson	7	14	Cohen
9	12	Martin	9	14	Jensen	9	16	Brown
11	14	Rodriguez	11	16	Gordon	11	18	O'Brien
13	16	Lane	13	18	Martin	13	2	Johnson
15	18	Cohen	15	2	Rodriguez	15	4	Jensen
17	2	Brown	17	4	Lane	17	6	Gordon

Prepared by Marnell Fliger, State University of Iowa

Cancellation or withdrawal of a debate team from a tournament after the pairings and schedule are completed can play havoc to the pairings and to the schedule of teams and judges assigned with reasonable conformity to the four-step procedure set forth immediately above. Although a tournament manager can prepare, in advance of the tournament, alternate plans for different numbers of teams in an effort to avoid irreparable damage to the schedule, he can hardly hope to avoid insoluble problems, because he cannot anticipate which team or teams may cancel or withdraw. He can, of course, resort hopefully to such alternatives as the following:

1. Invite directors of debate to agree on the substitution of one or more of their own extra teams in the place of the team, or teams, which cancels or withdraws.

2. Invite the directors to agree to the tournament manager's inviting one or more teams from a nearby school which is not entered in the tournament to substitute for any team, or teams, which cancels or withdraws.

3. Give a "bye" to the team or teams scheduled to debate a team, or teams, which cancels or withdraws and declare each team which draws a "bye" to be a winner for the rounds and determine its team and individual speaker ratings on the basis of the number of rounds in which it actually debates.

4. If practical, the tournament manager will be wise either to use an alternate plan prepared ahead of the tournament or re-do the pairings and assignment of judges.

If a tournament manager and the directors of debate who have teams entered in the tournament are not concerned about the safeguards listed above being applied to the pairings and to the assignment of judges, the tournament director can determine the pairings and formulate a schedule well ahead of the tournament by using the following method illustrated by a sample worksheet.

ORGANIZING AND CONDUCTING A DEBATE TOURNAMENT 331

PAIRINGS WORKSHEET

Pairings Schedule

Round I			Round II			Round III		
Aff.	Neg.	Judge	Aff.	Neg.	Judge	Aff.	Neg.	Judge
1	4	1–O'Brien	1	6	4–Gordon	1	8	8–Cohen
3	6	2–Johnson	3	8	5–Martin	3	10	9–Brown
5	8	3–Jensen	5	10	6–Rodriguez	5	12	1–O'Brien
7	10	4–Gordon	7	12	7–Lane	7	14	2–Johnson
9	12	5–Martin	9	14	8–Cohen	9	16	3–Jensen
11	14	6–Rodriguez	11	16	9–Brown	11	18	4–Gordon
13	16	7–Lane	13	18	1–O'Brien	13	2	5–Martin
15	18	8–Cohen	15	2	2–Johnson	15	4	6–Rodriguez
17	2	9–Brown	17	4	3–Jensen	17	6	7–Lane

Judging Assignments

Judges	Round I	Round II	Round III
1	1 – 4	13 – 18	5 – 12
2	3 – 6	15 – 2	7 – 14
3	5 – 8	17 – 4	9 – 16
4	7 – 10	1 – 6	11 – 18
5	9 – 12	3 – 8	13 – 2
6	11 – 14	5 – 10	15 – 4
7	13 – 16	7 – 12	17 – 6
8	15 – 18	9 – 14	1 – 8
9	17 – 2	11 – 16	3 – 10

Prepared by Marnell Fliger, State University of Iowa

1. The first step of this method is exactly the same as the third step of the recommended method above. Steps one and two of that method are omitted because code numbers are assigned to schools only after a representative from each school draws for a set of numbers upon his arrival on the day of the tournament.

2. The second step is to assign numbers, beginning with 1, to the names of judges which the schools submit on the registration forms.

3. The third step is to assign the judges to the debates which they will judge. In round I, judge number 1 will judge the debate between teams number 1 and number 4; judge number 2, the debate between teams number 3 and number 6, et cetera, until all judges have been assigned. For succeeding rounds, the assignment of judges becomes a trial and error procedure until judges have been assigned to judge debates between teams which they will not have judged in preceding rounds and teams from schools whose other teams he will have already judged in preceding rounds.

Then simply record the judge by either number or name on the schedule of pairings opposite the debate to which each has been asigned to judge. If judges are assigned by number only, they too can draw when they arrive at the tournament.

This procedure overcomes easily the problem of late cancellations or withdrawals since, if either occurs, the last set of team numbers and the last judge number can be omitted from the drawing and the pairings can be adjusted accordingly. Obviously, however, this method does not overcome the problem of withdrawal after the tournament begins nor does it solve any of the problems against which the manager should guard in making pairings and assigning judges.

Although either method can be used in making pairings, it is important to remember that both require time and effort to apply and that neither will overcome all problems inherent in conducting a well-organized tournament. Both require much trial-and-error work because of the varying number of schools represented in various tournaments, their various degrees of ability and competence, and the special limitations on which judges can be assigned to which debates for which no pat rule of thumb procedure can guarantee satisfaction. However, with experience and practice, any director of debate can learn to make pairings and to assign judges in a way which will minimize foreseeable problems and maximize the probability of students achieving the desired outcomes of the tournament.

Distribution of materials. When directors of debate, debaters, judges, chairmen-timekeepers, and other personnel arrive to register at a central location on the day of the tournament, detailed schedules, regulations, appropriate instructions, and so on should be distributed to them. A responsible person other than the manager can be appointed to stay at the registration desk throughout the day to distribute materials, make authorized changes in the schedule, answer questions, and act as "public relations man" for the tournament. It is a good idea to post in a central location a copy of the schedule on which changes can be recorded. Copies of a clear, detailed schedule, a sample list of regulations, a sample instruction sheet for judges, and a sample instruction sheet for chairmen-timekeepers are presented on the next pages.

Before the first round of the tournament and prior to each succeeding round, a ballot in an unsealed envelope should be delivered to each judge. The envelope should be marked clearly with information concerning his assignment for the round such as the name of the judge, the time of the round, the number of the round, the number of the room in which the debate will be held, and the code numbers of the affirmative and negative teams. Each judge can call at the headquarters of the tournament ahead of each round of debate to pick up his unsealed envelope and ballot or he can, before the first round, pick up his ballots and envelopes for all debates in all rounds which he will be judging. At the end of each debate, the judge can place his completed ballot in the envelope, seal it, and return the sealed envelope to the registration desk at headquarters.

Invitational Debate Tournament
Midtown High School
December 7, 19___

SCHEDULE

Welcome to the Midtown High School Invitational Debate Tournament. We trust each of you will have an enjoyable and profitable experience in this tournament. To that end, we seek your cooperation and pledge ours.

Personnel in Charge

Mr. Mittendorf, manager of the tournament.
Miss Wade, registration clerk.
Miss Kyle and Miss Ludno, tabulation clerks.

PROGRAM
Registration, 9:30–10:30 A.M.
Round I, 10:45–11:45 A.M.

Aff.	*Neg.*	*Room*	*Judge*
1	4	123	O'Brien
3	6	125	Johnson
5	8	127	Jensen
7	10	209	Gordon
9	12	213	Martin
11	14	215	Rodriguez
13	16	217	Lane
15	18	225	Cohen
17	2	227	Brown

Lunch, 11:45 A.M.–1:00 P.M., School Cafeteria
Round II, 1:00–2:00 P.M.

Aff.	*Neg.*	*Room*	*Judge*
1	6	123	Cohen
3	8	125	Brown
5	10	127	O'Brien
7	12	209	Johnson
9	14	213	Jensen
11	16	215	Gordon
13	18	217	Martin
15	2	225	Rodriguez
17	4	227	Lane

(et cetera)

Invitational Debate Tournament
Midtown High School
December 7, 19___

DEBATE REGULATIONS

1. No director of debate is to attend debates in which his school is not represented.
2. No director of debate is to impart information or give suggestions to any debater during the course of a debate.
3. The debaters shall be separated from the audience, and they shall receive no signals from the audience or a director of debate while the debate is in progress.
4. Each team shall consist of two members. Each constructive argument, beginning with the first affirmative speaker and alternating, is to be for 10 minutes. The first rebuttal will be the negative, and will be for 5 minutes.
5. Time lost in unavoidable interruptions shall be made good to the speaker.
6. Cheering a debater while he is speaking is forbidden. Time so consumed shall not be made up to a speaker.
7. No new argument may be introduced in the rebuttal speech.
8. Speakers shall not be interrupted by their opponents at any time. Should any problem arise, a debater may appeal to the judge at the end of the debate.
9. Debaters shall be entitled to warning signals which shall be at the ninth minute in the constructive and at the fourth minute in the rebuttal.
10. Debaters shall cease speaking when the signal is given.

* * * * *

Each team has been assigned a Code Number by which the teams will be judged. No student or director of debate need divulge the Code Numbers of the teams from his school. It is preferable to have the teams remain anonymous as far as possible until after the last debate so as to insure all teams against any possibility of partiality in judgment. Please respect the Code Number of any team whom you happen to recognize during the tournament.

Invitational Debate Tournament
Midtown High School
December 7, 19___

INFORMATION FOR JUDGES

1. Each judge will judge three rounds of debate.
2. After receiving his ballot at Headquarters, each judge will go to the room to which he is assigned for any particular round.
3. Judges are to fill in each ballot and, after the close of the debate, deliver it in a sealed envelope to Headquarters.

ORGANIZING AND CONDUCTING A DEBATE TOURNAMENT

4. Criticisms may be written as specified on the ballot. Extra sheets of paper are available to judges for use in making notes and criticisms.
5. Decisions are to be kept secret until the end of the tournament.
6. Questions should be answered by the Tournament Manager, in order to be official.
7. The following rules should be observed by the debaters, and the judges should see that there are no infractions.

CRITERIA FOR JUDGING

8. The judge must remain neutral throughout the debate and evaluate only the debating skill being displayed between the affirmative and negative teams.
9. A judge should be prone to penalize a team which resorts to sarcasm but he should not base his decision on whether one of the teams used sarcasm, except in the case of a tie based on all points other than sarcasm. However, obviously, bitterness manifested by a team can result automatically in its being disqualified.
10. The affirmative team may either debate principle or present a plan.
11. The negative team may argue a straight negative case, the status quo with repairs, or offer a counterplan.
12. No new argument may be introduced in the final rebuttal speech.
13. Judges for the tournament were selected and assigned to debates based on their competency, impartiality, and availability with the belief that each judge will make every effort to render competent, fair, and impartial judgments and decisions, ratings, and criticism.

Invitational Debate Tournament
Midtown High School
December 7, 19___

INFORMATION FOR TIMEKEEPERS

1. After having been given your room assignment and time cards, go to your appointment. Remain there for all rounds of debate.
2. If, after ten minutes past the designated time for a debate to begin, a debater, team, or judge is missing, report the discrepancy to Headquarters. Instruct those present in the room to remain until you get back with further instructions.
3. The constructive speeches, the first four speeches in the debate, are of ten-minute duration. The rebuttal speeches, the last four speeches in the debate, are of five-minute duration.
4. You are to hold, in full view of the debater, a time card designating the amount of time left in the debate speech as each minute expires. At the end of the allotted time for the speech, you are to signal the speaker that his time has expired. (Please stand to signal the end of the time.)
5. You are responsible for the room in which you are officiating. Do not let

the students tamper with equipment, bulletin boards, or blackboards. At the *end of the tournament, check your room* to be sure that everything is in order—chairs, desks, et cetera.
6. Remember that you are a representative of this high school. Be a courteous host whenever possible. Your cooperation will help to make this tournament a success.
7. Return the time cards to Headquarters at the close of the tournament.

Your help and cooperation in conducting this tournament is greatly appreciated. THANK YOU.

* * * * *

If a debate tournament is to be an educational experience, the debate ballot or rating form should provide each team and individual debater with some suggestions as to their strengths and weaknesses and reasons for the judge's decision. Most judges agree that they desire a ballot which gives them an opportunity to award the decision, write some comments on crucial points of the debate and on the debating by each debater, and indicate team and speaker ratings. The sample debate ballots on the succeeding pages are typical of the kind being used at present in high school debate tournaments. They range from ballots which include specific and detailed criteria for the judge to use to numerical ratings of the teams and debaters. Obviously, there is no one debate ballot which is superior to the others. Each director of debate should decide for himself which is best and use that ballot for his practice debates and for his own invitational debate tournaments.

Iowa High School Forensic League
State University of Iowa

OFFICIAL DEBATE BALLOT

Instructions: At the conclusion of the debate, the critic shall award his decision by writing "Affirmative" or "Negative" in the space provided on page 6. In addition to awarding his decision, he shall *rate each team* and *rate each debater* as: 5–Superior, 4–Excellent, 3–Adequate, 2–Fair, or 1–Unsatisfactory. During or after the debate, he shall, please, write his criticism for each debater, using one criticism sheet for each debater, clearly designating the name of each debater and his position on a team, i.e., first affirmative, first negative, et cetera, in the appropriate places.

The critic shall consider the *merits of the debate; not the merits of the proposition.* He shall weigh content, organization, phraseology, and projection or delivery. He shall, *please,* consider *matter to be more important than form or manner.* He shall discount speeches that are obviously memorized. He shall distinguish genuine argument from mere declamatory embellishment. He shall award his decision to the team which better presents *clear, logical, and sound thought.* He shall weigh carefully excellence in thinking and excellence in speaking.

Criteria

1. *Knowledge and Understanding of Proposition:* Extent of investigation as indicated by analysis, argument, evidence, rebuttal, and familiarity with all aspects of the proposition.
2. *Analysis of Proposition:* Adequacy of definition, limiting of the proposition, history of the proposition as necessary, grasp of main and sub-issues, and statement of issues and sub-issues.
3. *Argument:* Effective use of specific instances, analogy, authority; causal reasoning; testing of assumptions or general statements; and team consistency.
4. *Amount and Value of Evidence:* Relevant, accurate, reliable, abundant, consistent, and persuasive.
5. *Organization and Composition:* Interest, order, force, unity; originality and resourcefulness; excellence of outlining; effectiveness of sentence construction; use of summaries and similar elements; and vividness of language.
6. *Adaptation to Opposing Case and Refutation:* Selection of points to be refuted, general and specific methods, position and amount, and inclusion of new evidence except in final rebuttal.
7. *Voice and Bodily Control:* Direct communication; conversational mode; structural emphasis; earnestness; sincerity; posture and effectiveness in bodily action; total bodily movement; appropriate voice and voice control; rate; force; quality; rhythm; and projection by devices other than voice and bodily action.
8. *Audience Adaptation:* Appeal of the argument to the audience intellectually, emotionally, and imaginatively; effectiveness in the use of motivating appeals; adjustment of argument to the audience; evidence and analysis and other elements of the speech; and appeal of the speaker through sincerity, earnestness, and humor.

Prepared by Hugh F. Seabury

Iowa High School Forensic League
State University of Iowa

CRITICISM FOR FIRST AFFIRMATIVE SPEAKER ONLY

NAME _____ TEAM CODE NUMBER _____
ROUND: I II III IV V VI   PLACE _____ DATE _____
(Circle the correct number)

[Page 3 of this ballot should be prepared exactly like this page except that it should be entitled "Criticism for First Negative Speaker Only"; pages 4 and 5 should be prepared accordingly with page 4 entitled "Criticism for Second Affirmative Speaker Only"; and page 5, "Criticism for Second Negative Speaker Only."]

338   DIRECTING A CO-CURRICULAR SPEECH PROGRAM

(Continue on back of this sheet as desired)
CRITIC _____ *Please seal* in envelope and return to
(Signature)
Tournament Headquarters after the debate. *Please do not reveal either decision or rating to debaters or to their teachers.*

Iowa High School Forensic League
State University of Iowa

OFFICIAL DEBATE BALLOT

Instructions: The critic shall, *please,* rate each team and *rate each debater* as 5–Superior, 4–Excellent, 3–Adequate, 2–Fair, 1–Unsatisfactory, and *award his decision* to the *affirmative* or *negative* team. He shall, please, fill out this ballot *accurately* and *completely* and honor the request in the *note to the critic* at the bottom of this ballot.

Round: I II III IV V VI   Place: _____ Date: _____
(Circle the correct number)
Affirmative Team Number _____   Negative Team Number _____

(First Affirmative)   (Rating)   (First Negative)   (Rating)

(Second Affirmative)   (Rating)   (Second Negative)   (Rating)
Affirmative Team Rating _____   Negative Team Rating _____
The *better* debating was done by the _____ team.
(Please write "Affirmative" or "Negative")
Critic _____ Address _____ Phone _____
(Signature)

Note to Critic

1. Please check this ballot to make sure that you have completed it accurately.
2. Please check to see that the team with the higher team rating is consistent with the decision. It is difficult to accept the team with the higher team rating as loser of the debate.
3. Please check to see that the sum of the ratings of the debaters on the team which did the *better* debating is at least as high as the sum of ratings of the debaters on the other team.
4. Please check to see that the individual ratings of each debater on each team is consistent with the ratings of the team as a whole or that the difference between the individual ratings of the debaters on a team and the team rating is, for some good reason, justifiable.
5. Please be sure that you have signed your ballot and given an address and telephone number where you can be reached if a challenge or question arises.
6. Please deliver this ballot, the pages entitled *Criticism,* and the time cards if there is no timekeeper to Tournament Headquarters.
7. *Please do not reveal either your decision or your ratings to the debaters or to their teachers.*

Minnesota State High School Speech League
Minneapolis, Minnesota

CRITIC SHEET FOR DEBATE

Round _____ Room _____ Judge _____

Affirmative Team Number _____ vs. Negative Team Number _____

I. Team Scoring (5–Superior)   Affirmative Team   Negative Team
                                5 4 3 2 1   5 4 3 2 1

Organization
   Overall team planning
   Basis strategy
   Case structure

Evidence
   Selected information, its
   quantity and pertinence
   Documentation

Reasoning
   The individual debater's
   skill in interpreting
   evidence

Refutation
   Answering opposing arguments in constructive
   or rebuttal speeches

Delivery
   Voice, bodily aciton,
   language usage

II. Total Effectiveness
   (Circle one for each team)   5 4 3 2 1   5 4 3 2 1

III. Win-Loss (If the debate is close, give the winner 2 points, the loser 1 point. If one team wins by a substantial margin, award it 3 points and the other team 0.)

Affirmative Team   Points _____   Negative Team   Points _____

IV. Individual Debater Ratings   (Circle one for each speaker)
Affirmative Team Members   Superior Excellent Very Good Good Fair
1. _____   5   4   3   2   1
2. _____   5   4   3   2   1
Negative Team Members
1. _____   5   4   3   2   1
2. _____   5   4   3   2   1

Judges Comments for Team (Use reverse side and/or extra clearly marked sheets.)

    Adapted with the permission of William S. Howell, Donald K. Smith, and David W. Thompson from *Speech—Debate—Drama in Contests and Festivals*. Minneapolis, Minnesota: Minnesota State High School Speech League, 1953. p. 95.

Oklahoma High School Speech League
University of Oklahoma   Norman, Oklahoma

OFFICIAL DEBATE BALLOT
Affirmative

Class _____ Round No. _____ Place _____ Team No. _____

Judge's comments to the *Affirmative* team: Rank the speakers 1, 2, 3, 4 in the
Below rate each team as follows: order of their effectiveness. Also,
S–Superior; E–Excellent; G–Good;   rate each on the basis indicated
F–Fair; P–Poor.   in the opposite column.

A. Organization and Analysis _____   1st Aff. _____
B. Use of Evidence _____   1st Neg. _____
C. Argument-Reasoning Ability _____   2nd Aff. _____
D. Adaptability and Extemporaneity _____ 2nd Neg. _____
E. Rebuttal Strength _____
F. Courtesy and Attitude _____

The better debating was done by _____ Team No. _____
                      (Affirmative or Negative)
                  Signed _____, Judge

Negative

Class _____ Round No. _____ Place _____ Team No. _____

Judge's comments to the *Negative* team: Rank the speakers 1, 2, 3, 4 in the
Below rate each team as follows: order of their effectiveness. Also,
S–Superior; E–Excellent; G–Good;   rate each on the basis indicated
F–Fair; P–Poor.   in the opposite column.

A. Organization and Analysis _____   1st Aff. _____
B. Use of Evidence _____   1st Neg. _____
C. Argument-Reasoning Ability _____   2nd Aff. _____
D. Adaptability and Extemporaneity _____ 2nd Neg. _____
E. Rebuttal Strength _____
F. Courtesy and Attitude _____

The better debating was done by _____ Team No. _____
                      (Affirmative or Negative)

Used with permission of James Robinson, Director, Oklahoma Speech and Drama Services, University of Oklahoma, Norman, Oklahoma.

Tabulation and posting of results. As soon as the first round of debates ends and judges return their completed ballots to the registration desk at tournament headquarters, the tabulation and posting of results begin. A tournament which appears to be well organized and efficiently and skillfully managed can quickly give an impression of a lack of organization and inefficient management if the operation of the tabulation room is not

ORGANIZING AND CONDUCTING A DEBATE TOURNAMENT

also well organized, efficient, and accurate. The tabulation room itself should be a room which is reasonably well isolated from the main activity in corridors and other rooms to make it possible for the tabulators to work in quiet surroundings and with a minimum of interruptions. The tabulators should be responsible persons who can cooperate with each other in tabulating results quickly and accurately.

To facilitate the tabulation and posting of results, a tabulation form such as the one which appears below can be mimeographed on 5" × 8" cards. Two of these forms can be completed for each school represented

Debate Tabulation

Team Number

Aff.	Neg.	School				City			
AFFIRMATIVE	RI	RII	RIII	RIV	RV	RVI	WINS		LOSSES
W-L Record:									
Team Ratings:									
Student Ratings:	RI	RII	RIII	RIV	RV	RVI	TOTAL		COMPOSITE
1.									
2.									
3.									
4.									
5.									
6.									
NEGATIVE	RI	RII	RIII	RIV	RV	RVI	WINS		LOSSES
W-L Record:									
Team Ratings:									
Student Ratings:	RI	RII	RIII	RIV	RV	RVI	TOTAL		COMPOSITE
1.									
2.									
3.									
4.									
5.									
6.									

Prepared by Mr. and Mrs. Donald E. Malmgren
Colorado State College for Women at Denver

at the tournament with the names of its debaters and the code numbers of its teams. The copies of the forms can be separated into complete sets, reassembled in numerical order, and attached in that order on two large pieces of cardboard. One set attached to one cardboard can be used as a poster to be displayed in a central location after the tabulation for each round has been completed and before or during the succeeding round. The other set, on which schools can be identified by name also, should be kept in the tabulation room as a cross-reference set and later as the manager's permanent record of the results.

The tabulators should record carefully in ink all the necessary information including team ratings, individual ratings, and the decision on each set of cards when the judges return their completed ballots after each round of debate. The two sets should be cross-checked against each other and against the original ballot before one set is posted in a central location. Ballots which have been tabulated should be either stapled or paper-clipped together, labeled with the number of the round for which they were completed, and put in a place where they will not be lost but will be available for later reference. If written criticism sheets are used, they should be distributed to the *appropriate* directors of debate *personally* or deposited in *envelopes* labeled with the name of each school, which each director can obtain at the end of the tournament.

When the final round of debate is completed and the results are tabulated, the tabulators in cooperation with the tournament manager should calculate the composite team and individual ratings and determine the "winners" if "winners" are to be declared. It is then a good idea for the tournament manager to hold a general meeting in which winners are announced, awards are presented, gratitude is expressed to judges, timekeepers, directors of debate, debaters, and other personnel for their cooperation and effort, and achievement of desired outcomes is recognized.

Post tournament. Of course, the job of the efficient and effective director of debate who is tournament manager does not end as soon as the general meeting is adjourned, visiting directors of debate and their debaters have departed, and the premises have been tidied. A complete and accurate report giving a detailed summary of the results of each school's debating and further recognition of outstanding achievement should be prepared and mailed to each director of debate to enable him and his debaters to have a permanent record for their analysis and file. A portion of such a report is presented on page 343. Briefer reports of achievement might also be prepared and mailed to high school or community newspapers for each high school represented. Letters of congratulation should be prepared and mailed to one of the administrators of each school represented by debaters whose achievement was meritorious. Thank-you letters should be mailed to all

ORGANIZING AND CONDUCTING A DEBATE TOURNAMENT

Department of Speech

Midtown High School

Midtown, _____

FINAL REPORT

Invitational Debate Tournament

Saturday, December 7, 19__

Tournament Champion
Riverview High School, 6–0, 5.00

First Runner-Up
West High School, Central City, 5–1, 4.83

Champion Affirmative Debaters
Wesley Elliott, Riverview, 5.00
Lynn Lohring, Riverview, 5.00
Wayne Ritter, Central City, West, 5.00
Linda Watson, Central City, West, 5.00

Champion Negative Debaters
Gertie Karn, Lakeville, 5.00
Connie Lei, Riverview, 5.00
Ben Marston, Riverview, 5.00
Marty Pollock, Central City, West, 5.00

Results by School

School and Debaters	I	II	III	Composite Rating	W–L
Benton, Mrs. Martha Riley					
5 Affirmative	L–3.00	W–4.00	L–4.00	3.66	1–2
Tom Werges	3.00	4.00	4.00	3.66	
Pam Tanberg	3.00	4.00	3.00	3.33	
6 Negative	W–4.00	L–4.00	W–5.00	4.33	2–1
Ron Polanski	4.00	4.00	4.00	4.00	
Kathy Johnes	5.00	4.00	5.00	4.66	
Central City, East High School, Mr. Kyle Smith					
9 Affirmative	L–3.00	L–3.00	L–4.00	3.33	0–3
Bob McGregor	4.00	3.00	4.00	3.66	
John Fox	3.00	3.00	4.00	3.33	
10 Negative	L–3.00	L–3.00	W–4.00	3.33	1–2
Peg Gasperlin	3.00	3.00	4.00	3.33	
Matt Felix	4.00	4.00	4.00	4.00	
Central City, West High School, Miss Leona Rasmussen					
1 Affirmative	W–5.00	W–5.00	W–5.00	5.00	3–0
Linda Watson	5.00	5.00	5.00	5.00	
Wayne Ritter	5.00	5.00	5.00	5.00	
2 Negative	W–5.00	W–5.00	L–4.00	4.66	2–1
Marty Pollock	5.00	5.00	5.00	5.00	
Sue Winn	5.00	5.00	4.00	4.66	

Prepared by Marnell Fliger, State University of Iowa

personnel who served the tournament. Judges and other personnel may be given a token payment for their services. Any and all other debts should be settled as soon as possible and the "books" closed. The tournament manager who is himself well organized will probably find other details which may require a follow-up and will see that the follow-up is accomplished.

Organizing and managing a debate tournament is not easy. It should be undertaken by a person only if he plans to give it a great deal of conscientious thought and effort. However, anyone willing to cooperate with other directors of debate in providing profitable and rich experiences for debaters can learn to organize and manage it. He will need to heed the magic words, "anticipation" and "planning," and work diligently to attain objectives through a well-organized and well-managed tournament.

Extemporaneous Speaking

Extemporaneous speaking is the one method by which a speaker can prepare best to *talk* with an audience without being committed to the language of his manuscript and without being dependent on his memory. This method, unlike the methods of speaking impromptu or from a manuscript or memory, permits a speaker who is proficient in its use to focus his attention on his audience, to convey to his audience the impression that he knows his subject and is well prepared, to react to responses by his audience, and to make adjustments in *what* he is saying and in his use of language. If members of his audience seem puzzled, he can rephrase what he has said, add an example or illustration, define a term, and, within his capabilities, make whatever other adaptations are necessary and desirable. Without notes or with the skillful use of brief notes, an extemporaneous speaker has opportunity to give evidence of his sincere interest in both his audience and his subject.

Good extemporaneous speaking depends on the kind and quality of preparation, information, abilities, and personal attributes needed by effective conversationalists and by most effective public speakers. The speaker needs a broad background, acquired from extensive preparation, and organized information which comes only from intensive preparation. He should be able to analyze his audience, to determine his purposes in speaking, to select and narrow his topics, to organize his ideas, to select developmental and supporting materials with which to give meaning and vividness to his ideas, and to adapt himself, his ideas, and his language to the audiences. He needs the personal attributes of confidence, poise, humility, and other socially acceptable qualities which can help him to become increasingly secure, free, and otherwise able to talk with deliberation, enthusiasm, and effectiveness.

Mastery of the extemporaneous speaking method is beneficial and even basic to excellence of speaking by any other method. Until a student develops his abilities and personal attributes necessary for extemporaneous speaking, he might well be stimulated and guided by his teacher to develop these abilities and attributes before he is encouraged to speak from a manuscript or from memory. Until he has developed a degree of proficiency in extemporaneous speaking, the student will likely "hide behind" his manuscript, rely on his memory of words rather than on his thinking, develop affectations in his delivery, and, worst of all, learn these poor speech habits to the point that they must be unlearned before he can ever become an effective and secure extemporaneous speaker. On the other hand, after he learns to speak extemporaneously, he should be encouraged and perhaps required to learn to talk from his prepared manuscript and from his memorized compositions prepared by other speakers and writers.

Since extemporaneous speaking is the method of speaking used by most people in our society and since proficiency in extemporaneous speaking has good effects on the use of other methods and forms of speaking, it is most often included in interscholastic speech tournaments sponsored by high school forensic associations and leagues. Although procedures and methods for teaching students to speak extemporaneously vary, teachers of speech can find the following suggestions to be helpful and desirable in working with students who aspire to become effective extemporaneous speakers.

1. Extemporaneous speaking is probably unsurpassed by any other form or method for its demand for extensive preparation. The speaker must decide on a topic and must prepare his material intensively during the time allotted to him before he begins to speak.

2. Since topics for extemporaneous speaking usually involve either a general topic or numerous specific topics of current interest, students should be encouraged at the beginning of the school year to build and to expand continuously their storehouses of ideas and information. If the state forensic association or league has selected such a general topic as "International Communication," "Educational Opportunity," "Utilization of Natural Resources," or "Governmental Regulation of Television," the teacher of speech should, of course, guide his students in their definitions and analyses of the topic and in their building a bibliography on it. If the association or league has selected a number of specific topics, the teacher should, likewise, guide students in their study of periodicals, newspapers, and books which present ideas and information on them. If topics are not available at the beginning of the school year, the wise teacher of speech

will guide his students to survey the latest issues, for perhaps two or three months, of such publications as the *National Observer, Newsweek, Time,* and *U. S. News and World Report* to identify topics on problems of current interest. Students aspiring to excel as extemporaneous speakers should be, and oftentimes are, avid readers who seek to "furnish their minds" on a variety of topics. Therefore, the wise teacher will not hesitate to guide them to periodicals and books which treat general topics thoroughly.

3. The teacher should consider how the topics are framed. They should be timely, challenging, worthwhile for study by students, and manageable. If a topic is manageable, it is probably limited in its scope and indicative of some line of development that means something to the students. A good topic encompasses valid and reliable material accessible for study. It should challenge the student to solve for himself a problem involved in the topic, rather than enable him to take a stand for or against a proposition embodied in it; and it should give him impetus to seek further argument and evidence to support his position. Ideally, each topic should be framed as a question which cannot be answered by a "yes" or "no." Finally, each topic compared with others should be equally difficult or else the student, when he chooses one, should be able to draw from enough topics to represent the various degrees of difficulty in all of the topics.

4. Students should receive necessary guidance in the use of library facilities for research. The teacher of speech should not assume that his students are familiar with the resources of a library which is well-stocked with materials to make it possible for students to become knowledgeable on many topics. An effort should be made to acquaint the students with the resources of the library and with the various procedures for locating readily information vital to their comprehensive study of each topic. Students would profit much by instruction and a conducted tour of the library by the librarian. The teacher of speech may sometimes join his students in using of the library. He can gain a great deal of satisfaction from knowing that each topic is covered adequately by materials in the library and that the needed materials are accessible.

5. Some students will quickly learn a system for note taking, note filing, and note organizing. Others will need help on how to record, organize, and preserve for future reference ideas and information essential for their future use. It is probably a good idea for the teacher to insist that each student develop an acceptable system and that he use it habitually. Even then, the teacher may well check to assure himself that students record accurately the sources of their ideas and information and that they develop judgment in selecting points, illustrations, examples, quotations, statistics, and anecdotes to serve in developing ideas.

6. A basic aspect of extensive preparation by students is the selection

and organization of ideas. Too often this is overlooked in the emphasis on collecting ideas and information. The teacher should talk with the students and have them read a good deal about speech composition. The students can profit much by their study of outlining in textbooks in pubic speaking and in their own outlining of speeches on a number of topics. The teacher should impress upon his students the need for an effective introduction and conclusion of each of his speeches. Likewise, students should develop an understanding of the various patterns in organizing the body of a speech. Patterns of organizations such as problem-solution, chronological, spatial, and topical should be discussed by the students and the teacher. The students may well be invited to apply each of the patterns in organizing their ideas for speeches on various extemporaneous speaking topics.

7. The teacher should schedule all students interested in extemporaneous speaking in weekly sessions beginning early in the school year. In these weekly meetings, the teacher should call upon students to give progress reports on what they have read, problems they have encountered, any shortages of material on a topic or topics, especially meritorious ideas and developmental materials related to topics, and outlines which they have constructed. Each student should be encouraged and, in fact, be expected to share his ideas and information with other students. Although the students should exercise initiative in these meetings, the teacher should be quick to help students gain insights, analyze the results of their research, define terms, see the need for investigating all phases of each problem or topic, find new sources of information, and evaluate segments of information relating to a topic.

8. Extemporaneous speakers need much participation in practice sessions which are conducted according to the procedures in the next three sections of this chapter. The procedures are like those for conducting contests in extemporaneous speaking in interscholastic tournaments. Practice sessions can be held during some of the weekly sessions already indicated. In each practice session, each student should draw three to five topics, choose one, and return the others to the teacher. He should be expected to prepare intensively for an hour. At the end of the hour, he should deliver his speech to the group and to the teacher. At some of these practice sessions, he should have an opportunity to record his speech on tape for later evaluation. The teacher should use a regular ballot or rating form in evaluating the speaker, his speech, and his speaking. The teacher should conduct a critique during which the speaker should be complimented sincerely on points of his presentation which deserve praise. Likewise, the speaker should receive a careful analysis of all phases of his presentation and be given suggestions for improvement where needed. Attention should be given to his ideas, his evidence and other developmental details, his analysis

and reasoning by which he arrives at his conclusions, his organization, his language, and his delivery. It is a good idea for the teacher to ask him questions to test his breadth and depth of knowledge of his topic and his analysis of it. Also, people who are not members of the group may be invited to participate as listeners and critics in these practice sessions. The teacher should try to help each student develop his inner compulsion to explore his topic thoroughly, exercise judgment in his selection of ideas and materials, organize his speech well, present his ideas effectively, and be prepared to answer questions and to stand cross-examination on his presentation.

Drawing of topics. The drawing of topics in an extemporaneous speaking contest seems to be a significant experience for extemporaneous speakers. In the first place, the speakers may draw numbers to determine the order in which they will draw topics. Or they may draw topics in the order in which they are listed on the program. The teacher, like the manager of a contest, may permit the speakers to draw numbers to determine the order of speaking and thereby determine the order in which the speakers will draw topics. Sometimes the speakers all draw their topics before any of them are permitted to begin their intensive preparation of their speeches. At other times, each speaker draws, in turn, at perhaps seven-minute intervals if the speeches are each five or six minutes in length. In any event, the teacher should manage the drawing of topics so that each speaker has an equal opportunity with other speakers to choose a single topic on which he can prepare and present an effective speech, provided he has done well during the period of his extensive preparation.

Intensive preparation. Intensive preparation refers to the preparation which the speaker accomplishes during the hour between drawing a topic and the time he is scheduled to speak. Sometimes each speaker is assigned to a room where he can take books, magazines, writing materials, and his file box containing information he has collected during his period of extensive preparation, but not speech outlines or manuscripts. He is to occupy the room alone with his topic and materials to prepare during one hour a speech for his presentation at the end of that time. No one is permitted to counsel or visit him.

At other times, by agreement of the speakers and their teachers, the speakers may be "on their own" to accomplish their intensive preparation during the hour between the drawing of the topic and the time set for the speech to begin. The speaker may be permitted to go to a library or to any other place of his choosing so long as he reports at the time and to the place set for his speech. In this case, each speaker is treated as a mature individual who will likely concentrate during the one hour on his topic and on his speech preparation.

In any case, each speaker who has prepared extensively during many weeks or months and who has an hour to prepare intensively is not likely to speak impromptu. On the other hand, only one hour of intensive preparation probably will not be enough for him to prepare a manuscript or to memorize any more than an outline of his speech.

Speaking. When the time comes for the event to begin, the first speaker reports to the appropriate room with each of the succeeding speakers reporting at approximately seven-minute intervals. Or if all speakers draw topics at approximately the same time, all speakers report to the appropriate room at the time for the event to begin. They speak in the order determined before the hour of intensive preparation. Each speech is limited to five minutes. After a speaker has spoken, he remains in the room until all the other speakers have spoken. Obviously, each speaker is expected to confine his speech to the topic. He may use notes of perhaps fifty words, containing necessary evidence of fact and authority. He is entitled to a timekeeper and appropriate time warnings. He is expected to make clear his analysis of the topic as it is stated and proceed to present a speech which contains only materials relevant to the topic as he analyzes it. As a result of his analysis, he may be wise in leading an audience to appreciate a problem and in helping the audience to see possible solutions to it. Possibly he will present the pros and cons of a single solution. Although he may hold his announcement of his position either for or against the solution, he will likely make clear his position before he concludes. In *talking* with his audience, he can probably do best to the extent that he succeeds in leaving the audience with the impression that he knows his subject, analyzes his topic, understands the problem, has a sound solution for it, is well organized, has ideas supported by evidence, needs no notes, enjoys talking with an audience, speaks with confidence and humility, knows much more than he has time to say, and is sincere in all that he says and does while he is on the platform.

Questioning. Each speaker may be questioned or cross-examined immediately after he speaks. If he is asked a single question, it should be designed to test his analysis of his topic, his reasoning, the relationship of one of his points to the topic, the relevance and significance of developmental details or supporting evidence in his speech, omissions of segments of information or of an aspect of his topic which would make a difference in his conclusions or to the solution of the problem, or his delivery if his speech appears to be memorized. If he is cross-examined, the questions are designed to test in depth his analysis of his topic, the relationship of his ideas and information to the results of his analysis, aspects of his topic which he may have neglected, consistency of his presentation, the soundness of his position on his topic, or any other point related to his ideas, organization, support, or delivery. If the speaker is asked a single question, he is allotted a couple of minutes to answer. If he is cross-examined, the questions and answers are allotted a maximum of three minutes. In either event, the questioner or cross-examiner should be selected before the speaker speaks. Another extemporaneous speaker may be designated or selected by lot to ask a question or to cross-examine the speaker. The judge may be designated. Of course, the judge or judges should consider the questions and answers as factors in the evaluation of each speaker.

Criteria used in evaluation. The criteria which are accepted usually for evaluating extemporaneous speaking, speeches, and speakers include:

1. Relevance. Did the speaker analyze the topic on which he spoke and did he relate the remainder of his speech to the results of his analysis and to the topic?

2. Use of information. Did the speaker present an effective selection of available information and use it to develop his ideas related to the topic?

3. Ideas and reasoning. Did the speaker demonstrate sound, careful, and original thinking and were his ideas clear, valid, and acceptable?

4. Organization. Was an appropriate pattern of organization used and did the speech reveal clarity, coherence, proportion, and unity?

5. Style. Did the speaker's choice of language and his use of language "stir up" in his audience the meaning which he apparently intended?

6. Delivery. Did the speaker's use of his body and voice respond to meaning as he spoke and, being relatively free from distracting mannerisms, promote effective communication with his audience?

7. Desired outcome. Was the speaker's objective stated or clearly implied and did the speaker seem to get from his audience the response sought by him as indicated by his objective?

Rating forms are presented at the end of this section which can assist teachers of speech in formulating their own ballots and rating forms for use in the evaluation and criticism of extemporaneous speaking.

Original Oratory

Oratory is a term which may mystify many high school students, especially as to the kind of speaking it implies. They may infer that it means exaggerated effects in language or delivery, or both. They may associate with oratory embellished, flowery, ornate, unnatural, and distracting language. Likewise, they may associate with the term high-sounding, bombastic, and unnatural delivery marked by a loudness level and other affectations which either obscure or at least detract from a speaker's message. Teachers of speech sometimes refer to "oratund" voices and "oratorical" speaking to

EVALUATION FORM
Extemporaneous Speaking

Speaker _____

Topic _____

Evaluation Scale: 5–Superior; 4–Excellent; 3–Good; 2–Fair; 1–Poor.

Factors Considered	Evaluation	Comments
1. Relevance		
2. Thought Content		
3. Organization		
4. Development of Ideas		
5. Use of Language		
6. Voice and Diction		
7. Bodily Action		
8. Communication		
Total Effect		

Criteria for Evaluation
1. *Relevance:* How relevant is the theme and content of the speech to the subject the speaker selected?
2. *Thought Content:* Does it have depth? Is it logical? Is the approach fresh and challenging?
3. *Organization:* Is the introduction adequate? Are points apparent? Are transitions clear? Is the conclusion adequate?
4. *Development of Ideas:* Is there an adequate use of example, illustration, etc., to clarify? If an argumentative speech, is there adequate evidence and reasoning to prove?
5. *Use of Language:* Does the wording have the simplicity, accurateness, vividness, forcefulness, and "communicative ease" to be expected in an effective extemporaneous speech?
6. *Voice and Diction:* Is the voice pleasant? Is there enough variety and emphasis? Is pronunciation acceptable and enunciation distinct without being pedantic?
7. *Bodily Action:* Does the speaker have "unobtrusive" poise and animation? Is he direct and physically communicative? Does he have distracting habits and mannerisms?
8. *Communication:* Does the speaker have conversational rhythm and fluidity? Mental directness? Does he talk *with* rather than *at* his audience?

Date _____ Judge _____

Adapted with permission by James Robinson, Director, Oklahoma Speech and Drama Services

CRITIC SHEET FOR EXTEMPORANEOUS SPEAKING

SPEAKER _____
TOPIC _____
JUDGE _____

5–Superior
Check each item

	5	4	3	2	1

I. Adherence to subject
   Is the speech a reasonable development of the exact topic selected?

II. Use of information
    Does the speaker present a good selection of available information? Does he use the information to develop his ideas?

III. Organization
     Does the speech reveal the development of an appropriate organizing principle?

IV. Thinking
    Does the speaker reveal sound, careful, original thinking?

V. Delivery
   Directness, spontaneity, control, clarity, appropriateness

Total Effectiveness (Circle one)   5   4   3   2   1

Additional Comments:

Adaptation of the critic sheet used in the Minnesota State High School League

OFFICIAL EXTEMPORANEOUS SPEAKING BALLOT

SPEAKER _____ ORDER OF SPEAKING _____
TOPIC _____

Instructions: The critic will *rate* and *rank* each speaker on his general excellence. He will consider such factors as quality of ideas expressed, integrity and sincerity of the speaker, soundness of thinking, clarity of organization, adequacy and concreteness of developmental or supporting details, comprehension and use of language, acceptability of pronunciation, clarity of enunciation and distinctness of articulation, control and use of body and voice, and general effectiveness as an *extemporaneous* speaker. The critic will *rate* each speaker: 5–Superior, 4–Excellent, 3–Adequate, 2–Fair, 1–Unsatisfactory. He will *rank* the speakers: 1, 2, 3, and so on. He will, please, write a criticism for each speaker. (Please use a separate ballot for each speaker.)

Rating _____ Rank _____

Criticism of the Speaker:

(Continue criticism on back as desired.)

Date _____ Critic _____

Place _____

Prepared by Hugh F. Seabury

suggest a lack of naturalness, flexibility, simplicity, unobtrusiveness, and communicativeness. A few teachers of speech seem to believe that the use of the term "oratory" causes students to demonstrate an attitude which results in practices unsuited to effective speaking and speechmaking. But oratory with its honorable history, significant tradition, and powerful impact on the affairs of men and their courses of action persists as a most challenging activity, especially for men and women in high places in democratic society. Likewise, original oratory is a challenging activity for which intensive preparation occurs in advanced units and courses in speech, in interscholastic forensic tournaments, and in most places in which students are free to exercise their mental and speech powers to persuade.

An *original oration* on an appropriate topic of a student's choice implies that the topic is important and that the speech is the result of the student's intensive preparation. Intensive preparation implies a clear statement of purpose to appeal to the best motives of men and to move them to high aspirations and action, sound reflection on the topic and detailed analysis of the subject matter encompassed by it, judicious selection and arrangement of ideas in a meaningful pattern of organization to enable the speaker to attain his purpose, imaginative and sound choice of developmental and supporting materials with which his ideas are documented, a high degree of compression of thought with no irrelevant or distracting ideas or language, and meaningful and correct language which says exactly and interestingly what the speaker means to say to get from his audience the response he desires.

Original oratory implies that the oration is a product of the student's thinking, writing, and speaking. The assumption is that the student selects a topic, analyzes it, develops a central theme, and writes and memorizes a speech which satisfies the criteria of oratory as he delivers it from memory.

The fact is that the student may prepare extensively on topics on which he expects to speak extemporaneously and, during preparation, may become motivated to prepare intensively on one or more of the topics and, as a result, present an original oration which meets the criteria of oratory. In such an exceptional case, the student does not speak from memory and he may not have written his speech but, being full of his subject, aroused by it, and successful in his choice of language, he is effective in moving his audience to high aspirations and noble action. Nevertheless, each student who expects to achieve the desired outcomes of original oratory is expected to write his "oration" and to memorize it. During the process, he is expected to avail himself of the opportunity to profit by his intensive experience in research, assimilation and organization of his ideas on a topic, precision in his choice and use of language, delivery which manifests thought and conviction, and a presentation which arouses his audience.

Sometimes it is difficult to determine what is original and what is not. A student who abstracts an article, merely paraphrases the language of another, or who uses, as his own, excerpts from an article or articles can hardly be credited with originality. The term "original" implies:

1. That the student does not copy extensively from any source or sources.

2. That he credits all identifiable sources from which he draws ideas and passages.

3. That he emphasizes an aspect of a topic which is not ordinarily the focal point of attention.

4. That he uses a new and unique approach or viewpoint in developing a theme.

5. That as a result of his thinking and imagination he presents unique divisions of a subject and succeeds in revealing new relationships within the subject.

6. That he adapts and applies an old idea or truth to a new set of circumstances.

7. That he reasons from a set of facts and opinions which have not been weighed heavily in consideration of a problem.

8. That he gives emphasis to an idea by his correct and unique choice and use of language and thereby gives new meaning to the idea.

9. That he identifies a socially significant problem, moves the audience to want the problem solved, and enables the audience to visualize a significantly improved people, institution, or situation as a result of his audience's facing the problem and helping to solve it.

10. That he shapes an idea in language which gives the clearest and best expression of the idea.

Although few high school students—or adults, for that matter—can successfully lay claim to originating an idea which is completely new, no high school student or teacher of speech should be frightened by the prospect of his qualifying for original oratory with ideas or the treatment of ideas which are new to him and probably also to his audience.

The selection of an appropriate topic for an original oration is, oftentimes, most difficult. The topic should grow out of the experience, thinking, and feeling of the orator. In selecting a topic, a student might well ask himself, "About what controversial issue, problem, or topic do I have the most knowledge and conviction? Is it the one topic with which I can most likely sustain my interest and arouse the interest of an audience? Can I, in the time allotted to me, make an audience see its significance?" An appropriate topic is one which will likely challenge the orator and his audience. It reflects good taste and lends itself to a significant and worthy purpose. It can be narrowed so as to be treated adequately in the ten minutes which are usually allotted to each speaker. It is one which the orator can likely keep fresh, new, and up to date.

Topics and titles may differ. A topic of an oration should indicate its subject and subject matter. A title of an oration should challenge attention, arouse curiosity, and stimulate the imagination. The title may allude to its topic but need not reveal either the topic or the subject matter of the oration. It may be selected after the oration is prepared. It should lend dignity to a printed program. Titles of orations of recent years include "Aristocracy in Thinking," "Civilized Brutality," "Death Has Favorites," "Failure Breeds Success," "Human Driftwood," "The Eleventh Volume," "The Golden Door," "The Mighty Pen," "The Negro Pursues Happiness," and "They Can Teach Us." Every oration should be given a title. Every orator should begin the preparation of an oration with a topic.

After an appropriate topic is chosen by a student, the wise teacher of speech will talk with him about some of the basic requirements of preparation: the need for thorough knowledge through research on the topic, the need to understand the basic principles of speaking, the importance of a suitable organizational pattern, the effect of "oral style" in oratory, and the need for suitable delivery. Basic considerations in the preparation of an oration include:

1. Determine the *purpose* of the oration. Is it to persuade, to inspire, to eulogize, to commemorate, or to actuate?

2. Determine the *central* or *controlling* idea or theme. Frame it in a single sentence. Fix the idea or theme firmly in mind and keep it in mind during the planning, organizing, thinking, writing, memorizing, and speaking.

3. Make certain that the purpose can be accomplished by the develop-

ment of the central idea or theme within the time limit. Otherwise, the topic needs to be limited further.

4. Work out a tentative outline utilizing information already possessed. If the topic embraces an important problem, state the problem and its significance, identify the causes of the problem, list possible solutions of it, analyze each solution to identify the advantages and disadvantages of it, and arrive at a solution which can be recommended with confidence. If a person, institution, or other object is chosen to eulogize or commemorate, list the attributes which are admirable and worth noting, significant achievements or contributions, and characteristics around which the oration can be built.

5. Recognizing that the outline is tentative, proceed with research. Read as many sources as possible. Don't rely on any one article for evidence and support. Don't ignore firsthand experiences and thinking which may offer the most important type of developmental material for the speech. Be ever mindful of the fact that unsupported generalizations have no place in oratory.

6. Reorganize the outline to the extent that its reorganization is suggested by the material which has been collected. Look carefully at the structure of the speech. Both the audience and the orator need clear, easy-to-follow organization. The introduction should gain the attention of the listeners, arouse their interest in the topic, and draw their attention to what is said. State or imply clearly the objective. Plan the speech around the central idea or theme and indicate clearly the main ideas joined together by logical transitions. Make sure that the supporting materials such as examples, illustrations, facts, statistics, quotations, analogies, anecdotes, and other details, relate clearly to the basic ideas underlying the theme. Identify the over-all organizational plan as chronological, spatial, topical, problem-solution, cause-effect, or a combination of two or more of these patterns of organization. Plan a conclusion to present a final summary related clearly to the theme, a quotation which carries the point of the message, an emotional appeal, a plea for action, or a combination of two or more of these possible parts of a conclusion. Determine the suitability and effectiveness of the conclusion and make sure that it does conclude.

7. After the organizational plan or pattern has been developed, "talk it through" to reveal any defects in organization, reasoning, or support. *"Talking* it through" can help the student remember that he is preparing a *speech* when he moves to the next step in writing his oration.

8. In writing an oration, emphasis on appropriate and meaningful language cannot be too great. The speaker should paint word pictures for his audience, and strive for vividness, imagery, and concreteness. As the student writes his oration, he will likely find it helpful to read aloud

while he is writing because his reading aloud what he writes tends to enable him to speak with an "oral flavor."

9. Once the rough draft of the oration has been written, it should be read aloud to the teacher, to friends, and to any others who are available for the purpose of criticism and evaluation to make certain that the ideas are clear, the language effective, and the delivery communicative.

10. Finally, through much practice, the student makes the oration a part of himself. He does much more than merely memorize words. He presents the oration so effectively that an audience feels he is inventing, developing, and projecting himself and his ideas as he talks. The use of a tape recorder to enable the student to listen to himself can aid him in achieving his goal of *talking* with his audience.

Original oratory requires practices and skills necessary for effective public speaking. It requires an original oration on a topic vital to the student who selects it. It requires him to analyze his topic, to select a central or controlling theme, to organize his ideas clearly, and to develop and support his ideas resulting from his research and reflection. The student becomes motivated to choose and use language with which to present meaning accurately and interestingly. He learns to become increasingly effective in persuasion. He develops, sooner or later, the attitude that original oratory at its best is the epitome of excellence in speaking.

Critic sheets used for evaluating the orator and original oratory show remarkable similarity. They set forth elements which qualified persons seem to accept as important criteria by which to determine the effectiveness of the orator and his oratory. Sample critic sheets are included at the end of this section to help the teacher of speech and his students focus on important elements of original oratory and on criteria by which it can be evaluated. The criteria may be used in studying the oration originated by Marlene Zwilling as recorded on pages immediately after the critic sheets in this section.

Non-original Oratory

Non-original oratory, called memorized oratory, oratorical declamation, or oral interpretation of oratorical prose, refers to the presentation, from memory, of another person's oration. For example, a student selects, perhaps with guidance by a teacher of speech, an oration delivered by some orator, masters its meaning and language, memorizes it, and presents it to an audience as if he composed it. The student prepares the oration so well by study and practice that he communicates to his audience the ideas of the orator who first spoke the oration.

358   DIRECTING A CO-CURRICULAR SPEECH PROGRAM

Minnesota State High School League
CRITIC SHEET FOR ORIGINAL ORATORY

SPEAKER _____

TITLE _____

JUDGE _____

5–Superior
Check each item

5   4   3   2   1

I. Central proposition
Does the speech reveal an explicit, reasonable central proposition?

II. Supporting materials
Does the speech present evidence and reasoning adequate to support its major assertions?

III. Organization
Does the speech reveal a useful organizing principle?

IV. Use of language
Is the language vivid, interesting? Is the language meaningful, free from vagueness and ambiguity?

V. Delivery
Directness, spontaneity, control, clarity, and appropriateness.

Total Effectiveness (Circle one)   5   4   3   2   1

Additional Comments:

JUDGE'S EVALUATION FORM

ORIGINAL ORATORY

ORATOR _____

TITLE OF ORATION _____

EVALUATION SCALE: 5–Superior; 4–Excellent; 3–Good; 2–Fair; 1–Poor.

FACTORS CONSIDERED	EVALUATION	COMMENTS
1. Suitability of Subject		
2. Thought Content		
3. Organization		

4. Development of Ideas	
5. Use of Language	
6. Voice and Diction	
7. Bodily Action	
8. Communication	
Total Effect	

Criteria for Evaluation
1. *Suitability of Subject:* Is the subject appropriate, timely, worthwhile?
2. *Thought Content:* Does it have depth? Is the approach fresh and challenging?
3. *Organization:* Is the introduction adequate? Are points apparent? Are transitions clear? Is the conclusion adequate?
4. *Development of Ideas:* Is there an adequate use of repetition, restatement, cumulation, example, illustration, evidence, and so on, for effective oratory?
5. *Use of Language:* Does the wording have the simplicity, accurateness, vividness, and forcefulness essential to effective oratory?
6. *Voice and Diction:* Is the voice pleasant and appealing? Is there enough variety and emphasis? Is there an adequate use of climax? Is pronunciation acceptable? Is enunciation distinct without being pedantic?
7. *Bodily Action:* Does the speaker have "unobtrusive" poise and animation? Is he direct and physically communicative? Does he have distracting habits and mannerisms?
8. *Communication:* Does the speaker have mental contact as well as eye contact with his audience? Is he sincere? Naturally direct? Persuasive? Is he talking *with* rather than *at* his audience?

Date _____ Judge _____

Adapted with permission by James Robinson, Director, Oklahoma Speech and Drama Services

Iowa High School Forensic League
State University of Iowa

OFFICIAL ORIGINAL ORATORY BALLOT

SPEAKER _____ ORDER OF SPEAKING _____

TITLE OF ORATION _____

Instructions: The critic will *rate* and *rank* each speaker on his general excellence. He will consider such factors as vital and stimulating ideas, soundness of thinking, excellence of structure, adequacy and concreteness of developmental details, excellence of language, pronunciation and articulation, control and use of body and voice, and general effectiveness as a *persuasive* and/or *inspirational* speaker whose speaking gives prominence to imaginative and emotional elements. Soundness of thinking and weight of content are supplemented by a degree of eloquence in delivery by a speaker who is stirred, aroused, and challenged by his subject and audience. The critic will *rate* each speaker: 5–Superior, 4–Excellent, 3–Adequate, 2–Fair, or 1–Unsatisfactory. He will *rank* the speakers: 1, 2, 3, and so on. He will, please, write a criticism for each speaker. (Please use a separate ballot for each speaker.)

Rating _____ Rank _____

Criticism of the Speaker:

(Continue criticism on back as desired.)
Date _____ Critic _____
Place _____

Prepared by Hugh F. Seabury

The Golden Door

You are hypocrites. You prove it every time you sing the words of our national anthem, "The land of the free and the home of the brave," or recite the Pledge of Allegiance to our flag, "One nation under God, indivisible, with liberty and justice for all." The time has come for you and me and every other person who professes to be an American to feel guilty and ashamed. If we could pause long enough in our self-glorification, we would hear the rest of the world laughing at us. Our Statue of Liberty stands in New York harbor, supposedly a symbol of freedom and democracy in America, the golden door which is open to all.

The golden door is a myth; it does not exist in America. Instead, there are two doors; they stand side by side; they look alike. Many people will swear they are the same, but examine them closely. You will find that one door is actually made of gold. The other is made of bronze, but it has been polished to look like gold with the most expensive polish man has ever devised. The polish is called, "Separate, but equal." One other characteristic distinguishes these two doors. The golden door is marked, "For whites only"; the bronze door is marked, "Colored."

In a short time, I will be given the right to vote. Along with countless other young Americans, I have been told that we are the hope of the future. The task of maintaining America's ideals will be in our hands. And that task assumes new responsibilities, for today a divided world looks to America for guidance. A world which stands at the crossroads between Communism and Democracy. In view of this crisis, we can no longer afford the cost of maintaining two doors. We cannot afford segregation.

Roughly one-third of the world's people have already turned left at the crossroads to communism. Another one-third has turned right to democracy. The remainder of the people who stand undecided hold the fate of the world in their hands, for it is doubtful whether one-fifth of the world could remain free if the other four-fifths embraced communism. It is here that we begin to pay the tremendous cost of the second door. The majority of the undecided people who hold our future in their hands are colored. How can they believe us when we tell them that democracy will keep them free and when behind our golden door they see small children turned away from our schools with bayonets?

Our recent ambassador to India reported that no American returning from Asia can doubt that the status of the American Negro is the key to our country's relationships with the awakening nations of Asia and Africa.

We must expand his theory to include the entire world. Hitler, so the story goes, once sent a mission to the United States to study our methods of discrimination.

The United States Army, marching into a small town in Germany during World War II, assembled the townspeople to explain what the occupation would mean to them. The first order given by a colonel from the Army Intelligence Corps was that German women were not to associate with Negro troops. The bewildered townspeople asked for an explanation and the colonel replied impatiently, "You must understand that the Negro in the United States is the same as the Jew in Germany."

Anti-American propaganda has an effective weapon in its hands when it attacks our "Achilles heel" of race relations. The prestige of the United States hit an all-time low in the fall of 1957 when Governor Orville Faubus defied openly the Supreme Court of the United States and closed the schools of Little Rock, Arkansas. The repercussions of this act were world-wide.

Pravda, noting that Secretary of State Dulles had said our foreign policy was based on moral and religious principles, commented acidly, "The pictures and illustrations from Little Rock show graphically that Dulles' precious morals are in fact bespattered with innocent blood." Communists in Italy published a cartoon showing our Statue of Liberty garbed in the robes of the Ku Klux Klan, holding a burning Negro child in place of a torch. The condemnation of the United States was not confined to Communists alone. The *London Daily Herald*, voice of Britain's Socialist Labor Party, stated, "There's something rotten in the state of Arkansas, rotten through and through, a white-skinned rottenness that oozes from an evilish, unseen pigment in their souls."

This, then, is the cost of our second door. As *Commonweal* magazine reported, "For many years the segregationists, whether they are disguised as states' rights or separate but equal advocates, have combined with out and out supremacists in subjecting millions of Americans to a state of degradation which has made the name of America, once a synonym with freedom, an abomination in the eyes of a large part of the human race."

The South is an old man, an old aristocrat, who stubbornly insists on maintaining the traditions of the past even though the foundation is crumbling away beneath him. Eventually, the traditions will die of themselves as the integration of Virginia's schools proves. Then, does it not seem sensible to wait for time to weather away our golden door? We cannot afford to wait. From somewhere amidst the chaos and hatred, we must find the tools to tear down the second door.

Booker T. Washington stated, "In all things purely social, we can be as separate as the fingers, but one as the hand in anything essential to mutual progress." This seemed to be the solution for him. However, we must find the way to be one as the hand in all things.

Perhaps the answer lies in the courts of law which are beginning slowly to outlaw segregation on state and local levels.

Perhaps it lies in education. The song from Rodgers and Hammerstein's *South Pacific* says, "You've got to be taught to hate." If you can be taught to hate, then you can also be taught not to hate.

There are many possible solutions, perhaps they will all work, perhaps an entirely new one will be introduced. Regardless of which we choose, our generation must seek to find one. We must end our discrimination of racial minorities or be content to surrender the moral leadership of the world.

We must break down these two doors and replace them with one large enough to accommodate all Americans, a door without a sign.

Prepared by Marlene Zwilling and presented by her at Saint Cloud State College

This activity can be valuable for any student of speech. He has an opportunity to study great speeches by great speakers whose impact on audiences and, later, on readers of the speeches, was profound. Although the student may be guided by his teacher to read speeches by British and even Greek orators, the student will likely select an oration by a contemporary American orator. Ideally, the student studies orators and their orations until he finds a speech that interests him greatly or in which he can develop and sustain much interest. He needs to select a speech with ideas with which he agrees, appeals which arouse him, support for ideals which are his or which can soon become his, and language within his capability but beyond his present level of language usage. The oration he selects should make it possible for him to speak with conviction and, at the same time, to grow in his knowledge, understanding, and ability, and thereby sustain and stimulate further his interest in oratorical prose and the ideas and language of it. A value of non-original oratory which the student will probably realize first is his own development of the finer points of delivery in his communication with an audience. Herein, as every teacher of speech probably knows, lies a danger for the student who recognizes a significant change in his delivery without realizing that he is developing affectations and other poor habits of speaking and, at the same time, not mastering what he has to say.

A student's first concern in choosing an oration should be his own mental and physical capability for understanding, maintaining interest, memorizing, and delivering the oration of his choice with profit for himself and his audience. Mentally, any contemplated oration must be within the scope of the student's understanding and imagination. This is of prime importance because the orator must be able to comprehend the meaning himself before he is permitted to attempt to "stir up" the meaning of the oration in an audience. To comprehend an oration of any consequence composed by a recognized orator, the student must be able to relate it to his own experience. To do so, he needs to be able, as he begins to work on it, to visualize the oration as his and himself as an effective speaker of the oration. Being able to compare and associate the material of the oration with segments of his experience can help the student to amplify and intensify the oration's full meaning. Since all of this is impossible if the oration is beyond his capability, he needs skillful guidance in selecting something suitable for him.

A student's interest must, of course, be considered in his choice of an oration. The teacher knows that the preparation of any significant oration composed by a person other than the student takes a great deal of time, effort, and achievement. Consequently, he knows that the student must have an interest in the oration if the finished product is to mirror his best effort and achievement. Therefore, the teacher should take pains to see that the student selects an oration which will enable him to communicate to the audience the message of the oration with enthusiasm, sincerity, and conviction.

In conclusion, the student should choose an oration which lies within his mental power, which interests him, and which contains a message accepted by the student as one he wants to communicate to an audience.

But mental capacity alone is not sufficient. The oration must be within the physical capability of the individual. A girl in high school trying to do an oration by William Jennings Bryan such as his "Cross of Gold" speech or Patrick Henry's oration entitled "Liberty or Death" is making a problem for herself. Most high school girls, or women for that matter, lack the vocal quality, variety, and power of these orators. Even if they had the voice properties, the effect would likely be greatly reduced or weakened compared to that presented by a man or boy, especially by a boy who fits the oration and, best yet, by a boy whom the oration fits. Of course, either of these orations might be presented well enough by some high school girl—perhaps better than by some boy. Nevertheless, the student should ask himself two questions, and, if he does not seem to find the answers, the teacher of speech should help him answer the questions: First, is it within my mental capacity and interests? Second, do I have the necessary physical characteristics and qualities to make an effective presentation of the selection to communicate in the language of the selection its meaning to an audience?

A student is, then, faced with a third criterion for choosing an oration. The message should also be interesting to listeners. Consequently, the message should be timely. No matter how tremendously important and effective an orator *may have been*, his oration should not be used by a high school student if it is outdated. But some speeches may be very old, even a century, and still be timely because the problems presented in the orations are still problems which concern and even baffle people today. Two examples tend to clarify both of these points. In 1896, William Jennings Bryan won the presidential nomination allegedly with his tremendous oration on bimetallism. Today, however, this particular subject is hardly compatible with current economic theories and is hardly a concern of people. Thus, the message is outmoded and the oration should be avoided even though the orator and his orations merit study. On the other hand, Abraham Lincoln faced a problem which is still prevalent, plaguing our country, baffling people today, and a likely issue which must be faced in a presidential campaign and election. An oration by Abraham Lincoln on the problem of civil rights and responsibilities is timely, intensely interesting to many people, and likely to be significant for a high school student to present and for an audience to hear.

Thus the student should be stimulated and guided to select a significant speech within his mental power, his physical capability, and within the interests of people today.

After he has selected an oration, the student should exhaust every means of learning the background of it, seeking out meaning of words, analyzing passages, and learning to know the orator whose oration he is making his own. For example, if the student is going to use an oration by Wendell Phillips, he should be aware that the orator was an antisegregationist, a "dry," and a socialist, that he was a champion of the "underdog," and that he was one of the finest orators of all times. Also, the student should learn that Wendell Phillips had definite ideas on phrasing and delivery, that he gave much thought to these ideas, and that he "practiced what he preached." Without such understanding, a high school student can hardly appreciate or even ascertain the significance of these factors as evidenced in the texts of the orations.

Obviously, it is difficult if not impossible to communicate the message of an oration if the speaker knows not of what he speaks. Therefore, the high school student has responsibility for knowing the subject matter of the oration and for understanding its exact meaning. Likewise, a teacher of speech knows that he is responsible for his student's grasp of the message. The teacher knows also that the student develops a mastery of the selection as suggested by his development of a sympathetic understanding of the imagery and of sensitiveness to the mood of the oration.

Preparation in delivery is also necessary. Although the oration falls within the student's potential capability, his voice and speech should show command of the oration's meaning and his delivery should stir up the meaning in the audience without imitating the originator. By developing his own delivery techniques, the student can "be himself" and, in no case, an exhibitionist. Until the student understands the oration and knows its meaning, masters it as if it were a product of his own thinking, and develops his own abilities to communicate to an audience the intended message and meaning, he should not memorize the oration, because all these elements should be a part of his memorization. Memorization should be accomplished by the "whole" method because piecemeal memorization tends toward piecemeal thinking, delivery, and mood. Therefore, the following principles of memorization should be applied:

1. Memorize out loud.

2. Read the oration through from beginning to end, think of the meaning, and gain the ideas and thought of the originator.

3. Keep the feeling and spirit of the oration alive by retelling it and working on it when the mind is fresh and alert.

4. Keep working on it, at many intervals, until it is memorized with its full meaning assimilated and its language mastered.

The student's success will be determined, ultimately, by his communication with his audience. Therefore, his success ties in directly with his delivery techniques. No pattern of delivery is certain in its effect. Of course, poise, sincerity, and spontaneity are essential. The student must, with the help of the teacher, learn to communicate ideas rather than to recite words, to give vigorous utterance to the oration rather than no emphasis, and to be conversational and direct rather than exhibit himself merely as an orator. Since audience contact is necessary for effective delivery, the student can find surprisingly helpful results if he practices with an actual audience or an imaginary one rather than listening to himself recite.

The role of voice in delivery is important. The volume, pitch, and inflection of the voice combine to effect obtrusive or unobtrusive delivery. The student needs to develop "vivid realization of the idea at the moment of utterance" characteristic of excellent conversational speech. Oftentimes, the best learning by the student occurs in delivery. For a student who is a "beginner" in speech, the results can be staggering. Again, the teacher of speech must make every reasonable effort to make the results staggeringly good in their effect on the student's speech and speaking.

Bodily action is a problem which each student with the aid of his teacher will need to solve. Gestures, referring to any bodily movement or action used for the purpose of communication, should never detract from the "spoken word" or its meaning. On the other hand, oral utterance should never suffer from a stiff, formal presentation when the meaning of the material lends itself to bodily action and possibly to bodily movement. Probably the teacher of speech will need to help the student to find his answers to these questions: "Does the student seem to be presenting the speech in a natural manner? Is it believable that the student might be trying to persuade a group of his acquaintances that what he is saying is worthy of their consideration?" If so, then the use of bodily action and movement is probably as good as the teacher can hope for. If not, then the teacher will need to continue working with the student to help him develop bodily action or movement which is natural for the student and which aids his persuasive power. With persistence, the teacher may elicit the student's bodily response to the meaning of what he is saying. An analysis of a sentence, a phrase, or a word which results in the student's grasp of the thought or feeling, or both, will likely cause him to respond bodily as well as vocally to the meaning. The teacher should not attempt to impose a gesture or bodily movement on the student. If the student cannot respond adequately to the meaning, probably the student should not continue to practice until he learns to respond naturally to the meaning of his oration. Until he further studies the oration or other similar material and learns to respond acceptably to the meaning, his delivery will develop poorly.

Any student is likely to ask, "Where can I find an oration that meets the necessary specifications?" A wise teacher should not direct him to any one oration. Instead, he will lead him to such current publications as the *Congressional Record, Vital Speeches of the Day*, volumes of *Representative American Speeches*, books of winning orations, newspapers that cover texts of speeches, and other publications in any well-stocked library. Material for students interested in non-original oratory can be found almost anywhere, for intelligent men and women are always thinking and communicating their ideas to others. Oratorical declamation is largely a recreation of this process.

The student of speech who is successful in *talking* with an audience to communicate ideas expressed by great speakers gains a special value that should not be overlooked. Every teacher who believes that a student can profit most by learning first to speak well extemporaneously recognizes the appeal of declamation to a student who is uninitiated in speech activities but interested in participating. The teacher understands that the student may choose to depend on the ideas and language of another person as a way of improving his speech delivery and for gaining self-confidence. The wise teacher of speech understands also that non-original oratory serves well in stimulating and guiding the student to other speech activities from which even greater benefits accrue. A well-qualified and dedicated teacher of speech would not be contented with a student's confining his speech enterprise to any one method of speaking or to any one speech form or activity.

The main purpose of a student speaking memorized oratory is to communicate with an audience. This goal should be uppermost in the student's mind whenever he "delivers" a speech. Every time the student speaks in the presence of his teacher, the student should feel that the teacher has not heard his speech before. The teacher should help him to maintain this feeling. Also, the teacher should stimulate and guide the speaker to convey the meaning of his oration as clearly and efficiently as possible.

Criteria for use in the evaluation of a student's effort in non-original oratory are set forth in the ballots and evaluation forms which follow.

ORAL INTERPRETATION OF ORATORICAL PROSE

ORAL INTERPRETER _____

TITLE OF ORATION _____ _____

(Speaker)

Instructions: The critic will rate each oral interpreter on his general excellence. He will consider such factors as (1) *Selection:* Is it oratorical prose? Is it worthy of study, because its ideas are vital and stimulating and because it challenges the abilities of the oral interpreter to interpret and communicate to a high level of his capacity? Does it present ideas clearly? Is it suitable for an educational activity, for the oral interpreter, and for the audience and occasion? (2) *Interpretation:* Has the oral interpreter analyzed his selection? Does he understand it? Does his interpretation seem to be informed and reasonable? (3) *Speaking:* Does the speaker command involuntary attention? Does he talk with his audience with suitable voice, bodily action, articulation, pronunciation, and general deportment? Does he seem to be stirred, aroused, and challenged by his subject and his audience? Does he seem to evoke the desired response?

Rate each oral interpreter as follows: 5–Superior; 4–Excellent; 3–Adequate; 2–Fair; or 1–Unsatisfactory. He will, please, write a criticism for each oral interpreter. (Please use a separate ballot for each oral interpreter.)

Rating _____

Criticism:

(Continue criticism on back as desired.)

Date _____ Critic _____
(Signature)

Formulated by Hugh F. Seabury

JUDGE'S EVALUATION FORM
Standard Oratory

Speaker _____

Title of Oration _____

Evaluation Scale: 5–Superior; 4–Excellent; 3–Good; 2–Fair; 1–Poor.

Factors Considered	Evaluation	Comments
1. Suitability of Selection		
2. Adequacy of Preliminary Remarks		
3. Apparent Understanding of Selection		
4. Communicativeness		
5. Voice and Diction		
6. Bodily Action		
Total Effect		

Criteria for Evaluation

1. *Suitability of Selection:* Does it have enough merit (as a speech rather than as an essay) to justify the time devoted to it by the speaker? If not dealing with a current significant problem, is it something that deserves preservation?
2. *Adequacy of Preliminary Remarks:* Does the speaker tell enough about the oration, orator, circumstances under which it was delivered, etc., to enable the audience to understand and appreciate the oration? Does the speaker give adequate reasons why he considered this oration worth the time necessary to memorize and practice it?
3. *Apparent Understanding of Selection:* Does the speaker appear to grasp the political and social significance of what he is saying? Does he appear to feel his subject matter? Does he appear to be speaking "from the inside out" rather than "from the outside out?"
4. *Communicativeness:* Does the speaker appear to be talking "with" rather than "at" his audience?
5. *Voice and Diction:* Is the voice pleasant and persuasive? Is there enough variety and emphasis? Is there an adequate use of climax? Is pronunciation acceptable? Is enunciation distinct without being pedantic?
6. *Bodily Action:* Does the speaker have "unobtrusive" poise and animation?

Is he direct and physically communicative? Does he have distracting habits and mannerisms?

Date _____ Judge _____

Adapted with permission by James Robinson, Director
Oklahoma Speech and Drama Service

CRITIC SHEET FOR ORATORICAL DECLAMATION

SPEAKER _____

TITLE OF ORATION _____

JUDGE _____

5–Superior
Check each item

5   4   3   2   1

I. Choice of selection
Is it appropriate to speaker and to the situation?

II. Communication of meaning
Does the speaker reveal complete understanding of the selection, and communicate this understanding?

III. Spontaneity
Is the speaker free, physically and vocally, to respond to the meaning of his selection?

IV. Control and clarity
Does the speaker use voice and action to make communication more complete and exact?

V. Audience contact
Does the speaker achieve significant identification with his audience?

Total Effectiveness (Circle one)   5   4   3   2   1

Additional Comments:

Adapted with permission of the Minnesota State High School League

Student Senate

Organization of people in groups to examine and weigh arguments and evidence for and against proposed solutions to problems and courses of action is basic to our American system of government. In our democracy mature men and women are privileged and obligated to participate in deliberative assemblies. Business sessions of city councils, school boards, parent teachers' associations, church societies, service clubs, political conventions, chambers of commerce, and many other community organizations need active men and women who know how to exercise their privileges and obligations efficiently, harmoniously, and beneficially. Likewise, men and women who respect and know how to protect the rights of the majority, of the minority, of individuals, of absentees, and of all people collectively are needed in deliberative assemblies on state, national, and international levels. Our governmental institutions and societal organizations are dependent on people who are prepared to assume their responsibilities in performing their deliberative and other duties in the councils of the state and nation and, increasingly, in world organizations and councils.

If a high school student is to prepare for active and effective participation tomorrow in private and public affairs on all levels of our government and society, he needs to learn today how to exercise his rights and perform his duties as a citizen and to respect the rights of others and to recognize their duties and responsibilities in all kinds of public assemblies. Perhaps this kind of preparation in citizenship and public service is the most significant and most needed part of his education. Only by being an active member of organizations in which reasonable rules of American democratic processes are observed and practiced can he become a useful school citizen and develop attitudes, understandings, abilities, and attributes as a foundation for useful citizenship and essential community enterprise.

A forensic enterprise sponsored most recently by some state forensic associations and leagues is a legislative assembly, student congress, or student senate. Its purpose is to provide opportunity for the high school student to meet with his peers in parliamentary assembly, to propose in legislative form bills containing their ideas on how best to solve current problems recognized by them as significant, and to debate and vote on the bills in accordance with acceptable parliamentary procedure based on standard rules as set forth in Robert's *Rules of Order*.

Although these assemblies vary in details of organization and in their minute procedures, the American Assembly founded in 1950 at Columbia University and sponsored in recent years in a number of states, the Student Congress of the National Forensic League, and the Student Senate of the Iowa High School Forensic League are examples of forensic group enterprises which provide opportunities for high school students to exercise themselves in the kind of deliberation essential for useful, public-minded citizens. In the Iowa Student Senate which meets each year in December and again in April procedures and regulations similar to those in other state and national forensic organizations apply. High school students propose, debate, and vote on bills of their own authorship with emphasis on deliberation and decision-making regulated by parliamentary law.

Bills. A bill submitted by a high school student for consideration in the student senate pertains to any timely and important problem. Each bill selected by a committee of students with faculty supervision for deliberation proposes a solution for the one problem stated in the bill. The sifting committee which selects bills for the docket of the student senate weighs each bill received by it by these criteria:

1. The timeliness and importance of the problem stated in the bill.

2. The appropriateness of the problem and its proposed solution for investigation, deliberation, and learning by high school students.

3. The relevance, practicality, and succinctness of the recommended solution as it is stated by the author of the bill.

4. Its potential for stimulating interest, at least adequate preparation, and imaginative thinking and deliberation by the peers of the author of the bill.

5. Its potential contribution to a docket of significant and challenging bills on a variety of state, national, and world problems.

6. The authorship of the bill including its form, organization, paragraphing, sentence structure, and preciseness of language. Although these criteria are used by the sifting committee in making the final selection of bills for the docket, each bill accepted by the committee for consideration is free from argument for or against the adoption of the bill; it is no more than 150 words in length; it is double-spaced on a typewritten sheet; and it is approved by a teacher of its author.

A sample student senate bill is presented at the end of this section. Perhaps the sample bill is indicative of the capabilities of some high school students for recognizing timely and significant problems, thinking imaginatively and realistically of solutions to the problems, and preparing bills which reflect excellence of authorship. During recent years the student senators have debated proposals to develop the world's food resources, establish uniform traffic signals throughout the several states, strengthen the United Nations, set minimum emergency requirements in hospitals, recognize Red China, provide for presidential succession in case of incapacity of the President of the United States, and others.

Preparation. Preparation for the deliberation of state, national, and world problems and their solutions needs to be a continuous process by citizens and potential citizens in a democracy. As in extemporaneous speaking, extensive preparation for participation in deliberative assemblies should begin early in the school year. Teachers of speech can stimulate students to become aware of significant social problems, to analyze the problems, to seek their causes, to propose in their discussions possible solutions, and to analyze the solutions in an effort to find the right and the best solution. Each of the problems lends itself to small group discussions which afford some preparation for debate. In some schools, main motions, resolutions, and bills for parliamentary debate are framed and local legislative assemblies are provided to give students opportunity to engage in mock legislatures and congresses. As a part of the preparation, teachers stress the importance of thorough understanding of parliamentary law and how to use it to facilitate free, informed, and responsible debate. These teachers are alert to counsel students who get the false notion that parliamentary procedure is a set of regulations for manipulating group action by confusing the group or interfering with majority rule.

As a result of the extensive preparation by students, bills are selected in each school and mailed to the state office of the student senate at least six weeks prior to the beginning of the first session of the student senate. The bills finally selected for the state student senate are reproduced in quantity and copies are mailed at least one month before the student senate convenes to all the schools which enter student senators in the state student senate. Then, students in each of the high schools begin intensive preparation on each of the bills. The preparation consists of each student marshaling argument and evidence for or against the bill as it is stated or as he chooses to amend it on the floor of the student senate.

Organization. The Iowa Student Senate is held at the State University of Iowa. Each member school sends a maximum of six students. At the opening session, the student senators hear a keynote speech and elect their officers: a speaker, speakers pro tempore, head clerk, reading clerk, recording clerk, and sergeants-at-arms. Graduate students in the university department of speech serve as both temporary and advisory officers during the three sessions of the student senate. Selected teachers of speech in high schools serve as parliamentarians.

Parliamentary debate. Parliamentary debate begins after the author of a student senate bill reads his bill to the senate, it is seconded, read again by the reading clerk, and declared by the presiding officer of the senate to be open to debate. The advisory officers of the senate work with the elected officers to maintain a climate for free and effective debate which is governed by specific parliamentary regulations with the head parliamentarian deciding, finally, on all questions of order. Some specific regulations governing debate include:

1. The author of each bill is entitled to the first and last speeches on it.

2. No speech on the floor of the student senate shall exceed three minutes in length.

3. The presiding officer shall recognize no student senator a second time until all other student senators who seek the floor have been recognized.

STUDENT SENATE

4. The head clerk shall maintain a roster of the authorized student senators and assist the presiding officer in recognizing them.

5. The recording clerk shall maintain a record of all action taken by the student senate and present the minutes of the sessions to the chairman of the league immediately after the close of the final session.

6. The presiding officer shall not debate a bill until he relinquishes the chair to a speaker pro tempore, and shall not vote except in case of a tie vote.

7. The presiding officer shall make every reasonable effort to stimulate the pro and con arguments on each bill and debatable motion before he "puts the question to a vote."

8. The presiding officer and the student senators shall recognize the decisions of the head parliamentarian as final on any questions of order.

9. The presiding officer shall demonstrate firmness, fairness, and friendliness as well as efficiency and effectiveness as the presiding officer of the student senate.

Criteria. Criteria for use by judges in evaluating the student senate are set forth at the end of this section.

Student Senate Bill Number _____

By Mr. Howard Berg of University High School, Iowa City

An Act to Admit Hawaii and Alaska to the Union of the United States of America

1. Be it enacted by the Iowa High School Forensic League
2. Student Senate:
3. That the Territory of Hawaii, consisting of the Hawaiian
4. Islands: Hawaii, Maui, Kahoolawe, Lanai, Molokai, Oahu, Kauai,
5. and Niihau; and the Territory of Alaska, consisting of Alaska
6. and the islands of Nunivak, St. Lawrence, Kodiak, and the
7. Pribilof and Aleutian Islands, be admitted to the Union of the
8. United States of America as the forty-ninth and fiftieth states
9. by not later than January, 1955.
10. The citizens of the above named shall be subject to the
11. Constitution of the United States, the Constitutional Amendments,
12. all acts and rulings of Congress, the decisions of the President,
13. and all rulings of the Supreme Court.
14. All statehood requirements and proceedings, as stipulated
15. by the Constitution and deemed necessary by Congress, shall be
16. met before the date of admission.

Submitted by Howard Berg, a student in University High School, to the Chairman of the Iowa High School Forensic League in February, 1954, for consideration by the 1954 Student Senate. A motion for its adoption carried.

Iowa High School Forensic League
State University of Iowa

OFFICIAL STUDENT SENATE BALLOT

Session: I II III IV Place _____ Time _____
(Circle one)

Approximate number present _____

Instruction: In evaluating the work of each student senator, including each officer, please keep in mind the following criteria: (1) The soundness of his position on a motion, resolution, or bill; (2) The relevancy, value, and soundness of his argument in support of his position; (3) The clarity with which his argument is organized; (4) The relevancy, value, and soundness of his development and support of his argument; (5) His analysis, insight, and ability in refuting argument by opponents and in resubstantiating his own arguments; (6) His reasoning ability; (7) His comprehension and use of language; (8) His purpose, understanding, integrity, and ability in the use of parliamentary rules and procedures; (9) His attitude and conduct in the Student Senate; and (10) Perhaps most important, *his over-all effectiveness as a person and student senator throughout the session for the best interests of the Senate and himself.* Please *rate* each student senator, including each officer, whom you have adequate opportunity to appraise: 5–Superior, 4–Excellent, 3–Adequate, 2–Fair, or 1–Unsatisfactory.

Please do not hesitate to interrupt the speaker when necessary to get the name of a student senator and his school. *Please write legibly or print.*

1. _____ _____ _____
   Student Senator   School   Rating
2. _____ _____ _____
3. _____ _____ _____
4. _____ _____ _____
5. _____ _____ _____
6. _____ _____ _____

Please designate below the names of one or more student senators, including officers, which you observe, who, in your judgment, were the best in the session and *rank* them: 1–Best, 2–Second Best, and so on.

                                                          Rank
1. _____ _____ ____1____
2. _____ _____ ____2____
3. _____ _____ ____3____
4. _____ _____ ____4____

Date _____ Critic _____
                                    (Signature)

Your comments concerning any student senator, student senate arrangement and/or procedure, and/or suggestions for improvement of the Student Senate will be appreciated. Use space on the back as needed or additional sheets as needed.

Prepared by Hugh F. Seabury

Oral Interpretation of Literature

Oral interpretation, sometimes called dramatic interpretation, interpretative reading, oral reading, or reading aloud, is the act of attaching to prose or poetry the meaning intended by the author or poet and using audible symbols and visible bodily action to elicit from an audience response to the meaning.

The desired outcome of the oral interpretation of literature is an audience's comprehension, understanding, and appreciation of the meaning and significance of prose and poetry through the communication of both by an oral interpreter. Therefore, the purpose of an oral interpreter of literature should be twofold: (1) to understand the meaning and significance of the prose or poetry as intended by the author or poet, and (2) to communicate the meaning of it to members of the audience so that they can respond to it. Although an oral interpreter can seldom be sure of the precise meaning of the prose or poetry intended by the author, the oral interpreter can be responsible for making every reasonable effort to understand the exact meaning before he attempts to communicate it.

Oral interpretation is one extra-class and interscholastic speech activity which has a curricular base in most high schools. Often it is a part of a course in literature or a course in basic speech development, or both. In a course in literature, the emphasis may be on the *interpretation* of literature with little effort given to *communication* to an audience. In a course in basic speech development, the emphasis may be on *communication* to an audience with too little effort given to the *interpretation* of the literature. In both courses, students could probably gain greater information, insight, inspiration, and pleasure from studying prose and poetry if both teachers were to emphasize "good reading, both silent and oral, of good literature."

Suggested principles and procedures. Principles and procedures are suggested as guidelines in helping students to realize desired outcomes of oral interpretation:

1. Choose selections which are worthy of study, suitable for oral interpretation, and appropriate for the interpreter, the audience, and the occasion.

2. Make every reasonable effort to understand the purpose, theme, and plot of the author or poet as means of developing understanding and

appreciation of the meaning, both logical and nonlogical, of the selection.

3. Study the selection for the purpose of gaining insight into its meaning and realize, as you study it, that what the author or poet had in mind when he wrote it may challenge your imagination in gaining insight into his meaning.

4. Master the words, phrases, and sentences in the selection with the aid of a good dictionary and any other available reference which may be helpful to you in realizing the precise meaning in the mind of the author or poet when he used the words, phrases, and sentences.

5. Study your selection of poetry to recognize and appreciate the full richness of imagery, metaphor, simile, rhythm, and meter of poetic form.

6. Determine early in your study of the selection the method which you will employ to stir up in your audience the meaning of the selection and, if your decision is to speak from a manuscript or book or from memory, practice using the method in time to develop proficiency and confidence in its use.

7. Form in your mind the bodily action suggested by your insight into the meaning of the selection and plan to respond to the meaning rather than to recreate the action per se.

8. Respond to the meaning and inner feeling of the selection during your study and rehearsal of it and avoid extravagant and, if possible, obtrusive bodily action, vocal expression, and speech sound formation.

9. Use bodily action, vocal expression, pronunciation, and speech sound formation which are suited to the selection and its meaning, the author's purpose, the interpreter, the audience, and the occasion.

10. Describe and suggest the bodily action of characters rather than pantomime it because any impersonative treatment tends to direct the attention of the listener to *how* the selection is being read or spoken rather than to *what* the meaning of the selection is.

11. Speak with a voice which is audible, clear, flexible, well modulated, and responsive to meaning.

12. Use pronunciation which is correct and acceptable.

13. Enunciate clearly your vowel and vowel-like sounds and articulate distinctly your consonant and consonant-like sounds.

14. Concentrate on the literature, avoid exhibition and exploitation of yourself, and develop through your practice good art and good taste in talking *with,* not *at,* your audience.

15. Reveal your enjoyment of the selection and your desire to share its meaning with your audience.

Choice of selection. The choice of selection by a student for oral interpretation in interscholastic speech contests and festivals should be approved by his teacher. A student and his audience can benefit by his teacher's stimulating and guiding him to select prose or poetry considered as "the best expression of the best thoughts of the best authors" within the mental and physical capability of the student to interpret and communicate. Without such guidance, the student is likely to choose a selection which is hardly challenging to him beyond his first reading of it and, as a result, neither he nor his audience is likely to find either the selection or his communication of its meaning to be inspiring or worthwhile. Sometimes a student will choose a selection which is beyond his capability, even though this is seldom the case, memorize the words, and speak words without meaning for himself or his audience. Although the student needs to recognize and select prose and poetry of interest and value to himself and his audience, the wise teacher of speech will guide the student in his choice so that the selection meets at least the minimum requirements, which can be determined by criteria such as the following:

1. The selection should fall clearly within the type required for oral interpretation in the contest or festival: humorous, serious, narrative, oratorical, dramatic literature, Bible, and other sorts.

2. The selection should lend itself well to oral interpretation by virtue of its meaning, organization, development to a climax if it has a plot, movement of the audience to understand and appreciate its theme, and communicativeness without obtrusive delivery by the interpreter.

3. The selection should challenge the interest of the student by its ideas which relate to his background of experience and by its meaning which is likely to sustain his interest.

4. The selection should be one which is within the student's capability, both mentally and physically, without likelihood of either the student or his audience feeling that it is unsuitable for him.

5. The selection should challenge the understanding, insight, ability, and pleasure of the student by leading him on to new ideas and new emotions which result in new knowledge and new experiences.

6. The selection should offer the student a satisfying experience as he grasps its meaning, interprets it imaginatively, and communicates it successfully to an audience.

7. The selection should be one which has ample potential to enable the student and his audience to gain immediate and lasting pleasure.

8. The selection should contain elements which relate and appeal to the thinking or feeling of people in general and hold significance for each of them.

9. The selection should be significantly unique either for what it says or the way its meaning is expressed, or both.

10. The selection should have a purpose or theme, balance, proportion, mood, coherence, and unity.

11. The selection should contain well-chosen words, and sentence structure, phrasing, and paragraph patterns which contribute to its clarity, force, and beauty.

12. The selection should challenge the powers of concentration by the student and thereby cause him to forget himself as the meaning of the selection challenges the audience's powers of concentration.

13. The selection should hold potential for leading the student to significant growth in his ability to comprehend and communicate meaning and for leading him to set a new goal or goals for himself.

Although a teacher should weigh each selection by applying to it these criteria or similar ones before he approves it, he should, of course, help the student to apply at least minimum criteria in making his own selection. As the student develops his own standards by which to evaluate selections, the teacher should stimulate and guide him to make choices of prose or poetry, or both, and refer him to anthologies, literature texts, and current periodicals and publications in which he can find selections potentially acceptable for oral interpretation. Without a doubt, the student can find selections which are acceptable to him and for him, except that they may be too long.

Abridging and arranging selections. Many otherwise acceptable selections will be too long to be presented within the time limit of perhaps eight to ten minutes in interscholastic contests and festivals. Although the time limit frequently poses for the student and his teacher the problem of cutting the selection, probably some of the finest selections available are not used because they are not "ready-made," even though the "ready-made" ones may be overworked and, therefore, trite for teachers, older and regular members of audiences of oral interpreters, and perhaps for the student who is permitted to use a "ready-made" selection. Considerations in addition to a time limit encourage wise teachers of speech to guide students to choose new, fresh, and long selections with a view to abridging and arranging each of them. Gilbert[12] outlined procedures for abridging and arranging literature:

> How to cut: 1. Mark off in parentheses the words to omit, and draw a line from the last word before the cut to the first one after it. [It should not be necessary to tell the student not to mark a book which does not belong to him.] 2. Cross out paragraphs or pages to omit. 3. If you are to use a book and will cut several pages, clip the omitted pages together.
>
> What to cut: 1. When possible, cut whole incidents which are not essential to understanding the portion you will read. 2. Cut out characters

[12] Edna Gilbert, "Oral Interpretation and Speech Festivals," *Speech Teacher,* vol. 5, no. 2 (March 1956), pp. 117-120.

who are not essential to the part you will read. . . . 3. Cut any description unnecessary to the setting or the mood. . . . 4. Cut any repetition unless it is necessary for emphasis or for some other obvious reason. . . . 5. Cut the "he said's" once you have established the characters by voice patterns. . . . 6. Cut descriptions of action or manner of speaking: "Mary looked up shyly." Imply this action with voice and movement. 7. Cut profanity or any comparable element which may offend your audience. 8. When necessary, provide transitional words or sentences to avoid any possible lack of clarity which may result from cutting. 9. If the selection is still not within the time limit, cut every other nonessential item.

Another aspect of oral interpretation often criticized is impersonation or acting by the student rather than "reading." Each student should understand that he is expected to recognize his audience and "read" to it without any impersonation or acting. He should know that he is to retain his own identity. The oral interpreter is the communicator of the author's or poet's ideas, moods, and feelings, and he should never lose sight of his role. He appears and speaks, not as someone else, but as himself. He asks his audience to re-create imaginatively what he reads. His vocal and bodily techniques are used only to aid members of the audience in this process of recreation as the oral interpreter employs unobtrusively and skillfully the process of suggestion. Members of the audience interpret the audible symbols and visible bodily action which are perceived by them. The use of a manuscript or book can help the student maintain an awareness of his role as an *oral interpreter*.

Preparation. For effective oral interpretation, the following suggestions for the student's "analysis" of the selection can be helpful:

1. Read the selection, first, in an effort to react to it as a whole.

2. Read the selection again slowly to identify parts of it which you suspect you do not understand, and make a note of these parts for special study.

3. Study the life of the author or poet to learn how his life related to his writing and, if possible, to your selection.

4. Learn the significance of the title of the selection.

5. Use a dictionary to learn the meaning and pronunciation of unfamiliar words.

6. Notice the punctuation marks to see how they help to make the meaning clear.

7. If the selection is a "cutting" of a longer selection, study the longer selection to see how your "cutting" is related to the entire selection.

8. Discover the purpose of the author or poet for writing the selection.

9. Read the entire selection again for the purpose of finding out if it has new meanings for you and if you have a different reaction to the whole selection.

10. State in one sentence the central or controlling idea of the selection.

11. Read a geographical, historical, Biblical, or other literary reference or references to find information which may be helpful to you in understanding the selection and its significance.

12. Study the author's or poet's style of writing and his use of rhythm, rhyme, and other literary devices.

13. Determine the form of literature used and develop your understanding of the limitations and problems of the form: essay, speech, short story, play, poem, and so on.

14. Study the subordination of words and phrases, the organizational pattern, and the climax if the selection has a climax.

15. Look for "key" words which suggest emotion in order for you to be able to respond to the meaning of the selection by your voice usage.

16. Read the selection as a whole with imaginative insight for the purpose of understanding the meaning of the selection.

After careful analysis of the selection by the student, the next step is to help him with his communication. This is based, of course, upon his thorough understanding and appreciation of the selection he is reading. He will probably need to be helped to become aware of such factors as timing, inflectional range and flexibility of the voice, voice quality, patterns of emphasis and stress, spontaneity of expression, acceptable use of bodily action, and freedom from the manuscript even if he will "read" from the manuscript to the audience. The student must be well aware of how communication is affected by facial expression, bodily attitude and posture, voice, and enunciation and articulation. Although the student may practice frequently alone, the teacher should be alert to the student's need for responding to the meaning as he practices. Therefore, the teacher should hear him often enough to correct poor habits of speaking, "mechanical reading," or mannerisms. Thought-provoking questions about the meaning of a sentence, a phrase, or a word asked by the teacher can challenge the student to respond to the meaning of his selection during his practice. A recording of one or more of his practice sessions played back to him and analyzed by him and the teacher can be efficient and effective in focusing his attention on the meaning of a phrase, sentence, or paragraph. The recording can, of course, be used to analyze his communication. Every effort should be made by the student and his teacher to prevent the student from appearing to give a "public exhibition" of oral interpretation and to assure unobtrusive communication of the meaning of his selection.

During his preparation, beginning at least two months before an interscholastic contest or festival, the student should grow as an oral interpreter of literature for the information, insight, inspiration, and pleasure of himself and his audience. The student has an opportunity to grow by his intensive preparation of a single, short selection of literature. He can analyze his selection in its every detail, gain insight into each detail as it relates to the selection as a whole, and assimilate its meaning. Besides understanding and appreciating his selection, he will learn to perfect his speech abilities and attributes, enabling him to evoke from his audience a full appreciation of the selection.

Ideally, his selection will be of such high quality and his stirring up in his audience the meaning of the selection will be accomplished so effectively and, therefore, unobtrusively and with good taste, that the audience and the oral interpreter are interested solely in the meaning and significance of the selection, *not* in the oral interpreter, his skills, or his techniques. A qualified teacher of speech will make every effort to help the student realize this ideal desired outcome. This is not easy to do, because the student can hardly accept or even realize that he is the agent of the author or poet; *not* an actor, impersonator, or public speaker. He is an oral interpreter of literature who seeks no approval or admiration for himself or his performance per se, but one who seeks only to help his audience understand and enjoy the selection. Until the student accepts his role, the teacher is confronted with the challenge of stimulating and guiding the student to re-examine his selection and its purpose, to prepare a précis, to paraphrase the language, and to discuss its meaning. As the teacher tries to get the student to focus on the *meaning* of his selection, the teacher may use other measures to stimulate the student to *talk with* his audience and thereby help the student to get it across to his audience. The teacher may encourage the student to sit down and talk with the teacher in the language of the selection as it is recorded in a book. He may suggest that the student talk from a typed copy of his selection in a notebook or on cardboard. The teacher has the task of helping the student to realize that his goal is to respond to his own understanding and inner feeling, to be refined, natural, and restrained in his physical and vocal response and expression, to avoid extravagant facial expression and all other extraneous bodily action and movement, and to avoid any vocal expression not in keeping with the meaning of what he is saying. At the same time, the teacher can encourage the student to use purposeful bodily action and vocal expression which enhance understanding and appreciation.

The student and his teacher can give much time and effort to preparation of a single selection for oral interpretation in a contest or festival in which the student does superior work. If the selection is one which challenges the understanding, ability, and potential of the student, he can realize much satisfaction from his achievement and his teacher can be equally satisfied by the student's development and growth. However, neither the teacher nor the student should conclude as a result of the student's accomplishment with one short selection that he is, really, an oral interpreter of literature. That should be held in abeyance until the student has had more extensive preparation, which will be achieved through experience in extemporaneous oral interpretation.

Extemporaneous oral interpretation. Extemporaneous oral interpretation refers to a student's analyzing many different selections of literature over a period of months or even a year, preparing intensively for an hour or so any one of the selections, and communicating to an audience the meaning of the selection.

In some interscholastic contests and festivals in oral interpretation, each student interprets orally (1) a selection which he has had opportunity, perhaps during months, to prepare and practice intensively with the stimulation and guidance by a teacher; and (2) a selection which is one of many he has had opportunity to study, analyze, and perhaps practice since the beginning of the school year but which is drawn by lot about an hour before he is scheduled to communicate its meaning to an audience.

For extemporaneous oral interpretation, the students know by the beginning of the school year that selections will be chosen from a general area of literature such as the Bible, plays by Shakespeare, plays by another designated playwright, a designated collection of prose, a designated collection of poetry, or other source. Each student is expected to accomplish extensive preparation for oral interpretation by studying and analyzing the literature in the area designated for extemporaneous oral interpretation during the school year.

After the student arrives at the site of the contest or festival, he draws three to five selections from the area of literature which he has studied since the beginning of the school year, chooses one, prepares intensively during approximately one hour, and reports promptly to the room in which he is to appear. Then, he interprets orally the selection which he prepared before he came to the contest or festival. Immediately thereafter, he interprets orally the selection which he drew about an hour before he was scheduled to appear in the event. He may have five to seven minutes for his oral interpretation of each of the two selections.

In extemporaneous oral interpretation, the emphasis is on each student's understanding the meaning and significance of an area of literature and on his ability to communicate any selection within the area rather than on only one selection which may reflect the analysis and communicative ability of the teacher more than of the student.

The teacher should, of course, concern himself with helping each student develop his understanding and application of basic principles of interpretation, communication, and abridgment and arrangement of selections because these understandings and abilities by the student are the outcomes desired in teaching oral interpretation of literature. In fact, a student's preparation and experience in extemporaneous oral interpretation may afford him learning experiences of greater value than that of working intensively on a single selection. The issue involved here is, of course, moot but the values to be derived by the student who participates successfully in both kinds of experience are hardly debatable.

Criteria and sources. Criteria for use in evaluating oral interpretation of a single, intensively prepared selection and extemporaneous oral interpretation based on extensive preparation of numerous selections of literature are set forth on the next three pages. Sources of literature for oral interpretation are included in the selected bibliographies at the ends of this chapter and Chapter 5.

JUDGE'S EVALUATION FORM

___ *Oral Interpretation of Humorous Literature*
___ *Oral Interpretation of Dramatic Literature*

ORAL INTERPRETER _____

TITLE OF SELECTION _____

EVALUATION SCALE: 5–Superior; 4–Excellent; 3–Good; 2–Fair; 1–Poor.

Factors Considered	Evaluation	Comments
1. Choice of Selection		
2. Adequacy of Introduction		
3. Apparent Insight and Understanding		
4. Characterization		
5. Voice and Diction		
6. Bodily Action		
Total Effect		

Criteria for Evaluation

1. *Choice of Selection:* Is the selection appropriate to the speaker and occasion? Does it have enough merit to justify the time and effort devoted to it in a contest of this sort?
2. *Adequacy of Introduction:* Does it give enough information about the author, setting, and circumstances to establish the proper mood and understanding on the part of the audience? Does it arouse attention and interest? Was the transition from introduction to selection smooth?
3. *Apparent Insight and Understanding:* Does the interpreter appear to have an insight into the mood and emotional implications of the selection? An appreciation of the author's theme, purpose, and point of view? An understanding of the intent of unusual words, allusions, figures of speech, and the like?
4. *Characterization:* Is character delineation vivid and consistent? Is it

secured largely through vocal and facial suggestion rather than through "impersonation" and "acting"? Are transitions between characters smooth without being obscure?
5. *Voice and Diction:* Is pronunciation acceptable? Is enunciation distinct without being pedantic? Is voice clear, resonant, pleasant, and flexible enough to be responsive to mood and meaning? Are these projected adequately?
6. *Bodily Action:* Is there physical poise as shown in posture, gesture, and movement? Does the interpreter avoid distracting mannerisms and other unmotivated activity? Does he avoid "extravagant theatrical projection" although otherwise motivated and appropriate?

Date _____ Judge _____
Adapted with permission of James Robinson, Director, Oklahoma Speech and Drama Service

OFFICIAL BALLOT
Oral Interpretation

Oral Interpreter _____

Selection _____ Author _____

Instructions: The critic will rate each oral interpreter on his general excellence. He will consider such factors as (1) *Selection:* Is it worthy of study because it challenges the abilities of the oral interpreter to interpret and communicate? Does it present ideas clearly? Does it have continuity, theme, and proportion? Is it suitable for an educational activity; for the oral interpreter; and for the audience and occasion? (2) *Interpretation:* Has the oral interpreter analyzed his selection? Does he understand it? Does his interpretation seem to be informed and reasonable? (3) *Speaking:* Does the speaker command involuntary attention? Does he talk with his audience with suitable voice, bodily action, articulation, pronunciation, and general deportment? Does he communicate the meaning with clarity and sincerity? Does he seem to evoke the desired response? Does he seem to "read" or "act" or interpret orally and visually as is expected of him?

Rate each oral interpreter as follows: 5–Superior, 4–Excellent, 3–Adequate, 2–Fair, or 1–Unsatisfactory. Please write criticism of this oral interpreter. (Use a separate ballot for each oral interpreter.)

Rating _____

Criticism:

(Continue criticism on back as desired)

Date _____ Critic _____
(Signature)
Prepared by Hugh F. Seabury

CRITIC SHEET FOR MANUSCRIPT READING

READER _____

TITLE _____

JUDGE _____

5 – Superior
Check each item

	5	4	3	2	1
I. Choice of Selection Suitable, and yet challenging, for reader and audience?					
II. Communication of the Author's Meaning Firm grasp of the author's attitude or tone (comic, serious, satiric, and so on)? Appreciation of the author's manner or style (realistic, poetic, fantastic, and so on)? Clear indication of the author's theme or central idea?					
III. Spontaneity Does the physical and vocal delivery give "an illusion of the first time?"					
IV. Control and Clarity Does the reader manage his body and voice with exactness and precision?					
V. Audience Contact Do bodily action, eye contact, and vocal projection help communicate the selection to the audience?					

Total Effectiveness (Circle one)   5   4   3   2   1

Additional Comments:

Adapted with permission of Minnesota State High School League

Speaking on Radio

Speaking on radio in interscholastic forensic tournaments consists of a variety of speaking experiences such as announcing, newscasting, news commentary, and expository speaking. In one state forensic organization, each student who participates in speaking on radio is invited (1) to read a prepared script, either original by the student or an adaptation of material written by somebody other than the student, not to exceed four minutes in length on an appropriate topic other than a news item; (2) to read at sight a typical press release of news, travel, science, et cetera; and (3) to "ad lib" an announcement provided for the speaker immediately before he goes on the air. In another state forensic league, each student who enters an event called "News Commentary on Radio" is presented with a news story (or stories), given exactly one hour to read it and to prepare his news commentary based on the story which, incidentally, is just off the press, and invited at the end of his preparation to present within five minutes his news commentary. As he speaks on radio, the student may speak from a manuscript if he prepared one during his hour of preparation, from memory if he prepared and memorized his news commentary, from an outline or notes, or with no notes.

In at least one state speech association, each student who enters the radio event is expected to be prepared with an original speech of a kind which he and his teacher choose and on any appropriate topic of the student's choice. The student may speak from a manuscript, from memory, or extemporaneously. After he has spoken for not more than six minutes, he reads news material presented to him immediately after he finishes his original speech.

Finally, one state forensic league sponsors an event called "Expository Speaking on Radio" in which each student presents, within a maximum time of six minutes, an original, expository speech in which his purpose is to explain a process or a concept such as democracy, communism, extremism, civil responsibility, education, or religion.

Although the requirements for speaking on radio vary from state to state and even from tournament to tournament, the objectives to be attained by each student and the desired outcomes to be realized by him are either identical or very similar.

Preparation. The teacher realizes, in helping a high school student prepare to speak on radio, that the basic principles apply underlying the preparation of an effective original oration or speech. The choice of a suitable topic may be peculiarly crucial because a high school student may choose a topic which enables him to attempt to imitate a "performer" whom he has heard on radio or seen on television, who impressed him as easy to do and extremely entertaining, and which is beyond his capability. A professional speaker succeeds oftentimes in making exciting and vivid in radio broadcasts and in telecasts automobile races, athletic games, feats of astronauts, world championship boxing, horse races, and political conventions. From his carefully chosen vantage point and with his professional skill, he elicits from listeners and viewers deserved admiration as a result of his stirring up in them vivid mental pictures of the event as it is in progress. However, a high school student can seldom achieve similar success. The topic should grow out of the student's background of experience, thinking, and feeling. Although it should not be limited to his too mundane experience, neither should it be one which extends beyond his imaginative, mental, and speech powers. It must be held to the time limit for his speech. It should be appropriate and challenging for the speaker and for his audience and, of course, worthy for both. Perhaps unfortunately, *his* audience is unlike audiences which listen to radio broadcasts and, therefore, his teacher of speech can help him to analyze his likely audience in the interscholastic forensic activities.

A student who is required to do "sight" reading on radio can profit from experience in which a teacher of speech stimulates and guides him in analyzing news stories and in preparing and presenting his news commentaries. With a public address system or a tape recorder, or both, the teacher can help the student to duplicate or at least to simulate a radio studio. By obtaining from a local radio station news stories just off the press, the teacher can help the student to gain experience which is similar or identical to that afforded by a radio studio. Schools with modern communication systems often afford students opportunities to present announcements, read brief manuscripts, present short commentaries, and make different kinds of short speeches. In some schools, the teacher will find it possible to arrange with a nearby radio station to use its facilities to give his students the kind of experience needed in preparation for speaking on radio as if in the league event.

A student can profit from encouragement and assistance in learning how to use a microphone. Although the student who is uninitiated in the use of a microphone may have "mike fright," his apprehension about eliciting the desired response from his audience may be greater than his apprehension about using a microphone. Nevertheless, he will need instruction and some practice in speaking into a microphone. He needs to understand that a microphone will pick up his audible symbols only within its range and that it will give amplification and prominence to audible breathing, vocalized pauses, rattlings of scripts, or any other sounds within its range. The student will normally use a bi-directional velocity microphone, which means it is "live" on two sides opposite each other and "dead" on the other two. Therefore, the student needs to be able to stand directly "on beam" or in front of a "live" side. Also, he needs to learn that his voice and speech will be reproduced with greater fidelity or naturalness in some positions within range of the microphone than in others. His lip distance from the microphone should be constant. His script level should be approximately at the microphone level. If he holds it too low, his voice and speech will likely be directed at the script and away from the microphone. If he permits his script to come between his lips and the microphone, it will "cut him off" or tend to interfere with his talking into the microphone. Although these techniques are simple, they may call for much correct practice by a student to enable him to use them habitually and to maintain his confidence and poise in speaking on radio.

Effective speakers on radio maintain lively and communicative conversation in a friendly and informal manner with their out-of-sight audiences. During his practice, a high school student can become increasingly effective by developing a clear, flexible, well-modulated voice responsive to the meanings of what he says. His control and use of his voice, the clarity of his enunciation, the distinctness of his articulation, and the correctness of his pronunciation are invaluable assets in focusing audience attention on the subject matter of his speech. In both speaking and reading from a manuscript, emphasis should be placed on his timing, rate of utterance, inflections, pauses, and emphasis of what is important and subordination of what is less important. Too often when a student reads from a manuscript, it seems easy for him to become monotonous and mechanical in his presentation. His teacher can help him, early in his practice, to mark his script as he tries to speak from a manuscript with vocal variety and with accuracy in stirring up in his audience the exact meanings intended.

During his preparation, a student should learn to apply basic principles of both public speaking and oral interpretation. He needs a speech which is attention-holding from its beginning to its end. The introduction of his speech should open with a statement designed to express a thought which commands attention. As the student leads his audience to his topic or to the controlling idea of his speech, the idea should be one which appeals to a fundamental human motive or *need*. By his statements, the speaker should imply and enable his audience to infer some prospect of satisfying that need or motive. He should not "talk down" to his audience, but his points should be clear and his developmental details relevant, concrete rather than abstract, vivid, and believable. The central idea should pervade the whole speech. His transitions should cause his audience to progress with him in the development of his points and in "moving" with him to his conclusion. His language should be intelligible, tasteful, and interesting. His conclusion should give especial emphasis to the central idea, should again refer to the need or motive, should be brief and pungent, and should conclude with a statement of an idea which is likely to have a lasting effect on his audience. The student should learn to apply the principles of speaking and speechmaking so well that they can guide him during his intense preparation of his speech even if his preparation is accomplished after he draws a topic or materials shortly before he goes on the air. Likewise, he should be able to apply principles of oral interpretation during any short period in which he prepares to speak from a manuscript when he goes to the microphone. And finally, he should be aware that his effect on his audience is dependent on his usage of audible symbols and that he should, therefore, use his voice and audible speech skillfully and unobtrusively to hold attention on what he says or reads.

Standards. Standards are essential for evaluating speaking on radio. Although an understanding of these standards is essential for teachers and critics, each student has a right and an obligation to understand these yardsticks by which his achievement and development are measured. The standards are set forth on the following pages.

JUDGE'S EVALUATION FORM
Radio Speaking

SPEAKER _____

TITLE OR TOPIC _____

EVALUATION SCALE: 5–Superior, 4–Excellent, 3–Good, 2–Fair, 1–Poor

Factors Considered	Evaluation	Comments
Prepared Script		
1. Introduction		
2. Choice of Material		
3. Wording		
4. Communicativeness		
5. Voice and Diction		
Cold Script		
Ad Lib Period		
Total Effect		

Criteria for Evaluation
1. *Introduction:* Does the introduction capture the attention before the listener has a chance to turn the dial?
2. *Choice of Material:* Does the material have enough human interest, personal appeal, and attention value to hold an audience without benefit of a crowd or the physical presence of the speaker? Is it suitable to the speaker?
3. *Wording:* Are the words simple, forceful, vivid, conversational; are sentences easily followed and "digested"; is there freshness and variety in the wording of the script?

4. *Communicativeness:* Does the speaker seem to be talking "with" rather than "at" the listener? Is his rhythm in a "conversational mode?"
5. *Voice and Diction:* Is the pronunciation acceptable? Is enunciation clear and articulation distinct without being pedantic? Are some defective sounds magnified and others distorted?

Date _____ Judge _____

Adapted with permission of James Robinson, Director, Oklahoma Speech and Drama Service

OFFICIAL BALLOT

NEWS COMMENTARY ON RADIO

COMMENTATOR _____

TITLE OR TOPIC _____

Instructions: The critic will *rate* each commentator on his general excellence. He will consider such factors as quality of ideas expressed, appropriateness of his commentary for radio, integrity and sincerity of the commentator, soundness of thinking, clarity of organization, adequacy and concreteness of developmental details, comprehension and use of language, control and use of the voice, clarity of enunciation, distinctness of articulation, correctness of pronunciation, use of the microphone, and general effectiveness as a news commentator on radio.

The critic will rate each news commentator: 5–Superior, 4–Excellent, 3–Adequate, 2–Fair, or 1–Unsatisfactory. He will write a criticism of each commentator.

Please consider carefully whether the speech on radio is a *news commentary.*

Rating _____

Criticism of the Commentator:

(Continue criticism on back as desired.)

Date _____ Critic _____
(Signature)

Prepared by Hugh F. Seabury

Speaking on Television

Speaking on television may consist of a variety of speaking experiences such as announcing, newscasting, news commentary, expository speaking, and others. In one state forensic league, the announced purpose of the television event, beginning in 1954, was (1) to provide experiece for each student to speak before cameras; (2) to provide opportunity for the student to speak extemporaneously *or* from memory with one or more visual aids; and (3) to provide each student with an evaluation of his speech, his speaking, and his use of visual aids.

Choice of topic. The choice of topic for use in this popular event is made by each student with his teacher's counsel and approval. Each student chooses an appropriate topic for a "how to do it" expository speech. Topics which have been selected are indicated by such titles as "The Art of Cartooning," "Hula Dancing," "Developing a Character in a Play," "The Art of Ventriloquism," "Tips on Life Saving," "What's Proper for Her to Wear," "How to Make a Corsage," and "What's Proper Diet." In fact, a variety of interesting and worthwhile concepts and processes have been explained clearly, interestingly, and effectively by high school students who have participated in this event on closed circuit television.

Preparation. The preparation of a five-minute expository speech by a student who plans to speak on television is basically identical to that of a speech for presentation in a classroom, on a public platform, or on radio. Each student who plans to speak on television should be stimulated and guided by his teacher to recognize and to apply the basic principles underlying speech preparation as he plans for his "appearance" and "performance" on television.

Each student is likely to be motivated to prepare intensively during a period of weeks or even months in advance of the date set for his expository speaking on television. Having heard and seen speakers on television, he has probably obtained some background and appreciation of their speech performances. This has challenged his imagination of opportunities for much satisfaction from his own successful speaking on television. Therefore, he is likely to want the chance to prepare more intensively for his "performance" on television than for his speechmaking in a classroom or in any other nontelevised speech situation. Now he is ready to receive help from a teacher who knows procedures for preparing an expository speech and for speaking effectively on television, who can guide the student in systematic use of such concepts and procedures as the following during his period of preparation:

1. Determine and clarify the controlling purpose of his speaking which, to the extent that it is achieved, will effect the response desired by him from his television audience.

2. Analyze the likely television audience and the television studio with its intense lighting, cameras, "boom" microphone, visual stands, studio props, directors, cameramen, and floor crew busily employed and coordinated to give prominence to the speaker and meaning to his speech.

3. Select and narrow a topic which will lend itself to exposition of a concept or process vitally interesting and worthwhile for television audiences viewing on numerous television sets.

4. Prepare a tentative outline in which are enumerated a few main ideas with which to explain the concept or a few steps by which to explain a process.

5. Choose and arrange developmental materials with which to make clear, concrete, and vivid each of the main ideas basic to an understanding of the concept or the steps in the process.

6. Plan visual aids and the use of graphic materials in accordance with specifications enumerated later in this section to hold the attention of the television audiences and to give clarity, concreteness, vividness, and emphasis to the points of the speech or to the steps in the process.

7. Plan a conclusion to give especial emphasis to the central idea and to conclude with a statement of the concept or process to reinforce it as lastingly as possible in the minds of the viewers and listeners.

8. Plan an introduction with an attention-getting and attention-holding opening statement, with reference to the controlling idea of the speech, and with suggestion of satisfaction to be derived by viewers and listeners tuned to the channel on which the speaker speaks.

9. Talk it through in an effort to follow the sequence of the main ideas or steps, to choose language which expresses precisely and interestingly the meaning, and to *talk* extemporaneously with the imaginary viewers and listeners.

10. Write a script of the entire speech with the aid of its outline and the sample form and sample television dictionary recorded later in this section.

11. Prepare visual aids which meet the requirements indicated in paragraph six above and plan to use them during rehearsals of the speech.

12. Rehearse or practice the speech until the ideas and their sequence, the developmental details, the visual aids, and the language are mastered for talking extemporaneously or from a memorized script.

13. Give the speech a title which is likely to attract attention of potential viewers and listeners, arouse their curiosity, and stimulate their desires to see and hear the speaker.

14. Assume responsibility for sending two typed, triple-spaced copies of the script to the director of the television event at least ten days in advance of the event so that he can coordinate the efforts of his production staff to rehearse and televise the speaker when he appears in the studio.

15. Plan to appear in the television studio at least thirty minutes before the time set for the speaker to "go on the channel," to be dressed in attire suitable for television as described on page 396, and to be in control of a copy of the script, visual aids, special props, and of the speaker himself and his speech.

Although these concepts and procedures can serve as guidelines for a student during his preparation, a teacher needs to help him understand the meaning of the concepts and to apply the procedures successfully before the student can realize the potential satisfactions of his "appearance" in expository speaking on television.

Visual aids. Visual aids are used in all kinds of speechmaking and in all kinds of speech situations. They are used in classrooms and on public platforms to aid speakers in their efforts to hold and focus the attention of their audiences on the meaning of what they say, to add concreteness and clarity to their expositions, and to emphasize points to which the aids can be significantly related in their speeches. Except for speakers on radio, visual aids are used to appeal to the sense of sight of each member of an audience as a speaker's audible symbols appeal to the sense of hearing. In most speech situations, a speaker has a "captured" audience because most people are courteous enough to "hear him out" even when they are not interested. However, a speaker on television may have many small audiences sitting in front of television sets which can easily "turn him off" and shift to another channel. Therefore, a speaker who wants to be heard needs to utilize every available means for "keeping" his audience with him. Visual aids which are well prepared, which are significantly related to the points of his speech, and which are used well constitute one means for holding his audience.

Visual aids may take the form of objects which are demonstrated, charts, graphs, blackboards, slides, film strips, and the like by which a speaker illustrates a point. In planning visual aids and in using graphic materials, the student should keep in mind a few specifications of aids required for the benefit of viewers of the television screen. The television picture is a third wider than it is high and, therefore, visual aids which are to fill the screen completely should have a width-to-height ratio of 4 to 3 inches. They must be large enough so that the camera can easily focus on them. They should be small enough so that they are easy to handle. A good size for a visual aid is approximately 16 inches wide by 12 inches high. Each aid should have a 2-inch border so that the cameramen have enough room to focus on the important part of it. Letters and figures should be printed in large block letters and arabic numerals so that they can be seen clearly on a medium "shot" of the speaker and his visual aid. Simplicity in style and detail is a key to good graphic art in television. The student should be sure that his visual aids are *4 units wide by 3 units high.*

Manuscript. A manuscript, or script, is very necessary for directors, cameramen, and members of the floor crew, and very beneficial for the speaker who hopes to realize success and satisfaction on television. In fact, the director and his staff need at least two typed, triple-spaced copies of the complete manuscript consisting of both video directions and cues and audio requirements at least ten days in advance of the date on which the speaker is to appear on television. In addition, the student and his teacher need an exact duplicate of the manuscript received by the director.

The director and his staff need two copies of the manuscript for at least three reasons: (1) After two members of the staff study the manuscript, the director may find it necessary to write to the teacher to request more adequate video direction, to suggest either slight changes or major revisions in either the video or audio portion of the manuscript, or both, with a view to improving the final production, or to indicate that the manuscript is acceptable; (2) after the manuscript is acceptable in its content and form, the director and his staff need to plan the camera "shots" and the floor work necessary to help the speaker succeed; and (3) after the plan is complete, the director and each member of his staff need to know exactly what is going to happen, when the camera "shots" are to be called in a "split-second" sequence, and how to give the speaker and his visual aids adequate television coverage.

SAMPLE TELEVISION SCRIPT

APPRECIATION OF GREAT MUSIC

Fade in title on camera 2
Dissolve to
No. 1 CU of bands playing _____
Table No. 2 waist shot of speaker ____

Follow as he moves to piano

Take No. 1 pianist at piano
Medium Shot (MS)

Take camera No. 1 _____
CU of Bach

(*Play few bars* of "Rhapsody in Blue")

In order to understand the Gershwin music we've just heard, it is essential to know something of the history of modern music so that we can see how the elements developed which really make up this music.

The years from 1700 to the present day (this is the period of modern music) are divided into four ages—classical, romantic, impressionistic, and modern. During the first of these, classical composers adhered strictly to set time and allowed no emotion in their music. In the place of emotion they gave their music an elegance, a polish, a simplicity that has hardly ever been equaled. The most representative composer of this time was Johann Sebastian Bach. (*Pause*) In his "Gavotte" you can see this definite elegance and simplicity.

By courtesy of Dennis Franke, Newman High School, Mason City, Iowa

The student who is to speak on television needs an exact copy of his manuscript so that he can know the plans of the production staff and be cooperative and effective during the rehearsal beginning at least thirty minutes ahead of the time when he "makes his first appearance on television" and ending with the "black out" of the screen after his speech.

The form of the manuscript is important. In order for the student to prepare the manuscript of his speech in a correct and usable form, he will probably need stimulation and guidance by a teacher who knows the correct form and why it is necessary. *In a sample, first-page manuscript on page 394, a correct and usable form is recorded.* Video terms are recorded on the *left side of each page* of the manuscript and the audio terms *on the right.* The video terms give clear direction to the cameramen and members of the floor crew. Lines are drawn from video terms to positions in audio terms in the script to aid the directors. Television terms are used to describe the presentation. The speaker's action is recorded in parentheses and capital letters within the audio portion of the script, so that the directors can direct the cameramen to focus on all changes by the speaker throughout his speech.

Television terms may not be understood by the student but his teacher can obtain for him either a television dictionary or a list of television terms important for use in preparing his script. The following list of terms and their definitions is indicative of those used to facilitate mutual understanding in television:

A Visual	Any pictorial sequence.
Angle Shot	A camera shot taken from any position except straight on the subject.
Aspect Ratio	Proportional relationship of the width of the television picture to its height which should be four units wide to three units high.
Black	Darkest part of the gray scale or, in its extreme, a black screen; "to black" means to fade the television receiver to black.
Control Room	A room adjacent to the television studio from which the program is coordinated.
Cover Shot	A projection shot usually wide enough to cover every performer or object in a scene on television and used when other cameras are devoted to close-ups or tight shots.
CU—Close-Up Shot	A narrow angle picture used for a full screen image of the shoulder and head of a speaker or of another object.
Cue	A signal for the start of shooting, music, narration, or action.
Cutting	A reference to camera transitions; also elimination of undesirable motion.

Dolly Shot	Shot taken while the camera is in motion.
Fade In	The gradual increase from a black screen to a bright and clear picture.
Fade Out	From a bright and clear picture to darkness of the screen.
Floor Manager or Director	Production man who heads the crew in a live television studio and transmits the control director's instructions to actors and speakers on a set.
Monitor	A control kinescope used by personnel to check and preview camera pick-ups or on-the-air pictures.
Pan	To follow the action to the right and to the left by swinging the camera horizontally.
Stand-By	Cue to talent, cast, or crew that the program is about to go on the air.
Take	Signal to "cut" from one camera to the other.
Tilt	Camera movement up or down.
Truck	Movement of camera left or right parallel to the performer.

Appearance and attire. The appearance and attire of a speaker make the difference, other things being equal, in a student's effectiveness in talking with an audience. His posture, clothes, features, eye contact, cleanliness and neatness, and self-control are important. A teacher of speech will recognize much of what is written here as merely a suggestion of good taste for a speaker in any speech situation. However, the teacher can help the student to be aware of the importance of his appearance and attire, especially on black and white television—where, for example, stark black and stark white should be avoided.

For men who speak on television, shirts should be blue, green, or tan, *not* white. Ordinary collars look better than button-down collars which often give the impression on television that they are too tight. If a speaker is standing, his coat and trousers should not appear noticeably different in color unless a specific "sporty" effect is desired. A smaller-sized coat looks better than one that is too large because a large coat appears to sag. The coat should be buttoned. Clothes should be kept in the middle contrast range. The ideal attire for men on television, in both color and texture, is a medium gray flannel suit.

For women who speak on television, suits and tailored dresses are generally more flattering than skirts and loose or bloused jackets unless a special effect is desired. White collars should not be worn. Sheer nylons, satins, velvets, or shiny taffeta should be avoided. Again, clothes should be in the middle contrast range. Ordinary make-up may be used but not rouge. Shiny jewelry is usually distracting. Pearls are good for television.

Both men and women need to understand that the cameras will pick up visible bodily action and status within its range and will give amplification and prominence to every feature, gesture, and facial expression. Likewise, the cameras focus the attention of the television audience on the visual aids and on manuscripts and their use if manuscripts are used. At the same time, a microphone will give amplification and prominence to audible breathing, vocalized pauses, rattling of scripts, or any other sounds within its range.

All of these unique requirements for successful and effective expository speaking on television suggest some values which can be realized by a student who chooses to prepare thoroughly and to meet the standards.

Criteria. Criteria for evaluating expository speaking on television are, for the most part, identical to criteria for evaluating expository speaking in a school classroom, on a public platform, or on radio, except that emphasis is placed on the selection and use of audible symbols in speaking on radio and that special emphasis is given to the selection and use of both audible symbols and visible bodily action in speaking on television. Since a camera can give prominence to visual aids, they are weighted heavily in the list of criteria. Yardsticks of expository speaking on television are set forth below.

EXPOSITORY SPEAKING ON TELEVISION

SPEAKER _____

TOPIC _____

Instructions: The critic will *rate* each speaker on his general excellence. He will consider such factors as *clarity,* including organization, language, and visual aids, *control and use of body and voice, skill at using the television medium for exposition,* and *over-all effectiveness*—the latter having to do mainly with whether the viewers were probably enlightened by the presentation. The critic will concentrate on constructive criticism, including either compliments or suggestions, or both, for the speaker. The critic will *rate* each speaker: 5–Superior, 4–Excellent, 3–Adequate, 2–Fair, or 1–Unsatisfactory.

He will, please, write a criticism for each speaker. (Please use a separate ballot for each speaker.)

Rating _____

Criticism of the Speaker:

(Continue criticism on back as desired.)

Date _____ Critic _____

(Signature)

Prepared by Hugh F. Seabury

Conducting a Speech Contest or Festival

Much of the basic information, which was presented earlier in this chapter for organizing and conducting a debate tournament, applies to conducting a speech contest or festival. "Anticipation" and "planning" are no less "magic" words in conducting a speech contest or festival than in organizing and conducting a debate tournament. A letter of invitation and registration form, pre-planning, schedules of students and judges, preparation and distribution of materials of various kinds to all personnel involved in the contest or festival, tabulation forms for each of the various events, ballots, and a final report are all necessary. Although neither the necessary forms and procedures nor a discussion of them need be presented here, considerations peculiar to contests and festivals in which students participate in various speech events may bear analysis.

Contest or festival. A speech contest implies earnest and perhaps vigorous competition and contention for victory, superiority, first place, highest rank, and recognition for having qualified for an award such as a scholarship, trophy, key or pin, or other prize, including a proclamation of a contestant's having won an event in, or having won, the contest.

A speech festival implies earnest and perhaps vigorous endeavor by each student to achieve excellence in an event and perhaps to be recognized as qualifying for an award by virtue of his measuring up to the criteria of excellence.

Speech contests and speech festivals are not mutually exclusive terms. In fact, some teachers of speech use the terms interchangeably. But two concepts might well be considered in using the two terms: (1) The "contest" implies that each student in an event *competes* with each of the other students in the event for the topmost *rank*. (2) The "festival" implies that each student in an event, *without competing* with any other student in it, strives for the topmost *rating* and that a number of students in the event may attain the topmost rating. Theoretically, the topmost rank, or first place, in a *contest* is assigned to only one student, and each of the other students is assigned his rank order with one student assigned the bottom rank, or last place; but the topmost rating in a *festival* is assigned to each of any number of students who qualify for assignment to the topmost group and each of the other students is assigned to the group for which he qualifies.

Which is the better procedure: (1) To ask judges to *rank* each student in a speech event and thereby assign each student to his rank order? (2) To ask judges to *rate* each student in an event on, for example, a five-point scale with 5.00 high and 1.00 low and thereby assign each student to a group such as topmost, above average, average, below average, or bottommost?

Probably the less one analyzes each of these procedures and its likely effect on the speech behavior of high school students, the more certain he is of his answer. If a teacher of speech has confidence in the abilities and desirable attributes of his students, their preparation, satisfactions to be realized from their successful achievement, their power to excel, and recognition for their speech behavior in a speech event, he will likely prefer that each student be assigned a rank order. His preference is likely to be shared by each teacher of speech who is confident of his students' power to excel in one or more speech events.

Conversely, if a teacher of speech dislikes competitive education and enterprise, extensive and intensive effort, maximum achievement, development of the speech behavior of students to the highest levels of their capacities, or the consequential results of the assignment by a judge or judges of each student to his rank order, he will prefer that each student be assigned to his quality group, especially if few or no students are assigned to either the "below average" or "bottommost" group. His preference bears careful consideration by the teacher of speech whose students are "beginners," unprepared, and lacking in confidence, and who are not likely, for whatever reason or reasons, to be stimulated and guided to greater effort and participation in a speech event by virtue of their assignment to low rank orders.

Neither the procedure for assigning a student to his rank order in an event nor the procedure for assigning a student to his quality group in a festival-contest seems to be the answer. If the purpose of a speech contest is to effect maximum improvement of the speech behavior of the students, neither procedure alone is acceptable. Assigning eight to ten students in a speech event to his rank order is the better procedure for effecting maximum self-effort, self-preparation, self-achievement, and self-development of speech behavior by these students and for giving recognition to their attainment. However, the use of this procedure alone has its shortcomings because (1) it does not reveal to the student, or to his teacher, anything about the quality of his speech behavior except as compared with the other students, which may be high, medium, or low; (2) its successful use depends partly on the questionable assumption that a judge, or even as many as nine judges, can assign each student to his rank order; and (3) it may cause a student with much potential for development who is assigned a low rank order to "drop out" of speech education.

On the other hand, assigning perhaps eight to ten students in a speech event to his quality group is the better procedure for encouraging the greatest number of students in speech education, for effecting improved speech behavior of students assigned to the lower quality groups, and for giving recognition to students for their attainment in relationship to criteria by which their speech behavior is evaluated. However, the use of this procedure alone has its shortcomings because (1) it does not reveal to the student, or to his teacher, anything about his speech behavior compared to that of the other students assigned to the same quality group; (2) it does not challenge maximum self-anything by each of the best students in an event; (3) it probably does not challenge a judge, or even as many as five judges, to be most attentive to each student in an event, most analytical of each student's speech behavior, or most discriminating in his judgment; and (4) it may cause, and probably does, students who have undeveloped potential for improved speech behavior and who are no longer challenged by their assignment to the topmost quality group to "drop out" of speech education.

Since the shortcomings of assigning each student to his quality group tends to be offset by his assignment to his rank order and vice versa, the following procedure is designed to give equal value to the *quality rating* and to the *rank order* of each participating student in a speech contest:

1. Divide the total number of students entered in the event by eight or preferably by six, even though a larger number may be used, to determine the number of groups needed to give each student the best opportunity for both valid judging and for instruction.

2. Assign to each group at least one competent and impartial judge and instruct each judge to *rate* each student on a 5.00 scale with 5.00 high and 1.00 low, to assign each student to a *rank order* after he has heard all students in the group, to write on a separate card or sheet of paper correctly labeled succinct criticism for the benefit of each student, to *teach* the students as if they were his own during approximately thirty minutes as scheduled for him, and to deliver to contest headquarters his sealed ballot and written criticisms without having revealed to any student or teacher any quality rating or rank order and with the understanding that his written criticisms of students' work in the event *will be* presented to the respective teachers.

3. Determine the number of students who *actually appeared* in the group.

4. Determine each student's *rank value* by consulting the correct horizontal line and vertical column on the table below.

5. Add the sum of each student's *rank values* to the sum of his *quality ratings*, assuming more than one judge in the group; otherwise, add his rank value to his quality rating.

6. Assign first place to the student with the higher or highest total, second place to the student with the next highest total, and so on, until ranks are assigned to all students *in the group* and *in the event*.

7. Determine the composite quality rating and rank order of each student by dividing his total by the number of quality ratings and ranks included in his total.

CONDUCTING A SPEECH CONTEST OR FESTIVAL 401

*Table of Ranks Adjusted to a 5.00 Scale
with 5.00 High and 1.00 Low*

Rank Values of Students

*1	1	2	3	4	5	6	7	8	9	10	11	12
If 2:	5.00	1.00										
If 3:	5.00	3.00	1.00									
If 4:	5.00	3.67	2.33	1.00								
If 5:	5.00	4.00	3.00	2.00	1.00							
If 6:	5.00	4.20	3.40	2.60	1.80	1.00						
If 7:	5.00	4.33	3.67	3.00	2.33	1.67	1.00					
If 8:	5.00	4.43	3.86	3.29	2.72	2.15	1.50	1.00				
If 9:	5.00	4.50	4.00	3.50	3.00	2.50	2.00	1.50	1.00			
If 10:	5.00	4.56	4.11	3.67	3.22	2.78	2.33	1.89	1.44	1.00		
If 11:	5.00	4.60	4.20	3.80	3.40	3.00	2.60	2.20	1.80	1.40	1.00	
If 12:	5.00	4.64	4.28	3.92	3.56	3.20	2.84	2.48	2.11	1.74	1.37	1.00

* Number of Students in Each Group

Conceived by Paul Heinberg, devised by Marnell Fliger, and used in the Iowa High School Forensic League, State University of Iowa

The advantage of this procedure for evaluating a student's speech "performance" in a contest event is, obviously, that it gives equal value and emphasis to both *quality* of the student's speech "performance" and its *rank* among others of its kind by the student's peers in a speech contest. However, its use, even on an experimental basis, by a teacher whose objective is to stimulate and guide students in effecting improvement in their speech behavior will likely lead to changes in other contest procedures such as those mentioned above for the benefit of students who participate in speech contests.

Primary objective of a speech contest. The primary objective of a speech contest should be identified and kept very much in the forefront as the manager organizes and conducts the contest. Probably the manager, the teachers, and the judges subscribe to the proposition that each contest should provide the students with the best learning experiences, instruction, evaluation, and new and renewed goals. In a sub-district, district, or regional contest, the manager can easily lose sight of the primary goal of a contest as he concentrates on organizing and conducting "his" contest to determine which students are to advance to the next contest in the state series ending in a state finals. Although he will need to understand and apply the current official rules of the state speech association or league governing the contest, the official rules are not likely to interfere with his organizing and managing the contest to serve its primary objective. In fact, the selection of the best speaker or speakers in each event to advance to the next contest should be interpreted as an immediate, enabling objective which, to the extent that it is served well, contributes to the achievement of the primary objective.

With the primary objective foremost, the current official rules as his guide if the contest is one of a state series, and with understanding of such principles and suggested practices as are presented already in this chapter, a teacher of speech can plan his contest program, beginning by deciding such questions as the following:

1. What kind and how many events are to be included in the contest? If the contest is one of a series in a state association or league, the kind and number of events are probably prescribed in a bulletin or handbook prepared and distributed by the state organization. If the contest is not one of the state series, the teacher who is manager of the contest needs to decide what and how many events are likely to provide the best educational experience for the greatest number of students who may participate. In making his decision, he needs to be realistic in including only the kind and number of events likely to appeal to the educational interests of students and their teachers and which he can manage adequately and efficiently with the room space and facilities, personnel, and time available to him.

2. What room space and facilities are available as needed to enable him to manage a contest consisting of such events as the ten enumerated and discussed in foregoing sections of this chapter? If one event consists of one-act plays, it is necessary to have a stage which provides adequate on-stage and off-stage space and equipment, an auditorium or equivalent space accommodation suitable for an audience, and a very large room or rooms for assignment to schools to enable play directors, casts, and crews to meet their rehearsal and production schedules. If discussions and debates are a part of the contest, the number of suitable rooms available may put a limitation on the number of discussions and debates which can be scheduled. A legislative assembly or student senate makes necessary a large and otherwise suitable room. Speaking on radio and on television requires, obviously, special equipment which can possibly be simulated with much ingenuity and effort. Finally, the manager should exercise his imaginative insight in determining the kind and number of suitable rooms and facilities which can be made available for each event.

3. What personnel are needed and available? A sufficient number of competent and impartial judges who are especially interested and qualified and whose judgments are likely to be accepted and respected must be

available when they are needed. For some events, technicians are needed. Capable, dependable, and informed persons are needed to serve as responsible and tactfully firm chairmen and advisers for one-act play production, student senate, discussion, and speaking on radio and on television, and, if the contest is a very large one, for each event. Of course other responsible people are needed at the registration desk, in the tabulation room, and as hosts, hostesses, and timekeepers. Again, the manager will need to exercise his judgment in selecting and assigning people to ensure efficient, effective, and satisfying conduct of all events in the contest.

4. What amount of time during which to conduct the contest is available and desirable? If the contest is one in a series in a state association or league, the day or days during which to conduct it may be specified and, if so, the manager may find it necessary to adapt his program to the specification. If it is not a contest in the state series, and perhaps even if it is, the manager should plan to provide sufficient educationally productive experiences for the participants. If available time conflicts with the amount of time necessary and desirable for conducting the contest, the manager should, obviously, make his decisions to serve as best he can the primary objective of speech contests.

Ideally, the manager should plan his program to include the speech events which are likely to challenge the best interests, adequate preparation, significant and satisfying achievement, and maximum improvement and development of the greatest number of students. For these reasons, he should provide a variety of events but, at the same time, limit the number as necessary to enable him to manage well the events which are included in the contest.

A manager of a speech contest is fortunate if each event begins on time, runs smoothly, ends on time, and presents no problems. Such a feat may deserve praise, but it does not necessarily indicate or recognize the most praiseworthy outcome of contest management. If, for example, extemporaneous speaking were one of the "smooth-running" events in which each of fifteen or even fifty students drew a topic, prepared intensively for an hour to speak on the topic, spoke for five or eight minutes, was questioned or cross-examined for two or three minutes, received from a critic judge or from three judges assignment to a quality rating and to a rank order, and an excellent analysis of his "performance" and excellent constructive criticism, the feat of management is hardly praiseworthy compared to that of another manager who organized the extemporaneous speaking event to provide the same number of students three similar opportunities in three well-spaced rounds on three different topics and with three different judges or three different boards of judges. If this latter feat of management is accomplished in each of five or more events during a one- or two-day contest, the most praiseworthy outcome of management may be realized even if the events hardly run smoothly and do not end on time. In the first place, the fifteen to fifty students are provided three opportunities each to prepare and to speak on three different topics, to be questioned or cross-examined three different times on three different topics, and to be judged by at least three or possibly nine different critic judges. In the second place, his assignment to a quality rating and possibly to a rank order by at least three and possibly nine judges is much more likely to render for him a valid judgment than he could get from three judges or even nine judges who were to hear him speak once. In the third place, the fifteen to fifty students are provided opportunity to demonstrate improvement in speech behavior and "performance" during the three rounds. And in the fourth place, if the manager gives careful consideration to the selection and assignment of judges, they too may become increasingly well qualified and increasingly interested in helping to effect speech development by high school students.

The manager who has had experience in conducting speech contests knows that it may not be practical or even possible to schedule each student in each of the ten events discussed in this chapter in three rounds during a day or even two or three days. In a one-act play event each play is usually presented once; and on radio or television, more than one performance by a student may not be feasible. However, debate teams participate oftentimes in three or four rounds of debate during a single day and sometimes in eight to twelve rounds during a single tournament.

The question to be answered by a manager of a contest is how best to use the amount of time available to conduct the contest. The answer may lie in his planning, organizing, and conducting the events to use the time available to effect the greatest educational advantage for the students, teachers, and judges.

Having considered the kind and number of events to be included in the contest, the room space and facilities available as needed, the personnel who are needed and who are available, and the time which can be allotted to the organization and management of the contest, the manager is in a position to proceed to the next stage.

Invitation to the school. The invitation to the schools should be mailed, at least two months in advance of the contest, to the principal, teacher of speech, or other responsible teacher or administrator in each high school. The envelope should be addressed to the responsible person by *name and official position* rather than by either name or official position only.

The invitation should be designed to achieve three objectives: (1) To enable the teacher and the administrator to decide whether to enter students in the contest, based on information about it necessary for them to make an informed decision; (2) To enable the teacher and his students who enter the contest to prepare at least adequately for effective and satisfying participation and achievement in the events of the contest; and (3) To enable the teacher who enters students in the contest to cooperate with the manager, based on the teacher's understanding of the information included in the invitation.

The letter of invitation should, therefore, include all information such as the following:

1. Site, date or dates, and time, both beginning and ending, of the contest.

2. Statement of eligibility requirements that representatives in any event in the contest shall be bona fide high school students doing passing work in three of their subjects of the regular curriculum, undergraduates of their school at the time of the events, and under twenty years of age.

3. Statement of the objective of the contest.

4. Name of each event, explanation of the nature of it as necessary, requirements of each student who enters it, number of students who may represent a school in it, regulations governing it, time limits of each performance in it, criteria for evaluating each student's speech behavior and performance, and an indication of any special preparation expected of each student who enters it.

5. The number of events each student may enter.

6. Tentative schedule of the contest arranged chronologically, hour by hour, and showing the number of rounds of each event.

7. An indication of who the judges will be.

8. An indication of any awards in recognition of meritorious achievement by students, such as books, certificates, keys and pins, scholarships, and trophies.

9. Information concerning dining accommodations and housing facilities.

10. Invitation to luncheon or other special event.

11. Amount of individual student entry fee.

12. A statement of any requirements for each school to furnish for its students a judge, a chaperone or chaperones, and a teacher in charge.

13. Time, place, and procedure for registration of personnel upon their arrival for the contest.

14. A reminder that the rules and regulations of the state association or league will apply if the contest is one of the state series or if the rules and regulations apply to the contest which is not one of the state series.

15. An entry form or forms and an entry fee form which indicate clearly all the information and fees needed from the school and with the

deadline for complete registration and fee for each student stated on both forms.

16. Emphasis in the letter of invitation on the deadline for entries and entry fees.

Letter of acceptance. The letter of acceptance by a school of an invitation to enter students in a contest should present all the information and materials required from the school to enable the manager to schedule its students in the events. If the teacher has the necessary information and entry forms at least two months ahead of the deadline and if no real emergencies occur, the letter of acceptance should present all the information and materials required by the manager to proceed with his pre-planning of the contest:

1. The name and address of the school and, if the contest is one in a state series, the district in which the school is located, the name of the teacher in charge of students who enter the contest, and the name and address of each critic judge to be furnished by the school.

2. The name and grade level of each student, the name of the event or events which he intends to enter, and all other information and materials required from him before his entry can be accepted.

3. For a one-act play event, the title of the play, the name of the playwright, a list of the characters and the names of students portraying the characters in the order of appearance on stage, the name of the director and of any other members of the production staff, a diagram of the set plan, information peculiar to the production of the play, a signed statement that the royalty will be paid in advance of the date of the contest, and any special requests by the director are needed by the manager of the contest before he accepts the entry.

4. If discussion is an event, each school which enters students in it is expected to present a list of the names of the required number of discussants, the names of students who may be substituted in a round of discussion, the name of any student qualified to lead a discussion, the name of a student qualified to serve as a recorder, and the name of a faculty member qualified to serve as a moderator of a discussion group.

5. If debate is a part of the contest, each school submits to the manager information as indicated in an earlier section of this chapter on organizing and conducting a debate tournament.

6. For extemporaneous speaking, each school submits a specified number of topics to be consolidated by the manager into a list of topics for use in conducting the event.

7. For original oratory, the title of each oration and, if required, a copy of the oration correctly labeled with the name of the orator, the school, and the director for easy identification are submitted to the man-

ager for his use in preparing program copy, determining that the oration is original with no more than the maximum number of words quoted, and planning the schedule.

8. If non-original oratory is one of the events, the school submits the title of the oration and, if required, the name of the speaker who originated it, and perhaps a citation of the source from which it was taken.

9. If a student senate is included in the contest, each school submits a bill or bills, the names of its student senators, the names of alternates who may be substituted for one or more of its senators in one or more sessions of the senate, and, if required, the names of students qualified to serve as officers of the senate. Probably the manager obtains the names and services of parliamentarians by special invitation to teachers who are qualified.

10. For oral interpretation as an event in the contest, each school submits the title and author of the selection or selections and, if required, a citation of the source of each selection or a copy of it correctly identified with the name of the student, the school, and the teacher.

11. If speaking on radio is one of the events, the school may submit only the name of each student who plans to enter it or, depending on the nature of the radio event, a copy of a prepared speech.

12. For speaking on television, each school submits to the manager two copies of the manuscript prepared by each student in accordance with the specifications set forth in the sample television script presented earlier in this chapter.

13. The completed entry form or forms, the completed entry fee form, the student entry fees, housing reservations if needed, and any luncheon reservations are included in the letter of acceptance by the school which should, of course, reach the manager of the contest in time to meet the deadline for entries.

Although information and materials required from each school are indicated above, each manager determines, of course, the information and material he needs to plan and conduct the contest. He needs to exercise his insightful imagination and ingenuity to obtain from each school the necessary information in a form which can serve him best as he engages in the next stage of his pre-planning of the contest. For example, he may use a 5″×8″ card on which a teacher may submit to the manager necessary information about a single student entering an event. If a card is completed by the teacher for each of his entries and all cards mailed to the manager by the deadline, the cards can serve the manager well in grouping students in each event and in scheduling all students in all events. However, a card will need to be designed by the manager to solicit the information necessary for each event. The following form of a card is designed for use in oral interpretation.

MIDTOWN HIGH SCHOOL

100 Central Avenue   Midtown, _____

ORAL INTERPRETATION   ENTRY FORM

Please type or print.

City _____ School _____ District_____
Teacher in Charge _____ Critic _____
                                              Required if, as, and when needed.

Oral Interpreter (Not to exceed 3. Use a copy of this form for each interpreter. Give the grade level in school: 9, 10, 11, 12.)

Last	First	Middle	G.L.
Title of Prose Selection		Author	
Title of Poetry Selection		Author	

Completed Entry Fee Form must accompany this entry. *The deadline* for entries is stated on the Entry Fee Form.
Mail to: (Name and address of the manager)

Chairmen and judges. Chairmen and judges for a contest should be secured well in advance of the contest for their planning and for the convenience of the manager in assigning them to the various events as he organizes his program and prepares his schedule.

Chairmen of some events may consist of high school students but a faculty member is probably needed as chairman in charge of each of such events as the one-act play event, student senate, and perhaps television. Each chairman is likely to appreciate receiving from the manager, well in advance of the contest, an outline of his procedure and instructions to enable him to carry out his assignment with understanding, ability, and confidence. Each chairman should, of course, be familiar with the details of the event which he is to chair as well as with the duties of his chairmanship.

Each school may furnish a competent and impartial judge to serve one or more events in which his school is not represented by students. The wise manager prepares a list of names and addresses from which to select competent and impartial judges. After he knows the number of judges needed in each event, he may send an invitation to the judges he selects. The letter should state the site of the contest, the date or dates, the event

CONDUCTING A SPEECH CONTEST OR FESTIVAL

or events which the judge is invited to serve, and the starting time and ending time of each. In addition, the judge should be informed of any provisions for lunch, fee arrangements, and instructions including especially those procedures peculiar to each of the events which he is to judge. The invitation should be accompanied by a sample ballot and criticism sheet. The enclosure of a stamped, self-addressed envelope will facilitate an immediate reply.

The schedule. The schedule of a speech contest is crucially important in conducting a well-organized, smooth-running, and, above all else, a most effective and educationally satisfying set of speech experiences for the students. It should be a dependable guide for students, teachers, and all other personnel concerned with the contest. It should include all information necessary to enable each student, chairman-timekeeper, judge, and even the manager and each member of his staff to be at the right place at the right time throughout the contest by his following the schedule hour by hour from beginning to end. It should be accurate in detail, clear, and complete.

If possible, the manager should send a copy of the detailed schedule to each school so that the teacher and students become familiar with it before they arrive at the contest site. Also, at least one copy of the schedule should be posted in a central location at the contest site so that the manager can record on it any necessary changes and so that all personnel can be informed of the changes. In addition, it is desirable for a copy of the detailed schedule to be placed in the hands of each student entered in the contest and in the hands of all other individuals concerned.

Final details in preparation. The final details of preparation are many and time-consuming. Just a few are enumerated below:

1. Make arrangements for a registration center equipped with a desk, identification badges, forms on which to record the names of all personnel from each school as its representatives arrive, a large envelope including at least one copy of the detailed schedule, a map if necessary, and instructions for the teacher in charge of each school delegation. A competent and informed person should be in charge of the registration desk.

2. Set up a tabulation room staffed with personnel equipped and prepared to tabulate the quality ratings and rank order of each student in each event, to retain ballots in order, to distribute criticism sheets to the teachers of students, and to record and post the results of each round of activity in each event in a central location.

3. Set up and staff in a central location an information desk equipped with copies of the detailed schedule, envelopes prepared for chairmen-timekeepers, envelopes prepared and arranged by rounds of events for

judges, a list of chairmen and judges arranged by rounds so that personnel at the desk can check off each one as he reports in advance of each round for duty, a list of extra judges and extra rooms, and information to enable the personnel in charge to answer questions by students, teachers, visitors, and others.

4. If possible, assign a "home room" to each school which may serve as its headquarters during the contest.

5. Make available a bulletin board at a central location reserved for special notices to all personnel involved in the contest.

6. Prepare and post in a central location large envelopes with the names of teachers on the envelopes for their convenience in receiving criticism sheets prepared by judges and delivered to the envelopes by personnel in the tabulation room.

7. Prepare materials and set up procedure for using the materials in each of the events such as extemporaneous speaking topics and procedure for students to draw topics, late news releases or other materials for use by students preparing to speak on radio, and instructions for officers in the student senate.

8. Have available the awards for distribution to students who achieve meritoriously in each of the events.

9. Arrange for publicity in the local school, in the local newspapers, and in the local newspapers of the schools represented in the contest.

10. Arrange for the preparation of a final mimeographed report of all results including the names of students, schools, and teachers for distribution immediately at the close of the contest.

11. Recheck before the end of the day preceding the contest to see that it is organized and ready.

Ideally, a speech contest should function so smoothly that the people involved in it are not aware of "the way it works." By "anticipating" problems, careful "planning" and organization, selecting and assigning dependable and efficient people as members of the staff of the contest, and by being alert to emergencies which may arise, the manager has an opportunity to keep the thoughts and energies of participants and their teachers directed toward excellence of achievement and maximum educational development of students rather than toward expediting events in the contest.

Projects

1. Prepare to present to the class the results of your analysis of desirable and undesirable relationships between curricular, co-curricular, extracurricular, and interscholastic speech education. Be prepared to support or modify your conclusions.

2. Present to your teacher your paper in which you identify problems and their causes in co-curricular speech programs and propose possible solutions for three or four of the most serious problems. Indicate benefits to be derived by students by your proposed solution to at least one of the problems.

3. Prepare to present to the class your statement of guidelines which should, in your judgment, direct the thinking and practice of a teacher of speech in developing and executing a co-curricular and interscholastic program including events such as the ten discussed in this chapter. Support your guidelines and indicate the benefits which you believe could be derived by their application.

4. Review the standards of play selection discussed in this chapter, choose at least one one-act play which, in your judgment, measures up well to the standards, and prepare to explain to the class why the play or plays could be produced to contribute significantly to one or more of the educational objectives of a high school.

5. A director of a one-act play has the task of conducting a try-out or try-outs for the ostensible purpose of casting the play. Explain considerations and problems with which the director is confronted in casting. State your position on each of the most controversial issues involved and support your position.

6. Discussion seems to be a lost event in interscholastic forensic tournaments. Why? Present to your instructor a plan for conducting in a tournament a discussion event which you believe would be educationally productive for students in the event. Indicate the benefits likely to be realized by students.

7. Prepare an outline of procedure which you would recommend for use in working with high school students preparing to participate in two of the individual speech events discussed in this chapter. Indicate differences and similarities in your two outlines. Explain why the differences are significant.

8. In debate, five different plans are explained in this chapter. What are the advantages and disadvantages of each of the plans for high school students? Teachers of debate? Judges of high school debating? Which plan, in your judgment, has the greatest potential benefits for high school students?

9. Assume that you are to serve as manager of an interscholastic debate tournament in which each of nineteen high schools has entered two debate teams. Prepare pairings of all teams for five rounds of round-robin debating. Explain in class how you have the teams paired and the procedure which you used in pairing them.

10. Examine a copy of a bulletin or handbook of regulations of each

of two or three state high school speech associations or leagues. As a result of your examination, explain differences and similarities in the regulations governing interscholastic contest events. Then, explain to the class how you believe the regulations in your own state bulletin or handbook should be improved.

11. Investigate the program of speech education in a high school, perhaps in your home town. Interview the teacher. Present to your instructor a paper in which you evaluate the program. Be prepared to present your report to the class.

12. Outline a suitable plan for initiating and developing a program of debate in a high school. Consider: objectives, ways to stimulate interest, plans for the initial meeting, student activities, ways of sustaining interest and effort by students, and instruction by the teacher.

13. Prepare to present to the class your outline of a plan for working with high school students who are interested in developing their abilities to speak extemporaneously. Include examples of topics, sources of information on the topics, a study plan, note taking and filing, and practice sessions.

14. Choose a one-act play suitable for study and production by high school students. Present to your instructor a prompt book for use in directing the play.

15. As a class in methods of teaching speech, organize and conduct an original oratory contest open to all freshmen on campus. Prepare an announcement of the contest. Plan for each freshman who enters original oratory to have an opportunity to speak two or three times before students are selected to advance to the final round or rounds. Award certificates to the highest rating and ranking speakers.

16. Prepare your analysis of an original oration such as "The Golden Door" in this chapter. Consider title, content, organization, analogies, theme, figures of speech, introduction, and conclusion. Prepare to present to the class the results of your analysis.

17. Outline a plan for organizing and conducting a student senate in a high school.

18. Examine such anthologies of prose and poetry as the ones cited in the bibliography of this chapter. Propose at least four selections which you believe would be suitable for oral interpretation by high school students. Be prepared with reasons for your selections.

19. Outline a plan for working with students who are interested in preparing to speak on television.

20. Present in class the results of your evaluation of a speech contest consisting of at least five different events. Suggest ways in which the contest should be improved.

Selected Bibliography

ARMSTRONG, CHLOE, and PAUL D. BRANDES, *The Oral Interpretation of Literature.* New York: McGraw-Hill, Inc., 1963.

BOWEN, ELBERT R., "Promoting Dynamic Interpretative Reading," *Speech Teacher*, vol. 7, no. 2 (March 1958), pp. 118–120.

CAPP, GLENN R., ROBERT HUBER, and WAYNE C. EUBANK, "Duties of Affirmative Speakers—A Symposium," *Speech Teacher*, vol. 8, no. 2 (March 1959), pp. 139–149.

CATHCART, ROBERT S., "The Case for Group Discussion Contests," *Speech Teacher*, vol. 6, no. 4 (November 1957), pp. 315–318.

COFFIN, CHARLES N., *The Major Poets: English and American.* New York: Harcourt, Brace & World, 1954.

COGER, LESLIE IRENE, and MELVIN R. WHITE, *Studies in Readers' Theatre.* New York: S and F Press, 1963.

COLE, WILLIAM, *The Fireside Book of Humorous Poetry.* New York: Simon and Schuster, Inc., 1959.

COMPERE, MOIREE, *Living Literature for Oral Interpretation.* New York: Appleton-Century-Crofts, Inc., 1949.

GEHRING, MARY LOUISE, "The High School Oration: Fundamentals," *Speech Teacher*, vol. 2, no. 2 (March 1953), pp. 101–104.

GILBERT, EDNA, "Oral Interpretation at Speech Festivals," *Speech Teacher*, vol. 5, no. 2 (March 1956), pp. 117–120.

HARGIS, CLARA N., and DONALD E. HARGIS, "High School Literature and Oral Interpretation," *Speech Teacher*, vol. 2, no. 3 (September 1953), pp. 205–208.

HOOPES, NED E., "What Literature Should Be Used in Oral Interpretation?" *Speech Teacher*, vol. 10, no. 3 (September 1961), pp. 206–210.

HUNSINGER, PAUL, "Festivals and Changing Patterns," *Speech Teacher*, vol. 7, no. 2 (March 1958), pp. 93–98.

KERMAN, GERTRUDE LERNER, *Plays and Creative Ways with Children.* Irvington-on-Hudson, N.Y.: Harvey House, Publishers, 1961.

KLINE, H. CHARLES, and DONALD L. HOLLEY, "A Contest Workshop in Television Speaking," *Speech Teacher*, vol. 12, no. 2 (March 1963), pp. 119–122.

KRUGER, ARTHUR N., "The Extempore Speaking Contest," *Speech Teacher*, vol. 5, no. 3 (September 1956), pp. 214–222.

———, "Logic and Strategy in Developing the Debate Case," *Speech Teacher*, vol. 3, no. 2 (March 1954), pp. 89–106.

MOHRMANN, G. P., "Children's Literature and the Beginning Class in Oral Interpretation," *Speech Teacher*, vol. 13, no. 2 (March 1964), pp. 128–132.

MUSGRAVE, GEORGE M., *Competitive Debate: Rules and Techniques*, 3rd ed. New York: The H. W. Wilson Company, 1957.

NEBERGALL, ROGER E., "The Negative Counterplan," *Speech Teacher*, vol. 6, no. 3 (September 1957), pp. 217–220.

Portire, Dorothy Gamewell, "Selecting the High School Play," *Speech Teacher*, vol. 2, no. 2 (March 1953), pp. 109–113.

Quimby, Brooks, "Is Directing of Forensics a Profession?" *Speech Teacher*, vol. 12, no. 1 (January 1963), pp. 41–42.

Ried, Paul E., "A Spectrum of Persuasive Design," *Speech Teacher*, vol. 13, no. 2 (March 1964), pp. 88–95.

Reutter, D. C., "Providing High School Students with Debate and Discussion Topics," *Speech Teacher*, vol. 12, no. 3 (September 1963), pp. 233–237.

Roberts, Mary M., "Planning a Forensic Workshop," *Speech Teacher*, vol. 12, no. 2 (March 1963), pp. 115–116.

Shepard, David W., and Paul H. Cashman, *A Handbook for Beginning Debaters*. Minneapolis: Burgess Publishing Company, 1957.

Simley, Anne, "Hints for Student Readers," *Speech Teacher*, vol. 6, no. 3 (September 1957), pp. 233–236.

———, *Oral Interpretation Handbook*. Minneapolis: Burgess Publishing Company, 1960.

———, *Stories to Tell or Read Aloud*. Minneapolis: Burgess Publishing Company, 1962.

Speech Association of America, "Dramatics in the Secondary School," *The Bulletin of the National Association of Secondary-School Principals*, vol. 26, no. 166 (December 1949), 272 pp.

———, "Public Address in the Secondary School," *The Bulletin of the National Association of Secondary-School Principals*, vol. 32, no. 187 (May 1952), 318 pp.

———, "Speech Program for the Secondary School," *The Bulletin of the National Association of Secondary-School Principals*, vol. 38, no. 199 (January 1954), 296 pp.

Spolin, Viola, *Improvisation for the Theatre: A Handbook of Teaching and Directing Techniques*. Evanston, Ill.: Northwestern University Press, 1963.

Summers, H. B., F. L. Whan, and Thomas A. Rousse, *How to Debate: A Textbook for Beginners*, 3rd ed. New York: The H. W. Wilson Company, 1954.

Weaver, Carl E., "Coaching the Contest Orator," *Speech Activities*, Spring, 1949.

APPENDIX

Checklist for Teachers of Speech

Self-examination is a necessary step towards improvement. Probably no teacher of speech can answer all of these questions to his complete satisfaction. They are intended merely to suggest practices and attitudes which may be useful, possible, and necessary for many teachers. If shortcomings are found, reasons for the shortcomings should be determined. Their causes may lie in the need for curriculum revision, better teaching methods, additional subject matter preparation, more or better teaching materials, smaller classes, reduced teaching loads, or better communication within the school.

I. Personal and Professional Growth of the Teacher.
   A. How many professional journals in speech and drama do I read regularly? _____
   B. How many professional meetings have I attended in the last five years? _____
   C. How many books not required for courses have I read in the past year? _____
   D. How many plays have I attended during the past year? _____
   E. How many public discussions, debates, and speeches have I heard during the past three years? _____
   F. Other evidence of my personal and professional growth as a teacher? _____
   _____
   _____
   _____

II. Attitudes of the Teacher.
   A. Am I really interested in teaching speech or is it just another chore for me? _____
   B. Am I punctual in getting to class and do I start and close my teaching in the time allotted? _____
   C. Am I reasonably friendly and cordial with my students or am I impersonal and distant? _____
   D. Do I have patience with slower students? _____
   E. Am I easily irritated? _____

III. Classroom Management.
   A. Do I systematically check ventilation, lighting, heating, and cleanliness of my classroom? _____
   B. Am I in full control of my class at all times? _____
   C. Am I fair and reasonably firm, friendly, and enthusiastic during my teaching? _____
   D. Are my assignments definite and regular and do I hold all students accountable for their preparation? _____
   E. Have I learned to ask questions effectively to stimulate thinking and learning by my students? _____
   F. Do I check, through my questioning, whether students really understand what I say, what they say, and what they are invited to do? _____

IV. Preparation Prior to Teaching.
   A. Do I study my students as individuals so that I can help them to learn? _____
   B. Do I prepare my lessons carefully before each class to achieve a specific objective or objectives? _____
   C. Before introducing a new lesson or topic, do I prepare the class for it by reviewing what they have learned as background for the new lesson? _____

V. Teaching Methods and Materials.
   A. Do I make the provocation of thought a basic and primary objective in my teaching? _____
   B. Do I really teach speech so that its values are clearly recognized in the lives of my students? _____
   C. Do I make sufficient and effective use of illustrations, examples, and audio-visual aids in my teaching? _____
   D. Do I use language precisely and tastefully? _____
   E. Do I do too much talking? _____

F. Do I help students correct their mistakes and misunderstandings or do I merely reveal them? _____
G. Do I accept the proposition that if I am not careful in the organization of my teaching most of my better students will likely do well without me? _____
H. Do I provide opportunity for each of my students to bring his own interests and problems into the work of my class? _____
I. Do I help students set up standards by which to evaluate their performances, study, achievement, and development? _____
J. Do I use a positive approach in evaluating students and their work and thereby help them to improve? _____
K. Do I use a textbook as a reference work and supplement it with other appropriate books and other materials? _____
L. Do I use drills only as the need for them arises in the group or in an individual student? _____
M. Do I use the results of my evaluations of my students' achievement and growth for further planning of what and how to teach speech? _____

VI. Appraisal of Results.
 A. Are my students developing as a result of their experiences in my class their powers of discrimination and thereby becoming better listeners and observers? _____
 B. Do my students show their growth in their development of ideas? _____
 C. Are my students improving in their ability to summarize materials accurately and concisely? _____
 D. Are my students improving in their ability to organize materials effectively? _____
 E. Do my students realize that improvement in the various fundamentals of speech such as bodily action, voice usage, language comprehension and usage, adjustment to speech situations, ideas, organization, and speech sound formation contribute to the effectiveness of their speech and speaking? _____
 F. Do my students take pride in effective speech, speaking, and speechmaking and demonstrate their ability and willingness to assume their responsibilities toward their listeners? _____
 G. Are my students learning to listen to detect speakers' purposes and thereby to participate thoughtfully and critically in speech situations? _____
 H. Are my students improving in their use of speech fundamentals? _____

APPENDIX

I. Do my students who are in need of help with their speech problems have opportunity for improvement through extra-class activity under my supervision? _____

J. Does my instruction provide opportunities for learning by students with speech problems and handicaps, the "average" students, and students with special interests and ability in speech? _____

K. Are my students increasingly respectful of the ideas and opinions of others? _____

L. Are my students showing their increasing awareness of the responsibilities of the oral communicator in this age in which mass methods of communication are powerful? _____

M. Are my students growing in their independence and intellect to evaluate their own work and in finding ways for improving it? _____

N. Do I measure the success of my teaching by what my students know, understand, and do as the result of my having worked with them? _____

O. Are my students becoming increasingly self-directive in their thinking, in exercising their initiative and imagination, in their effective cooperation with others, in their courses of action, and in their compulsion to learn, and are they thereby developing adequately their potential and desirable personal attributes as persons? _____

Index

Entries in small capitals indicate forms, outlines, or word lists.

ACHIEVEMENT RATING, 259
ACHIEVEMENT IN SPEECH MAKING, 265
"Activity" approach to teaching, 184–198
Activity programs, speech, 284–290
  co-curricular, defined, 284
  COMPOSITE RESULTS form for use in, 289–290
  events in, 289
  extra-curricular, defined, 284
  philosophy of, 286–287
  role of, 285–286
  suggestions for directors of, 287–289
  weaknesses of, 284–285
  See also Contest or festival, conducting a speech; Debate tournament
Adams, Mary E., quoted, 197
Adjustment to speech situation, 132–143
  activities for development of, 141–143
  basic to learning, 132
  before and after meeting audience, 178–179
  defined, 132–134
  experimental studies in, 133–137
  maladjusted speaker, described, 133
  philosophy of teachers toward, 137–139
  subject to teaching, 140–141
  success in, 133
  suggestions for teaching, 179–181
  speech fright, 132–143
Administrators:
  attitude toward speech education, 47–48
  guiding factors for, 42–60
  habits and voices of speech teachers as concerns of, 49–50
  philosophy of speech teachers, 46–47
  planning and scheduling for speech teachers, 56–58
  preparation for speech teachers, 50–54
  qualifications of speech teachers, 54–56
  See also Teachers of speech
Adolescents, 67–73
Aggressiveness, 68
Alberty, Harold, quoted, 222
Alexander, William M., quoted, 221
Allen, Gracie, quoted, 141
Allen, Kenneth D. A., 158

American Assembly, 7, 370
American democratic society, 1–5, 9–19
  defined, 2
  Greek origin of, 3
  practicability of, and respect for, 3, 5
  success dependent on, 4, 9–19
  ultimate objective of, 2–3
  See also Speech education
American Educational Theatre Journal, The, 105, 276
American Speech and Hearing Association, 52
American Tape Exchange Service, 205
American Telephone and Telegraph Company, 170
Andersch, Elizabeth G., quoted, 163, 173
Appraisal of speech, means for, 71–91
  AUTOBIOGRAPHICAL FORM, 72–79
  autobiographical talk, 72–75
  confidential letter, 72–75
  cumulative records, 72–75, 90–91
  DIAGNOSTIC BLANK FOR VOICE AND SPEECH, 72–75, 84–85
  DIAGNOSTIC FORM FOR SPEECH AND HEARING, 72–75, 81–82
  PROFILE RATING FORM, A, 264
  READING ALOUD RATING FORM, 87
  recording, 72–75, 79–81
  SPEAKER RATING FORM, 72–75, 85–86
  SPEECH ANALYSIS FORM, 72–75, 83–84
  SPEECH INTERVIEW OUTLINE, 72–75, 87–90
  VOICE AND ARTICULATION EVALUATION FORM, 72–75, 82–83
  See also Students

Approaches to teaching speech, 116–220
  activities, 184–198
  fundamentals, 116–184
  subject matter, 198–203
Aristotle, 20
Articulation:
  consonants, concepts and features, 163–164
  consonants, variation in acceptable articulation, 165
  criteria by which to evaluate, 162
  defined, 162
  descriptive elements of, 164
  pattern for teaching, 164–165
  relation to loudness, 163
  unit on voice and articulation, 170
  word list as a teaching aid, 171–172
  Young American Films, 170
Ashbaugh, Kraid I., 185
Attitudes, desirable, 242
Auston, John T., 104
AUTOBIOGRAPHICAL FORM, 72–79
Autobiographical talks, 72–75
Auvitor, 168

Baird, A. Craig, quoted, 20
Bandini, A. R., 175
Barnes, Harry G., quoted, 133
Barnes, John, 154
Basic content and ideas, 118–124
  assigned by the teacher, 118–119
  control patterns for, 119–120
  responsibility of the teacher for, 117–118
  selected by students, 118–120
  suggestions to teachers of, 121–124
  topics to challenge students, 121–122
  topics from speech content, 118
Baskerville, Barnet, quoted, 241, 242

INDEX

Bavely, Ernest, 291
Beecher, Henry Ward, 142
Behavioral goals in the high school, 31
Berg, Howard, quoted, 373
Bills, 371
BIOGRAPHICAL INFORMATION, LIST OF, 129–131
Bird, Donald E., 227
Black, John W., quoted, 162–163
Bodily action for purposes of communication, 143–149
   asset in speaking, 145–146
   basic concepts of, 144–145
   objectives in teaching, 147
   program for development of, 146–147
   suggestions to teachers of, 147–149
   See also Oral interpretation of literature; Plays, one-act
Borchers, Gladys L., 40, quoted, 29, 157
Brandeis, Paul D., quoted, 173–174
Breathing, 153–157
BRIEF PERSONAL INVENTORY, 99
Brigance, William Norwood, quoted, 20–21, 153
Briggs, Thomas H., quoted, 39
Brockriede, Wayne E., 302
Brown, Marion A., 187
BROWN-CARLSEN, LISTENING COMPREHENSION TEST, 183
Bryan, William Jennings, 142
Bryant, Donald C., 63
Buck, Paul H., 13
Buehler, E. C., quoted, 103
Burke, Edmund, 173

Canham, Erwin D., 7
Card Catalog, 129
Cardinal Principles of Secondary Education, 9

Carr, Wilbur L., quoted, 174–175
Cathedral High School at St. Cloud, 273
Central States Speech Association, 108
Central States Speech Journal, 276
CHECKLIST FOR TEACHERS OF SPEECH, 415–418
Chenoweth, Eugene C., 133
Choral speaking:
   pattern for teaching, 194
   suggestions to teachers of, 194
   synonyms for, 193
   values of, 194
   variations of, 193–194
Churchill, Winston, 142, 173
Cicero, quoted, 142
Citizenship, 26
Civil responsibility, objectives of, 11
Clark, John Kirkland, quoted, 24
Classroom control, 95–105
   getting class started, 98–105
   motivation, importance in, 97
   principles of, 96
   suggestions to teachers for, 97–98
Classroom for speech, 269–275
   characteristics of, 270–272
   equipment of, 272–275
   location of, 270
   sketches of, 273
Commission on the Reorganization of Secondary Education, 9
Communication:
   defined, 24
   oral and written, the problems of, 21
   significance of satellites for, 22–23
   See also Speaking; Speech
Conant, James Bryant, 7, 12
Condescending attitude toward students, 98

422 INDEX

Contest or festival, conducting a speech, 397–414
  advantages and disadvantages of, 398–400
  chairman and judges for, 408–409
  concepts of, 398
  entry cards to facilitate management of, 407–408
  invitation to schools, 404–406
  letters of acceptance by schools, 406–408
  planning a speech contest, 402–404
  preparation, final details for, 409–410
  primary objectives of, 400–403
  procedure for equating quality rating and rank order, 400–401
  schedule of a contest, 409
  TABLE OF RANKS ADJUSTED TO QUALITY SCALE, 401
  See also Activity programs, speech; Debate tournaments, organizing and conducting
Confidence and poise, 140, 141–143
Confidential letter, 72–75
Congressional Record, 366
Contributions of speech education, 19–25
  See also Speech education
Conversation, 186–188
COURSE OF STUDY OUTLINE, 184, 197–198
Cousins, Norman, quoted, 27
Criteria for oral communication critique, 262–263
  See also Communication
CRITIC SHEET FOR DEBATE, 339

CRITIC SHEET FOR DISCUSSION, 304–305
CRITIC SHEET FOR EXTEMPORANEOUS SPEAKING, 352
CRITIC SHEET FOR DRAMA, 300
CRITIC SHEET FOR MANUSCRIPT READING, 385
CRITIC SHEET FOR ORATORICAL DECLAMATION, 369
CRITIC SHEET FOR ORIGINAL ORATORY, 358–359
Criticism, 98, 241–251
  art of, 243
  basic principles of, 244
  class, 245
  focus of, 98
  methods of, 246–250
  purpose of, 241–242
  self-, 250
  standards of, 241–243
  student, 248–250
  suggestions for effectiveness of, 245–246
  time for, 247–248
  training of listener-critic in, 244–245
  See also Evaluation
CRITICISM FOR FIRST AFFIRMATIVE SPEAKER ONLY, 337–338
Cronbach, Lee J., 120
Cross-examination debate, 321–322
Crowell, Laura, quoted, 102
Cumulative record system, 72–75, 90–91
Curricular speech patterns, 115
  See also Courses of study; Fundamentals of speech; Program of speech education; Speech activities

Dallinger, Carl A., quoted, 40
Dann, Matthew L., quoted, 44–46

INDEX 423

Debate, 190–191, 308–323
 basic principles of, 312
 cross-examination plan of, 321–322
 direct clash plan of, 322
 discussion basic to, 310
 first meeting for, 315
 heckling plan of, 322–323
 national proposition for, 312–314
 Oregon plan of, 321–322
 organizing for, 315
 problem-solving plan of, 323
 rationale for, 308
 relation to discussion, 190
 responsibilities of speakers in, 319–321
 responsibilities of teachers of, 310–312
 running rebuttal in, 318
 starting the program of, 314–315
 suggestions to teachers of, 191
 topics of a unit in, 191
 traditional plan of, 319
 types of values of, 309–310
DEBATE-DECISION RATINGS, 289
DEBATE REGULATIONS, 334
Debate tournament, organizing and conducting, 323–344
 announcement and invitation to schools, 324
 assignment of judges to, 327
 ballots for, 336–340
 canceling of teams in, alternatives, 330
 CRITIC SHEET FOR, 339
 distribution of materials for, 332
 fees, method of payment, 324
 FINAL REPORT OF, 343
 information for judges in, 334
 LETTER OF INVITATION FOR, 325
 pairing of teams in:
  with safeguards, 327–330
  without safeguards, 331

Debate tournament (continued)
 post tournament activities by the manager of, 342–344
 preplanning for, 325
 regulations governing, 334
 REGISTRATION FORM FOR, 326–327
 SAMPLE INFORMATION SHEET FOR, 315
 schedule of, 333
 TABULATION FORM FOR, 341
 tabulating and posting results of, 340
 timekeeper's information for, 335
Declaration of Independence, quoted, 4
Dedmon, Donald, quoted, 289–290
Deductive and inductive teaching, 109
Democratic processes, 370
Democratic society. See American democratic society
Demos, Raphael, 13
Desirable outcomes of speech education. See Speech education
Detroit Lakes High School, 273
Development, variations in, 69
Details in speaking, 128–132
 assistance in locating, 129
 defined, 128
 developmental and supporting, 128
 responsibility of the teacher for, 129
 sources, classified and specified, 129–131
 suggestions to teachers, 131–132
 system for recording and filing of, 131
Dewey, John, 5, quoted, 21, 26, 88, 175, 189
Diagnosis:
 speech and hearing, 72–75, 81–82
 voice and speech, 72–75, 84–85
 See also Appraisal of speech

DIAGNOSTIC EVALUATION OF DISCUSSION LEADER AND LEADERSHIP, 306–307
Dialect regions of the United States, 166
Dickens, Milton, quoted, 136, 137
Dietrich, John E., 296
Diphthongs, 162
Direct clash debate, 322
Direction of a co-curricular speech program, 285–414
  debate, 308–344
  discussion, 299–307
  extemporaneous speaking, 344–350, 352
  nonoriginal oratory, 357–369
  one-act plays, 291–299
  oral interpretation of literature, 375–385
  original oratory, 350–357
  radio, 385–390
  student senate, 369–375
  television, 390–396
Discipline, 96
Discussion, 189–190, 299–308
  criteria for evaluation of, 303–304
  CRITIC SHEET FOR, 304–305
  defined, 189
  diagnostic evaluation of leaders and leadership of, 306–308
  errors and weaknesses of, 302–303
  OFFICIAL BALLOT FOR, 305
  path to national consensus, 7
  pattern for, 189–190
  place in forensic programs, 303
  procedures in, 299, 302
  suggestions to teachers of, 190
  time limit of, 302
  topics of a unit in, 190
DISCUSSION—SPEECH PROGRAM, 290
Dodge, Emelie Ruth, quoted, 96

Dorden, Colgate W., Jr., 7
Douglas, Jack, quoted, 251, 253
DRAMA, CRITIC SHEET FOR, 300
Dramatic Index, 130
Dramatics, 276
Dramatics, 195, 291–299
  classroom activities in, 195
  objectives of a unit in, 195
  one-act plays, 291–299
  topics of a unit in, 195

Economic efficiency, 11, 31
Ecroyd, Donald H., quoted, 156
Education, 3–19
  imperative needs of youth, 12
  objectives and desired outcomes, 9–19
  primary function of the state, 4
  supreme values of, 4
  system of, 3
  See also Educational objectives
Educational objectives, 9–19
Educational Policies Commission, 28, 32, quoted, 9–12
Effective speech. *See* Speech
Effective thinking. *See* Thinking
Eisenhower, Dwight D., 7
Eisenson, Jon, quoted, 152
Emotional characteristics, 70
Encyclopedias, 130
English and Speech; differences in teaching, 53–54
English Journal, 105, 276
Enunciation:
  Conditions necessary for, 162–163
  criteria by which to evaluate, 162
  defined, 162
  dipthongs, explained, 162–163
  dipthongs, production of, 162
  unit on voice and articulation, 170

Enunciation: (*Continued*)
  word list as a teaching aid, 171–172
  Young American Films, 170
Erickson, Marceline, quoted, 108–109
Ethical character, 28
Evaluation, 241–251
  importance of, 241–243
  methods of, 246–250
  personal conference for, 250–251
  purposes of, 241–242
  role of teacher in, 242
  standards of, 241–242
  times for, 247–248
  written, 246, 247, 248, 249–250
EVALUATION FORM—EXTEMPORANEOUS SPEAKING, 351
Everett, Samuel, quoted, 75
Extemporaneous speaking, 344–353
  BALLOT FOR, 352–355
  basic to other methods, 345
  benefits derived from, 344
  criteria for evaluation of, 350, 351, 352–353
  drawing topics for, 348
  EVALUATION FORMS FOR, 351, 352, 353
  preparation for, 348
  questioning in, 349–350
  speaking in, 349
  suggestions to teachers of, 345–347
Eye, Glen C., quoted, 29, 44

FACTORS FOR ANALYSIS AND REVIEW OF SPEECH TEXTS, 277–279
"Fairness," 98
Familiar Quotations (Bartlett), 130
Featherstone, W. B., quoted, 24
Festivals. *See* Contest and festival, conducting a speech

Film Distributors, 281
FINAL REPORT—INVITATIONAL DEBATE TOURNAMENT, 343
Findlay, John H., Jr., 13
First speech, 102
Fliger, Marnell, 330, 331, 343, 401
Fort, L. M., quoted, 44–45
Franklin, Benjamin, 173
French, Will, quoted, 31–32
Fundamental processes, command of, 23
"Fundamentals" approach to teaching, 116–184
"FUNDAMENTALS" COURSE OF STUDY, 184
Fundamentals of speech, 2, 117–184
  adjustment to the speech situation, 132–143, 178–181
  basic content or ideas, 117–124
  bodily action for purposes of communication, 143–149
  developmental and supporting details, 128–132
  enunciation, articulation, and pronunciation, 161–172
  language, 172–178
  listening, 181–184
  organization of content or ideas, 124–128
  voice usage, 149–161

General education. *See* Education; Educational objectives
Getting a class started, 103–105
Gibson, Francis, quoted, 136
Giffin, Kim, 302
Gilbert, Edna, quoted, 378–379
Gilkinson, Howard, quoted, 135
Givens, Willard E., 5
Goals for Americans, 7. *See also* Societal objectives

"Golden Door, The," 360–362
GRADE REPORT FORM, 259
Grading, 253, 254–258
  bases for, 254–255
  frequency of, 254
  importance of teachers in, 257–258
  purposes and significance of, 254
  sources of assistance for, 254–255
  standards of, 254
  suggestions for, 255–258
  validity and reliability of, 253
Gray, Giles Wilkeson, quoted, 22, 153–154, 155
Greek philosophers and statesmen, 3
Greenewalt, Crawford H., 7
Greenleaf, Floyd I., quoted, 133–134, 135
Gruenther, Alfred M., 7
Guidance programs, 16
GUIDE FOR RECORDING SPEECH OF STUDENT, 80–81

Haefner, John M., quoted, 222
Hahn, Elise, quoted, 156, 162, 165
Hand, Learned, 7
Hanley, Theodore D., 153, quoted, 155, 164
Hargis, Donald E., quoted, 156, 162, 165
Hart, Frank W., quoted, 43–44
Harvard Committee of Twelve, quoted, 12–14
Havighurst, Robert J., quoted, 16–17
Hayakawa, Samuel I., quoted, 174
Health, 23
Heckling plan of debate, 322–323
Hedde, Wilhelmina G., quoted, 153
Heinberg, Paul, 401
Henrikson, Ernest H., 63, quoted, 140

High school, objectives of. See Educational objectives
Hitchcock, Orville A., quoted, 52–53
Hoadley, Leigh, 13
Hochmuth, Marie, quoted, 21
Hollinshead, Byron S., 13
Holtzman, Paul D., quoted, 244
Home membership, 26
Housman, Arthur L., quoted, 58
How We Think, 21, 26
Howell, William S., 339
Human relationships, 10, 30
100 TOPICS DESIGNED TO CHALLENGE HIGH SCHOOL STUDENTS, 121–122
Huyck, E. Mary, 158

Ideas, 25. *See also* Basic content ideas
Idol, Harriett R., 154
Inductive teaching, 109
Informal speaking, 185–188
  conversation, 185–187
  interviews, 187
  social introductions, 186–187
  telephone usage, 187–188
INFORMATION FOR JUDGES—INVITATIONAL DEBATE TOURNAMENT, 334–335
INFORMATION FOR TIMEKEEPERS, 335
INFORMATION SHEET SAMPLE—DEBATING, 315
Insecurity, feeling of, 68
Intellectual interests, 68
International Phonetic Alphabet, 167–168
International Phonetics Association, 168
Interviews, 187
Introductions, 186–187
INVITATIONAL DEBATE TOURNAMENT, 333

INDEX

Iowa High School Forensic League, quoted, 275, 287–289, 336–338, 359, 370, 374, 401
Iowa State Department of Public Instruction, 18–19

Jacks, L. P., quoted, 27
Jewett, Arno, 221
Jordan, Wilbur K., 13
Journal of Speech and Hearing Disorders, 276
Journal of Speech and Hearing Research, 276
JUDGE'S EVALUATION FORM—ONE-ACT PLAY, 301
JUDGE'S EVALUATION FORM—ORAL INTERPRETATION, 383
JUDGE'S EVALUATION FORM—ORIGINAL ORATORY, 358
JUDGE'S EVALUATION FORM—RADIO SPEAKING, 389
JUDGE'S EVALUATION FORM—STANDARD ORATORY, 368
Judges, information for, 334–335

Kelly, Fred J., 5
Kenyon, John Samuel, quoted, 166
Kerr, Clark, 7
Killian, James R., Jr., 7
Kilpatrick, William H., quoted, 19
Klohr, Paul R., quoted, 222
Knott, Thomas Albert, quoted, 166
Knower, Franklin H., quoted, 134–135
Konigsberg, Evelyn, quoted, 157
Kramer, Magdalene, quoted, 15
Kramer, Rita Lee, quoted, 156

Language, 172–178
 basic principles of, 173
 defined, 172–176
 means for improving, 173
 objectives in teaching, 176–177

Language (*Continued*)
 problems of grammar in, 173–174
 suggestions to teachers of, 177–78
LEADERSHIP, DIAGNOSTIC EVALUATION OF DISCUSSION LEADER AND, 306–307
Learning experiences, characteristics of, 221
 See also Education; Educational objectives
Le Gallienne, Eva, quoted, 142
Leisure time, 27
Lesson plan, 237–238
 examples of, 238–239
 typical form of, 237–238
 See also Listening
LETTER OF INVITATION—DEBATE TOURNAMENT, 325
Librarian as teacher, 129
Lindsley, Charles F., 154
Linkletter, Art, 101
LIST OF WORDS FOR PRONUNCIATION, 171–172
Listening, 25, 181–184, 235–239
 comprehension test for, 183
 counterpart of speaking, 25
 defined, 25, 181
 lesson plans for, 238–239
 listeners, responsibility for, 182
 objectives in teaching, 182
 rationale for teaching, 181–182
 resource unit in, 224–235
 speaker's responsibility for, 182
 suggestions to teachers, 182–184
 teaching unit for beginners, 235–236
 teaching unit, advanced, 236–237
Literature, oral interpretation of, 375
Lomas, Charles W., quoted, 156, 162, 165
Loudness, 151
Low, Gordon, quoted, 134

Maladjusted speaker, 133
Malmgren, Donald E. and Rene L., 341
MANUSCRIPT READING, CRITIC SHEET FOR, 385
Marshall, Leon C., 5
Mast Teaching Machine. *See* Auvitor
Meany, George, 7
Memorization, principles of, 365
Michigan Speech Association, 198
Minnesota State High School Speech League, 299, 339, 358, 369, 385
Mitchell, Wanda, 110
Monthly Catalog of U.S. Government Publications, 129
Monthly Labor Review, 130
Moodie, Elizabeth, quoted, 60
Moore, Robert C., 5
Moore, Wilbur E., quoted, 162–163
Morgan, Joy Elmer, quoted, 5–6
Motivation, 97
MY AUTOBIOGRAPHY, 76–79

National Association of Secondary School Principals, 12, 21
National Council of Social Studies, 222
National Council of Teachers of English, quoted, 66–71
National Education Association, 9, quoted, 5
National Forensic League, 108, 370
National Thespians, 108
Needs of Youth, 16–17
Neher, Nancy, 119
Nehru, Jawaharlal, 142
New York State Board of Law Examiners, 23
New York Times Index, 130
Nichols, Ralph G., quoted, 181, 228–229

Niles, Doris, 107
Nonoriginal oratory, 357, 363–369
 ballots for, 367–369
 bodily action in, 366
 building background for, 364–365
 capabilities of students in, 363–364
 choosing an oration for, 363
 criteria for evaluation of, 367–369
 critic sheet for, 369
 defined, 357
 JUDGE'S EVALUATION FORM FOR, 368–369
 memorization of oration for, 365
 oral interpretation in, 367–368
 talking with an audience in, 366–367
 values for students of, 362
 voice in delivery of, 365
North Central Association, 314

Objectives. *See* Societal objectives; Educational objectives; Speech education, objectives and outcomes
O'Connell, William V., quoted, 22
OFFICIAL BALLOT—NEWS COMMENTARY ON RADIO, 390
OFFICIAL BALLOT—ORAL INTERPRETATION, 384
OFFICIAL DEBATE BALLOTS, 336–340
OFFICIAL DISCUSSION BALLOT, 305
OFFICIAL EXTEMPORANEOUS SPEAKING BALLOT, 352–353
OFFICIAL ORIGINAL ORATORY BALLOT FORM, 359–360
OFFICIAL STUDENT SENATE BALLOT, 374

Oklahoma High School Speech League, 340
Oklahoma Speech and Drama Service, 351, 359, 368–369, 389–390
Oliver, Robert T., quoted, 256–257
One-act plays, 291–299
ORAL COMMUNICATIONS CRITIQUE, 261–262
Oral interpretation of literature, 375–385
  abridging and arranging selections for, 378–379
  ballots for, 383–385
  choice of, criteria, and sources of, 383–385
  curricular base for, 375
  defined, 375
  desired outcomes of, 375
  extemporaneous reading in, defined, 382–383
  judge's evaluation form for, 383
  preparation of selection for, 379–382
  principles of and procedures in, 375–376
  purpose of, 375
ORAL INTERPRETATION OF ORATORICAL PROSE, 367
Oral reading, 192–193
  basic concepts of, 192
  benefits of, 193
  principles of, 192–193
  suggestions to teachers of, 193
  topics of a unit for, 193
  See also Oral interpretation of literature
ORATORICAL DECLAMATION, CRITIC SHEET FOR, 369
ORATORY:
  meaning, 350, 353

Oratory: (*Continued*)
  nonoriginal. *See* Nonoriginal oratory
  original. *See* Original oratory
ORATORY, CRITICAL SHEET FOR ORIGINAL, 358–359
Oregon plan debate, 321–322
Organization, principles of, 124–125
Organization of ideas, 124–128
  importance of, 124–125
  outlines, dittoed for, 126
  plans of, 126
  suggestions to teachers of, 127–128
Orations, titles of recent, 355
Original oratory, 350, 353–362
  ballot for, 359–360
  critic sheet for, 358
  "Golden Door, The," model of, 360–362
  judge's evaluation form for, 358–359
  meaning of, 353–355
  preparation for, 355–357
  selection of topic for, 355
  topics and titles for, 355
  See also Nonoriginal oratory
Outsider looks at education, 24

Pace, Frank, Jr., 7
PAIRINGS WORKSHEET, 323
Parker, William R., quoted, 137
Parliamentary procedure:
  basic concepts of, 191
  rationale of, 191
  suggestions to teachers of, 192
  topics of a unit in, 191–192
  See also Student senate
Paulson, Stanley F., 140–141
Pei, Mario, quoted, 176

Personal conference, 250
PERSONAL INVENTORY, 99–101
Personal speech attributes, 36, 37
Phelps, Waldo, W., 103
Phifer, Gregg, quoted, 316
Philosophy of speech teaching, 58–60
　See also Teachers of speech
Phonetic Alphabet, 167–168
Physical changes, 69
Pitch, 151
Pitfalls, 106–107
Place of speech in an integrated program, 24
　See also Speech education
Planning by teachers, 56–58
Plato, quoted, 3
Players' Magazine, 276
Plays, one-act, 291–301
　analysis and criticism of, 299
　casting, 295–296
　JUDGE'S EVALUATION FORMS FOR, 301
　performance of, 297
　rehearsing of, 296–297
　REHEARSAL SCHEDULE FOR, 298
　selecting of, 293–295
　standards of, 291–292
　TRYOUT FORM FOR, 295–296
　See also Dramatics
Prall, Caleb, quoted, 136
Preparation by speech teachers, 54–55
President's Commission on National Goals, 7–8
Problem-solving debate, 323
PROFILE RATING FORM, A, 264
Program of speech education, elements of, 22
　See also Activity programs, speech; Speech activities; Speech education

Pronouncing Dictionary of American English, A, 166
Pronunciation:
　colloquial pronunciation, defined, 166
　compared in dictionaries, 165–166
　correct pronunciation, defined, 167
　criteria by which to evaluate, 165
　dialect regions, 166
　LIST OF WORDS FOR, 171–172
　pronunciation, defined, 162–170
　recordings as teaching aids, 170
　responsibility for eight processes of, 164
　selection and accentuation, 165
　suggestions to teachers, 169–172
　teaching unit in, 167
　word list as a teaching aid, 171–172
　Young American Films, 170
Przybilla, Arthur, quoted, 298
Public Affairs Information Service, 130
Public speaking, 188–189
　methods of, 189
　speaker's bureau in, 189
　suggestions to teachers of, 189
　topics of a unit in, 188–189
　types of speeches in, 189
　See also Speech activities
Purposes of Education in American Democracy, The, 9

Qualifications of speech teachers, 54–56
Quarterly Journal of Speech, 105, 276
Questioning, 349
Quintilian, 173

INDEX

Radio:
  acting and speaking, 195–196
  NEWS COMMENTARY ON, OFFICIAL BALLOT, 390
  speaking on, 385–390
  topics of a unit in, 196
Rasmussen, Don, 167
Rating techniques, 136
Reader's Guide to Periodical Literature, 129
READING ALOUD, RATING FORM, 87
  See also Oral interpretation of literature; Oral reading
READING AND SPEAKING DIAGNOSTIC BLANK—VOICE AND SPEECH ANALYSIS, 85
Readings in drama, 28
Readings in public address, 28
Record distributors, 280–281
Recording guide, 79–81
Reflective thinking. *See* Thinking
REGISTRATION FORM—INVITATIONAL DEBATE TOURNAMENT, 326–327
Reid, Loren D., 96, 103, quoted, 153
Reid, Ronald F., quoted, 58–59
Reprimand, 98
Representative American Speeches, 366
Resource unit, 221–235, 239–240
  characteristics of, 222
  definitions of, 222
  elements of, 222–223
  pattern for, 223–224
  SAMPLE OF, 224–235
  suggestions to teachers for, 239–240
  unit, defined, 221
  UNIT OUTLINE, 223–224
Richards, Ivor A., 13
Richey, Robert W., 62
Roback, A. A., quoted, 134

Robert's *Rules of Order,* 370
Robinson, Edward R., quoted, 141
Robinson, James, quoted, 301, 340 350, 358–359, 368–369, 389–390
Rodgers and Hammerstein, quoted, *South Pacific,* 362
Ross, Edward A., 5
Ross, F. Fulton, quoted, 59–60
Rules of Order, Robert's, 370
Rulon, Phillip J., 13
Rupp, A. E., quoted, 44–46

SAMPLE INFORMATION SHEET FOR DEBATE PROGRAM, 315
SAMPLE LESSON PLAN, 237–239
SAMPLE RESOURCE UNIT, 225–235
SAMPLE TEACHING UNIT, 235–237
Santiago, Florence M., 277
Saylor, J. Galen, quoted, 221
SCHEDULE FOR A ONE-ACT PLAY PRODUCTION, 298
Schlesinger, Arthur M., 13
Schmidt, Ralph N., 126
Scott, Harry F., quoted, 174–175
Seely, H. F., quoted, 24
Seiger, Marvin L., quoted, 244–245
Selections:
  abridging and arranging, 378
  choice of, 377
  criteria and sources, 383
Self-criticism, 250
Self-realization, 10, 29
Sequential Tests of Educational Progress: Listening 1A and Listening 1B, cited, 183
Sheets, Roberta D., quoted, 291–292
Shepard, David W., quoted, 302
Simley, Anne, 193
Slang, 71
Smith, Carney C., quoted, 318
Smith, Donald K., 339, quoted, 157

Societal objectives, 2–17
  defined, 2
  emphasis on dignity of man, 3
  evolution and endurance of, 3–8
  guide for educational planning, 3, 17
  listed, 5–8
  Plato's conception of, 3–4
  stated in Preamble, Constitution, and Bill of Rights, 4–5
  See also American democratic society
Southern Speech Journal, 276
Speaker's bureau, 189
SPEAKER RATING FORM, 86
Speaking, defined, 24–25
Speaking on radio, 385–390
  BALLOTS FOR, 389–390
  consists of, 385–386
  JUDGE'S EVALUATION FORM FOR, 389–390
  preparation for, 386–389
  standards of, 389–390
  See also Radio; Television
Speech, 21–31, 53
  basic elements of, 29
  defined, 25
  as foundation of activities and relations, 21
  free, 31
  instrument of social adaptation, 21
  keynote of mental life, 21
  not oral English, 53
  need for, defined, 25
  object of study, 21
  outward marks of an inward grace, 30
Speech activities, 184–198
  choral speaking, 193–194
  debate, 190–191
  discussion, 189–190

Speech activities (*Continued*)
  dramatics, 195
  informal speech, 185–188
  oral reading and interpretation, 192–193
  parliamentary procedure, 191–192
  public speaking, 188–189
  radio and television acting and speaking, 195–196
  storytelling, 194–195
  See also Directing a co-curricular speech program; Fundamentals of speech
SPEECH ANALYSIS FORM, 84
Speech Association of America, 33–34, 51, 198, 314
Speech education, 1–36, 107–109
  beginning of, 20
  contribution to:
    citizenship, 26–27, 31
    democracy, 20
    economic efficiency, 31
    education, 19–34
    ethical character, 28
    freedom of speech, 31
    fundamental processes, 23–24
    health, 23
    home membership, 26
    human relationships, 30–31
    self-realization, 29–30
    society, 22
    use of leisure, 27–28
    vocational achievement, 26
  function of education, 19–21
  defined, 1–2, 20, 25, 35
  need for emphasis on, 19–34
  objectives and outcomes of, 19–25, 34–36
  significance to the teacher, 2
  suggestions for up-grading, 107–109

INDEX 433

Speech fright, 132–143
  asset or liability, 133
  causes of, 139
  identification and measurement of, 134
  symptoms of, 135, 139
  therapies for, 139
  See also Adjustment to the speech situation
SPEECH AND HEARING DIAGNOSTIC FORM, 81–82
Speech Index, 130
SPEECH INTERVIEW OUTLINE, 87–90
SPEECH MAKING, 265–266
Speech making, 20, 265–266
  achievement in, 265
  achievement ratings, 259
  beginnings in self-government, 20
  forms, 264–268
  inherent in a free society, 20
  RATING FORM FOR, 265–266
Speech Monographs, 105, 276
Speech need, defined, 25–26
SPEECH PROGRAM—DEBATE FORM, 289–290
SPEECH RATING FORMS, 263–264, 266–268
SPEECH OF STUDENTS, GUIDE FOR RECORDING, 80–81
  See also Contest or festival, conducting a speech; Debate tournament
Speech Teacher, 105, 276
SPEECH TEXTS, FACTORS FOR ANALYSIS AND REVIEW OF, 277–279
Staats, Lorin C., quoted, 163, 173
Statesman's Yearbook, 130
Statistical Abstract of the United States, 130
Storytelling, 194–195
  benefits of, 194, 195
  criteria of a story for, 194

Storytelling (Continued)
  dangers of, 195
  importance of voice in, 195
  kinds of stories for, 194
  procedure in preparation for, 194–195
Strang, Ruth, 187
Stratton, Dorothy C., 187
Stroud, James B., 119
Student senate, 369–375
  bills for, 371, 373
  criteria for judging, 373–375
  OFFICIAL BALLOT FOR, 374
  organization of, 372
  preparation for, 371
  purpose of, 370
  values of, 369–370
  See also Parliamentary procedure
Students, 23, 66–92
  all-round and continuous development of, 23
  characteristics of, 66–71
  individual needs of, 71–73
  language characteristics of, 69–71
  orientation of, 91–92
  See also Societal objectives; Educational objectives; Contributions by speech education
STUDY COURSE OUTLINES, 184, 197–198
Subject matter approach to teaching, 198–203
  basic assumptions of, 199–200
  defined, 198
  rationale of, 198–199
  readings in drama, 203
  readings in public address, 202–203
  topics for units for, 200–203
Superior teacher, concepts of, 44–46
Survey of Current Business, 130

Tau Kappa Alpha, 316
Teacher, reasons for liking, 43–44
Teachers of speech, 23–34, 46–61, 415–418
  administrators concepts of, 44–45
  appraising results of teaching by, 417–418
  attributes of, 42–47, 58–60
  awards for outstanding achievement by, 58–60
  best (student opinion), 43–44
  best liked (student opinion), 42–49
  as bookkeepers and recordkeepers, 56
  certification of, 51–52
  classroom management by, 47, 416
  friendliness of, 54–55
  importance of their work, 23–34
  judgment of, 47
  liked least (student opinion), 43
  as learners, 55–56
  needs of students, respected by, 71–73
  opportunities to contribute, 23–34
  personal and professional development of, 52, 415
  philosophies of, 46–47
  planning and scheduling by, 56–57
  professional preparation of, 50–53, 416
  public relations by, 50
  research, understanding by, 61
  specialization in seven topics by, 51
  speech and voice habits of, 49–50
  teachers' judgment of, 44, 58–60
  teaching methods and materials for, 416–417

Teaching aids:
  sources of, 276
  types of, 275
Teaching speech:
  approaches to, 116–220
  deductive and inductive methods of, 109–111
  suggestions for improvement of, 105–109
  See also Teaching aids
Teaching unit, 235–237
  SKELETON OUTLINES OF, 235–237
  See also Listening
Telephone usage of speech, 187–188
Television:
  appearance and attire for, 396–397
  cameras and microphones in, 396–397
  choice of topic for, 391
  consists of, 390–391
  criteria for evaluation of, 397
  manuscript required for directors of, 393–395
  preparation for, 391–392
  speaking on, 390–397
  terms used in, 395–396
  visual aids for, 393
  See also Radio acting and speaking
TERMS TO BE DEFINED, LIST OF, 123–124
Testing:
  factors of, 251–252
  instruments of, 252–253
  procedures for improvements of, 253
  purposes, scope, and significance of, 251
  validity and reliability of, 223
  See also Criticism; Evaluation

Textbooks:
  factors for analysis and review of, 277–279
  recent, in speech education, 279–280
THEATER—SAMPLE BLANK FOR DIRECTOR, 295–296
Theatre Arts, 276
Thinking, 13–14, 26
  characteristics of, 14
  defined, 13–14
  reflective, five steps in, 26
  tests of, 14
Thompson, David W., 339
Thonssen, Lester, quoted, 20
Thurman, Wayne L., quoted, 155, 164
TIMEKEEPERS, INFORMATION FOR, 335
Today's Speech, 276
Tones, duration of, 151
Topics, drawing of, 348
TOPICS DESIGNED TO CHALLENGE HIGH SCHOOL STUDENTS, 100, 121–122
Twain, Mark, 142

Ulich, Robert, 13
Unit. *See* Resource unit; Teaching unit
United States Office of Education, 275
Universal education, goals of, 15

Vandraegen, Daniel, quoted, 156, 162, 165
Vertical File Catalog, 130
Vital Speeches of the Day, 130–131
Vocation, 26
VOICE AND ARTICUALTION EVALUATION FORM, 82–83

Voice usage, 149–161
  breathing, importance of type for, 155–156
  concepts basic to development of, 151–152
  drill, its significance for, 156–157
  listening, its relation to, 151
  lung capacity, importance for, 153–155
  objectives in voice training for, 152–153, 157–158
  problems in voice training for, 151, 152–156
  suggestions to teachers of, 158–161
  test of, 153
  training, 157–161

Wald, George, 13
Washington, Booker T., 362
Watts, A. F., quoted, 29–30
Weaver, Andrew T., quoted, 29, 157
Webster, Daniel, 142
Western Speech, 276
White House Conference on Education, 17
Wiksell, Wesley, quoted, 181
Wilkinson, Gerald T., quoted, 174–175
Wilson, Woodrow, 173
Wise, Claude Merton, quoted, 22, 153–154, 155
Woolbert, Charles H., 30
Wright, Benjamin F., 13
Wriston, Henry M., 7
Writing standards, 257

Young American Films, 170
Youth, problems of, 16–17

Zwilling, Marlene, original oration, quoted, 360–362

Date Due

JUN 14 '67			
DEC 19 72			
APR 09 78			

Demco 293-5